VINCENNES UNIVERSITY LIBRARY

PREGNANCY, DELIVERY, CHILDBIRTH

This book reconstructs the history of conception, pregnancy and childbirth in Europe from antiquity to the 20th century, focusing on its most significant turning points: the emergence of a medical-scientific approach to delivery in Ancient Greece, the impact of Christianity, the establishment of the man-midwife in the 18th century, the medicalisation of childbirth, the emergence of a new representation of the foetus as "unborn citizen", and, finally, the revolution of reproductive technologies.

The book explores a history that, far from being linear, progressive or homogeneous, is characterised by significant continuities as well as transformations. The ways in which a woman gives birth and lives her pregnancy and the postpartum period are the result of a complex series of factors. The book therefore places these events in their wider cultural, social and religious contexts, which influenced the forms taken by rituals and therapeutic practices, religious and civil prescriptions and the regulation of the female body.

The investigation of this complex experience represents a crucial contribution to cultural, social and gender history, as well as an indispensable tool for understanding today's reality. It will be of great use to undergraduates studying the history of childbirth, the history of medicine, the history of the body, as well as women's and gender history more broadly.

Nadia Maria Filippini was Lecturer in Women's History in the Department of Humanities at Ca' Foscari University of Venice. She obtained her PhD in history at the École des Hautes Études en Sciences Sociales in Paris. Her research concerns the history of women and the history of mentalities. She has published books, essays and articles, in Italian and other languages, on topics such as the history of Caesarean sections ("extraordinary birth"), childbirth and the body, as well as the history of medicine, and women's social history. She is a founding member of the Società Italiana delle Storiche (Italian Society of Women Historians).

PREGNANCY, DELIVERY, CHILDBIRTH

A Gender and Cultural History from Antiquity to the Test Tube in Europe

Nadia Maria Filippini

Translated by Clelia Boscolo

LONDON AND NEW YORK

First published 2021
by Routledge
2 Park Square, Milton Park, Abingdon, Oxon OX14 4RN

and by Routledge
52 Vanderbilt Avenue, New York, NY 10017

Routledge is an imprint of the Taylor & Francis Group, an informa business

© 2021 Nadia Maria Filippini

Translated by **Clelia Boscolo**

The right of **Nadia Maria Filippini** to be identified as author of this work has been asserted by her in accordance with sections 77 and 78 of the Copyright, Designs and Patents Act 1988.

All rights reserved. No part of this book may be reprinted or reproduced or utilised in any form or by any electronic, mechanical, or other means, now known or hereafter invented, including photocopying and recording, or in any information storage or retrieval system, without permission in writing from the publishers.

Trademark notice: Product or corporate names may be trademarks or registered trademarks, and are used only for identification and explanation without intent to infringe.

First published as Nadia Maria Filippini, *Generare, partorire, nascere. Una storia dall'antichità alla provetta*, Roma, Viella, © 2017 - Viella s.r.l.

British Library Cataloguing-in-Publication Data
A catalogue record for this book is available from the British Library

Library of Congress Cataloging-in-Publication Data
Names: Filippini, Nadia Maria, author. | Boscolo, Clelia, translator.
Title: Pregnancy, delivery, childbirth: a gender and cultural history from antiquity to the test tube in Europe / Nadia Maria Filippini; translated by Clelia Boscolo.
Other titles: Generare, partorire, nascere. English
Description: Milton Park, Abingdon, Oxon; New York, NY: Routledge, 2020. | Includes bibliographical references and index.
Identifiers: LCCN 2020010004 (print) | LCCN 2020010005 (ebook) | ISBN 9780367211073 (hardback) | ISBN 9780367211080 (paperback) | ISBN 9780429265457 (ebook)
Subjects: LCSH: Childbirth—History. | Obstetrics—History. | Motherhood—History.
Classification: LCC RG511 .F4513 2020 (print) | LCC RG511 (ebook) | DDC 618.2—dc23
LC record available at https://lccn.loc.gov/2020010004

ISBN: 978-0-367-21107-3 (hbk)
ISBN: 978-0-367-21108-0 (pbk)
ISBN: 978-0-429-26545-7 (ebk)

Typeset in Bembo
by codeMantra

To my son Pietro

CONTENTS

List of figures   xi
Acknowledgements   xiv
List of abbreviations   xv

Introduction   1

PART I
Cultural representations   7

1 Gender dichotomies   9
   1 *Introduction* 9
   2 *The earth and the sower* 10
   3 *Man as the "origin of generation": generated by man, born by woman* 13
   4 *Sons and daughters: hierarchies in generation* 17
   5 *Generating with the body, generating with the mind* 19
   6 *Zeus' cephalic delivery: Athena's birth* 21
   7 *Childbirth vs war, childbirth as war* 22
   8 *Eve's pains* 26
   9 *Mary's virgin delivery* 29

PART II
Giving birth and being born from antiquity to the 18th century   41
Foreword 41

2 Pregnancy   45
   1 Being pregnant 45
   2 The foetus: its development and ensoulment 49
   3 Making a beautiful baby: the power of the gaze and cravings 54
   4 Precepts, practices and prohibitions between medicine and tradition 58
   5 Not only babies: "monsters" and moles 62
   6 The fight against abortion and the defence of the venter *66*
   7 Institutions for unmarried mothers ("fallen women") 69

3 Childbirth   76
   1 A painful test, a risky journey 76
   2 Preparing for the event 79
   3 The childbirth scene: places, people and practices 82
   4 "Natural" versus "unnatural" childbirth: the doctors' discourse 90
   5 "Sacrificing the fruit to save the tree": the priority of a mother's life 95
   6 The "second delivery": the placenta 97

4 Birth and post-natal period   103
   1 The birth setting 103
   2 Breastfeeding and wet nurses 109
   3 Impurity: a period of time between life and death 112
   4 Beliefs and rules 115
   5 Purification rituals 118
   6 Infanticide and abandonment 120

5 Social birth   128
   1 Rites of passage 128
   2 In the ancient world 129
   3 In the Christian world 130
   4 Baptism between the Reformation and the Counter-Reformation 134
   5 The dual death and the construction of Limbo 136
   6 Rituals which replaced baptism 137
   7 Post-mortem Caesarean sections 139

6 The midwife   143
   1 Features and skills 143
   2 The "midwife-witch" 148

3 The control of the Church 149
   4 Control and regulation of political institutions 151
   5 A variety of figures 153

PART III
The 18th-century juncture   159
   Foreword 159

7 The institutionalisation of midwives   161
   1 Childbirth: public and political interests 161
   2 Midwives on trial 163
   3 "The light of knowledge": the creation of midwifery schools 166
   4 A new model of midwife 168
   5 Qualified versus unlicenced midwives: an age-old competition 170

8 Man-midwives on the childbirth scene   174
   1 The establishment of man-midwives 174
   2 Forceps and vectis: the "iron hands", symbols of the
      new midwifery 176
   3 Active versus waiting obstetrician: a conflict of
      perspectives and practices 180
   4 European differences 183
   5 Midwives and man-midwives: the issue of manual interventions 185

9 Lying-in hospitals   192
   1 Unmarried and poor mothers in the service of training 192
   2 New midwifery rituals and practices 197
   3 Childbed fever and Semmelweis's 'indecent' discovery 200
   4 Puerperal insanity and infanticide: new medical, legal and social
      perspectives 202

10 The "foetus-as-citizen"   207
   1 New theories about generation 207
   2 The birth of embryology and the personification of the foetus 208
   3 Theologian F. E. Cangiamila and the campaign for post-mortem
      Caesarean sections 211
   4 The protection of "unborn citizens" 213
   5 Caesarean sections on living women 215
   6 Saving the mother or the child? 219
   7 Defending (the foetus') life: the verdict of the Holy Office 221
   8 Breastfeeding and new forms of childcare 222
   9 Reforms and laws in defence of newborns 226

PART IV
The contemporary age   231

11 The many revolutions of the 20th century   233
    1 Maternity protection 233
    2 Maternity and nationalism: the Italian case 235
    3 Eugenics, sterilisation and forced abortions 240
    4 The Catholic Church and the Protestant Churches 242
    5 The delocalisation of childbirth to hospitals 243
    6 "My womb is mine": contraception and abortion in the feminist movement 248
    7 "Of woman born": a new perspective on childbirth 250
    8 Pain-free childbirth: chloroform, epidural anaesthesia and psycho-prophylaxis 252
    9 "Let's take childbirth back!" 255
    10 Revealing the secrets of the womb: ultrasound scans 258
    11 The new frontier of artificial insemination 260
    12 Conclusions: at the dawn of the third millennium 264

Bibliography   *273*
Index   *311*

FIGURES

1.1 Uterus and "penile" vagina: "matrix cavity" (= uterus cavity, A), neck of the matrix (B), "female testicles" (= ovaries D), "pudendo, or nature of the woman" (= vagina, C), from Scipione Mercurio (1618), *La Commare o riccoglitrice*, Milano: Giob. Bidelli, p. 19. Reproduced with permission of the Biblioteca Pinali antica (Padua) 15

2.1 Female figure with pregnant uterus, from Jakob Rueff (1587), *De conceptu et generatione hominis*, Francofurti ad Moenum: P. Fabricium: c 10. Reproduced with permission of the Biblioteca Pinali antica (Padua) 50

2.2 Foetus with placenta outside the uterus, from Jacob Rueff (1587), *De conceptu et generatione hominis*, Francofurti ad Moenum: P. Fabricium: c19r. Reproduced with permission of the Biblioteca Pinali antica (Padua) 51

2.3 The female organs of generation, from Giovanni Raffaele (1841), *Ostetricia teorico-pratica. Atlante*. Note the position of the foetus in the uterus, with the face facing the back of the mother. Reproduced with permission of the Ministero dei Beni e delle Attività Culturali e del Turismo – Biblioteca Nazionale Marciana (Venice) 52

2.4 "Superstitions" (betting on the sex of the foetus), from Giovanni Grevembroch [1754] (1981, vol. IV, p. 87). Reproduced with permission of the Ministero dei Beni e delle Attività Culturali e del Turismo – Biblioteca Nazionale Marciana 56

2.5 Examples of "monsters", from Jakob Rueff (1587), *De conceptu et generatione hominis*, Francofurti ad Moenum: P. Fabricium: c 44r. Reproduced with permission of the Biblioteca Pinali antica (Padua) 62

3.1 Tool for vaginal fumigations, from Scipione Mercurio (1618), *La Commare o riccoglitrice*, Milano: Giob. Bidelli, p. 294. Reproduced with permission of the Biblioteca Pinali antica (Padua) 80

3.2 Birthing chair, from Jakob Rueff (1587), *De conceptu et generatione hominis*, Francofurti ad Moenum: P. Fabricium, c18r. Reproduced with permission of the Biblioteca Pinali antica (Padua) 86

3.3 Childbirth scene, from Eucharius Rösslin [1513] (1910: ch. III). Reproduced with permission of the Ministero dei Beni e delle Attività Culturali e del Turismo - Biblioteca Nazionale Marciana (Venice) 87

3.4 Childbirth scene, from Jakob Rueff (1587), *De conceptu et generatione hominis*, Francofurti ad Moenum: P. Fabricium, 3r. Reproduced with permission of the Biblioteca Pinali antica (Padua) 89

3.5 Foetus in cephalic ("natural") presentation, from Eucharius Rösslin [1513] (1910, p. 27). Reproduced with permission of the Ministero dei Beni e delle Attività Culturali e del Turismo - Biblioteca Nazionale Marciana (Venice) 91

3.6 Foetus in breech ("unnatural") presentation, from Eucharius Rösslin [1513] (1910, p. 30). Reproduced with permission of the Ministero dei Beni e delle Attività Culturali e del Turismo - Biblioteca Nazionale Marciana (Venice) 92

3.7 Manual extraction of the placenta, from Cosme Viardel (1748), *Observations sur la pratique des accouchemens naturels, contre nature et monstrueux*, Paris: chez d'Houry. Reproduced with permission of the Biblioteca Pinali antica (Padua) 99

4.1 *Birth of the Virgin*, Venetian School (1589), oil painting on wood, in Venice, Church of Santa Maria Formosa. Reproduced with permission of the Curia Patriarcale of Venice, Ufficio Beni Culturali 104

4.2 Tintoretto, *Birth of St John the Baptist* (about 1546–1548), oil on canvas, in Venice, Church of San Zaccaria (chapel of Sant'Attanasio). Reproduced with permission of the Curia Patriarcale of Venice, Ufficio Beni Culturali 105

4.3 Title page of Eucharius Rösslin (Rodhion) (1537), *De partu hominis et quae circa ipsum accidunt libellus*, Venice, Bernardinum Bindonis, in Eucharius Rösslin [1513] (1910) 106

4.4 The wet nurse from Giovanni Grevembroch [1754] (1981), vol. III, p. 155 111

5.1 Pietro Longhi, *The Baptism* (1745), oil painting. In the background, a female figure is hiding; many critics think this is the mother, who could not attend the baptism because she was considered impure. Reproduced with permission of the Querini Stampalia Foundation of Venice 133

6.1 The midwife ("counsellor"), from Jakob Rueff (1587), *De conceptu et generatione hominis*, Francofurti ad Moenum: P. Fabricium: c 17r. Reproduced with permission of the Biblioteca Pinali antica (Padua) 144

6.2 A midwife with her servant carrying a birthing chair, from Giovanni Grevembroch [1754] (1981, vol. III, p. 55). Reproduced with permission of the Ministero dei Beni e delle Attività Culturali e del Turismo - Biblioteca Nazionale Marciana (Venice) 147

7.1 Manual midwife operation in a difficult birth, from Scipione Mercurio (1618), *La Commare o riccoglitrice*, Milano: Giob. Bidelli, p. 176. Reproduced with permission of the Biblioteca Pinali antica (Padua) 165

8.1 Title page of Cosme Viardel's (1748), *Observations sur la pratique des accouchemens naturels, contre nature et monstrueux*, Paris: chez d'Houry. The caption says: *"Non impar Lucianae"* ("not inferior to Lucina", the Roman goddess of childbirth). Reproduced with permission of the Biblioteca Pinali antica (Padua) 175

8.2 Deployment of forceps, from Giovanni Raffaele (1841), *Ostetricia teorico-pratica. Atlante*. Reproduced with permission of the Ministero dei Beni e delle Attività Culturali e del Turismo - Biblioteca Nazionale Marciana (Venice) 178

8.3 Title page of John Blunt's book (1793), *Man-Midwifery Dissected*. The book has the licence: Creative Commons Attribution (CC BY 4.0) 187

8.4 Versions and extraction, from Giovanni Raffaele (1841), *Ostetricia teorico-pratica. Atlante*. Reproduced with permission of the Ministero dei Beni e delle Attività Culturali e del Turismo - Biblioteca Nazionale Marciana (Venice) 188

9.1 Obstetric examination by a man-midwife, from Giovanni Raffaele (1841), *Ostetricia teorico-pratica. Atlante*. Reproduced with permission of the Ministero dei Beni e delle Attività Culturali e del Turismo - Biblioteca Nazionale Marciana (Venice) 199

10.1 Table of embryological development by anatomist Gian Battista Bianchi, revised by theologian Francesco E. Cangiamila, from Cangiamila (1775). Reproduced from my collection 210

10.2 Detail of the illustration, figure XV: a foetus at 2.5 months. Reproduced from my collection 211

10.3 Caesarean section on living woman, from Scipione Mercurio (1618), *La Commare o riccoglitrice*, Milano: Giob. Bidelli, p. 269. Mercurio was a supporter of the Caesarean section, although he had never performed it. Reproduced with permission of the Biblioteca Pinali antica (Padua) 217

11.1 'Number is power! Celebration of mother-and-child's day', article from fascist journal *Il Popolo di Romagna*, 17 December 1938, XVII. Reproduced with permission of the Gambalunga Library (Rimini) 237

ACKNOWLEDGEMENTS

The book is the revised and expanded version of the book *Generare, partorire, nascere. Una storia dall'antichità alla provetta* (2017), published by Viella in the series 'Storia delle donne e di genere' (History of Women and Gender) of the Società Italiana delle Storiche (Italian Society of Women Historians).

I wish to extend my special thanks to those who have supported the translation of this book with their encouragement and help: Anna Bellavitis, my friend in life and in research; Sandra Cavallo, Raffaella Sarti, Perry Wilson and Francesca Medioli for their help and valuable advice; Gianni Moriani and Silvia Carraro for their help with the editing; Alessandro Ambroggi for helping with image resolution; and Clelia Boscolo for her translation work.

I am grateful to the anonymous English referees who, with their constructive critical remarks, have directed me to review or expand some parts of the original Italian text.

Special thanks to the institutions and libraries that welcomed me and provided invaluable help in the final stages, especially the British Library and the Wellcome Library. The Biblioteca Nazionale Marciana in Venice, the Patriarchal Curia of Venice, the Querini Stampalia Foundation of Venice, the Biblioteca Pinali antica of Padua (special thanks to Giulia Rigoni) and the Gambalunga Library in Rimini kindly allowed me to reproduce valuable images from their collections.

ABBREVIATIONS

ACBg	Archive of the Municipality of Bergamo (Italy).
AIPMI	Archive of the Provincial Institutes for Childcare Assistance of Milan (Italy).
APlatt	Aristotle, *On the Generation of Animals*, transl. by Arthur Platt.
ASVe	Venice State Archives (Italy).
Did.	*Didaché. The Teaching of the Twelve Apostles.*
Epith.	Thucydides, *Peloponnesian War ('Pericles' Epithaph').*
Eum.	Aeschylus, *Eumenides*, transl. by Herbert Weir Smyth.
Exc.	[Hippocrates], *Excision du Foetus*, texte établi et traduit par Florence Bourdon.
FS	[Hippocrates], *Femmes Steriles*, texte établi et traduit par Florence Bordon.
GA	Aristotle, *De la Génération des animaux*, texte établi et traduit par Pierre Louis.
Gen.	[Hippocrates], *De la Génération*, texte établi et traduit par Robert Joly.
Genesis KJV	*Genesis*, Old Testament, King James Version.
Gyn.	Soranos d'Éphèse, *Maladies des femmes*, texte établi et traduit par Paul Burguière, Danielle Gourevitch, Yves Malinas.
HPott.	[Hippocrates], *On Generation. Nature of the Child. Diseases 4. Nature of Women and Barrenness*, ed. and transl. by Paul Potter.
Lev. KJV	*Leviticus*, Old Testament, King James Version.
Luke KJV	*Luke Gospel*, King James Version.
LG	*Lumen Gentium* (Dogmatic Constitution).
Med.	Euripides, *Medea*, transl. by David Kovacs.
Nat. H.	Pline l'Ancien, *Histoire naturelle*, texte établi et traduit par A. Ernout.

NE	[Hippocrates], *De la nature de l'enfant*, texte établi et traduit par Robert Joly.
PMG	*Pseudo-Matthew Gospel.*
Polit.	Aristotle, *Politique*, texte établi et traduit par Jean Aubonnet.
San.	Galen, *De sanitate tuenda*, transl. by Robert Montraville Green.
Superf.	[Hippocrates], *Superfétation,* texte établi et traduit par Florence Bourdon.
Sym.	Plato, *Banquet*, texte établi et traduit par Paul Vicaire.
Symp. J.	Plato, *Symposium*, ed. by Rhonda L. Kelley, transl. by Benjamin Jowett.
Summa	Thomas Aquinas, *Summa Theologiae*, transl. by Fathers of the English Dominican Province.
Temp.	Soranus of Ephesus, *Gynecology*, transl. by Owsei Tempkin.
Theae.Fow.	Plato, *Theaetetus*, transl. by Harold N. Fowler.
Théét.	Plato, *Théétète*, texte établi et traduit par Augene Diès.
Tim.	Plato, *Timée*, texte établi et traduit par Albert Rivaud.
Tim.Lamb.	Plato, *Timaeus*, transl. by W.R.M. Lamb.
Trach.	Sophocles, *Trachiniae.*
Trot.	*The Trotula: A Medieval Compendium of Women's Medicine*, ed. and transl. by Monica H. Green.
WHO	World Health Organization (UN).

INTRODUCTION

The history of childbirth is a fundamental chapter in women's history, not only for the obvious reason that, in the past, women give birth and gave birth much more frequently than they do today, spending many of their fertile years being pregnant. There is also another reason, related to the codification of gender itself: for centuries, being a woman coincided with being a mother. Motherhood was an expression of sexual identity. The value of women, their position and role within their families, in some societies even their actual acceptance into their husbands' families, were measured against it.

Thus, individual, familial and societal expectations converged on this capacity, but so did forms of control, discipline and protection that were centred on the family, with its internal hierarchies, and on ecclesiastical and political institutions. Over time, multiple powers have acted and interacted upon the fertile female body in different ways, either within alliances and in synergy, or in conflict, sometimes directly, but more often indirectly, through controlling figures (such as midwives or doctors). For centuries, the birth scene (to employ a useful metaphor drawn from microsociology) has been the field of invisible battles aimed at asserting normative hegemonies or more trivial professional hierarchies. The clashes that in recent decades have broken out over the question of abortion or reproductive technologies are not a peculiarity of our days, but a recurring element in history which became more accentuated in the 20th century. Women have not been mere passive objects: they have been able to promote forms of solidarity and complicity, create alliances so much more feared because they were secret, circumvent the norms and carve out independent spaces, often relying on the exclusively female features of the scene, which, for centuries, they managed alone. In fact, it was precisely this fact which, in some historical periods, gave rise to a proliferation of institutional regulatory measures. More recent historiography has placed more emphasis on these aspects, correcting the excessive victimisation of early feminist research.

However, the history of childbirth is not only inscribed in social and institutional history, but also in the broader landscape of the history of culture and mentalities. It was the very idea of generation and birth that changed over time, as did that of the foetus, forcing a reassessment of its relationship with its mother's body. Over time, representations of motherhood in its various facets have constantly changed, albeit in anything but linear and progressive ways, with periods of sudden acceleration and long continuities, alongside innovations and changes.

These cultural representations are at the root of the rituals that accompany motherhood and birth and of the deontological principles that have guided practice. On the other hand, the medical concepts themselves, in both anatomy and obstetrics, have been an integral part of the cultural construct, and are inscribed within more complex systems of thought and depend on them. This aspect has often been overlooked by the traditional histories of obstetrics, mostly characterised by evolutionary and celebratory readings.

To underline these aspects, some historians have spoken of *Kulturgeschichte*.[1] This cultural perspective has also included imagination, fears and obsessions: the suspicions of magical practices, witchcraft, and child murders, carried out within that sphere of action that has always eluded male control, haunted Western thought for a long time, sometimes exploding in forms of violent repression. Significantly, the vast majority of women sent to their deaths on charges of witchcraft between the 15th and 17th centuries were midwives. Dreams and fantasies speak to us of medicine's long-held desire not only to remove death from the birth scene or to "see" what happened in the secrecy of the womb, but also to discover the secrets of life, to reproduce it artificially outside the female body, thus also showing men's subconscious envy of something that was inaccessible to them (it must be remembered that for centuries, women were excluded from the practice of medicine). In this perspective, the recent frontiers of reproductive technology appear as the fulfilment of a utopian dream long held before science and technology made it actually possible.

In short, the figures, rituals, therapeutic practices and places that have characterised childbirth are the outcome of a complex series of (scientific, religious, social, political) factors and represent a privileged vantage point to analyse not only the history of women, but also social and cultural history. Being aware of this means sheds light not only on the past, but also on the present and its future prospects.

In writing this book, I have attempted to explain these multiple facets, highlighting cultural representations, as well as medical-scientific ones, investigating rituals alongside therapeutic practices, considering public initiatives and institutional regulations, the figures involved and the peculiarities and characteristics of the places. I have tried to capture – as far as the sources have allowed – the experience of women. This is why I have used a range of sources, including legal, medical and social texts; visual sources; folklore; women's writings and oral testimonies, gathering the outcomes of more than 30 years of research.

I have chosen a very long-term perspective, from the ancient world to the 20th century, because of the foundational nature of Greek thought on this issue and due to the many continuities that exist between the Greek-Roman, medieval and modern worlds not only on the medical and scientific levels, but also in terms of representation and practices, despite some significant changes introduced primarily by Christianity. I also wanted to point out how certain beliefs, even when they were abandoned by scientific thought, persisted far longer in popular traditions, in some cases right up until the 20th century and even today.

Choosing such a broad perspective has obviously entailed the need to leave out some aspects, underlining, on the one hand, the elements with greater continuity, and, on the other, the most significant junctures and changes to provide more general keys for interpretation. In choosing what was relevant, I have taken as fundamental benchmarks the crucial characteristics of the birth scene as a set of figures, places and practices. In this perspective, some historical periods seem particularly important: first and foremost, the ancient world and Greek culture, for its founding value; the advent of Christianity, with the changes introduced by its new ethics and by ecclesiastical control; the 18th century, which saw the first male midwives and *accoucheurs*, surgeons experienced in assisting women in childbirth, who joined the traditional figure of the midwife. Their growing influence, although very uneven in Europe, was encouraged by the emergence of biopower, according to Foucault's well-known definition.[2] Finally, I have considered the 20th century, which saw some radical changes: the delocalisation of birth from homes to hospitals that, albeit with different time-scales, affected almost all contexts and social classes, becoming ubiquitous in the Western world. The rapid proliferation of reproductive technologies, extended to the various phases of reproduction, is intertwined with this. Their application in the social reality has not only triggered profound changes in the way procreation, pregnancy and childbirth are experienced, but has also led to radical transformations in terms of sexuality, parenting, family and even gender representation.

The resulting picture does not claim to be exhaustive and is obviously open to question in its choice of relevant elements, as well as those inevitably left out, but I have tried to explain the criteria and motivations of my choices.

I wanted to consider the event of birth from the points of view of the two main figures involved: the mother and the child, often linked to the same destiny of life or death, or, on the contrary, opposed in painful deontological choices: in difficult births, for centuries, the midwifery practice has had to deal with the dramatic choice of sacrificing either the mother's or the child's life, so as not to lose them both, and in this matter religious currents and medical schools faced one another and bitterly clashed all over Europe. To what extent the representation of the foetus affected this has been another aspect that I have tried to focus on: the history of the embryo and foetus is in fact one of the most recent topics of research recently tackled by the humanities and which has proved particularly fruitful. This reconstruction could not fail to pay attention to the figure of the father, not only for his obvious role in conception (particularly emphasised in ancient medical thought and up to the 17th–18th centuries), but also for the role he played in terms of "social birth", power and forms of control.

As can be gleaned from this brief presentation, childbirth is a complex story that involves different actors and institutions and reflects cultures, mentalities, religious beliefs, scientific knowledge and technological innovations. I have tried to explain this complexity because therein lies its peculiarity, its charm and its past and present relevance.

In the first part of the book, *Cultural Representations*, I analyse the main representations of gender difference, starting from those concerning the reproductive capacity of women's bodies, in a mirroring game of male/female bias and juxtapositions. Originating in the ancient Greek world, these ideas are at the root of Western gender culture and have been reproduced in different forms in myths, pictorial representations, language and metaphors over a very long period of time. They were intertwined with Jewish religious views, linking the 'original sin' and the pains of childbirth, and with the complex theological construction of the figure of Mary in Christianity, involving the belief in her virginity "before, during and after childbirth".

In the second part, *Giving Birth and Being Born from Antiquity to the 18th Century*, I analyse the foundations of ancient medical and philosophical thought and its endurance in the medieval and early modern Europe. I have considered the ethical principles, social practices, rituals and beliefs concerning pregnancy, delivery and childbirth, the different attempts at disciplining these practices over time, paying particular attention to the transition to Christianity and the control established by Church over sexuality and reproduction. In particular, I have highlighted long-term continuities and their re-elaborations. In addition to childbirth, a baby's birth has been considered in its own right as a social event accompanied by specific rituals both in the ancient and in the Christian worlds. Finally, I have focused on midwives, who were at the centre of an exclusively female scene and therefore perceived as ambivalent figures, the object of appreciation and social esteem but at the same time – especially in certain historical periods – suspected of witchcraft and magical practices.

In the third part, *The 18th-Century Juncture*, I consider the radical transformations that characterised this century: they affected both the realm of science (with the emergence of new theories on reproduction and foetal development) and the socio-political context (with the rise of a new idea of national state and citizenship and, in parallel, a new political attention to birth and the establishment of what Foucault has called 'bio-power'). Within this context, the book has analysed the emergence of man-midwives and their growing influence, in a break with the centuries-old tradition of female presence; the creation of lying-in hospitals and midwifery schools; the institutionalisation of midwives; public and political interventions in the area of childbirth and the process which has transformed the embryo/foetus into a real person, into an "unborn citizen".

The fourth and final part, *The Contemporary Age*, addresses another crucial step in this story, characterised by key political and social transformations. On the one hand, this period saw the full development of biopower practices, which led to the eugenic and demographic policies of totalitarian regimes in the early 20th century. On the other hand, there was the beginning of a process of hospitalisation of childbirth, which became a common practice after the Second World War. In this context, a series of techniques were introduced that would have a profound impact on the experience of motherhood: from ultrasound scans to pain relief, from psycho-prophylaxis to in-vitro fertilisation and finally, to the legalisation of contraception and of voluntary terminations in most Western countries. These more recent transformations emerged in the context of and prompted by a feminist movement that identified in these matters one of its crucial areas of reflection and political action, claiming women's right to motherhood as a free choice and a change in the practices of childbirth.

Notes

1 Schlumbohm *et alii* (1998).
2 Foucault (2008).

PART I
Cultural representations

1
GENDER DICHOTOMIES

1 Introduction

We are all born from a woman's body, men and women: there is no birth without a woman's pregnancy and labour. This evidence (in the etymological sense of the word, from the Latin *video*) highlights another piece of evidence: only the female body is able to divide itself and give birth while remaining whole. In Western culture, however, this fact has not been given a symbolic representation of adequate significance, at least not since Indo-European society imposed its own male gods, downgrading the mother goddesses of more ancient tradition, such as Isis, Ishtar and Demeter.[1]

On the contrary, a substantial cultural construct, rooted in Greek culture, has consistently played down its value in a variety of ways, for example, by overstating men's contribution to generation, or by contrasting it with other abilities and generative powers in a subtle game of hierarchies and supremacy, which ended up causing a "philosophical removal" of birth.[2] Women's capacity to give birth has been countered by men's capacity to "generate"; the capacity to produce bodies by the superior one to produce thoughts; the capacity to give life by the ability to bring death, as we shall see in the following paragraphs.

These cultural constructs, as several feminist scholars have highlighted, reveal the unconscious envy of an exclusively female prerogative, as well as an attempt to inscribe this difference within a hierarchical scale, an asymmetric gender codification that would reinforce and consolidate male supremacy, extolling its peculiarities.[3]

The outcome has been a dichotomy, to a large extent influenced by Greek thought, between generation and birth, body and mind, motherhood and war, which has permeated the whole of Western culture, characterising gender and fostering a system with many additional oppositions: matter/form, nature/culture, body/spirit.[4]

From the symbolic point of view, Christianity brought about a profound change, but in ambivalent and contradictory ways. The mystery of the incarnation put birth, which was totally marginal in the ancient world, at the centre of the sacred representation, and extolled the figure of the Virgin Mary. But this became intertwined with a theological construct aimed at removing any trace of physical childbirth from her image, exonerating her from the pains of childbirth, from blood and suffering, reserved instead for Eve and her descendants. It was the scene of the birth that was glorified; it was all about the child who was coming into the world, and not about his mother in the act of giving birth to him, with a focus connoting every level of this representation, including the pictorial one. With increasing emphasis in the transition between the medieval and early modern ages, what Christianity valued about motherhood was, above all, the spiritual aspect or the maternal function. The very term "*maternitas*" emerged with this meaning: it was coined in the ecclesiastic circles of the 12th century to refer to the symbolic motherhood linking the Church, Christ's bride, to the wretched.[5] The physical aspects of motherhood were increasingly left in the shadows and laden with negative connotations, as something animalistic or shameful; childbirth was surrounded by the taint of impurity.

It is a concept already articulated by various philosophers in Roman times, but taken up and reworked by Christian theologians, to the extent that it became a real medieval trope.[6]

A rift was therefore established, destined to continue for centuries, although with different emphases and re-elaborations, between two aspects of the same event. These were given different relevance, with a celebration of the role and function of motherhood on the one hand, and a devaluation of the physical aspects of motherhood and therefore of childbirth on the other.

In this chapter, we shall analyse some of these representations, being well aware that they are not the only ones and that others were added over time, but, equally, that they have deeply marked our culture, with important repercussions in women's lives.

2 The earth and the sower

Let us begin with the concept of generation and look first of all at its representations and metaphors. An analogy which is deeply rooted in Western culture (but also found outside Europe) has linked a woman's body to earth in terms of fertility: a woman was earth, field, furrow; like the earth, she welcomed and cared for the seed, fed it and made it germinate in a continuous generative cycle; she was a tree bearing fruits. She was also a vase (made of earth as well), where the male-deposited seed was protected and helped to develop, or even an oven, where the food placed within rose and cooked.[7]

In turn, the earth was often represented as a mother who guarded the seeds in her womb, who bore fruits to men and nourished them.[8] From its innermost self came living beings, just as the dead would return to it when buried for their eternal sleep. The earth was a mother, as was Nature (Mother Nature) in the widest sense of the word, which included celestial and terrestrial bodies, animate and inanimate ones. And, by analogy, since the Middle Ages, in some European languages, such as French and Italian, even female genitalia were referred to as "nature": for example, by Italian physician Michele Savonarola (1384–1466) in his *Ad mulieres ferrarienses De regimine pregnantium* (circa 1460)[9] or Scipione Mercurio (1540?–1615) in *La Comare o Ricoglitrice* (The Midwife) (1596).[10]

We are dealing with a strong metaphoric element running continuously through the centuries, reclaimed and reworked over time in various fields and disciplines with different emphases and meanings, like a symbolic alphabet forming the weft and weave of different articulations of discourse. Beyond their apparent uniformity, in the various historical contexts, analogies and metaphors obviously took on specific meanings in relation to the general ideas of nature and its holiness at that time, the interconnections established between macro- and microcosms and the narratives and correspondences that linked the human body and its parts to the sky, the stars and the planets. This is why analogies and metaphors are important indicators of continuity and change, as Carolyn Merchant has shown when discussing the ideas of Organicism and Mechanism, or as I have sought to highlight concerning 18th-century Vitalism and its implications in the field of obstetrics.[11]

When analysing the analogies related to the female body and to generation, Page duBois has identified an important metaphoric rewriting in 5th-century Greece, destined to endure through the centuries. While in earlier centuries the earth, as a representation of the female body, was frequently described as a virgin territory that spontaneously produced every nourishment for mankind, in subsequent writings, this had become "a field, a(s) space marked off by culture and by human labour [..] the space in which he labours" (cited by duBois 1988: 65–77). This is the metaphor that took shape in Greek literature: Deianeira, according to Sophocles (*Trach.*, 31–33), is "an outlying field", that her husband Heracles "sees (it) only when he sows and when he reaps" (cited by duBois 1988: 73).

On the one hand, this important rewriting assigned women a more passive role in procreation, and, on the other, it presented them as property of a farmer-husband, who tills and sows 'his' field to produce fruits that belong to him: the earth opens up under his labour, welcomes the seeds, grows them and makes them germinate. This metaphoric variation accounts for a profound change in Greek society, in an imperialistic sense. The implicit consequences furthermore highlight the supremacy of the patrilineal relationship compared to the matrilineal one, namely the greater significance of the father–son/daughter relationship. Aeschylus stated this very clearly in the *Eumenides*, the third and final part of the *Oresteia* trilogy, a work symbolic of the changes that marked the passage from pre-Indo-European matrilineal society to the Indo-European patriarchal and patrilineal one.

In his reply to the Erinyes (ancient goddesses wishing to avenge his mother), and speaking before Athens' Areopagus council for Orestes' acquittal of his mother's murder, the god Apollo uses precisely this analogy which sees a father as the 'sower', and therefore the main 'procreator' (procreator is he who sows the seed) and a mother as the mere 'host' of the embryo:

> The mother of what is called her child is not the parent, but the nurse of the newly-sown embryo. The one who mounts is the parent, whereas she, as a stranger for a stranger, preserves the young plant, if the god does not harm it.
>
> *(Eum., 657–661)*[12]

This reiterates the blood tie directly uniting children to their father, and not their mother who gave birth to them, in practice, the superiority of the paternal bond, as Aristotle claimed, giving a scientific base to this representation.[13]

The metaphor of the earth and the sower was used repeatedly not only in literature,[14] but also in medicine and philosophy. For Plato, for example, men "sow upon the womb, as in a field, animals unseen by reason of their smallness and without form" (*Tim.* 91 d).[15]

From ancient Greece, through the Roman Empire, this metaphor reached medieval and early modern times. Soranus of Ephesus (98–138 AD), author of the *Gynaecia*, one of the most important ancient texts on obstetrics, considered the founder of scientific obstetrics and gynaecology, "Methodicorum princeps",[16] for example, to give advice on how to best prepare for intercourse (which he calls "sowing"). For it to result in conception, he suggests relaxing massages and taking light meals, preparing the body as the farmer prepares the field before sowing it:

> As a farmer sows only after having first cleansed the soil and removed any foreign material, in the same manner we too advise that insemination for the production of man should follow after the body has first been given a rubdown.
>
> *(Gyn, I, 40)*[17]

In the progress of this metaphor, when the seed develops, it becomes a 'flower' and then a 'fruit' and this is the term used to refer to the foetus developing in the womb. Recalling a metaphor used in the Hippocratic Corpus, in the Middle Ages, in the *De passionibus mulierum*, a famous set of texts by the *schola medica Salernitana* attributed to figure of Trotula or Trota de Ruggiero (11th century), but certainly written by several people and collected in the 12th century,[18] an embryo in the first phases of its development was compared to a fragile and very tender flower: "the fetus is attached to the womb just like fruit to a tree, which when it proceeds from the flower is extremely delicate and is destroyed by any sort of accident" (*Trot. 99, par. 88*); the umbilical cord represented its stem. If the foetus is the fruit, the mother is the tree from which it sprouts and where it grows: this is definitely the most recurrent metaphor to describe pregnancy and the relationship between mother and foetus during gestation: the development and growth of a living being in a body finds in this vegetal image its most congruous symbolic depiction with the representation of conception.[19] Birth was therefore seen as the falling of a ripe fruit. For this reason, too, the duration of pregnancy was taken to be variable, from seven to nine, ten months (as in the Hippocratic Corpus or in Aristotle's *The Generation of Animals*). The fruit detaches itself when it is fully ripe, and this process does not take place within a set time, but a variable one.

This metaphor, like the previous one, is also recurrent in several fields, and was constantly used in art, literature and religion. "Blessed is the fruit of thy womb", exclaimed Elizabeth upon seeing Mary in the Gospel of Luke (Luke, 1, 42),[20] and "fructus ventris tui" is what Jesus is called in the Latin version of the *Hail Mary*.

It's interesting to see how this metaphor was widely used by medieval theologians in their detailed formulation of the norms regarding sex. In his *Paidagogos*, Clement of Alexandria (c.150–215 AD), in banning sexual intercourse during pregnancy, wrote that, like a farmer does, man must only sow where the soil welcomes the seeds.[21] Regarding the positions during intercourse, the only one allowed was the one traditionally referred to as the 'sower's', not only because it was deemed more appropriate to achieve conception from the physiological point of view, according to doctors, but also because it respected the natural order; the medieval Penitentials, in fact, punished any other position as 'against nature'. In this sense, we can agree with J.-L. Flandrin that in the Christian world, copulation had the features of a fertilisation rite.[22]

In this perspective, the rewriting of this metaphor by some physicians many centuries later, in the late 1700s, when a new political interest in birth arose, is extremely significant. Johann Peter Frank, the founder of "medical police" and a pioneer of public health, a consultant and minister of various European sovereigns, always represented a woman's body as a field, not as any field or a privately owned plot of land, but as the 'seedbed of the state', where "unborn citizens" grow like tender seedlings (see Chapter 10.4).[23] This is an important turning point, as we shall see, accounting for the new public importance of birth, and for the establishment of biopower, namely the political control over people's bodies.[24]

3 Man as the "origin of generation": generated by man, born by woman

From the very beginning, the attention of Greek medical and philosophical thought was on generation, the initial moment of the reproductive process, on which family and social expectations were focused.

Many philosophers, such as Parmenides, Anaxagoras, Empedocles and Democritus, broadly agreed that conception was the outcome of the combination in the uterus of male- and female-produced seed. It was also strictly linked to sexual pleasure, essentially an effect of this fusion.[25] We find the same theory in the Hippocratic Corpus, a collection of some 70 medical texts, written between the 5th and 4th centuries BC and attributed to Hippocrates of Kos, but actually written by different authors and with uneven content.[26] The subject is dealt with in detail in *On Generation* and *Superfetation*. In the first, we read that both man and woman contribute to generation by releasing a fluid, where both male and female seeds are contained. However, the two sexes do not have equivalent roles, since their bodies are hierarchically different from a biological point of view. This hierarchy was founded on a different combination of the four fundamental base elements of the universe (earth, air, water and fire), which were associated with the qualities of warmth, cold, humidity and dryness, and also with the bodily humours, according to the 'theory of bodily humours' (blood, phlegm, yellow bile and black bile), which, as developed by Galen together with the theory of 'temperaments', would be the basis of medical thought for many centuries.[27]

The female body was considered colder and more humid compared to the male; this caloric insufficiency translated into a different degree of strength and activity, and even determined several physiological peculiarities such as menstruation. Ultimately, it was an imperfect copy of the male body, characterised by a sequence of shortcomings, although some *Corpus* writings talk of the female body in terms of difference.[28] The male seed was therefore usually more powerful than the female one, and its superiority determined the birth of a boy: "The male is stronger than the female: it must follow that it is engendered from a stronger seed" (*Gen.* VI, 478).[29]

Aristotle (384–322 BC) applied a significant change to this view. For him, generation was the exclusive outcome of the action of the male seed on the material supplied by the female body, which didn't produce any seed, but only a secretion. In his *On the Generation of Animals*, he explained that in virtue of its greater heat, in the male body the residue of nutrients was filtered and refined, turning from blood to semen. In the female, this process of "concoction" did not occur precisely due to its thermal impotence. The residue would collect in the womb to be later expelled as menstrual blood. The male seed was composed of an immaterial substance, *pnéuma*, "analogous to the element of the stars" (*GA*, II B, 3, 736 b),[30] and possessed in itself the three principles of form, mutation and soul. Upon entering the uterus, it would set the residue of blood in motion, activating it like rennet in milk: "the material secreted by the female in the uterus [is] fixed by the semen of the male (this acts in the same way as rennet acts upon milk)" (*GA*, II B, 4, 739 b).[31]

The roles of the two sexes in the process of generation were therefore strongly hierarchical and consistent with the founding principles of his philosophy, which rested on the active/passive and form/matter dichotomies: in generation, the male provided the form, the female the matter, "the female always provides the material, the male that which fashions it" (*GA*, II B, 4,738 b).[32] Essentially, the capacity to generate was attributed only to the man, while the woman's role was devalued, reduced to that of a mere receptacle: her body fed what the male seed had generated. The male was active, "agent and mover"; the female was passive, in the etymological sense of the Latin *patire* (endure). In short, the male generated. He was *arché tes genésos* (origin of generation), while the woman welcomed, fed and birthed.[33]

Aristotle's theory, by stressing the role of the father, provided the patriarchal system with a solid scientific base: sure enough, if the male was the "origin of generation", while the woman only provided matter, it would follow that children belonged *in primis* to their father, not only according to social norms, but also by the law of nature.[34]

These different theories on generation continued to be the object of broad discussions and re-elaborations in the following centuries. In particular, Aristotle's theory was criticised by Galen, who in his *De semine* went back to Hippocratic theories on the combination of both seeds (even if still characterised by a qualitative difference, developing them into a symmetrical view of the two bodies, according to which the male, external sexual organs found their mirror-like correspondence in the female, internal ones: to the testicles, for example, corresponded the ovaries, called "female testicles". This reinforced the "one-sex model", which remained a foundation of medical thought for many centuries, right up to the 18th century, as shown by historian Thomas Laqueur (Figure 1.1).[35]

FIGURE 1.1 Uterus and "penile" vagina: "matrix cavity" (= uterus cavity, A), neck of the matrix (B), "female testicles" (= ovaries D), "pudendo, or nature of the woman" (= vagina, C), from Scipione Mercurio (1618), *La Commare o riccoglitrice*, Milano: Giob. Bidelli, p. 19. Reproduced with permission of the Biblioteca Pinali antica (Padua).

Even the theory of pleasure fitted with and was confirmed by this approach: without pleasure, there could be no generation, because that meant that there had been no emission of semen; in turn, conception was proof of the emission of semen, the result of shared sexual pleasure, with all the consequences that this would entail even on a legal level. For example, if a woman had conceived after being raped, it meant that she had enjoyed it, emitting the seminal fluid, as stated in the *Corpus iuris civilis*, Justinian's important collection of laws (6th century AD) and foundation of medieval and early modern legislation.[36] This principle was also later taken up in a variety of ways in legal medicine. Even the timing and simultaneity of pleasure were important: a qualitative or temporal difference could represent an objective obstacle to generation.

Galen's approach therefore reassigned an important role to the female in the process of procreation, to the extent that he was considered a "proto-feminist" by some historians,[37] even though the gender hierarchy in generation was still reiterated in the codification of the different contribution of the two seeds: the male seed determined the specific identity of every single animal, and the female seed its individual identity (the male determined, for example, the eyes, and the female their characteristics).[38]

Aware of these discrepancies, in his *Canon of medicine*, Avicenna tried to reconcile these two views, on the one hand, developing his theory of "radical humidity", indispensable to conception as fuel is to fire, but, on the other, denying a woman's contribution to the production of seed.[39]

Aristotle's theories, however, were not set aside, but had renewed success in the late medieval period: scholasticism brought Aristotle's theories on generation back, in the context of an overall reappreciation of his philosophy and its common ground with Christian thought. In his *Summa Theologiae*, quoting Aristotle, Thomas Aquinas (1225–1274) stated that, following natural law:

> In the generation of an animal the female supplies the matter, while the male is the active principle of generation; woman's semen is not apt for generation, but is something imperfect in the seminal order, which, on account of the imperfection of the female power, it has not been possible to bring to complete seminal perfection. Consequently this semen is not the necessary matter of conception.
>
> *(Summa, III, 31, art. 5, 2–3)*[40]

This concept was also reiterated by Dante Alighieri (1265–1321) in his *Convivio*.[41]

In practice, the discussion remained open and both theories continued to be followed with alternating progress and fortune, both in medicine and in theology. Galen's theory would come to fore again in the 16th century, further developed by authoritative philosophers and physicians, such as Girolamo Fabrici d'Acquapendente (1533–1619).

It was given credit even by various theologians, since it helped to better explain a phenomenon that was otherwise unacceptable in their eyes: that an act as shameful and animalistic as sexual intercourse could generate such pleasure.[42]

The procreative purpose of enjoyment motivated it, absolved it and for some allowed them to accept as legitimate even those sexual practices which allowed it to be reached simultaneously, even with all the limits and distinctions, more or less marked in the different theological schools of thought. Jesuit theologian Tomás Sánchez (1550–1610), for example, one of the most open-minded of his kind, author of the *De sancto matrimonii sacramento*, wrote that in marriage, "sexual pleasure is not a bad thing in itself, given that nature itself has bound it firmly to the act for the purpose of procreation" (cited by Pelaja and Scaraffia 2008: 121).

Only during the 17th century were these theories gradually considered obsolete and abandoned: the new era of scientific progress based on experimental methodologies brought new ideas on generation, as we shall see in Chapter 10.

It's curious to observe how, despite the radical change in the scientific perspectives on generation, remains of these ancient theories emerge even nowadays in some popular beliefs used especially in the debates on abortion or sexual violence. When, in 2012, Todd Akin, US senator and fanatical anti-abortionist, declared in a televised interview that pregnancies resulting from sexual assaults were 'really rare', since "if it's legitimate rape, the female body has ways to try and shut the whole thing down" (cited by Filippini 2012), he essentially did nothing but re-propose an entirely anachronistic belief linked to a view of conception that comes from antiquity, and which has remained rooted in the cultural background of people even in our time.

4 Sons and daughters: hierarchies in generation

From Aristotle's theory, which put the father as the only 'origin of generation', derived a precise hierarchy in its outcome, namely children, asserting not only the male supremacy over the female, but also a ranking based on similarity to the father and/or the mother.[43]

Since, as Aristotle explained, "the one who is generated resembles the one who generated it" (*GA*, IV, 1, 766 b),[44] and since the generating one was the father, it followed that the ultimate aim of generation, that is a perfect being, was the production of a male child resembling the father. The birth of a female child represented in itself a departure from the aim, although "necessary to nature" to preserve the species in animals where male and female were separate. In practice, the ideal reproductive model was a "generation of identicals" and generation coincided, in fact, with fatherhood.[45]

The way sex was determined was explained by Aristotle through the principle of the heat of the seed: the hotter seed gave rise to a male, whereas the birth of a female was the result of a colder, second-rate (*deficiens*) seed:

> when the first principle does not have strength and cannot concoct the nourishment through lack of heat nor bring it into its proper form, but is defeated in this respect, then it must necessarily change into its opposite. Now the opposite of the male is the female.
>
> (*GA, IV, 1, 766 a*)[46]

The theory contemplated further specifications, considering in addition to sex the characters of physical resemblance. Besides the gender principle, two other factors were decisive: the individual character and the impulse. In case the principle of gender prevailed, but that of the individual character was weak, a boy resembling his mother would be born. If the principle of gender did not prevail but was in the presence of a strong individual character, the outcome would be a girl resembling her father. Finally, if the impulse was also weak, a girl resembling her mother would be born.[47] Four levels were thus presented in the hierarchy of generation: a male resembling his father, a male resembling his mother, a female resembling her father and a female resembling her mother. The final and greatest degradation of the generative process was "animal matter", a "monster", an expression of the absolute "prevalence of brute matter".[48] Aristotle therefore dissociated himself from those who believed that monsters were the outcome of the union of different animal seeds, i.e. the result of the copulation between animals and women, a recurrent trope in the ancients' imagination and in myth; he did not believe in the possible fertilisation of a woman with the seed of another animal.

In conclusion, a minimal gap separated the female who resembled her mother from the degeneration of matter, from monstrosity, as the prevalence of the feminine, in gender and in likeness, was at the lowest level in the hierarchy of generation. In this sense, we can say, in Rosi Braidotti's words, that "the monstrous as the negative pole, the pole of pejoration, is structurally analogous to the feminine" (Braidotti 1994: 80), not only as other-than the established norm, but precisely because of its physiological closeness.

During the Middle Ages, Aristotle's theory was revised in a variety of ways. Theologian and naturalist Hildegard of Bingen (1098–1179), for instance, added a spiritual element, virtuous love, which was very original, but ultimately stressed the negative connotations in the birth of a girl: in fact, the outcome of the union between poor semen and weak affection was a "*foemina amare complexionis*".[49]

Other theories, still affected by hierarchical approaches and implicit gender supremacy and based on the predominance of the right side over the left and/or on the degree of warmth of the "matrix", i.e. the womb, correlated the determination of sex to where conception had taken place inside the womb and/or its temperature. Anaxagoras and Parmenides, for example, believed that it depended on the origin of the semen: a product of the right testicle would generate a boy, whereas a girl would be born from semen coming from the left testicle.[50] This theory recurs in some books of the Hippocratic Corpus, next to others that indicate the time of sexual intercourse as important.[51] Galen also considered the right/left opposition to be fundamental, but as related to the womb: since this organ was believed to be divided into separate chambers[52] (in a way which mirrored the breasts), with the right chamber warmer than the left, if the embryo developed in the right chamber, a boy would be born, and vice versa. The different nuances in this location determined resemblance and personality. This belief reached the Middle Ages, thanks to the mediation of Arabic medicine and Avicenna in particular.

Some of these theories remained deeply rooted not only in science, but also and above all in popular belief. As Thomas Laqueur has argued, the theory according to which the ovaries were counterparts of the testicles, the "female testicles", even outlasted the practice of anatomical dissections, remaining popular until the end of the 17th century.[53] The theory connecting sexual pleasure and procreation lasted even longer, as we have seen, despite the evidence of new theories on generation at the end of the 17th century.[54] In 1740, the young empress of Austria Maria Theresa, anxious to get pregnant as soon as possible after her marriage, was advised by her court physician to dwell more on the preliminaries and on sexual enjoyment, the same advice given by Soranus of Ephesus in his writings. Various 19th-century books on obstetrics, such as Giovanni Raffaele's *Ostetricia teorico-pratica* (1841), still stated that the more intense the sexual pleasure was, the more likely the conception would be.[55]

5 Generating with the body, generating with the mind

In Greek culture, women's ability to give birth with their bodies was juxtaposed to men's ability to "give birth with their minds" in a gender representation which assimilated procreation to creation, giving birth to one's children to generating ideas, be they artistic, literary or philosophical ones. This is a case of "appropriation by metaphoric transfer", a "symbolic theft" (Rigotti 2010: 24–25), particularly frequent in Greek culture, especially in Greek philosophy, resumed and revised by Christianity to represent one of the metaphorical cornerstones of Western culture. Needless to say, this analogy also fits in with gender hierarchies which see what (the best of) men generate with their minds as nobler and of a superior nature to what women generate with their bodies.[56]

The broadest conceptualisation of this is in Plato's (428–347 BC) *Symposium*. When reasoning about love, Diotima asks Socrates: "What is the cause, Socrates, of love, and the attendant desire? See you not how all animals, birds, as well as beasts, in their desire of procreation, are in agony when they take the infection of love, which begins with the desire of union?" (*Symp.* 207 a/b).[57] Diotima herself finds the answer in the rejection of death, in the desire to defeat it through procreation, ensuring the continuity of life so deeply felt in all societies: "the mortal nature is seeking as far as is possible to be everlasting and immortal: and this is only to be attained by generation" (*Symp.* 207 d).[58] Those who are

> full of generative power in the body only, betake themselves to women and beget children; this is the character of their love; their offspring, as they hope, will preserve their memory and give them the blessedness and immortality which they desire in the future.
>
> (*Symp. 208 e*)[59]

But Diotima goes further and points out that this is only the first and most basic way in which people try to overcome death; there's another and superior kind of generation, because it is less ephemeral: the generation of the spirit. As well as in the body, a person can be fecund in the spirit; and the mind needs to find a spiritual match in order to be productive, too, in other words, a "beautiful person" to help us "bring to light" what has been conceived in a fruitful spiritual union. The mind alone conceives what grants fame and immortal memory to its creators, such as poets, legislators and philosophers. So, reproduction and spiritual creation are linked by a mirroring analogy that marks all the stages: desire, search for the loved one, carnal or spiritual union, conception and birth. But the offspring of the spirit are far more beautiful – says Plato – because they are immortal: "Who ... would not rather have their children than ordinary human ones?" (*Symp.* 209 d).[60]

The lack of qualitative symmetry in reproduction is obvious in the light of the intrinsic purpose that determines it, the desire to overcome death: those "born of women", in fact, are destined to die, whereas the offspring of the mind are immortal. So, male generation is the only one that can guarantee a person's immortality, while the female body shows its limitations. Giving birth to imperfect children, destined to die, is the limit of what women can achieve.[61]

Precisely in the context of this analogy, in a well-known passage from Plato's *Theaetetus*, Socrates called his philosophy "maieutics", stating that he practised the same art (*tékhne*) as his mother Phaenarete, a midwife (*maîa*). Just as she helped women to give birth, Socrates helped his pupils to produce something which was "vital and true", that is concepts and ideas, through a kind of intellectual labour. Therefore, a philosopher is like a midwife, but he practises his art on the minds, not on the bodies; on men, not on women, showing that thought is sexually masculine: "All that is true of their art of midwifery is true also of mine, but mine differs from theirs in being practised upon men, not women, and in tending their souls in labor, not their bodies" (*Théét.*, 150 b).[62]

The analogy is enriched by further details: as a woman who is about to give birth is supported by a woman who helps her, so a man who produces thoughts is supported by another man who helps him, through questions, to work out concepts in an intellectual labour through which truth is produced. And as a midwife is an older, no longer fertile woman, Socrates calls himself "barren", but in wisdom, because his art consists of questioning others, not producing thoughts himself.

This is another analogy which was transferred from the Greek and the Roman world to Christianity and then throughout Western culture: what the spirit produces is often referred to with terms drawn from the field of generation. Francesca Rigotti has gathered examples of this from every age and intellectual or artistic activity: Catullus called his poems *dulces musarum fetus* ("sweet children of the Muses"); Ovid (and afterwards also Montesquieu) referred to his work as a "child conceived without a mother"; and Alessandro Manzoni presented his *Promessi Sposi* as "my rough childbirth".[63] Even a religious conversion process, often connoted as a re-birth, draws on this metaphor: in his Letter to the Galatians, St. Paul describes his effort to prepare the catechumens in the same terms.[64]

This is a strong and diachronic feature of gender representation in the Western world and is also symbolically connected to the marginalisation of women from higher intellectual professions and universities. The deeply rooted conviction of their intellectual inferiority, based on the overall minority attributed to the female nature, was certainly reinforced by this representation placing giving birth with the body and giving birth with the mind, motherhood and thought in opposition to each other, as irreconcilable events.

A female figure, fruitful in both body and mind, would have been too powerful and therefore threatening to the male imagination, thereby highlighting the envy and unconscious fear which underlie these constructs.

6 Zeus' cephalic delivery: Athena's birth

The myth of Athena's birth from Zeus' head is in many ways remarkable for its multi-faceted symbolism, expressing at the same time envy for the female reproductive capacity and male desires to take possession of it and to give birth to offspring without the mediation of women's bodies.

Before analysing the myth in detail, it is important to stress that the representation of divine births in many myths involves both heroes and gods coming into the world not "in the common and vulgar way of men" in the words of the medieval Persian poet Firdowsi (10th–11th centuries).[65]

Their "extraordinary" birth (from the Latin *extra ordinaria*, out of the ordinary) is at the same time an expression and a mark of their superiority: they can be born from the head or the thigh, like Dionysus, or from the side, like Adonis, Asclepius or Julius Caesar, who, according to a medieval tradition, was born by Caesarean section. In this sense, Athena's birth is no exception.[66]

However, as Carles Miralles has pointed out,[67] there is much more in this myth, and to fully understand it, we must go back to the beginning. According to Hesiod's *Theogony*, after defeating his father Cronus and becoming king of the Titans, Zeus married Metis, the goddess of wisdom, who possessed an intelligence superior to all men and gods and a metamorphic capacity Zeus did not have.[68]

Fate had foreseen that she would give birth to equally powerful children: a girl, equal in her wisdom and strength to her father, and a son of immense physical strength, destined to become the king of men and gods. To avoid it, following the advice of his mother Gaia, Zeus decided to do away with Metis, swallowing her while pregnant. He certainly did it so as not to be overthrown by his son, but also to absorb the goddess' power. He thus acquired at the same time her wisdom and her procreative capacity. On a symbolic level, he incorporated the female-generating principle, continued with the pregnancy within himself and, when its time is up, gave birth through the head, not just because this was deemed the noblest part of the body, but also because it was the seat of intelligence, a prerogative of his daughter Athena.

The male symbolic element is also reiterated by the background to the scene of this birth: by Zeus' side, to assist him, we do not find one of the Eileithyiae, the Greek goddesses of childbirth, in passive attendance, but the god Hephaestus (or, according to other versions of the myth, Prometheus and/or Hermes) opening Zeus' skull with a hatchet, a typically male tool, as seen on various Greek vases.[69]

Hesiod's narrative shows not only resistance against women's role in procreation, but also a desire to take possession of it and procreate "all alone", an expression of the dream of a reproduction totally free from women, which we find in various works, as, for instance, in Euripides' *Medea*, where Jason states: "Mortals ought, you know, to beget children from some other source, and there should be no female sex. Then mankind would have no trouble" (*Med.*, 573–575).[70]

Athena's traits, ambiguous from a gendered point of view, also emphasise this symbolic aspect: she was born armed, so in a male connotation; she is *Métis* (knowledge) like her mother, but a *métis* subdued to her father; she is a virgin, therefore has no bridegroom, but, most of all, she is only her father's daughter, a motherless goddess, as she herself says in Aeschylus' *Eumenides*, the final play of the *Oresteia*: "For there was no mother who gave me birth; and in all things, except for marriage, whole-heartedly I am for the male and entirely on the father's side" (*Eum.* 736–739).[71]

This is the reason why she is the one who decrees the end of the priority of blood ties between mother and children, in the Areopagus court, casting the decisive vote to acquit the matricide Orestes, against the Erinyes, ancient goddesses of maternal revenge. It is no coincidence that Aeschylus uses her as a symbolic figure of the transition to a patriarchal and patrilineal society, with a consequent change in the hierarchies of blood ties and the set of prohibitions and taboos. The symbolic mother–daughter couple of pre-Indo-European civilisations (Demeter/Kore) is replaced by the father–daughter couple (Zeus/Athena), which forestalls a break of identity and decisive alliances in the history of women.

As a corollary to this myth, we should also remember that in a sort of rivalry with Zeus, Hera tries to generate alone, too, but gives birth to Hephaestus, a god so ugly as to be unbearable to look at even for his own mother, who throws him off Mount Olympus, making him lame: in symbolic terms, the outcome of any motherhood, even a divine one, occurring without male approval and contribution, could only be monstrous (as pointed out by M. Detienne).[72]

7 Childbirth vs war, childbirth as war

"Men say that we live a life free from danger at home while they fight with the spear. How wrong they are! I would rather stand three times with a shield in battle than give birth once" (*Med.* 249–251).[73] The famous words pronounced by Medea in Euripides' tragedy are not just the spontaneous outburst of a desperate woman, betrayed by her husband and about to lose everything, including her children. First and foremost, they belong to a more complex discourse, denouncing the unhappiness of women and giving the reasons for this, starting with having husbands who are also masters (*despótes*) they themselves bought with their dowries. They also belong to a wider discourse on the subordination and suffering of women, which also includes childbirth as a peculiarly feminine experience.

By assimilating childbirth to war, Medea presents a gendered representation deeply rooted in Greek culture, which linked the two experiences in more complex ways (and not only because women obviously brought warriors into the world). In practice, childbirth was for women what war was for men: evidence and proof of their nature, identity and value. In this sense, childbirth was configured as "women's war", to use an extremely enduring metaphor in the representation of genders throughout Western culture.

In Greek culture, this correlation features repeatedly and in many different forms, as Nicole Loraux has pointed out in her detailed analysis.[74] Childbirth and war even shared a common term, *pónos*, used to identify both labour pains and a long conflict such as the Trojan war (*Troikós pónos*), and even a strenuous effort such as Heracles'; just like its synonym *lóchos*, it was used to refer to labour, an ambush or armed troops.[75] A woman in labour was said to be fighting against the pains of childbirth. Even the pain of a fighter wounded in battle could be likened to that of a woman in labour: in the 11th book of the *Iliad*, Agamemnon is said to be suffering a pain, as "sharp dart striketh a woman in travail, the piercing dart that the Eilithyiae, the goddesses of childbirth, send" (*Iliad.*, XI: 222).[76]

If childbirth was a fight, it is not surprising that the goddess overseeing it, together with the Eileithyiae, was armed with arrows: Artemis, virgin goddess of the hunt, an ambiguous figure who dragged women into fights, which might be fatal to them and where their courage and strength were tested: womanhood was proved only by motherhood and we shouldn't forget that in Greek society, childbirth marked a girl's transition from *pàrthenos* (virgin) to *gyné* (mature woman).[77] Similarly, men showed their courage and valour (*andréia*) in battle: the equation man = warrior was fundamental to their gender representation.[78] And just like women in childbirth, soldiers in war staked their bodies, "offered their bodies to their country", as Thucydides wrote (*Epith.* II, 43.2).[79] In this sense, their war wounds were symbols of their valour (*symbola tes andréias*), to be exhibited, Plutarch wrote, as happened in Rome when it was a republic during electoral campaigns.[80]

The analogy is strengthened by the fact that both events took place in separate gender groups: only men participated in war; only women (midwives, female relatives or neighbours) in childbirth: the exclusion of men from childbirth, which lasted up to the 17th–18th centuries, was mirrored by the exclusion of women from the battlefield. Breaking either of these bans would arouse suspicion or accusations of witchcraft, as evidenced, to some extent, by the life of Joan of Arc.

Both trials involved not just experiencing pain, but also, potentially, death. Women faced it so as to give life, men in order to bring death, by killing their enemies. In the Greek world, this was considered the most beautiful death, the one bringing honour and fame not just to the warrior himself, but also to his family and his entire city, as Pericles declares in Thucydides' famous epitaph (*Epith.*, II, 43.1).[81]

In Sparta, such an honour was rewarded by inscribing the hero's name on his tombstone, despite the rules dictating that all burials should be nameless. Women who died in childbirth were honoured in the same way: their names, too, were reported on their graves. Likewise, in Athens, where different funeral laws were in force, warriors who died in battle and women who died in childbirth shared a distinction: their funerary reliefs portrayed their deaths, whereas the practice was to represent scenes from the life of the deceased.[82]

Men and women could be so distinguished by the two opposite and specular capacities of giving life and giving death. Anthropological studies showed that since the beginning of humanity, male identity found its basis in the ability to confront death by fighting against animals and men (in hunting and war).[83] The German scholar Walter Burkert pointed out how, in the ancient world, "hunting, sacrifice and war are symbolically interchangeable"[84] and how sacrifice represented a transposition of this symbol to a sacred context: a sacred killing was offered to God as an act of reparation. In Burkert's view, this explains the persistence of war in all civilisations, its constant reoccurrence throughout history, despite the evidence of its disastrous consequences for both winners and losers, all due to war being the ritual self-representation and self-validation of male society. Even though Burkert's analysis underestimates the impact of other important factors in wars, it undoubtedly captures a crucial aspect of the male identity and representation also analysed in a long-term perspective by historians such as George Mosse.[85]

To return to Euripides, what is Medea complaining about, if the analogy between childbirth and war was a regular trope? In actual fact, Medea's complaint is that childbirth is not valued as highly as fighting, and that women are accused of leading a safe and peaceful life within their homes, living free from dangers, a recurrent accusation in literature and in philosophy.[86] In other words, in her speech, Medea repeats the well-known metaphor, but in order to denounce its representation of social inequality and, in so doing, she dwells upon one of the crucial and peculiar facets of Greek culture: the extolling of battle which turns a warrior into a hero and war into the most exciting event in history, a symbolic pinnacle permeating art, literature and myth. From the Trojan to the Persian wars, the war fought by men (or by the gods) has been extolled as the pinnacle of human experience, the foundation of civilisation. Armed conflict has been the topic of historical narrative, and has been held out as a supreme example of values and civilisation. "Women's war", however, fought within their homes, in a wholly internal and carnal battle to give life and not death, is excluded from public discourse, from pictorial representation and from the symbolic sphere; it becomes neither symbol, nor *lógos*.

Nevertheless, it is important to stress the huge success of this analogy and its crucial importance in Western culture, where for a very long time childbirth and war have been recurrent, essential features of gender representation, despite being articulated in a variety of ways at different times and in different contexts.

We find it in medical language and illustrations. For instance, the first printed anatomical drawings, collected by German physician Johannes de Ketham in the *Fasciculus medicinae*, show the "wounded man" as a warrior, pierced by all kinds of cutting weapons, whereas a woman is portrayed as pregnant and in the typical childbirth posture.[87] Other physicians likened the condition of a woman after childbirth to that of a warrior who had survived a battle, comparing the puerperium period to the condition "of a seriously wounded man, for whom a slight disorder might lead to death" (Mahon 1820: 403). In the 18th-century debate on Caesarean sections, its supporters stressed the duty of a mother's sacrifice, likening it to that of soldiers making the ultimate sacrifice for their country.[88]

Until recently, it also featured in popular culture: in some regions of northern Italy, such as Friuli, if the newborn was a boy, people would remark that "an alpine soldier" had been born[89]; "He will have to fight in the war", French midwives would say, whereas, in the case of a girl, they would say: "she will suffer what I have suffered to give birth. Isn't childbirth for women what war is for men?" (Laget 1982: 172).

We also find the same analogy in the autobiographical accounts of female peasants from the early 20th century: they describe childbirth precisely as a war, with the drama of a deadly challenge often taking place in the worst conditions, in cowsheds, in the cold and without any assistance. The analogy was not lost even on an expert narrator of war events such as Nuto Revelli, who commented: "Childbirth was often just like war, the real one!" (Revelli 1985: LXXII).

The nationalist avant-gardes of the 19th and 20th centuries resumed and re-elaborated this analogy in a redefinition of gender models which emphasised war-like traits and physical strength. Friedrich Nietzsche stressed both the correlation between man and warrior and that between woman and mother, intended as a "maker of warriors". Nietzsche's superman is first and foremost a warrior seeking his war and his enemy, in a monosexual union with his "brothers in war", whereas "everything about woman is a riddle, and everything about woman has one solution: that is pregnancy" (Nietzsche [1881–1885] 1995: 47 and 66).[90] A woman is "a warrior's rest" and the mother of his children. Benito Mussolini reiterated the essential elements of this analogy in a 26 May 1934 speech to the Italian Parliament, saying: "War is to a man as motherhood is to woman" (cited by Meldini 1975: 85).[91] The Fascist project of national education hinged precisely on the two figures of the woman as mother and the man as warrior, and was supported by a pervasive propaganda which juxtaposed the image of a warrior, with his set of symbols (the colour black, skulls, daggers, etc.) to that of a fertile and nurturing mother.

8 Eve's pains

Over time, the suffering of childbirth has been culturally re-elaborated in a variety of ways, both from the philosophical/scientific and, above all, from the religious point of view. Ancient physicians, well aware of the difference between humans and animals in childbirth, remarked upon the peculiarity of women's suffering, even in natural childbirths, however varied individually.[92] In fact, this was much more obvious in agricultural and pastoral societies, thanks to their daily contact with animals.

In *On the Generation of Animals*, Aristotle speculated on the reasons for the labours of pregnancy and the "exhausting pains" of childbirth in humans, observing that it is the only physiological event to cause such suffering and suggesting that it may be linked to women's lifestyle, in particular to their extreme lack of physical activity causing a detrimental stagnation of "residues". He concluded that "among nations where the women live a laborious life gestation is not equally conspicuous and those who are accustomed to work bear children easily; for work consumes the residual matter" (GA IV, D, 6, 775a),[93] thus ascribing the change to a more favourable natural state to social habits.

Centuries later, and in particular in the 18th and 19th centuries, this view was proposed again, in the wake of Jean-Jacques Rousseau's glorification of the state of nature, in a polarisation which saw society as corrupting an original state of balance. It was further strengthened by the incorrect interpretation of anthropologists studying African tribes, who misinterpreted the silence of women in labour as an absence of pain, so as a physical rather than a cultural trait, as we shall see later (Chapter 3.3).[94]

Religious thought tended to associate pain to a punishment by the gods and this punishment to men's crimes: the box Pandora opens despite Prometheus' prohibition contains suffering and death, the unleashing of which was punishment for Prometheus, benefactor of humanity.[95] Judaism went beyond this association, with a genderised explanation dealing precisely with the matter of suffering in childbirth. The story is well known and is one of the central passages in the book of *Genesis*: God's punishment for the original sin, in addition to banning mankind from Earthly Paradise, thereby decreeing their mortality, is differentiated by gender: Adam will suffer the exertion of work, Eve the pains of childbirth and the submission to her husband:

> I will greatly multiply thy sorrow and thy conception; in sorrow thou shalt bring forth children; and thy desire shall be to thy husband, and he shall rule over thee.
>
> (*Genesis KJV*, 3, 16)[96]

The pains of childbirth were thus ascribed to the will of God, as a supernatural decree uniting all women to Eve, in an enduring memory of the original sin, perpetuated through pain. Not only was suffering inescapable, it also required a woman's full acceptance.

This view was kept and enriched by further elements in the transition to Christianity, particularly after the 4th century, when misogyny and disgust towards sexuality intensified. In the Middle Ages, a great deal of theological texts stress the crimes committed by Eve in her role as prototype of womankind, her greater responsibility for the original sin, her moral weakness and frailty, and her propensity to forge links with the devil: all these traits made her a *ianua diaboli*, in Tertullian's definition in the *De cultu feminarum* (On Women's Dress).[97] The parallel theological construct of the figure of the Virgin Mary only stressed these negative traits even further, in an ever increasing polarisation. Eve's sin was charged with sexual connotations, particularly connected to the sin of lust which drove women to desire men. Through the pains of childbirth, women thus atoned not just for her original disobedience, but for the carnal sin which was one of the main consequences of her downfall. Moreover, the greater importance given to chastity in the Church's moral hierarchy made this sin ubiquitous even within marriage. The manner of the birth itself, *intra faeces et urinam*, was increasingly looked upon with disgust by medieval theologians and taken as a symbol of the stain of the original sin and of the miserable nature of mankind, taking up and developing the thought of various Stoic philosophers.[98]

The Church therefore encouraged women to fully accept the pains of childbirth as atonement for their sins: for centuries, the prayers written for pregnant women reinforced these concepts, stressing different aspects depending on the particular religious denomination and reaching intimidating tones in the 16th and 17th centuries, with the Augustinians and Jansenists. The *Prayer of an Expectant Mother* by Saint Francis de Sales, written at the height of the Counter-Reformation, but also popular in later centuries, states:

> In as much as your just anger made the first mother of human beings along with her sinful posterity subject to the pain and suffering of childbirth, O Lord, I accept all the pain that it will please you to permit me to experience on this occasion. I only ask by the sacred and joyful birth of your innocent Mother, to be merciful to me, a poor and worthless sinner, at the time of my painful delivery. Bless me with the child it will please you to give me with the blessing of your eternal love. I ask you this very humbly and with perfect trust in your goodness[99]

Even death in childbirth fitted within this perspective, as supreme atonement for carnal sins, as a prayer from 1646 reads:

> for although holy matrimony has made my conception legitimate, I confess that concupiscence mingled its venom therewith and that it has urged

me to commit faults which displease you. If it be you will that I die in my confinement, may I adore it, bless it and submit to it.

(Cited by Gélis 1991:155)

In the 18th century, the correlation between crime/suffering/atonement was drawn even in theological debates on midwifery practices, particularly when discussing the choice between the life of the mother and that of the child, as an argument in support of the latter: in other words, the difficulties experienced in childbirth were interpreted as signs of God's will, special punishment for the mother's sins. It is no coincidence that this argument returned in 1889, in the reflections of some theologians of the Holy Office [the Supreme Sacred Congregation of the Roman and Universal Inquisition] condemning embryotomies: "The many ways used by divine justice to carry out the terrible sentence pronounced to Eve after her sin, "multiplicabo aerumnas tuas et conceptus tuos: in dolores paries filios", include ectopic pregnancies" (cited by E. Betta 2006: 304).

Such arguments were not limited to theology: they appeared in medicine, too. In *La Comare o ricoglitrice*, the first midwifery manual written published in Italy in 1596, Scipione Mercurio, after listing some natural causes of pain in childbirth, reported the words from *Genesis* and the authoritative opinion of theologians, in whose view a woman in childbirth had to go through "such woes because of the original sin", as she had been "an instrument of the devil" (Mercurio [1596] 1713: 5).[100] Similarly, in 1773, during the debate on Caesarean sections on living women, Sicilian physician and theologian Giuseppe Carbonajo was in favour of a mother's ultimate sacrifice, commenting that in a difficult birth, "she must deems herself to be a victim of divine wrath" (cited by Filippini 1995: 266).

In Western culture, suffering has thus been naturalised, in the sense that it has been seen as intrinsic to a nature regulated by divine law, and as such fixed and not subject to change. A woman giving birth without suffering (especially to her first child) would be suspected of consorting with the devil, contravening both God's and natural laws.[101]

This view had considerable repercussions in the medical and scientific fields, too, diverting research both from investigating the causes of pain and from developing techniques and medication to fight it. Only with the Enlightenment and later with Positivism was there a reversal in this trend. The question asked by Aristotle in the 4th century BC was officially taken up as a topic of scientific discussion by the Paris *Académie de médecine* as late as 1783, with the following formulation: *Pourquoi la femme a-t-elle besoin de secours pour accoucher, alors que les femmeles des bêtes accouchent seules*? (Why do women need help to give birth, whereas female animals give birth unaided?).[102] And only half-way through the 19th century, in Anglo-Saxon countries first and communist ones later, did the trialling of practices and techniques aimed at reducing the pain of childbirth openly begin (as we shall see in Chapter 11.8).

For centuries, such a representation has encouraged a pain-driven view, an extolling of suffering which appears to be one of the primary features in the

Western image of childbirth and which, in turn, stresses and substantiates a representation of women as giving themselves freely and self-sacrificing.

It is found in the autobiographical accounts of many early 20th-century women; it formed the basis of certain forms of sadism used with women in labour,[103] especially in hospitals, where vulgar remarks were rather widespread in some countries right up to the 1960s. And even in the 1990s, it was suggested in some currents of thought in Catholic Ecofeminism advocating natural childbirth, where suffering was extolled as a precious experience for women, an essential and positive rite of passage towards motherhood, almost granting moral superiority, denying the religious matrix of this stance and the centuries of history that have bound it to the destiny of women as an unavoidable sentence.[104]

9 Mary's virgin delivery

Christianity brought about a profound breech with the ancient world in the representation of birth: the mystery of God's incarnation, in fact, places the event at the core of the religious context. Jesus Christ's *Dies Natalis*, set in the 6th century AD to coincide with the Roman *Saturnalia* celebrations, from the 12th century onwards, together with Easter, became one of the most important liturgical celebrations. The veneration of the nativity scene, promoted by St. Francis of Assisi, experienced extraordinary development, becoming, in the following centuries, one of the favourite topics of religious pictorial representation, too.

With Christianity, therefore, birth took on a relevance and symbolic codification which was totally absent in the Greco-Roman world, as Yvonne Knibiehler has shown.[105]

But with the Virgin Mary's physical motherhood, however, it was a very different story: not only was it not represented, but was actually symbolically removed in the process of theological construction of Mary's virgin birth. In fact, Mary conceived "knowing no man" and gave birth to Jesus Christ whilst remaining a virgin: the glorification of Jesus' birth became intertwined with the symbolic erasure of her childbirth and her motherhood was purged of its bodily features: Mary was a mother, but did not give birth like other women. Thus, the two sides of this event have opposite symbolic meanings.

This process was achieved through a complex construct by Mariology, the powerful branch of theology which defined the features and traits of the Virgin Mary, integrating the limited information contained in the Gospels. This long theological path aimed to purge the figure of Mary from every physical and spiritual impurity or corruption, asserting her perfection and eternal virginity: Mary is *virgo virginum, turris eburnea, mater inviolata*, to recall some of the most recurrent attributes from the *Laurentian Litany*.[106]

The idea of a virgin conception, however, was not new on the religious front: the trope of a virgin birth occurs in many ancient mythologies; it belongs to the "extraordinary births" theme, which characterises especially gods and heroes, as already mentioned (par. 1).[107] Therefore, Christianity did not invent, but rather reused and reworked an older theme.[108] The novelty it introduced lies in the eternity of the mother of God's virginity, preserved even after the birth of her son, *post partum*, a totally unprecedented and original trait in the religious landscape.

The first stages of this theological construct date back to the early centuries of the Church and go hand in hand with the definition of Mary as *Theotókos* (mother of God), declared as dogma by the council of Ephesus (431 AD). This sanctioned the dual nature of Christ, both divine and human; Mary was the "mother of God" because Christ was both true God and true man: as a man, he had grown in a woman's womb and had been brought into the world by her according to nature.[109]

But how could both events, conception and birth, be explained and reconciled with Mary's virginity? The matter became the subject of elaborate interpretations of the holy texts which even covered physiological details, in an attempt to reconcile faith with philosophical and scientific principles and with the evidence of childbirth.[110]

On the matter of conception, the subtlest analysis is that by Thomas Aquinas in his *Summa Theologiae*, where the mysteries of the incarnation and of Mary's virginity are explained resorting to Aristotle's theories about generation: at the moment of conception, Mary had supplied the matter (i.e. the blood from her womb), whereas, in place of the male seed, God had infused the active principle (i.e. the form); as He was the Word (*logos*), He had impregnated Mary with His spirit through her ear:

> And consequently it belongs to the supernatural mode of Christ's generation, that the active principle of generation was the supernatural power of God: but it belongs to the natural mode of His generation, that the matter from which His body was conceived is similar to the matter which other women supply for the conception of their offspring. Now, this matter, according to the Philosopher (*De Gener. Animal.* 1, 19), is the woman's blood, not any of her blood, but brought to a more perfect stage of secretion by the mother's generative power, so as to be apt for conception. And therefore of such matter was Christ's body conceived.
>
> (*Summa, III, 31, art. 5, 3*)[111]

Virginity in childbirth was posited as completing the construct of virginity upon conception, in the sense of maintaining the absolute integrity of the mother of God's body, which had to represent perfect physical integrity, free from both sexual penetration and the lacerations of childbirth.[112] How could the mother of God have given birth in pain, contaminating herself and her child with the blood which a deeply rooted tradition looked at with horror, as the most unclean and corrosive bodily fluid? And how could the son of God have been born *intra faeces et urinam*? Furthermore, how could Jesus' natural birth be reconciled with Mary's eternal virginity? Did not his own passing through the birth canal and the vagina entail in itself the *apertio vulvae*, the rupturing of the very hymen seen by theologians as a seal (*signaculum*)? In fact, some claimed that Mary had been a virgin at the time of conception, but that she had lost her virginity in childbirth and that she had gone on to bear Joseph more children.

As far as the moment of delivery was concerned, the Gospels were very vague: about Mary, they said that "while they were there [in Bethlehem], the days were accomplished that she should be delivered. And she brought forth her firstborn son, and wrapped him in swaddling clothes, and laid him in a manger" (*Luke KJV*, 2, 2–6).

Some apocryphal gospels, however, mentioned a virgin birth: Pseudo-Matthew reported that at the time of delivery, Joseph had run to call a midwife. By the time they had returned to the cave, however, the baby had already been born and the midwife, examining Mary, was amazed to find that she was still a virgin:

> And when Zelomi had come in, Salome not having come in, Zelomi said to Mary: Allow me to touch thee. And when she had suffered herself to be examined, the midwife cried out with a loud voice, and said: Lord, great Lord, ave mercy! Never hath it been heard or suspected, that the breasts of any woman should be full of milk, and the child born show its mother to be a virgin.
>
> (*PMG, 13, 2–3*)[113]

The story had a further twist in the apocryphal gospel of James, with the episode of the "incredulous midwife" Salomé who, disbelieving Zelomi, had asked to verify Mary's virginity in person. For her doubt, she had been punished with the paralysis of her hand, from which she had been healed by touching the child, with Mary's intercession. The first revelation of Jesus' divine nature and his first miracle were thus linked precisely to the assumption of his mother's *post partum* virginity.[114] This episode is reproduced in various medieval and Renaissance frescoes and paintings showing the figure of the midwife, from Giotto's *Nativity* in the Scrovegni Chapel in Padua (1303–1305) to the more explicit one by Jacques Daret, *Nativity, from the Altarpiece of the Virgin* (1434–1435), Thyssen-Bornemernisza Museum, Madrid, evidence of the popularity of the story. Precisely, this version of the story, from the apocryphal gospels, was taken up by the Church Fathers.

As far back as the 3rd century, Origen of Alexandria had added the term *tuttasanta* to *theotókos*, advocating Mary's eternal virginity. In the 4th century however (in many ways a turning point in the history of the Church), this view became increasingly established, supported by a number of authoritative Eastern and Western theologians: Ephrem the Syrian, "Mary's Own Singer", Ambrose, Zeno of Verona, Pope Leo I. Gregory of Nyssa (4th century AD), recalling the prophet Isaiah, stressed the correlation between Jesus' conception and Mary's painless delivery:

> Just as the Virgin herself did not know how the body of God was formed in her body, so she did not feel his birth, as the prophet Isaiah

testifies: according to him, the birth was painless. In fact, Isaiah says: "before pain came upon her she delivered a son" (Isaiah, 66, 7). Therefore He was chosen to renew the order of nature in both senses: because he was not born thanks to human intervention, nor did he come out of the womb with difficulty.

(Cited by Bergamo 2003, note 22)

Even Augustine (354–430) considered the mystery of the incarnation intimately connected to that of the virgin childbirth: "For as a virgin she conceived Him, as a virgin brought Him forth, and a virgin she continued" (*Sermo*, I, 18).[115] In the *Enchiridion*, to explain the miracle, he used an analogy which would become very popular, assimilating Christ's birth from his mother's body to his exit from his tomb, which had left the seal intact, connecting the two events (birth and resurrection) by their miraculous occurrence. This argument was taken up by Jerome (4th–5th centuries AD), doctor of the church and foremost advocate of the perpetual virginity of the mother of God, in his *De verginitate Beatae Mariae*.[116] Another analogy used by theologians to explain the miracle of *post partum* virginity was that of the sun passing through a pane of glass, without breaking it.

Soon, these theological reasonings became church dogma: Mary's perpetual virginity "mother of God and forever a virgin" was ratified in 553 by the Second Council of Constantinople, the fifth ecumenical council called by emperor Justinian I.[117] The attribute given to Mary, *aeipàrthenos* ("ever virgin"), was drawn from the ancient world, where it had been associated with goddesses such as Athena or priestesses such as the Vestal virgins. In 649, Pope Martin proclaimed the dogma of the perpetual virginity of the Madonna in the Lateran Council, which also stressed the link between the true, but virginal conception and the true, but incorrupt birth, defining Mary as *àcrantos* (without blemish) and *panaghìa* (all saint).[118] The attribute "ever Virgin", included in the profession of faith by the Fourth Lateran Council (1215), was confirmed by Pope Paul IV (1555) in his Ecclesiastical Constitution *Cum quorundam*, which declared as an article of faith that Mary had been a virgin "before, during and forever after Jesus's birth", in a three-part wording later maintained and repeated.[119]

Mary's theological construct went hand in hand with the increasing popularity of her liturgical celebrations, from Antioch's Nativity to Jerusalem's Mary *Theotòkos*, dating back to the middle of the 5th century, to the *festivitas Sanctae Mariae*, celebrated in Rome and in other Western cities (6th century) to that of the Holy Mary *in expectatione partus* (awaiting childbirth), popular in Spain from the 7th century. In particular, especially from the 6th and 7th centuries, the Annunciation and the Nativity of the Virgin were celebrated with solemn processions and masses, which, in turn, strengthened her worship and were evidence of a devotion that had spread beyond the theological circuits, as the increasing popularity of the Byzantine image of the *Panagia Platytera* (Virgin of the Sign, depicted full length with a *clipeus* (medallion) on her chest containing the child) also attests.[120]

Her exclusion from the suffering of childbirth emphasised Mary's difference from Eve, according to a juxtaposition of the two women that medieval theologians were very fond of. Mary was the "other" woman, the one who had brought salvation to the world, whereas Eve had brought death: *"per feminam mors, per feminam vita"* (from a woman, death came, from a woman, life), St. Augustine had written.[121] And since the pain of childbirth was a consequence of the original sin, Mary's immaculate conception was also reiterated, which is not – as is widely thought – her virgin conception, but the absence in her of the original sin from her conception. Precisely because she was free from this sin, Mary did not have to suffer the punishment that God had given Eve and her descendants: the pain of labour.

More recently, Mary's perpetual virginity was confirmed by the Second Vatican Council: the Dogmatic Constitution *Lumen Gentium* (1964) reiterated that "Our Lord [..] did not diminish His mother's virginal integrity but sanctified it" (*LG*, VIII, 57),[122] as is also stated in the new Catechism of the Catholic Church.[123]

As we have seen, Mary's absolute and perpetual virginity, initially sated by the apocryphal gospels, was already consolidated in the High Middle Ages and constantly reiterated over time: her bodily virginity completed the mother of God's virginity, which includes her "virginity of the mind" (*virginitas mentis*), the constant desire to remain such and her virginity of the soul (*virginitas sensus*), the absence of lust.

The Catholic Church's successive dogmas, such as the Immaculate Conception (1854) and the Assumption (1950), perfected this representation of total purity of Mary's body and soul, making her a symbol and a metaphor of the Church, also considered mother of God's children.

Mary's representations in art have reflected this theological construct and its progress in a trajectory moving from emphasising her virgin body, to gradually removing the physical signs of motherhood from the representation, underlining its symbolic significance instead. The Byzantine representations of Mary as a new mother, lying next to Jesus like any other woman after the trials of labour and delivery (as in Giotto's Nativity in the Scrovegni Chapel in Padua), were gradually replaced by the image of the Madonna adoring the newborn child.[124]

The so-called *"Madonne del parto"* (Pregnant Madonnas), iconic depictions popular in Italy between the 14th and 15th centuries showing a heavily pregnant Mary holding a book (a symbol of the verbum incarnate), such as, for example, the frescoes by Taddeo Gaddi in the church of St. Francis de Paola in Firenze (mid-14th century) or Piero della Francesca's in Santa Maria da Momentana in Monterchi (1460),[125] gradually disappeared after the Counter-Reformation, as they were considered irreverent,[126] just like the *Vierges ouvrantes* or *Schreinmadonnen*, small wooden sculptures with an opening along the centre of the Virgin Mary's body and containing images of the passion or the Trinity, popular in northern Europe between the 13th and 14th centuries.[127]

The portrayal of breastfeeding lasted longer and was more widespread, but even these images of the breastfeeding Madonna (*Maria Lactans*), so explicit and obvious in medieval art, with her uncovered breasts spurting milk,[128] were eventually replaced by more symbolic portrayals, with covered breasts, removing from Mary's body every trace of the physical transformations of motherhood.

Some feminist scholars have analysed the contradictory features in this sacred figure which embodies both motherhood and virginity, focusing mainly on its cultural contents, the point of view and the inner motivations of the Fathers of the Church.[129] According to some psychoanalytical interpretations, Mary's figure would represent a form of the Oedipus complex: how a son would desire his mother to be, deprived of any sexual contact with his father, entirely devoted to him: "The Madonna – Ida Magli wrote – encompasses the desires, dreams, hopes related to femininity of men-males" (Magli 1987: 95).[130] She would therefore represent the female image cherished by medieval monks in their horror for sexuality and the female body: a woman completely and forever "closed", inviolate and obedient.[131] It should, however, be noted that ascribing birth to religious symbolism implies an appreciation of motherhood and of the mother–son relationship unknown to the ancient world and emphasised in the Christian, and above all Catholic one, even after the Counter-Reformation.[132]

The features ascribed to Mary by theologians, however, contributed to the emphasis of the emotional and spiritual dimensions of motherhood, not the physical one, which was not only excluded from religious representation, but confined to an animal-like dimension deemed unworthy of the Mother of God. Reaffirming the principle of Mary's *post partum* virginity indirectly emphasised the negative sense of the physical elements, confining the pain and loss of blood to the unmentionable bodily functions.

We might at this point wonder what the consequences of this representation might have been on women's lives, in their perception of their body, pregnancy and childbirth, even in their sexual identity.[133] This has clearly introduced elements of profound contradiction in the experience of motherhood: on the one hand, in fact, it was extolled as a crucial step in a woman's life, the fulfilment of a duty on which both family and social expectations hinged but which was also a divine commandment. On the other hand, however, it was physically mortified, loaded with negative connotations that Christianity certainly did not invent, but ended up confirming and emphasising.

In some parts of Italy, even in the early 20th century, women in their final months of pregnancy were discouraged from going to mass, for reasons of "decency" or "scandal", as evidenced by some oral sources.[134] Childbirth was a taboo subject, erased from language and storytelling: children were taught that babies were brought by storks or that they were born under cabbage leaves. For centuries and in many regions right up to the 20th century, new mothers were considered impure and dangerous to themselves and to others removed from people's gaze and confined indoors (as we shall see in Chapter 4.3). And a rather negative shadow was cast even on breastfeeding: the use of wet nurses among women of the *élites*, which in many contexts lasted to the mid-20th century, with many other different reasons was also ascribed to its perception as being "animal-like" and "unseemly", as many studies have highlighted.

It is precisely this contradiction in the experience of motherhood that emerges from the life stories of Italian country women and which undermines it, leaving it suspended between pride and shame, fulfilment and silence, making the representation of their bodies uncertain and contradictory, and consequently even their sexual identity.[135]

Notes

1 Graves (1948); Gimbutas (1982); Giani Gallino (1989); Rangoni (2005); Testar (2010).
2 As shown by Hanna Arent (1958); Zucal (2017: ch. 9).
3 Rich (1976); Braidotti (1994); Cavarero (1990b); Ribero (2011); Boccia (1998, 2018).
4 Badinter (1986); Héritier (1996).
5 Cesbron and Knibiehler (2004: 59).
6 As noted by Zucal (2017: ch. 5); Bettini (2013: ch. 3).
7 Sissa (1983); Gélis (1984a: ch. 2).
8 Merchant (1980: ch. 1); Daston and Pomata (2003). This is not the only representation of Nature, but one of the most recurrent ones. Another one, particularly frequent in the Middle Ages, represents it as a craftswoman building her creatures (Modershon 1977).
9 Savonarola [1460?] (1952: V–XXIII). Despite the title, the text is written in Italian. On this, see Zuccolin (2017: 88–93 and 2018).
10 Mercurio ([1596] (1713).
11 Merchant (1980); Filippini (2003).
12 Aeschylus, *Eumenides*, Transl. by Herbert Weir Smyth, Cambridge: Harvard University Press, 1926, lines 657–661. Taken from the online version. www.perseus.tufts.edu/hopper/text?doc=Perseus%3Atext%3A1999.01.0006%3Acard%3D640. Further quotations are taken from this edition (*Eum.*) For the Greek text, I used Eschyle, *Les Eménides*, texte établi et traduit par Paul Mazon, Paris: Belles Lettres 1972.
13 Pomata (1994b and 1996).
14 As Page du Bois has shown (duBois 1988).
15 For the Greek text, I used: Plato, *Timée,* texte établi et traduit par Albert Rivaud, Paris, Belles Lettres 1970 (Tim.). For the English translation: Plato, *Plato in Twelve Volumes*, Vol. 9, *Timaeus*, translated by W.R.M. Lamb, Cambridge, MA, Harvard University Press, 1925. Taken from the online version: www.perseus.tufts.edu/hopper/text?doc=Perseus%3Atext%3A1999.01.0180%3Atext%3DTim.%3Asection%3D91d. Further quotations are taken from this edition (*Tim.Lamb.*).
16 As pointed out by Hanson and Green (1994).
17 For the Greek text, I used: Soranos d'Éphèse, *Maladies des femmes*, texte établi, traduit et commenté par Paul Burguière, Danielle Gourevitch, Yves Malinas, Paris, Les Belles Lettres, 1988 (*Gyn.*) For the English translation: Soranus of Ephesus, *Gynecology*, transl. by Owsei Tempkin, Baltimora: Johns Hopkins Press, 1991 (n.e.) (Temp.: 39).
18 *The Trotula: A Medieval Compendium of Women's Medicine*, ed. and transl. by Monica H. Green, Philadelphia: University of Pennsylvania Press, 2001 (*Trot.*). As Monica Green has pointed out, the Trotula Corpus is a grouping of three different texts, each of separate authorship, that were probably produced in Salerno between the 11th and 12th centuries: the *Liber de sinthomatibus mulierum* (Book on the Conditions of Women), the *De curis mulierum* (On Treatments for Women), certainly by Trotula, and the *De ornatu mulierum* (On Women's Cosmetics). By the late 12th century, the three works were combined by an anonymous compiler (Green 2007; 2008). An Italian edition was edited by Cavallo Boggi Pina (1979).

19 This is in fact the metaphor chosen by French historian Jacques Gélis as the title of his book, *L'arbre et le fruit* (1984a).
20 *The New Testament, Luke*, 1, 42. King James version. Taken from the online version: www.kingjamesbibleonline.org/ Further quotations are taken from this edition (*Luke KJV.*).
21 Noonan (1965: ch. 2).
22 Flandrin (1981: 119, n. 40).
23 Filippini (1997: 111).
24 Foucault (1973, 2008).
25 Campese (1983); Sissa (1983, 1992); Laqueur (1992); King (1998).
26 King (1998: 21).
27 Thomasset (1992); Vigarello (1993); Arikha (2007); Flemming (2018b); Pomata (2018).
28 As has been shown by Helen King (1998: 11).
29 For the Greek text, I used: Hippocrate, *De la Génération*, in *Œuvres complètes*, texte établi par Robert Joly, Paris: Les Belles Lettres, 1970, t. XI. For the English translation: Hippocrates, *On Generation*, published in Loeb Classical Library, edited and translated by Paul Potter, Loeb Classical Library 520, Cambridge, MA: Harvard University Press, 2012, vol. X. This quote is: LCL520, VII, 478, p. 17. Further quotations are taken from this edition (HPott.).
30 For the Greek text, I used: Aristote, *De la génération des animaux*, texte établi et traduit par Pierre Louis, Paris: Les Belles Lettres, 1961 (*GA*). For the English translation, I chose: Aristotle, *On the Generation of Animals*, trans. by Arthur Platt. Taken from the English online version: https://en.wikisource.org/wiki/On_the_Generation_of_Animals/Book_II. This quote is: book II, section 3. Further quotations are taken from this edition: APlatt.
31 APlatt, book II, section 4.
32 APlatt, book II section 4.
33 Sissa (1992: 71–72).
34 Pomata (1996).
35 Laqueur 1992. In fact, Helen King contradicts Thomas Laqueur, stating that the models of the body are not to be understood as such a stark dichotomy, but in a more nuanced way (King 2013 and 1998, *Introduction*).
36 Laqueur (1992: 49, 162).
37 Maclean 1980; Pomata (2013, 2018).
38 Li Causi (2005: 103–105).
39 Pomata (2018).
40 "Whether the flesh of Christ was conceived of the Virgin's purest blood?", Thomas Aquinas, *Summa Theologiae*, translated by Fathers of the English Dominican Province (1920). Taken from the online version produced by Sandra K. Perry (2006): www.gutenberg.org/cache/epub/19950/pg19950-images.html. Further quotations are taken from this edition (*Summa*).
41 Prosperi 2005: 165.
42 Thomasset (1992).
43 Héritier-Augé (1993: 126–127).
44 APlatt: IV, 1. Taken front the online version: https://en.wikisource.org/wiki/On_the_Generation_of_Animals/Book_IV.
45 As pointed out by Li Causi (2005: 98).
46 APlatt: IV, 1.
47 Héritier-Augé (1993: 127, 1996: ch. 8).
48 Li Causi (2005: 98–101).
49 Moulinier-Brogi (2005: 147–148).
50 Sissa (1983: 89).
51 King (1998: 8).

52 In the Middle Ages, this division was extended to as many as seven chambers (two on the right, two on the left and one in the centre), due to the cosmological meaning of the number 7 (Flemming 2018), as you can see in Speert (1973: 8).
53 Laqueur (1992). On this, see also the observations by Ekholm (2018).
54 Berriot-Salvadore (1993).
55 Raffaele (1841, I: 103).
56 Cavarero (1990a: 102–105).
57 Plato, *Symposium*, transl. by Benjamin Jowett (1871). Taken from the online version produced by Sue Asscher, and David Widger: www.gutenberg.org/ebooks/1600, adobe Digital ed.: 53. Further quotations are taken from this edition (*Symp. J.*). For the Greek text, I used: Plato, *Le Banquet*, texte établi et traduit par Paul Vicaire, Paris: Belles Lettres 1970. Regarding this text, see Curi (2009).
58 *Symp. J.*: 54.
59 *Symp. J.*: 55.
60 *Symp. J.*: 56.
61 Cavarero (1990a: 104 and 132).
62 Plato, *Theaetetus*, translated by Harold N. Fowler. Cambridge, MA, Harvard University Press; London, William Heinemann Ltd. 1921. Taken from the online: www.perseus.tufts.edu/hopper/text?doc=Perseus%3Atext%3A1999.01.0172%3Atext%3DTheaet.%3Asection%3D150b This quote is: 150b. Further quotations are taken from this edition (*Theae.Fow.*).For the Greek text, I used: Plato, *Théétète,* texte établi et traduit par Auguste Diès, Paris: Belles Lettres, 1967 (*Théét.*).
63 Cited by Rigotti (2010: 86).
64 Ibidem (116–117).
65 Cited by Filippini (1995: 22).
66 Hartland (1894, 1909); Crainz (1986); Bettini (2015: ch. 6).
67 Miralles (1993: 17–44).
68 Graves (1992).
69 Speert (1973: 396–396); Zglinicki (1983); Fanos, Fanos and Corridori (2010: 53).
70 Euripides, *Medea*, Transl. by David Kovacs, Harvard University Press, 1994. Taken from the online version: www.perseus.tufts.edu/hopper/text?doc=Perseus%3Atext%3A1999.01.0114%3Acard%3D214. This quote is lines 573–575. Further quotations are taken from this edition (*Med.*).
71 *Eum.*, lines 736–739.
72 Detienne (1976).
73 *Med.:* lines 249–251.
74 Loraux (1995).
75 On the various meanings and facets of the word *pònos*, see also Loraux (1982).
76 Homer, *Iliad*, transl. by Augustus T. Murray, Cambridge, MA: Harvard University Press, 1946. This quote is XI, 222. Taken from the online version: https://archive.org/details/in.ernet.dli.2015.281509/page/n521?q=Iliad+XI.
77 As pointed out by Helen King (1998: 23).
78 Mosse (1996).
79 *Thucydides' Peloponnesian War*, translated by Richard Crawley, London: J.M. Dent and Co., 1903: 104.
80 Loraux (1995: 88).
81 As pointed out by Vernant (2001) and Longo (2000: 9–27).
82 Cantarella (1985); Loraux (1989).
83 Magli (1989); Corbin, Courtine and Vigarello (2011).
84 Burkert (1983: 47).
85 Mosse (1996).
86 Loraux (1995: 28–29).
87 Ketham [1491](1988). See Pesenti (1985).
88 Filippini (1995: 293).

89　Lanzardo (1985: 14).
90　Nietzsche ([1881–1885] (1995: 47 ("Of war and warriors") and 66 ("Of little old and young women").
91　On this topic, see also the observations by de Grazia (1992, chs. 1 and 5.6).
92　Aristotle speaks of a "Difference in suffering between animals and women" (*GA*, IV, 6, 775b).
93　APlatt: IV, 6.
94　Morel and Rollet (2000: 48).
95　Vernant (2005).
96　*Genesis*, chap. 3, King James version. Taken from the online version: www.kingjamesbibleonline.org/Genesis-Chapter-3/. Further quotations are taken from this version (*Genesis KJV*).
97　Duby (1996); Dalarun (1992); Frugoni (1992).
98　Zucal (2017: ch. V).
99　*Prayer of an Expectant Mother* of Saint Francis de Sales. Taken from the online version: http://hosted.desales.edu/files/salesian/library/Prayer-Pregnancy.pdf. This prayer is also reported in the famous book by theologian Francesco Emanuele Cangiamila ([1745] (1751: 276); see ch. 10.3.
100　Mercurio [1596] (1713: 5); translated from the Italian edition, like the following quotations. This book, published in Venice in 1596, has had great success in Italy, with many reprints in the following decades with slight spelling variations in the title. The 1713 edition is titled *La Commare o raccoglitrice*. On the various editions of this book, see Curatolo (1901: 163–176); Guzzoni degli Ancarani (1903 and 1912).
101　As pointed out by Laget (1982: 160).
102　Cited by Laget (Laget 1982: 163).
103　Farge (1976).
104　For example, Verena Schmid wrote: "Pain accompanies women in their experience of separation from their babies, of abandonment of themselves; it leads them to their essence, making them re-live a deep experience of themselves; it leads them to an intense sexual experience which has its climax at the moment of birth" (Schmid 1992: 125).
105　Cesbron and Knibiehler (2004: 55).
106　Magli (1987), Warner (1976); Accati (1998).
107　Sissa (1987: ch. 3); Hartland (1894 and 1909).
108　Van der Lugt (2004).
109　Söll (1981); Gonzales (1988); Muller (1994); Perella (2003).
110　Pelaja and Scaraffia (2008: ch. 2.3).
111　*Summa*, III, 31, art. 5, 3. See Zucal (2017: 141–142).
112　Bertelli (2002; ch. 2).
113　*The Gospel of Pseudo-Mathew (PGM)*, in *The Apocryphal Gospel and other documents*, by B. Harris Cowper, London: F. Norgate, 1881 (5° ed.): 51. Taken from the online version: https://archive.org/search.php?query=Gospel%20of%20Pseudo-Mathew&sin=TXT.
114　Lovato (2012).
115　*St. Augustine Sermons on selected lesson of the new Testament*, edit. and transl. by Library of Fathers of the Holy Catholic Church, Oxford: J.H. Porter, 1844: 16. Taken from the online version: https://archive.org/details/sermonsonselecte01augu/page/n9.
116　Söll (1981: 134).
117　In agreement with Perella (2003: 200–202), I consider this the decisive council, rather than the Chalcedon one, in 451, as Knibiehler has stated (Cesbron and Knibiehler 2004: 54).
118　Warner (1976: 73); Perella (2003: 200–203).
119　Roschini (1969: 366).

120 Ronchi (2000).
121 Warner (1976: pars. I, ch. 4); Dalarun (1992: 26–27); Duby (1996: vol. 3).
122 Dogmatic Constitution on the Church *Lumen Gentium*, 21 November 1964. Taken from the online version: www.vatican.va/archive/hist_councils/ii_vatican_council/documents/vat-ii_const_19641121_lumen-gentium_en.html.
123 Available online at: www.vatican.va/archive/catechism_it/index_it.htm, cap. III, 9, par. 6, 966.
124 Drobot (1980); Bergamo (2003).
125 Ronchi, Ravasi and Montagna (2000); Verdon (2004).
126 According to Bertelli (2002: 40), they were forbidden by the Counter-Reformation; Renzo Manetti (2005) gives, as other Catholics do, a different interpretation of this pictorial subject: he argues that this is a representative symbolic evolution of motherhood.
127 Visentin (2000: 38); Pancino (2006: 52–53).
128 Verdon (2004: 64).
129 Vantini Vignola (2007: 101–110) well summarises these positions at the European level.
130 See also Accati (1998: ch. 8).
131 Daly (1973: ch. 3); Warner (1976: 4° pars).
132 Accati (1998); Cacciari (2017).
133 Warner (1976); Fattorini (1999); Vantini Vignola (2007); Murgia (2011).
134 "Our priest did not want us to go anywhere, not even to church! He said: don't come to church as you are giving scandal and it's unseemly ... when a woman is beginning to show, and you can see she is expecting, she had better stay at home, because she's giving scandal ... a great scandal in the whole village" (Filippini Cappelletto 1983: 79).
135 Ibidem: 85–86.

PART II
Giving birth and being born from antiquity to the 18th century

Foreword

In this section of the book, I have taken into consideration the main views, social practices and rituals concerning pregnancy, childbirth and puerperium from the ancient world to the end of the 17th century.

The choice of this extended chronological span is fundamentally motivated by two criteria. The first is the enduring over these centuries of medical-scientific thought rooted in the ancient world. The Hippocratic Corpus and Aristotle's writings were taken up in Roman times by important physicians such as Soranus of Ephesus and Galen, whose texts were disseminated, the former's thanks to Muscio's translation (6th century), the latter's thanks to the compilation of Oribasius' *Collectiones medicae*, a seventy-volume medical encyclopaedia requested by emperor Julian the Apostate.

Subsequently taken up by Arabic physicians, they became the essential reference point for medieval and modern medicine: Avicenna's *Canon* was the most widely used medical manual in European universities up to the 18th century. In the 16th century, the emergence of anatomic dissections, and Vesalius' revolution in particular, certainly led to a revision of anatomical and physiological knowledge, but this did not dismantle a system which remained solid in its foundations, especially as far as the theories about reproduction and embryonic development, the formation of the foetus and the female body were concerned. Radical changes in these views would only come after the scientific revolution which diminished the authority of the ancient and marked the advent of the experimental method, paving the way to new theories about reproduction (the use of the term itself, in fact, became current around the mid-18th century),[1] with new, gender-based approaches even in anatomy.[2]

The second criterion is the significant permanence of the fundamental elements of the "childbirth scene" with its places, people and therapeutic practices. For many centuries, this was an essentially female scene, where the presence of and contact with any man (even a physician) was forbidden primarily for cultural reasons, primarily, but not exclusively, linked to modesty. This is not to say that doctors or practitioners did not offer therapeutic suggestions, but that assistance during childbirth and care in the period following it were entirely in the hands of women, be they educated, professional midwives or simple wise women. A doctor could be consulted, or intervene, as a surgeon, in extreme circumstances, for example, to carry out embryotomies or post-mortem Caesarean sections, but their presence was limited to these contingencies.

The emergence of man-midwives represents a fundamental turning point in this context, taking place between the 17th and 18th centuries, at different times in various parts of Europe, and starting with the northern countries. As we shall see in the third part of this book, this transformation took place against the background of wider cultural, social and political transformations, and tied in with a more complex change in the scene of childbirth, not only in terms of the people present, but also of therapeutic practices, places and main ethical codes. The social and professional profile of midwives was profoundly altered by the creation of schools of midwifery.

I have attempted to focus not only on the main scientific knowledge, but also on the entire set of practices, precepts and rituals which were the essential elements in the various forms of assistance and in material culture.

The relationship between them, between scientific culture and social practices, is a topic of discussion among historians, a reflection that concerns the permeation, interconnections and divergences between educated and folk medicine, and which is made ever more complex in this specific case by the gender difference which characterises this field. For a large part of this timeline, the so-called "haute medicine" was reserved for men, while assistance in childbirth was a task specifically for women. For this reason, there are still questions to answer, and in more directions, concerning both the relationship between physicians and midwives in the pursuit of further knowledge and treatments, and the correspondence between written recommendations and actual practice in real life.

To what extent were the large number of remedies and recipes in ancient and medieval gynaecological texts, for example, the outcome of male, erudite elaboration adopted by women?[3] Were they perhaps the male transcription of female knowledge passed on orally by women?[4] Were they the successful outcome of a mixture and mediation of these two sets of knowledge?[5] Similar questions can also be asked about gynaecological texts from the ancient world, such as that by Soranus of Ephesus addressed to midwives for their training, which contains details and indications which were certainly the result of discussions and exchanges of knowledge with the *obstetrices* who actually oversaw childbirth, but did not write about it.

Another issue is concerned with how information differs between scientific texts and actual practice in its various local contexts and depending upon the different kinds of midwives.

In order to recreate the social reality of childbirth, written sources are definitely insufficient, since for centuries, midwives did not leave notes and records of their work. It is necessary to make use, it need scarcely be said, of a complex series of sources: from legal documents to trial records, from visual sources to books of memoirs, from letters to family books, etc.

By the time the first texts written by midwives began to appear, especially from the 16th century, the overall picture had certainly become more detailed, finally restoring this important figure's own voice: the *observations* and memoirs of midwives such as the French Louise Bourgeois, Dutch Catharina Schrader or German Justine Siegemund (whose life and works archive research is gradually bringing to light) are invaluable sources for historical research. Nevertheless, they should be taken in full awareness that they necessarily reflect only part of society, the educated one, which represented the tip of the iceberg of a variety of multi-faceted practices and knowledge in the field.

In setting myself apart from a certain tradition of self-referential and positivist medicine history, aimed at outlining progressive paths of discovery and knowledge only belonging to the scientific world, I have attempted to highlight, even in this part of the book, how medical-scientific knowledge fits in a wider cultural context, reflecting its contents, and how these have important repercussions and implications in birth-assistance practices. In other words, cultural history supplies important interpretative clues.

The idea, for example, that a general natural order was reflected in that of the process of childbirth led to a distinction between "natural" and "unnatural" birth, which has been one of the essential foundations of medical-obstetric thought, and whose elaboration and re-elaboration have featured very prominently in obstetrics texts for many centuries. These views were clearly reflected in the practice and resulted in a series of directions and therapeutic practices intended to restore this natural order in the malpresentations of the foetus during labour, by advocating manual turnings (cephalic version). Breech births were broadly considered unlucky and harbingers of dangers for this reason, and also because they mirrored burial rituals. Another example is the ambivalent view of post-partum bleeding, strongly rooted in culture, derived from the ancient world and remaining unchanged until the 18th century.

We find this view not only in folk medicine, but also in physicians' texts, even those about the burgeoning discipline of occupational medicine: its founding father, Bernardino Ramazzini (1633–1714), lists post-partum bleeding with the causes of professional illness in midwives (see Chapter 4.3).

It should also be pointed out that several beliefs and remedies of the erudite tradition, which we have considered in this part of the book, remain as heritage of popular culture, even when they are abandoned by medicine and ascribed to "superstition": the medical knowledge based on popular tradition and passed on by the collections of the 19th–20th centuries is in many cases nothing more than what remains of much more ancient systems and pharmacopoeias, revised by physicians. This, for example, is the case of the belief associated to birthmarks, of the imaginative virtue of pregnant women, which survived the anti-imagination turning point in the second half of the 18th century, persisting in some popular contexts up to the 20th century. I thought it appropriate to point out these continuities.

In order to understand practices and rituals (above all those concerning childbirth and puerperium), suggestions coming from anthropologic studies are very important. Arnold Van Gennep's analyses of the rites of passage which mark the lives of individuals, for example, are essential in understanding several long-term aspects of childbirth and birth, which reintroduce the three identifying moments of these rituals: separation, liminality and incorporation.[6] This is an essential vantage point to examine the traditions of quarantine and the rituals surrounding new mothers and newborns and sanctioning their social birth (see Chapters 4 and 5).

Even in this case, I have sought to highlight the long duration of some of these rituals which, in some European contexts, lasted until after the end of the Second World War.

Finally, it was essential to pay particular attention to the influence of and role played by religion, in the forms of its control over practices and rituals. Attention to this context allows us to grasp both the elements of continuity and synchronicity between the ancient world and Judeo-Christian society, and the differentiations which, from the start, distinguish religious cultures in several essential points, such as suffering during childbirth, abortion or infanticide, or the consequences of the death of an unbaptised child.

The distinction grows more complex with the Reformation, in the different approaches taken by Protestants and Catholics on the question of the salvation of souls and on the importance of baptism, with the consequences and repercussions this has had on different levels: from the rituals designed to replace baptism, to the control over the scene of birth and over midwives.

Notes

1 As pointed out in Hopwood, Flemming, Kassell (2018: *Introduction*).
2 Laqueur (1992); Schiebinger (1989 and 1993).
3 As claimed, for example, by Manuli (1980).
4 As claimed, for example, by Rouselle (1980), or Riddle (1992).
5 Totelin (2009).
6 Van Gennep [1909] (1981).

2
PREGNANCY

1 Being pregnant

What happens in a woman's body after conception? What immediate transformations does pregnancy bring about? According to a deeply rooted medical thought, after sucking the seed (just like a greedy animal), the womb, called *matrix* precisely because it was *mater (métra)*, mother of all embryos as defined by Soranus (*Gyn*. I, 6), closed up immediately to prevent leakage: "The uterus, on receiving the seed and closing holds it inside itself – as stated in the Hippocratic texts *(On Generation)* – inasmuch as this mouth contract in response to the moisture" (*Gen*. V, 48).[1] The subject is dealt with in detail in *Superfetation* (*Superf*. VIII, 476, 10). Like the set of obstetrics beliefs which we will examine in this part, this idea was transferred from the ancient world to the medieval and modern ones through Arabic medicine and through Avicenna (980–1037) in particular.

This seal was so tight that not even a needle could pass through, nor an odour, to which the womb was so sensitive. In instances when it did not seal properly, there was a risk of superfetation, a later fertilisation, which was deemed dangerous. Odour permeability was one of the tests used to check for pregnancy: various physicians, such as Michele Savonarola (1385–1466) in his *De regimine pregnantium*, suggested, on the basis of the Hippocratic Corpus, inserting a clove of garlic or some odorous herb into the vagina and checking the smell of the woman's breath the following morning: if it was pleasant-smelling, it meant that the woman was pregnant; otherwise, the odour would have travelled to her mouth due to the opening of the womb and its link to the upper organs.[2]

In this sense, in many Romance languages, a pregnant woman is named '*incinta*' (in Italian), *enceinte* in French, and *encinta* in Spanish, terms derived from *incingo*, a medieval Latin verb, which meant 'girdled', 'tied', as Maurizio Bettini has pointed out, correcting an interpretation by Isidore of Seville, followed by many historians, which derived it from *incincta*, so "non-girdled" (*in-cincta*), or untied, alluding to the need to remove belts and girdles from clothes during pregnancy.³

In the Roman world, a refined symbolism related to knots, to be either tied or undone, accompanied a woman in her becoming a wife and mother: knots to be undone upon matrimony (*cingillum*), as a symbol of her virginity being taken away; knots sealing her womb again after fertilisation and leaving it impenetrable; knots that the mature foetus would have to undo again with its own pressure to come into the world. A woman's body was understood as something which opened and closed, only to re-open and close again: "a matter of knots", where husbands played a crucial role. In Rome, according to Pliny, in order to speed up childbirth, husbands would take off their belts and tie them around their wives' waists, subsequently untying them again.⁴ The custom of "tying" pregnant women with their husbands' belts has been a very long-standing tradition in Europe.

In the ancient world, much as in the Christian one, 'holy' belts and girdles played an important role in rituals aimed at protecting pregnancies. One of Juno's titles was *Solvizona* ('the one who unties belts', because pregnant women went to leave their belts in offering at her temple on the Esquiline hill).⁵ In medieval times, in Christian countries, rolls of parchment with sacred writings and images and birth girdles were used during childbirth,⁶ while the relics of the girdles belonging to the Virgin Mary or to Saint Margaret of Antioch, patrons of women in childbirth, were particularly sought-after and the shrines where they were kept were places of worship and pilgrimage destinations for pregnant women all through the early modern age. Saint Dominic's, Saint Augustine's and Saint Francis' waist-ties, well known throughout Europe, had a similar role.⁷

In addition to closing up like a wineskin (*uter*), a pregnant woman's womb was believed to take root in her body, putting an end to the moving about and instability which characterised it, and was considered the cause of most women's illnesses. This organ, in fact, was believed to be mobile, an 'animal' which hungered for motherhood, according to Plato, and which, if left unsatisfied, moved about inside a woman's body, pressing against vital organs and casing all sorts of illnesses such as hysteria (from *hystéra* = uterus), if it reached her brain:

> Whenever the matrix or womb, as it is called, —which is an indwelling creature desirous of child-bearing, —remains without fruit long beyond the due season, it is vexed and takes it ill; and by straying all ways through the body and blocking up the passages of the breath and preventing respiration it casts the body into the uttermost distress, and causes, moreover, all kinds of maladies; until the desire and love of the two sexes unite them. Then, culling as it were the fruit from trees.
>
> (Tim. *91c*)⁸

The idea, derived from the Hippocratic Corpus and from Plato, that considered this organ as autonomous was widely shared in medieval medical thought, becoming rooted even in popular tradition. This is also stated in *De passionibus mulierum*, the famous text by the Salerno school attributed to Trotula: "Sometimes the womb is moved from its place" (*Trot., 87, par. 52*).

In many ways, therefore, pregnancy was also considered a condition that sheltered women from the pitfalls that virgins were vulnerable to; hence, even Galen considered intercourse as a form of hygiene.[9]

Nevertheless, pregnancy was considered an altered state which necessitated surveillance and care.[10] The idea that nutrition destined for the embryo's growth was taken from its mother made pregnant women susceptible to imbalances and emaciation; therefore, they were "neither healthy, nor vigorous, nor strong", as even Vitruvius remarked (cited by Rubiera Cancelas 2015: 922), evidence of a more popular opinion in Roman culture. They might also suffer from 'pica' (*kissa*), a term used by Soranus to identify a series of digestive ailments which appeared from the 40th day and lasted up to the fourth month (nausea, vomiting, salivation, bloating, etc.) (*Gyn*. I, 48). In other words, in any condition, a woman's body was seen as unstable and potentially sick and "pregnancy as a long illness" (Gourevitch 1984: 149).

But how, and through what signs, did a woman know she was pregnant, in days before the stethoscope, invented at the beginning of the 19th century, even existed?

The answer relates to bodily signs and manifestations, which women themselves gathered and interpreted: an absence of menstruation was certainly one of the important signs, but not a decisive one in days when amenorrhoea was frequently caused by a series of factors, such as malnutrition, cold or prolonged breastfeeding. Other bodily changes were clues: the swelling of breasts, a change in appetite, nausea, a change in skin tone, etc. are described in the Hippocratic *Corpus*. In the Middle Ages, these were listed in detail in various *Secreta* which circulated precisely in an attempt to decipher the secrets of the female body. The most famous, *De secretis mulierum*, written between the 13th and 14th centuries and attributed to Albertus Magnus had 54 editions between 1476 and 1500 and greatly influenced medieval and early modern thoughts, prompting a production of *Secreta* that intensified between the 16th and 18th centuries.[11] The fact that the introduction to the first edition stated openly that information had been gathered from *esperimenta* written by women is significant, although this detail was removed in successive editions, addressed exclusively to male practitioners.

In medieval times, uroscopy, the observation of urine, used in the diagnosis of other illnesses, developed by the Byzantine school of medicine in the 6th–7th centuries and adopted by the Salerno school, became more established as well.[12] From the 16th century, it would be variously questioned in the scientific world: for example, Italian physician Scipione Mercurio, in *La comare o ricoglitrice*, called it a "false and deceitful (ploy) more suited to quacks than doctors" (Mercurio [1596] 1713: 53), but it would still continue to be used up to the 18th century.

There was then the greatest array of empirical methods both to ascertain the state of pregnancy and to guess the sex of the unborn child. There was only one decisive test, though: the perception of the baby's movement, which could be felt, according to the Hippocratic Corpus, at different times according to the sex of the foetus: around the third month if male, around the fourth if female (*Gen.* XXI, 1, 511).

The Gospel of Luke reports how Elizabeth, pregnant with Saint John the Baptist, upon meeting Mary felt her child moving inside her for the first time and exclaimed:

> And she spake out with a loud voice, and said, Blessed art thou among women, and blessed is the fruit of thy womb [..] For, lo, as soon as the voice of thy salutation sounded in mine ears, the babe leaped in my womb for joy.
> (Luke KJV, *I, 41–44*)

Similarly, many centuries later and in a different context, in 17th-century England, the King's mistress, feeling the baby moving for the first time during a banquet, had shouted to the diners the good news and all the gentlemen were asked to leave the room, while maidservants were called to assist her, according to Samuel Pepys' testimony.[13]

So it was a woman herself who had the first solid proof of her pregnancy from listening to what happened in her body; she informed her family and her community and these words had legal relevance. Starting from Roman law, in fact, a mother passed on to her 'issue' her own condition of freedom or slavery not at the moment of conception or birth, but during pregnancy, even if childbirth represented the crucial moment which made this right effective.[14]

Even when doctors or practitioners were consulted, their roles were to carefully record what the woman was reporting, note down her symptoms, consult astrological calendars and obtain recommendations and suggestions, as emerges from the 16th-century *Case Books* and *Records*.[15] Diagnosis, just like prognosis, was the outcome of a kind of dialogue and 'negotiation' between patients and doctors.

Barbara Duden, who studied German doctor Johann Storch's records from the early 18th century, has stressed the relevance of this fact, and the radical difference with the situation nowadays, when the relationship is reversed and it is instead the doctor to communicate to a woman – much earlier in a pregnancy than in the past – what is happening inside her body and what he sees on an ultrasound scan or in laboratory results.[16] The consequence is that the state of pregnancy is no longer a woman's subjective observation, but stems from the announcement of a chemical test result. This is a change which has had no small weight on women's experience of their own bodies and of pregnancy itself.[17]

Even women's direct testimonies actually demonstrate how they were keeping a careful track of their menstruation, recording and interpreting changes in their bodies.[18] Correspondence between aristocratic women is richly detailed in this regard: "The character supposed to turn up [i.e. her period] on the 25th has not made an appearance yet, I do not know what may be the cause because

I am fine, only sometimes my stomach is a bit troublesome", Roman noble woman Eugenia Spada Maidalchini wrote to her mother in 1656, for example (cited by d'Amelia 1997: 26, 1999: 284). There was no shortage of advice and suggestions exchanged with mothers or sisters, as evidence of an extensive network of information and female knowledge that was anything but trivial, and even evaded medical control: "no need to say anything to the doctor", Eugenia's mother specified while speaking of a certain therapeutic suggestion given to her daughter (to drink cedar juice against nausea).[19]

2 The foetus: its development and ensoulment

Ancient medicine understood foetal development as the succession of distinct and progressive phases.[20] The embryo would therefore begin to develop the various parts of its body starting from an undivided whole, "branch(ing) out, just as the very extremities of a tree" (déndreon), as we read in the books *on Nature of the child* from the Hippocratic texts (*NE*, XVII, 2, 498).[21] Soranus of Ephesus described it extensively in his *Gynaecia*: the first phase involved the formation of an extraembryonic or foetal membrane, the *chòrion* (*Gyn.* I, 57), which, according to Galen, formed a kind of armour securing the embryo inside the womb.[22] The umbilical veins, through which the creature was nourished, would grow in this membrane. In his *De Foetuum generatione* (*The formation of the Embryo*), Galen distinguished four stages in the development of the foetus: in the first one, it still had the obvious appearance of a seed (*goné*); in the second, the liver, heart and brain would be formed (*kùema*); in the third, all the other parts would begin to appear (*émbrion*); and in the final one, all limbs began to grow separately (*paidìon*).[23]

Hildegard of Bingen, the 12th-century theologian and composer who was also a healer and a naturalist, thus summarised this development:

> When the woman has absorbed the seed, then, it can be formed to bring forth a human being and a little skin (*pellicula*) grows from the woman's blood, like a little container for this figure and holds it fast and encloses it … so that the little being lies in the middle like a person in the chamber of his house.
>
> *(Cited by Duden 1993: 35)*

According to the Hippocratic Corpus (*Nature of the child*), this phase lasted 30 days for a male foetus and 42 for a female one (*NE,* XVIII, 1,500) following the well-known gender hierarchies which Aristotle differentiated even more (40 days for a male foetus and 80 for a female one).[24] After taking human form, the foetus began to move, still at different times, according to its gender: in the third month if male, in the fourth if female.

As for its posture, in the earliest medieval anatomical drawings and in 16th-century charts, it is shown with its head uppermost, its hands close to its eyes and its knees bent.[25] This is the image shown, within its mother's womb, for example in the *Fasciculus medicinae* by German physician Johannes De Ketham (1491), in *De dissectione* by Charles Estienne (1545) and in *De conceptu et generatione hominis*, by Jacob Rueff (1587) (Figure 2.1).

Its features are those of a miniature man, according to a long-standing medieval tradition dating back to Muscio and his drawings of foetal presentations during childbirth, which the first 16th-century printed manuals of obstetrics also drew upon.[26]

In the late Middle Ages and early modern age, the development of anatomical sections and post-mortem Caesarean sections certainly increased the knowledge of the characteristics of a foetus in the womb. The famous chart drawn by Leonardo da Vinci between 1510 and 1512 appears incredibly realistic (as pointed

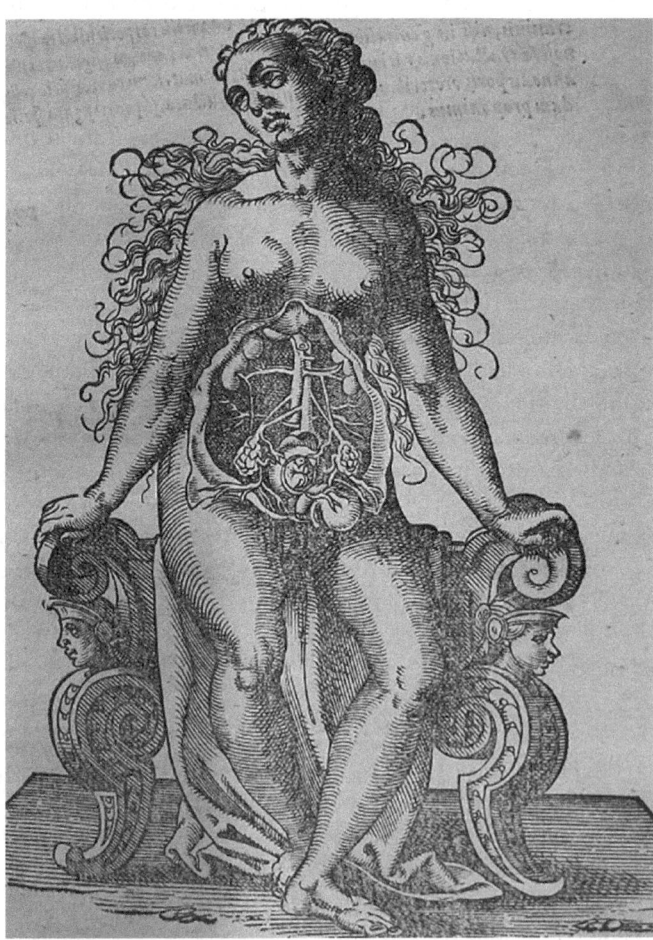

FIGURE 2.1 Female figure with pregnant uterus, from Jakob Rueff (1587), *De conceptu et generatione hominis*, Francofurti ad Moenum: P. Fabricium: c 10. Reproduced with permission of the Biblioteca Pinali antica (Padua).

out by Hilary 2018), as indeed does the one by Hieronymus Fabricius in his *De formatu foetu* (Venice, 1600).

In *De humano foetu libellus* (1564), Julius Caesar Aranzi also reported the observations made during anatomical sections performed in Bologna and noted by his pupil Scipione Mercurio, who recalls having witnessed the dissection of a nine-month pregnant woman. In *La Comare o ricoglitrice* (The Midwife) (1596), he described the position of the foetus in the womb:

> She holds [the creature] with its head in the upper part of the womb, where it has greater capacity. Its arms are folded in such a way that its elbows are placed near its hips: the palms of its hands are resting on its knees: its legs are bent, and crossed with the soles of its feet above its buttocks: its eyes rest on its knees and between them.
>
> *(Mercurio [1596] 1713: 15)*

The round position was explained, in the context of the Renaissance view, which saw a close link between macrocosm and microcosm and believed in a hierarchy of geometric figures (Figure 2.2).[27]

The womb was therefore represented as a sphere, in parallel to the universe, and the round position of the foetus was due to the fact that "the round figure is understood by Nature as the most perfect of all the other mathematical figures" (Mercurio [1596] 1713: 15). Moreover, this posture would give it greater protection, being "the only one designed not to be sensitive to damage" and would allow it to move without harming its mother or being harmed by her, "to always return to its centre and gradually resume the position most suited to rest", as stated by François Mauriceau, in *Traité des maladies des femmes grosses et des celles qui sont accouchées* (Mauriceau [1668] 1681: 228).[28]

The direction of its face was also discussed at length: Jacob Rueff and other physicians thought that it was turned towards its mother's back, while Scipione Mercurio, for example, claimed that it faced the outside (Figure 2.3).

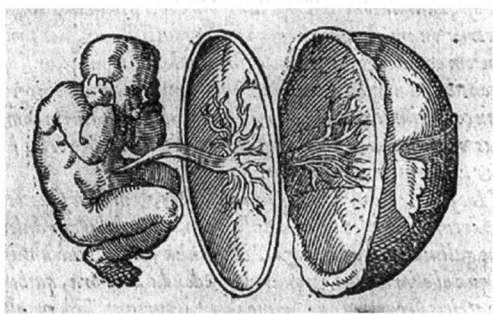

FIGURE 2.2 Foetus with placenta outside the uterus, from Jacob Rueff (1587), *De conceptu et generatione hominis*, Francofurti ad Moenum: P. Fabricium: c19r. Reproduced with permission of the Biblioteca Pinali antica (Padua).

FIGURE 2.3 The female organs of generation, from Giovanni Raffaele (1841), *Ostetricia teorico-pratica. Atlante*. Note the position of the foetus in the uterus, with the face facing the back of the mother. Reproduced with permission of the Ministero dei Beni e delle Attività Culturali e del Turismo - Biblioteca Nazionale Marciana (Venice).

In actual fact, with the exception of those by Leonardo da Vinci and Hieronymus Fabricius, 16th-century illustrations of the foetus continued to be very inaccurate and "abstract",[29] for two reasons. The first concerns the distance between what was seen and what was reproduced, the outcome of cultural mediation where imagination and the weight of tradition played a fundamental role: in other words, authors described what they expected to see.[30] The second reason concerns the fact that even in the early modern age, the opportunity to dissect deceased pregnant women was extremely rare. Famous anatomist Jacopo Berengario da Carpi bemoaned how difficult it was to obtain foetuses to dissect, despite the collusion of some midwives.[31] Since pregnant women could not be executed, anatomists lacked the "raw material" supplied primarily by the bodies of people sentenced to death. The only other sources were Caesarean sections carried out on deceased women, which were also rather rare, as we shall see (Chapter 5.7), or post-mortems granted by the families of deceased pregnant women.[32] They therefore resorted to dissecting animal foetuses, running the risk of making fundamental errors: it should be remembered that Vesalius himself portrayed a human womb with a dog's placenta.[33]

According to medieval thought, even the planets affected the development of embryos: "astrological medicine" suggested that every month was influenced by a different planet: identifying the month of conception was important to derive omens: for this reason, too, practitioners were consulted.[34] Towards the seventh month of gestation, so at an advanced stage of development, the foetus performed the *strophé* ("somersault"; *culbute* in French): it assumed a cephalic presentation, with its legs up and its head down. According to most ancient authors, this indicated that it was ready to be delivered. Some more mature foetuses, in fact, could already be born, in a delivery which was certainly risky, but not necessarily fatal. Foetuses born in the seventh month were actually considered viable, whereas those born in the eighth month were considered non-viable. This belief, dating back to the Hippocratic Corpus, would persist until the 17th century.[35] Many aspects contributed to it: for instance, the idea that the effort made by the foetus following the *strophé* made it too weak to survive childbirth; this was linked to the belief, shared by medieval physicians, in the negative influence of Saturn, the cold planet that presided over the eighth month.[36]

The length of pregnancy was considered variable: from seven to ten months; there was no fixed time for childbirth, as there wasn't for a fruit ripening on a tree. Due to the influence of the analogical naturalistic perspective, the decision on when the maturation process of a foetus was complete was left to nature: the foetus would make its own way out when space and food inside the womb were insufficient. Of course, different measuring systems also contributed to differing lengths: the solar month was advocated by doctors, but the lunar one was favoured by popular tradition, as J. Gélis has pointed out.[37]

Christianity combined this scientific view with the theory of the ensoulment of the foetus, which is the moment when God infused the soul into the new creature. In the early centuries of Christianity, this was the subject of bitter theological disputes, which also concerned the ways in which God created souls, whether all at the same time or one at a time, upon the creation of each single creature.[38] Despite different positions (such as Tertullian's), and Saint Augustine's hesitation, already from the 4th century, the so-called "delayist" thesis began to prevail; in line with Aristotle's views on the succession of souls, ensoulment was believed to take place after the formation of limbs: on the 40th day of gestation for a male foetus, on the 80th for a female one.[39] Resumed by Scholasticism, and in particular by Saint Thomas Aquinas, this view was sanctioned in 1211 by Pope Innocent III and in 1234 by Gregory IX with the papal constitution on abortion.[40] The matter, in fact, had some crucial implications on the seriousness of voluntary terminations, which were condemned in the Christian world: it was one thing to destroy some matter in formation, but an entirely different one to kill a foetus formed and endowed with a soul, as we shall see later (Chapter 2.6).

New interest arose in the question of the ensoulment of the foetus, both in the medical and theological worlds, during the Counter-Reformation, when a set of factors (such as the disagreement between Catholics and Protestants on the different value attributed to baptism for the purpose of salvation, or the debate on the fate of stillborn babies who had died without being baptised) prompted new investigations, aimed at clarifying the time of the ensoulment of the foetus.[41] The idea, supported by some scholars, such as Thomas Fyens (*De formatrice foetus liber*, 1620), of an early ensoulment, already on the third day of conception, which defined a foetus as a human person from the first few days of its life, began to take hold. In the mid-17th century, theologian Girolamo Fiorentini went further, supporting the duty to baptise all foetuses at any stage of pregnancy, following their extraction by Caesarean section after their mother's death. However, his book, *Disputatio de ministrando Baptism humanis foetibus abortivorum* (1658), was included in the Index of Prohibited Books and its author was forced to retract by saying that the treatise contained speculative discussions and the views presented were to be understood as possible and not as formal indications.[42] The times were not yet ripe for the kind of revolution in the thinking around reproduction, which, in the 18th century, led to the fall of the Hippocratic-Aristotelian theories and to the rise of new hypotheses on embryonic development, destined to influence theological thought as well.

3 Making a beautiful baby: the power of the gaze and cravings

Making a perfect baby meant first of all having a boy. The birth of a male did not only achieve the most fundamental aspirations of a patriarchal society, but also represented, as we have seen, the highest form of procreation, as the male body was the perfect prototype. Conceiving a girl was always poorly accepted and considered "contrary to the normal course of nature" (Laurent 1989: 122). The most frequent wedding wish in the popular traditions of some countries, "best wishes and many sons!", therefore expressed something deeper than a simple wish of a prosperous future, which in social reality turned into a real "rage de faire des males" (Darmont, 1979: 142).

Medical books and *Secreta* were also full of suggestions on ways to achieve this: they combined theories on generation with beliefs on the influence of stars, with powers attributed to traditional pharmacopoeia, ranging from the measures to be taken during intercourse to the benefits of taking certain potions. The treatise on *Superfetation* in the Hippocratic texts suggested that husbands tie up their left testicles during intercourse, in the belief that the semen from of the right testicle was responsible for a male child (*Superf.* XXXI.2).[43] In *De passionibus mulierum*, husbands were instructed to drink a decoction made with the desiccated vulva and womb of a hare, and wives to do the same with the testicles of a hare and to have intercourse at the end of their period.[44] Michele Savonarola instructed wives to lie on their right sides after intercourse, believing that a male foetus developed on the right side of the womb.[45] These different tips were often gathered in a set of instructions, such as, for example, those in Giovanni Marinello's *Le medicine partenenti alle infermità delle donne* (Medicines pertaining to women's illnesses).[46]

A male foetus would also make its mother more beautiful during pregnancy, improving her physical appearance; all the revealing signs on a mother's body would be positive, as opposed to those predicting a female foetus: if the skin of a pregnant woman's face was smooth and clear, she would have a boy; if, however, it was blotchy, a girl would be born, as we can read in the Hippocratic Corpus (*Barrenness*) (FS, IV, 1–2). This belief continued to exist in Italian popular traditions until the 19th–20th centuries, such as the one stating that, unlike a female foetus, "the male heals its mother, if she should have some disease" (Bernoni [1878] 1980: 14).

Even the shape of her breasts and/or belly revealed its contents: in some contexts, if a baby bump was pointed, a girl would be born, if it was round, a boy: "panza appuntuta, prepara lu fuso; panza chiatta, prepara 'a zappa" (pointed belly, prepare the spindle; flat belly, prepare a hoe), people said in the Naples area (Ranisio 1996: 46). But the opposite was believed elsewhere.

Bets would be placed on the sex of the unborn child, too, a popular tradition so rooted and widespread, especially in the Italian states, such as in the Venetian republic, that, between the 16th and 17th centuries, the political authorities had to intervene with severe repressive laws, often reiterated but just as often disregarded (Figure 2.4).[47]

As for a baby's features and perfection of its forms, they were believed to be determined by its mother, by virtue of the deep connection existing between the mother's and foetus' bodies. According to Galen, not only conception, as pointed out by Thomas Laqueur,[48] but also a child's beauty was related to the pleasure experienced during intercourse: the more intense it was, the more beautiful the child would be; in the 16th century, this idea was taken up by Ambroise Paré (1510–1590), the forefather of surgery in France and founder of new obstetric practices.[49]

But, above all, particular performative power was attributed to women's gaze and emotions. To support this belief, shared by other physicians, Soranus reported some examples, such as the ugly and deformed tyrant of Cyprus, who, during intercourse, forced his wife to look at beautiful statues and had from her well-formed children (*Gyn.* I, 39). This belief was also reported in Avicenna's *Canon of medicine*, thus developing a thought that would be deeply rooted in medieval and early modern scientific worlds. A mother's gaze was conceived as a kind of film imprinting on the "soft mass" of the foetus whatever she gazed upon, be it positive or negative, especially in the first months of pregnancy. For this reason, pregnant women were advised to always keep beautiful images before their eyes, so as to bring well-formed children into the world. On the contrary, seeing ugly or deformed objects or shapes was considered very dangerous: the negative impression could be reproduced in the foetus' body, causing deformity; for example, a cleft palate (also known as a "hare lip") was related, as the popular name suggests, to seeing a hare.

FIGURE 2.4 "Superstitions" (betting on the sex of the of the foetus), from Giovanni Grevembroch [1754] (1981, vol. IV, p. 87). Reproduced with permission of the Ministero dei Beni e delle Attività Culturali e del Turismo – Biblioteca Nazionale Marciana.

A similar power was attributed to a mother's imagination: so, not only could things which were actually seen be impressed on a foetus' features, but also those which were simply imagined. During the Renaissance, this belief in women's "imaginative virtue" extended widely. In the context of Renaissance organicism, this "virtue" was not interpreted in a negative sense[50]: it fitted within the Neoplatonic philosophical idea of an intimate and profound connection between macrocosm and microcosm, body and mind, thus resulting in greater unity between mother and foetus. In fact, imaginative virtue had a widely recognised value and was also considered the basis of artistic creativity. This view emphasised both the profound link between mother and foetus and also the power of a mother's body. The outcome was a strong image of female fertility, which attributed to women an active and decisive role, if not in its conception, at least in the development of the foetus.

Even women's unfulfilled desires could have negative consequences, and even cause miscarriages, as we read in the *De passionibus mulierum*, or cause blotches similar to whatever they had desired to become impressed on the foetus' body, the so-called "birthmarks" (*naevus* in Latin and *voglie* ("cravings") in Italian).[51] Hence, there was the recommendation, also present in many texts, to promptly satisfy a pregnant woman's desires, so as to prevent flaws on the unborn child:

> Note that when a woman is in the beginning of her pregnancy, care ought to be taken that nothing is named in front of her which she is not able to have, because if she sets her mind on it and it is not given to her, this occasions miscarriage.
>
> (*Trot.*, 95, par. 79)

Of course, these precepts could be skilfully exploited by women as blackmail, in dynamics played on the involuntary nature of desires, the apportioning of blame to the family and also threats, as fairy tales, stories and proverbs can attest.[52]

But power goes hand in hand with responsibility and stressing this aspect could also lead to apportioning blame to women, as happened, with a significant change in perspective, during the 17th century, when several authors insisted on women's unreliability, interpreting cravings as whims and desires as an indicator of poor self-control.

The imaginative-virtue theory was ultimately questioned in the mid-18th century and finally abandoned at the end of the century in scientific contexts, with the emergence of another view of embryonic development, characterised by greater autonomy and independence of the foetus from its mother's body (see Chapter 10.2). In the popular tradition, however, this belief lasted much longer, arriving almost intact as far as the 20th century: "What she gazes upon, remains imprinted and she will birth", a Venetian proverb said (Bernoni [1878] 1980: 12). For this reason, in the city, it was traditional for best men to give brides a "very beautiful sugar baby doll" to be kept in the bedroom, right under their eyes, so as "to make an equally beautiful baby" (Pancino and Pillon 1985: 120). Very

58 Giving birth and being born

similar was the function of the painted angels, wax or chalk dolls, or the plastic dolls proudly displayed in bedrooms up to very recent times, signs of a thousand-year-old tradition.

4 Precepts, practices and prohibitions between medicine and tradition

Pregnancy is a "long navigation" in an often stormy sea, where pregnant women and their babies roam over nine months, François Mauriceau wrote in his *Traité des maladies des femmes grosses*, employing a very effective metaphor.[53] Medical advice to see this risky "navigation" through, protecting the mother's health and preventing a miscarriage, was therefore plentiful throughout the ages, and featured prominently in medical texts, recipe books and medieval *Secreta*, in printed books of the 16th and 17th centuries.

Soranus divided pregnancy care into three parts: that aimed at preserving the foetus in the first stages of pregnancy, that aimed at alleviating ailments in the second part and finally that used to prepare women for childbirth (*Gyn*. I, 46). The first stage was particularly delicate: pregnant women had to avoid any kind of excessive movement or emotion, eat a balanced diet, avoid lifting weights or doing heavy work; these were Soranus' recommendations to his rich clients of the Roman aristocracy, repeated in later texts. Galen also suggested avoiding strong emotions, identifying even thunder among the causes of miscarriage, for the fright they caused, and, on his wake, at the end of the 16th century, Scipione Mercurio also recommended that pregnant women avoid "the passions of the soul", be they grief or excessive "cheerfulness", anger or melancholy. Pregnant women had to keep calm and be happy, "always hoping for a male child", as the author pointed out, identifying in this prospect one of the fundamental reasons for their good spirits.[54] They also had to try and avoid coughing and vomiting, which shook the diaphragm, and unpleasant smells. In fact, the "matrix" was believed to be particularly sensitive to smells, and therefore attracted by scents and disgusted by bad smells, which could even cause a miscarriage; vaginal fumigations, prescribed according to the circumstances, were therefore widespread practices.

Advice on clothing had been dispensed since antiquity: pregnant women should not wear excessively tight clothes that compressed their abdomen, and should use bandages or belts to support their bellies in the final months of pregnancy.[55] They had to avoid excessively hot or cold temperatures, which would alter the balance of humours and cause miscarriages. As far as food was concerned, they had to have a balanced diet, eating neither too little (so as not too starve the foetus), nor too much (so as not to suffocate it); excesses in either direction were to be avoided.[56]

As far as exercise was concerned, especially in the second stage of pregnancy, this was recommended, always avoiding excesses: both hard work and idleness would make "mothers and foetuses sluggish and weak" (Mercurio [1596] 1713: 80). Sharp movements, such as running, climbing or coming down the stairs quickly, dancing or the jolting of carriages, were to be avoided, "because they shake the women's wombs in the same way as trees are shaken, from which for such shaking the fruits fall".[57] This recommendation is also often found in female correspondence right up to the 18th century, such as, for example, Madame de Sevigné's to her pregnant daughter.[58] This was not the reason why the law that forbade Roman women to use carriages was passed, as some historians say:[59] the Oppia law (215 BC), contested by women, was in fact a sumptuary law, issued during the Second Punic War and aimed at cutting unnecessary expenditure at a difficult time, avoiding every display of wealth, such as the excessive use of carriages.

Sexual intercourse was considered harmful – as Soranus specified – throughout the pregnancy as, by causing a contraction of the matrix, it could cause a miscarriage, or a premature birth, by rupturing the membranes (*Gyn.*, I, 46). This belief was rooted in the idea of a fundamental incompatibility between husbands and sons, which characterised the availability of the female body and which is also found in relation to breastfeeding: women's bodies belonged either to their husbands or their sons; they could not be shared by both[60] (see Chapter 4.2). Farmers did not sow an already sown field where the shoots were growing, to use the naturalistic metaphor recurrent in many texts. In the Christian West, this medical precept was interwoven with a firm moral condemnation: as it was not aimed at procreation (already achieved and in progress) and moreover dangerous for the foetus, those indulging in sexual intercourse in pregnancy committed the serious sin of covetousness, made worse by the anomaly in human behaviour compared to that of animals:

> Men who say they have contracted marriage and are bringing up children, for the good of their country and of the race, should at least imitate the brutes, and not destroy their offspring in the womb; nor should they appear in the character of lovers, but of husbands.
> (Saint Jerome, Against Jovinianus, I, 49)[61]

This was the opinion of many important theologians such as Saint Ambrose, a position barely mitigated in the late Middle Ages by Saint Thomas Aquinas, who emphasised the risk of miscarriage and the priority of protecting the embryo to the detriment of conjugal duty.

In actual fact, all these recommendations were often ignored in real life, as the doctors themselves bemoaned. Scipione Mercurio raged against an "abuse so little taken into account in Italy and so rooted among almost all the nobility that practically no other amusements are offered to pregnant women than going out in carriages and to frequent parties" (Mercurio [1596] 1713: 152); he also recorded the widespread habit of making pregnant women eat for two, with harmful consequences for their health.

Working-class women, however, would continue to work hard and without precautions right up to the end of their pregnancies, both in the fields and in craft activities, as denounced in the 18th century, with new awareness, by the authoritative figure of Johann Peter Frank (1745–1821), medical advisor to many princes, director of medical affairs in Austrian Lombardy in 1786 and expert of 18th-century European social reality, in his famous work *System einer vollständingen medicinischen Polizey* (1779–1788) *(A system of complete medical police)*:

> Townspeople and peasants often burden their pregnant women, long after they have entered the second half of pregnancy, with much and difficult work. While the otherwise diligent peasant lies idle behind the stove in winter, his wife in advance pregnancy in the greatest cold and sometimes on dangerously iced paths, fetches water (in our country carrying it on the head, whereby the pail has to be lifted by the raised arms), brings firewood into the kitchen and lights the stove.
>
> *(Frank, Johann Peter [1779] 1976: 73)*[62]

Gender violence is equally dramatically documented by the sources, often compromising the lives of women and foetuses: Giovanni Marinello, in *Le medicine partenenti alle infermità delle donne*, lists one of the most frequent causes of miscarriage as violence "above the location of the matrix, just as some beastly husbands do, by punching and kicking their women" (Marinello 1574: 152). Louise Bourgeois reported a case of foetal malformation due to beatings received by the mother, which she revealed only after some time: "She told me that six weeks before giving birth, her husband had hit her lower back three times with a bludgeon" (Bourgeois [1606] 1992: 159).[63] Frank also complained about the husbands' habit, "among the coarser classes of people, especially the peasants [...] to chastise their wives by beating" to the point of causing miscarriages (Frank [1779] 1976: 74).

As far as medical practices were concerned, in cases of illnesses in pregnancy, bleeding was widely used, particularly in the early modern age. The theory of humours identified the causes of diseases in the imbalance of the four basic humours: excessive blood production, especially in women of "sanguine" temperament, was believed to cause excessive accumulation in the womb, a plethora that could even cause a "miscarriage due to suffocation" (Mercurio [1596] 1713: 158). Bloodletting was therefore considered a suitable way to rebalance the alteration of humours that was believed to be the cause of many illnesses and ailments in pregnancy. What varied over time was only the indication of its frequency and at what stage of pregnancy to perform it. The Hippocratic Corpus advised against it in the first months of pregnancy, a precept followed by many physicians even in the 16th century. But 17th- and 18th-century man-midwives, from G. Mauquest de La Motte to A. Levret, resorted to it more frequently, at least three times during the pregnancy, and F. Mauriceau recommended it even from the early months.[64] At the end of the 18th century, it became even more widespread, even at the beginning of childbirth, and acquired even greater importance at the end of the century, thanks to the "excitability theory" developed by Scottish physician John Brown.[65] What appears to our eyes as a misleading aberration, certainly harmful to women, was considered for centuries a healing remedy, on whose effectiveness there was full agreement between the scientific and the popular worlds.

Alongside bloodletting, a wide range of potions and remedies to prevent miscarriages is documented since antiquity: in his *Naturalis Historia*, Pliny included some of these recipes, based upon "analogical or sympathetic medicine", the foundation of medieval *experimenta* and *Remedy books*.[66] The underlying principle inspiring it was the use of plants, liquids and objects, linked in one way or another to the ailing body by shape, colour or other characteristics.[67] Very popular, for example, was the use of cereal germ or egg yolks: Louise Bourgeois, midwife to Queen Maria de' Medici, reported saving a woman from miscarrying by using them in a certain potion.[68]

A complex system of ritualistic prohibitions and obligations (persisting in the popular tradition in many contexts until the early 20th century, though with some local variation) regulated the lives of pregnant women, with the aim of protecting their babies and ensuring good deliveries. For example, pregnant women were not supposed to tie necklaces around their necks (because the umbilical cord would similarly be twisted around their babies' necks), or cross their fingers or legs, and neither were the people around them: according to Pliny, *Naturalis Historia* (XXVIII), it was *veneficium*.[69] In some contexts, such as in Italy, they were not supposed to leave skeins of wool on their reels, walk over reins or ropes tied to animals, or knit; nor were they allowed to see dead people.[70] The range of objects having to be worn around one's neck or on one's clothes to ward off bad luck also varied: for example, certain stones, such as the agate, were popular throughout Europe, or the eagle-stone (*lapis praegnans*), a geode whose shape recalls a pregnant uterus, which from antiquity was tied to pregnant women's arms to prevent miscarriages.[71] Clay was also supposed to have a special protective virtue: "if a woman carries some on herself when she is pregnant, she cannot miscarry" (Marinello 1574: 262). These were joined in the Christian West to devotional objects, such as relics of the Virgin Mary's or Saint Margaret's belts, or, as we have seen, of Saint Anthony's or Saint Francis' rope-belts. In the Middle Ages, in many contexts, there was a widespread tradition of wearing parchment scrolls with sacred images and prayers on one's body,[72] or a little cloth bag around one's neck: in Southern Italy, this was called the "little dress" and was also placed between a newborn's swaddling clothes.[73] To promote safe deliveries, special prayers (*Carmina*) or phrases were pronounced and sometimes, in the Middle Ages, if written, they were even chewed and eaten.[74] In short, the remedy books of medieval medicine were a mix of medicine, religion and magic.

In the 16th and 17th centuries, numerous *Remedia* for pregnant women were printed and distributed by parish priests and notables with the aim of helping the working womenfolk.[75] One of the best known in France, Marie Foucquet's, *Les Remèdes charitables*, had as many as 16 editions between the end of the 17th and the beginning of the 18th centuries.[76]

62 Giving birth and being born

Since the late Middle Ages, like in the ancient world, women, especially aristocratic ones and those from the urban middle-class, had also resorted to the advice of physicians and practitioners, though it should be noted that, for reasons of modesty, these consultations excluded any contact and/or view of the female genitalia.[77] Medicines and bloodlettings would be ordered, the latter performed by barber-surgeons.

What must be stressed is how, for the entire duration of a pregnancy and in order to ensure a successful outcome, a woman's body was subjected to strong family and social control, ubiquitous norms and constant monitoring.

5 Not only babies: "monsters" and moles

From the ancient world up to the 18th century, both the scientific and popular worlds shared the belief that women could conceive and bring into the world not only babies, but also "monsters", or shapeless masses of tissue called moles (Figure 2.5).

Whatever mysterious developments took place in women's bodies during pregnancy were the object of speculations or fantasies which, in different ways, depending on the times and contexts, articulated cultural representations, religious beliefs and collective anxieties and fears.

The representation of monsters does not have a linear or progressive evolution, correcting previous interpretations: it does not go from a fantastic thought towards a positive and rational one, but shows variations, coexistence and changing attitudes over time, both in science and in real life, with feelings ranging from horror to pleasure, from reluctance to fun, to rejection.[78]

FIGURE 2.5   Examples of "monsters", from Jakob Rueff (1587), *De conceptu et generatione hominis*, Francofurti ad Moenum: P. Fabricium: c 44r. Reproduced with permission of the Biblioteca Pinali antica (Padua).

Since Ancient Greek times, the view that monstrous beings (*téras*), half-human and half-animal, could be born, following the fusion of seeds of different species, had gained credit even in scientific circles, and this idea was reflected in myths which told of matings of women with animals.[79]

As mentioned (Chapter 1.4), Aristotle contested this view, explaining them as one of the disorders of fertilisation, in this case a deterioration of the seed that allowed matter to take over, in a progressive alteration of the forms. This conviction was also taken up by some Roman scientists, such as Pliny, who believed that the birth of monsters was connected to intercourse during menstruation and was due to the corrosive and destructive force attributed to menstrual blood (*menstruum quasi monstruum*), a belief that remained firmly rooted in subsequent centuries.[80] This view was the basis of the firm moral condemnation by medieval theologians, who viewed intercourse at this time as a mortal sin.

However, the idea of a possible mixed generation, *contra naturam*, remained rooted and was variously re-proposed in science even in the early modern age: an authoritative 17th-century German physician, Daniel Sennert, claimed that he had witnessed the case of a girl fertilised by the seed of a snake, dispersed in the water of a fountain.[81]

Since ancient times, in the social reality, the birth of a seriously malformed baby has always been interpreted, like other exceptional phenomena (invasions of locusts, epidemics, droughts, etc.), as a sign of the gods, who punished men even in their procreation, with infertility or the birth of monsters. The very etymology of the Latin term *monstrum*, connected both to *monere* (to warn) and to *monstrare* (to show), makes reference to this view. The deformed being was therefore often rejected and abandoned, in water or in an uninhabited place, rather than killed, fearing that its soul might haunt the living.[82]

In the transition to Christianity, this idea is taken up and expanded to underline the moral fragility intrinsic to human nature: the birth of a monster was connected to God's decision to send a sign to men and to punish them for their sins, in ways which varied in either direction, depending on the authors and the times. Monsters belonged to the system of prophetic signs indicating both God's will and his anger. Saint Augustine wrote in *De civitate Dei* that the birth of these beings was not a mistake or a defect of nature, but a sign sent by the Almighty to humankind to remind it of its condition as mortals, as a consequence of its original sin: therefore, they were caused not by individual sins, but by collective ones.[83]

The very characteristics of monstrosity were considered expressions of sins, which could be seen in the features of each deformation, according to a somatic interpretation which gained popularity from the Middle Ages. For example, in the features of a well-known "monster" born in Ravenna in 1512, a chronicler of the time identified the signs of the many moral evils that afflicted Italy: pride, greed, avarice and sodomy: "And on account of these vices, Italy is shattered by the suffering of war" (Daston and Park 1998: 182). For this reason, too, and for educational purposes, numerous printed flyers showed the images everywhere, and teratoscopy, the art of divination through monsters, became particularly popular.

The feeling they aroused was horror, a term that occurs in all the European languages, where these births were defined *dreadful or terrible, orrendi, espouvantables, grausames*.[84] This was often intertwined with an apocalyptic view: the birth of monsters was one of the signs of the end of the world, according to the *Apocalypse* of Ezra.

Starting from the second half of the 16th century and above all during the 17th century, in the scientific and philosophical worlds and within the view of nature expounded by organicism, a new approach took hold. Monsters were seen in a more positive light, as *mirabilia*, the wondrous works of an untiringly creative nature, which generated even in the strangest situations and with all the resources at its disposal: in this sense, they were seen as *lusus naturae* (play of nature), more astonishing than horrible: not *contra naturam*, but *praeter naturam*, as argued in Fortunio Liceti's *De monstris*.[85] This astonished gaze expressed itself in the fashion of collecting "monsters", which were included in the *Wunderkammern* just like other oddities and wonders of nature. The Gonzaga collection included a human foetus with four heads and two mouths, and another example was kept in the Ferrante Imperato museum in Naples. In fairs and in town and village squares, their performance also attracted crowds of curious visitors ready to pay to see them, according to an older custom which became more widespread throughout Europe in the 16th century.[86]

Of course, they often made their parents' or their keepers' fortune, so the birth of a human chimera was, in Liceti's opinion, a real blessing for poor families who could show them off for a fee. Not infrequently, behind these cases, there were organised scams, as shown by the story of a country woman from Godalming, a village in Surrey (1726), who had become famous for giving birth to several "rabbits", but later turned out to be a clever swindler.[87]

During the 17th century, they became the object of specific medical investigations, aimed at analysing their causes and also identifying their different types: specific publications appeared, such as Liceti's, which collected and summarised the different views. Ambroise Paré, in his *Des monstres et prodiges* (1573), summarised in detail the possible causes of monstrosity, listing, respectively:

> The Glory of God, His wrath, an overabundance of seed; an insufficient amount of it; the imagination [of the mother]; hypotrophy, or the small size of the uterus, the incorrect way in which the mother is sitting [...]; a fall or blows inflicted on a pregnant woman's belly; hereditary or accidental diseases; the putrefaction or corruption of the seed; the mixing of the seed; the deception of nasty beggars; demons or the devil.[88]

As far as the "wrath of God" was concerned, he stated that it was caused by the sins committed during intercourse (intercourse during menstruation or with animals) with a significant shift, now linking the event to an individual, rather than to a collective sin and its punishment. One of the causes given was also the "imagination of women", supported by various authors. A mother's performative force could go so far as to completely distort an embryo's forms, causing not only malformations or blotches, but real "monstrosities".[89]

In the second half of the 17th century, and especially in the 18th century, a new approach took hold among the educated élites, within a revival of Aristotle's philosophy; the "monsters" were thus naturalised: the causes of their birth were traced back to deteriorated matter in their conception, to defects in women's anatomy or in the foetus' development. The feeling they provoked was no longer fun or horror, but rather disgust for the deformities they showed. The interest of scientists and philosophers, such as R. Boyle and Voltaire, was limited to the chance of discovering more general laws on the functioning of nature, starting from the observation of deformity rather than normality. The emergence of a more strictly medical and scientific discourse in the analysis of their causes led, on the one hand, to the exclusion of God's direct intervention (which Paré and Rueff still included) and, on the other hand, to the disappearance of the admiration and amusement that had dominated in the 16th and 17th centuries.

Centuries-long scientific debates were also prompted by moles (*mylé*), a long-term notion in the history of medicine: fleshy masses, deformed pieces of tissue, in the most varied sizes and shapes. Unlike monsters, moles could not move, but, like monsters, they were considered by Greek medicine as the outcome of the deterioration of the product of conception, for poor quality or strength of the seed, as often stated in the Hippocratic Corpus (*Barrenness*) (FS, XXIII, 446, c.233), or for lack of heat in the womb, according to Aristotle: in short, they were the product of a nature "incapable and unable to perfect or to put the last touches to the process of generation", as Aristotle writes in the *Generation of Animals* (GA IV, 7–8, 775 b).[90] Despite Soranus' different interpretation (he thought that moles were due to an inflammation of the womb, or to an ulcer), the association between moles and childbearing continued in medieval and early modern medicines, albeit with different causes.[91] Charles de Saint-Germaine, in a 1651 text on the subject (*Traitté de fausse couches, enseignant la nature de faux germes, embryons, avortons et moles*), identified six types of matter delivered from the uterus: the seed, the false germ, the embryo, the miscarriage, the mole and the baby. This distinction was taken up and simplified by G. Mauquest De la Motte in pregnancies which were either "natural", "non-natural" and "against nature" (these included moles), or "false" (simple retentions of menstrual blood).[92]

But medical vocabulary, just like classifications, remained flexible. Much attention was always paid to this phenomenon: the research and debates on their causes, the identification of symptoms to distinguish true pregnancies from *faux germes* and from moles, reveal the anxiety and disquiet about whatever potentially threatening and deadly form might develop in the womb.

Women showed all the signs of pregnancy (nausea, vomiting, interruption of menstruation), but could not feel the movements of the foetus, and gave birth to a shapeless mass, often after several months or even years (unlike with *faux germs* that were expelled after three to four months). Alternatively, they would not give birth at all, thus putting their own lives in danger, as in the case of Madame Roger, dissected by Ambroise Paré in 1574, in whose womb a 17-year-old mole was found.[93]

In the 17th century, the presence of worms or snakes was also discussed, further increasing the range of possible living or non-living forms, that could be mysteriously generated within a woman's body. In short, knowing what was actually developing inside women's bodies before childbirth was impossible: "Affirmare quid intus sit divinare est" ("to say what may be inside is guessing"), as a 17th-century doctor called to pronounce on a case of false pregnancy had declared (Conforti 2009: 144).

Popular imagination embroidered on these fantasies, which went hand in hand with others that considered the womb as a restless and autonomous animal within a woman's body: moles were imagined as either vegetables or animals.[94] Some midwives reported seeing moles that could walk or fly or that had tried to return to the matrix once they had been extracted.[95] Italian man-midwife Giovanni Bigeschi, as late as the 19th century, referred to "empty-headed women" who "believed moles were animals that could move, fly, etc." (Bigeschi 1819: 104).

The existence of moles and monsters posed considerable problems to the practice of baptism. Were monsters to be considered human beings or not? Should priests or midwives (in emergencies) baptise them or refuse them this sacrament? In fact, baptism presumed the creature was human and alive. So, a mole should definitely not be baptised, but how should one behave with monsters? The view that prevailed in the Council of Trent was to baptise them *sub condicione*, with the formula "si tu es homo" (if you are a man). The *Rituale Romanum* advised exercising "great caution" in any case and seeking the "advice of the local Bishop" (*Rituale Romanum*, 'De baptizandis parvulis') [1614] (1740: 7).[96]

6 The fight against abortion and the defence of the *venter*

If the recommendations aimed at preventing miscarriages account for medical knowledge and the representation of pregnant women, then the normative system regulating abortion focused more precisely on the representation of the embryo and on power systems, i.e. the forms and figures of control surrounding women's fertile bodies.

In this field, a profound fracture separates the Greek and Roman world from the Jewish and, above all, the Christian one.[97] In the ancient world, abortion was morally accepted and lawful. Many medical texts, such as Soranus' to midwives (*Gyn.* I, 60), or Pliny the Elder's *Naturalis Historia*, contained indications and recipes, in addition to contraceptive methods, on how also to interrupt pregnancies, ranging from the use of poultices and mixtures taken by mouth (based on various herbs such as dittany, rue, mugwort, sylphium, etc.), to the jumping and shaking of the body, to the introduction of probes into the cervix.[98] So, it was equally well known that the skills of midwives also included the ability to abort a foetus, by administering *phàrmakon*, as Plato wrote in his *Theaetetus* (*Theae.Fow*, 149d) (see Chapter 6.1), without this affecting his good name.[99] How widespread this practice was is a matter of discussion among historians: if we lend credence to the accusations of Christians, we run the risk of having a distorted picture of reality, inflated by anti-pagan rhetoric.

There were, of course, criticisms as well, starting from the position taken by the Hippocratic Corpus in his famous oath (*Jusiurandum*),[100] variously taken up by authors such as Pliny the Elder, Ovid and many Stoics. In actual fact, however, abortion was used as a contraceptive practice, as Aristotle writes in his *Politics*, in a discourse on the need to control births (*Polit.* VII, 16, 1335b). No Greek or Roman law ever forbade it. A foetus was considered *mulieris portio vel viscerum*, or part of its mother's body, as long as it was in her womb, not yet a human being, but liquid matter like the "molten bronze" which could not be assimilated to a statue, to use the effective metaphor used by the philosopher Epictetus, who believed that "it was wrong to call molten copper a statue and man a foetus" (cited by Galeotti 2003: 23).

The first criminal law against abortion was issued during the Roman Empire, some time between 193 and 217 AD (during the reigns of Septimius Severus and Caracalla): it punished women who had had abortions without their husbands' knowledge. It is interesting to observe how the law was written not with the intention of protecting a foetus, but rather its father's *patria potestas* and his *ius vitae necisque* (right of life and death) on his wife and children, born and unborn, so also on the foetus contained in the womb: an abortion performed without his consent doubly violated this cornerstone of Roman law, since it implied a woman's unforeseen autonomy and deprived the father of every decision concerning the unborn child. Punishments were also imposed on those who had procured such abortions, but only if the women died.

Christianity brought about a radical change: abortion was condemned as the killing of a human being, equal to infanticide. For Christians, it was not just a violation of the divine precept of multiplication, but of a mortal aggression against a creature of God, on whose will every birth depended: a life did not belong to an earthly father, but to the heavenly one. The condemnation of the practice was therefore inscribed in a context where the figure of the natural father was somewhat diminished in its symbolic and real power.[101] As a creature of God, a foetus also belonged to that category of "neighbour", towards whom not only respect, but love was commanded. The *Didaché*, or *The Teaching of the Twelve Apostles* (end of the 1st century), the first document mentioning it, contains this motivation for its condemnation: "shalt not murder a child by abortion nor kill that which is begotten" (*Did.* 2/2).[102]

The seriousness of interrupting a pregnancy, however, took on a somewhat different connotation when, starting from the 4th century, the "delayist" view about the ensoulment of the foetus prevailed: aborting an unensouled foetus was not equivalent to aborting one already endowed with a soul and therefore in need of baptism. The early Middle-Ages Penitentials had different penances depending on whether the aborted foetus was in a "liquid state" or already ensouled.[103]

Saint Thomas pointed out that the first was to be understood as a violation of the divine commandment to multiply (analogous to the *coitus interruptus*), whereas the second was equivalent to an actual murder, as Pope Innocent III reiterated in his constitution *Sicut ex litterarum* (1211).[104]

This distinction was taken up by medieval civil laws. The *Leges Henrici Primi* (1115), the first English legal text, punished as quickening (i.e. murder) an abortion performed on an ensouled foetus, whereas if performed in the preceding months, it was considered as misdemeanour. Equally, the laws issued by Edward I (1239–1307) also considered murder the abortion of a foetus *formatus et animatus*. In Europe, starting from the 12th to the 13th centuries, a sin became a crime, in an important and significant process, and political institutions, at different times, issued laws condemning both abortion and infanticide, often joined in the wider category of "parricide" (the killing of blood relatives) and ascribed among the heinous crimes. This incurred particularly cruel capital punishments, even if their application was rather rare, at least up to the 16th century.[105]

The unanimous condemnation from both ecclesiastical and political institutions did not obviously entail a disappearance of the practice of abortion, but only its becoming a clandestine activity: that midwives and practitioners knew methods and herbs which could bring about the termination of a pregnancy (also clearly identified in medieval *herbaria*).[106] The repression directed at them obviously intended to discourage them from practising it: they were suspected not only of practising abortions, but also of witchcraft and magic based on the trafficking of aborted foetuses and stillborn babies.

In the early modern age, in a climate of increasing control over women's sexual lives, this condemnation was accompanied by attempts to prevent abortions by adopting measures to control the women considered at risk, such as unmarried girls and widows above all. The honour of women and the protection of children were no longer just a family concern, but involved the ecclesiastical and civil communities, too, joined in the shared supervision of women's fertile bodies, as argued by Adriano Prosperi.[107] Appropriate laws were used to monitor every pregnant woman considered at risk of committing abortion or infanticide in order to prevent such crimes. The first of these laws, passed by Henry II of France in 1556, forced pregnant women to present themselves before public officials to declare their pregnancies (*Déclaration de grossesse*), so as not to be accused of abortion or infanticide should the foetus die.[108]

The judicial precedent, appropriately reviewed and adapted, was an ancient Roman law that had fallen into disuse, passed by Marcus Aurelius at the request of a divorced husband (Rutilius Severus, after whom the law had been named), in defence of the *venter*, a Latin legal term indicating that, in addition to a pregnant woman, a foetus was placed under its father's authority. The first French law of 1556 was followed by a second one issued by Henry III (1586), who imposed its dissemination throughout France, then an English one issued by James I Stuart (1624), a Swedish one (1627) and a Danish one (1638).[109] In Switzerland, this control took on almost paradoxical contours, which included the *prevardatio*, forced periodic visits to which unmarried women were subjected which were aimed at ascertaining possible pregnancies.[110] In many German states, the control of unmarried pregnant women was entrusted to midwives.[111] In the Church State, this function was also entrusted to midwives, who had to report unmarried pregnant girls, under the penalty of their own indictment if they failed.[112]

Elsewhere, the figure of a replacement male was created for this purpose, acting as a "guarantor of childbirth": in 1701, in Tuscany, Cosimo III issued a rule that ordered pregnant women not only to present themselves to public officials to swear *De tuendo fetus* (to preserve the foetus), but also to nominate their "guarantor of childbirth", a public guarantor of pregnancy and birth.[113] This rule was everything but disregarded, as research has shown.

The State was clearly taking on the role of a replacement father-husband in cases where he did not exist or was temporarily unable to perform his function of controlling a woman's body before his community. This also highlights the sexualised nature of political institutions, understood as a male community, and the alliance established on this ground between Church and State, united in their common objective of preserving the honour of women (which reflected the honour of the whole community) and controlling their fertility.

Between the 15th and 16th centuries, in many European cities, these measures against pregnant women were accompanied by charitable initiatives in support of destitute mothers, started with the aim of preventing abortions and infanticide, well aware of how much poverty could be the origin of these choices even within families. They were generally supported by congregations and private foundations, but even public institutions began to take charge of this assistance, as, for instance, in Nuremberg, Lyon and Florence, where special subsidies were granted to poor and large families for each pregnancy and childbirth.[114] In Nuremberg, in 1461, a specific institution was founded, the Arme Kindbetterin Almosen, which continued to operate (though with various reforms) until the 19th century. In Basel, two private foundations were created, both lasting many years: the Erasmusstiftung, founded in 1538 according to Erasmus' wishes, and the Weissenburgsstiftung in 1523, which, in addition to providing poor girls with dowries, gave funds to women in labour and to new mothers.[115] It should be noted that the latter paid such contributions to their husbands or fathers, thus subjecting the new mothers to a double form of family and institutional control.

7 Institutions for unmarried mothers ("fallen women")

During the Counter-Reformation, the first institutes for unmarried pregnant women were created in Catholic countries. These were workhouses where unmarried girls, pregnant outside of marriage, were admitted, sometimes willingly but more often forcibly, leaving their babies to foundling hospitals. These institutions for abandoned newborns and young children had for some time also started to admit unmarried mothers who remained to work as free wet nurses for a period of time corresponding to their admission.[116]

The driving force behind these institutions was at the same time both moral and repressive: they removed every trace of scandal from the community, hiding 'fallen women' and the "product of sin" from the eyes of society, leading them from a life of sin back to a Christian life, and at the same time protecting the lives of unborn children. One of the first of these in Italy, the *Casa di Soccorso*, was opened in Ferrara in 1580 by Lucrezia d'Este, sister to Alfonso II, followed by the *Ospizio di San Rocco "delle Celate"* in Rome (1600) and the *Pia Opera Buon Pastore* in Asti (1693).[117]

Even in the cited cases, there was a close co-operation between the ecclesiastic and state institutions in the control of unmarried, pregnant women, a control which went as far as physically segregating them until the birth of their child.

These women, generally poor and marginalised, were usually brought by their families or admitted by law-enforcement officers at the request of the religious authorities, often during the night to avoid scandal. The Modena institution's rules even report the wording of such 'arrest warrant':

> If an illegally pregnant woman is reported, the entire Body of Presidents must investigate the matter and especially the birth, so that, ascertained first and foremost the illegitimate pregnancy, not knowing whether it will result in childbirth, they may proceed as cautiously as possible, in order to apprehend the pregnant woman and take her from where she is to the *Casa di Dio*, using the usual justice officers who will hand her to the male of female caretaker of the Casa.
> (Regolamento della Casa di Dio, 1759: I, XIV, 130)[118]

In these genuine correctional prisons, governed by a prioress, the women admitted were subjected to monastic discipline, without any obstetric care, nor contact with the outside. The reformative-punitive intent is clear in the strict rules which regulated a daily life of work and religious services: confessions, prayers, masses and vigils alternated with manual work and punishments, aimed precisely at atonement and reformation. The only freedom granted to the women in some institutes was cooking what they wished, in order to avoid the trouble for the foetus caused by their "imagination". On the other hand, as is clearly shown by the terms used in contemporary documents, these mothers were considered 'delinquent [girls]' and 'sinners' and their male partners 'accomplices' or 'criminals'.

During the 17th century, an increasing concern for the children's spiritual fate stepped up the foundation of these institutes: the one in Florence, for example, was created by priest Filippo Franci in 1679, right after the promulgation of Pope Innocent XI's papal bull on abortion and the ensoulment of the foetus, which boosted the fight against abortive practices.[119] Since according to canon law (and even many civil codes), the father of the newborn was required to provide for its sustenance even in the case of illegitimate children, women in labour had to report the 'perpetrator of the pregnancy' under oath at the moment of birth; this juncture had been specifically chosen to extract a truthful declaration from them, in *summis doloribus partus* (in the climax of childbirth pains), at a time when their life was in danger.[120] According to the laws of the time, the statement from the mother was, in fact, enough to attest paternity; this rule would generally disappear in the 19th century with the prohibition of paternity searches established by the Napoleonic code and other similar European codes.[121]

The statements reported in registers clearly show the wide range of situations that came before these 'illegitimate' pregnancies: from occasional encounters to abandonments, from liaisons with married men to rape and violence; there were even unions that could not bear the strain of a child, with men who backed out on their promises. Milan's Register of *Gravide, Balie e Comarine* gives us an idea of this wide range of cases:

> Giuseppa Scotti, 30 yrs old, unmarried, from Cura di S. Salvatore, declared that her baby's father is Giuseppe N.N., fled to Venice [...]. Giuseppa Barbarina, 21 yrs old, unmarried from Asago, admitted when pregnant, declared her baby's father is a peasant who lived in the house of the tenant farmer where she worked as a servant [...]. Elena Bossa, 35 yrs old, from the parish of S. Michele, declared that the criminal is Antonio Gian Luganese [...]. Giuseppa Bergoma, 40 yrs old, declared that her baby's father is an unknown peasant, who assaulted her in the countryside.
> (AIPMI, 130, 1.I.D, 1775)[122]

On the other hand, it should be remembered that pre-matrimonial sexual intercourse was, in many contexts, a long, community-accepted tradition, as research on the topic has revealed,[123] especially since marriage before the rulings of the Council of Trent was not a punctual and circumscribed event, but a process that consisted of successive phases, and that the Church sought to forcefully reform only after this Council.

The primary intent of these oaths, which unmarried women in labour had to swear, was forcing fathers to pay for the maintenance of the mother and especially the child, as pointed out by Lombardi.[124] In some cases, attempts were also made to persuade them, if not to marry the girl, then at least to provide a dowry for her; this was something that the institution itself undertook to do with 'converts', to whom a dowry would be given.[125]

In the opinion of several 19th-century physicians, who spoke of the obligation to swear such oaths as of real "moral torture", these rules actually served neither to prevent "illegitimate births", nor in many cases to identify "the partners in crime", but only to "increase the number of abortions, infanticide and dangerous abandonments of infants" (Buffini 1844: 92).

If we may agree with the first part of this opinion, the second is historically inaccurate: in actual fact, the number of foundlings significantly increased from the second half of the 18th century, when a culture of removal of a natural father's responsibility spread through society. Many 19th-century civil codes, modelled on the Napoleonic one, embraced and sanctioned this with their prohibition of paternity searches.[126] In exchange, unmarried mothers were given the opportunity of withholding their identities from the new lying-in hospitals which were founded in the 18th century, as we shall see in Chapter 9.

However, these institutions were not everywhere replaced by new lying-in hospitals: in some countries, these institutions remained throughout the 19th century and until the First World War. In Great Britain in the 1870s, around 75% of children born in workhouse lying-in wards were illegitimate.[127] In Catholic Ireland, they remained active until the 1970s, as the sad story of the Magdalene Houses, also known as Magdalene Laundries, for the work that the girls carried out, shows. This has been recently brought to the fore by research, surveys[128] and films[129] that have highlighted the tragic experiences of thousands of girls in these workhouses, the legacy of a past that was believed to have disappeared.

Notes

1. HPott LCL520, VII, 477,5, p. 15.
2. Savonarola [1460?] (1952: 52).
3. Bettini (2013: ch. 5).
4. Ibidem.
5. Curatolo (1901: 36); Belmont (1971: 161); Cid Lopez (2007).
6. Laurent (1989); Olsan (2018)
7. Bettini (2013: ch. 5); Gélis (1984a: 139).
8. *Tim. Lamb*, 91c.
9. Manuli (1983: 177).
10. Gourevitch and Raepsaet-Charlier (2001: 130).
11. Murray (2018).
12. Moulinier-Brogi (2004, 2010).
13. Duden (1993: 79).
14. Yan (1992).
15. Porter (1985); Kassel (2018).
16. Duden (1991).
17. Duden (1991, 1993).
18. McClive-King (2007); Berthiaud (2013, 2015); Castiglione (2017).
19. D'Amelia (1997: 27).
20. Laurent (1989); King (1998); Maire (2004); McClive and King (2007); Duden (2002); Papiernik et al. (2009); Frydman (2010); Casado and Savva (2017).
21. HPott: 53 (LCL520, VII, 506).
22. Marti Casado and Savva (2017: 32–54); Nardi (1954: 75–76).
23. Flemming (2018b).
24. Nardi (1954: 35).
25. Pancino (2006: 30–31).
26. Kassell (2018).
27. Pancino (2006: 26).
28. Translated from the French edition, like the following quotations from this text.
29. As stated by Pancino (2006: 38).
30. As also pointed out by Duden (1993, 2002).
31. Ekholm (2018).
32. Park (2006: ch. 3).
33. Ekholm (2018).
34. Laurent (1989); Kassel (2018).
35. Gélis (1984a: 131–132).

36 Laurent (1989).
37 Gélis (1984a: 129–130).
38 Laurent (1989); Brisson, Congourdeau and Solère (2008); Gongourdeau (2018).
39 Fischer (2010b: 115–117).
40 Noonan (1965); Galeotti (2003); Prosperi (2005), Betta (2010); Gongourdeau (2018).
41 Prosperi (2005: ch. 5).
42 Prosperi (2005: ch. 5); Filippini (1995: ch. 2.1).
43 King (1998: 8).
44 *Trot.*, 95, *par.* 76.
45 Savonarola [1460?] (1952: 56).
46 Marinello (1574: III, 245–246).
47 Grevembroch [1754] (1981), ("Avare superstizioni"); Vanzan Marchini (1985: 177).
48 Laqueur (1992).
49 Berriot-Salvadore (1993).
50 As pointed out by Pancino (1996: 79–80).
51 Laget (1982: 33).
52 Ranisio (1996: 52).
53 Mauriceau [1668] (1681: 192).
54 Mercurio [1596] (1713: 148–150).
55 Curatolo (1901: 59–62); Bettini (2013: ch. 5).
56 Mercurio (1658: V, 'Degli errori della gravidanza e del parto').
57 Mercurio (1658: 152).
58 Gélis (1984a: 148).
59 Galeotti (2003: 24).
60 Rollet-Morel (2000: 110–111).
61 "The Snares of Marital Love; Chastity Recommended to Women"; taken from the online edition: http://sites.fas.harvard.edu/~chaucer/canttales/wbpro/jerome.html. See Laurent (1989: 136) and Flandrin (2006: II, doc.2).
62 The text was republished in several volumes in Vienna (1787) and Berlin (1792). It was translated and published in Italy for the first time in Milan in 1807. In Italy, several editions of this work have been published because Frank taught at the University of Pavia (1785), held the post of inspector general in Austrian Lombardy (1786) and introduced reforms in medical instruction and practice. I have consulted the English edition by Erna Lesky (Frank 1976), with introduction by Erna Lesky, trans. from the German by E. Vilim, Johns Hopkins University Press. This and many of the following quotations are taken from this edition. For those missing from this translation, I referred to the complete edition published in Italy (Frank 1825).
63 Translated from the French edition, like the following quotations.
64 Gélis (1984a: 286).
65 In Italy, he became popular, thanks to "Jacobin" physician Giovanni Rasori, who also held political positions under Napoleon (Cosmacini 2002, 1987: 251–252).
66 Gourevitch and Raepsaet-Charlier (2001: 133–134); King (1998: 132–156); Barras (2004); Andò (2000).
67 As pointed out by L'Estrange (2010: 173).
68 Bourgeois [1606] (1992: 52–53).
69 Bettini (2013: ch. 5); Rollet, Morel (2000: 31–32).
70 De Gubernatis (1878); Pancino (1984: 187–195); Baldini (1991: 23–33).
71 Curatolo (1901: 60); Cavallo (2018).
72 Oslan (2018).
73 Ranisio (1996).
74 Green (2009); L'Estrange (2010: 174–177); Foscati (2014: 316–319).
75 Murray (2018).
76 Laget (1982: 49).
77 King (2018); Park (2006, 2018).

78 As shown by L. Daston and K. Park (1998).
79 Daston and Park (1998); Fischer (2010a).
80 Niccoli (1980).
81 Conforti (2009).
82 Lefaucheur (2010: 212 seq.).
83 Daston and Park (1998: 39–40).
84 Ibidem: 181.
85 Liceti [1616] (1665: I, XI, 41).
86 Gélis (1984a: 357–360).
87 Angelini (1997: 27–36).
88 Paré [1573] (1664): XXV, 645.
89 Fischer (2010a: 204); Pancino (1996: 97).
90 APlatt, IV, 7.
91 As pointed out by McClive and King (2007: 224).
92 La Motte [1715] (1989: 17–20).
93 McClive and King (2007: 234).
94 These popular beliefs were denounced as errors in the 16th century by Joubert (1578) and Mercurio Scipione (1658).
95 Gélis (1984a: 357).
96 Translated from the Latin edition, like the following quotations.
97 Noonan (1970); Feldman (1970); Sardi (1975); Riddle (1992); Gourevitch and Raepsaet-Charlier (2001); Kapparis (2002); Flamigni (2006).
98 Nardi (1971: 263–280 and 339–343); Gourevitch (1984: 207–209); Gourevitch and Raepsaet-Charlier (2001: 138); Riddle (1992).
99 On the ambiguous and ambivalent value of the term *phàrmakon*, in the wider context of the vocabulary of care, see Curi (2017).
100 Hippocrate, *Le serment, les serment cretiens, la Loi*. Texte établi et traduit par Jacques Jouanna, Paris: Belles Lettres, 2018: VIII and CXV. Jouanna presents and analyses the various versions of this famous text.
101 As pointed out by Cesbron and Knibiehler (2004: 51–52).
102 *Didaché. The Teaching of the Twelve Apostles*, ch. 2/2. Taken from the online edition, ed. by J.P. Audet 1958:,http://ldysinger.stjohnsem.edu/@texts/0095_didache/01_Didache.htm#CONTENTS.
103 Noonan (1970); Riddle (1992: ch. 10) Prosperi (2005: ch. 3); Der Lugt (2018); Muller (2012).
104 Prosperi (2005: 49–53 and 244); Galeotti (2003: 42).
105 Hoffer and Hull (1981: 22); Muller (2012: ch. 3).
106 Riddle (1992).
107 Prosperi (2005: 54–58).
108 Phan (1975: 61–88, 1986); Demars-Sion (1991); Lombardi (2018).
109 Hoffer and Hull (1981: 22); Prosperi (2005: 60–63); Muller (2012: ch. 3).
110 Ceschi (2011).
111 Flügge (1998).
112 Fiocca (1983); Pelaja (1994).
113 Zanotto (1996); Alessi (1989, 1995).
114 Felici (2005).
115 Ibidem.
116 Cappelletto (1983); Reggiani (2008); Hunecke (1987).
117 Grillenzoni (1868: 529–531); Curatolo (1901: 243–248); Garofalo (1949); Filippini (1992: 397–398).
118 Internal regulation of the so-called "House of God", an institution sheltering pregnant women bearing illegitimate babies.
119 Passerini (1853); Alessi (1995).
120 Reggiani (2018: 47).

121 Lombardi (1997, 2018).
122 AIPMI, corda 130, 1.I.D, Registro *Gravide, Balie e Comarine 1775–1776*, 27 ottobre 1775, 11 gennaio 1776, 13 luglio 1775, 11 marzo 1775. This important archive, catalogued and studied especially by Flores Reggiani (Reggiani 2008, 2014), holds the admission registers of pregnant women and their declarations on their children's fathers.
123 Flandrin (1975, 1976, 1981); Cavallo and Cerutti (1980); Phan (1986).
124 Lombardi (2018).
125 Pelaja (1994); Reggiani (2014).
126 Laslett (1977); Stone (1977); Cavallo, Cerutti (1980); Demars-Sion (1991); Lombardi (1997, 2018).
127 Rose (1986: 32).
128 Like the documentary film *Sex in a Cold Climate*, made by Steve Humphries in 1998, based on interviews with women who had been incarcerated there. The story of the Magdalene Laundries was brought to public attention in 1993, when, during work on a plot that had been owned by the Convent of Our Lady of Charity of Refuge, at High Park in Dublin's Drumcondra, the remains of hundreds of women and children were found, buried anonymously between 1866 and 1984.
129 For example, *The Magdalene Sisters* by Peter Mullan (2002) or *Philomena* by Stephen Frears (2013).

3
CHILDBIRTH

1 A painful test, a risky journey

The metaphor of childbirth as "war", which, as we have seen, was so deeply rooted in traditional culture, conveys some representations of childbirth that profoundly influenced the lives of women. Being a "test" was one of these representations: a particularly important test, when a woman's worth and her capacity to bear pain and to face fear were truly 'put to the test'. The gaze of both her family and her community would be focused on this moment; their appreciation or blame, praise or contempt would follow it. A lack of social value marked women who were either barren or unable to get through pregnancy, while respect and honour surrounded those who died in childbirth.

Childbirth was therefore an expression of a woman's mettle, but also of her sexual identity: a woman was not truly a woman if she did not become a mother: this event fulfilled family and social expectations, redefined her place in the family and consolidated her marriage to the extent that in some societies, such as in Greece, marriage was only fully achieved with motherhood and in Rome a woman who had not given birth to a child was often repudiated.[1]

This test, therefore, was a rite of passage, individual but not solitary: women in labour did not "fight" alone; they were assisted by multiple female figures, primarily midwives: the childbirth scene – as we have said (Chapter 1.7) – was a female one, from which men, including the unborn child's father, were generally excluded for modesty's sake. This gender separation reiterated the peculiar nature of the event. Even when, from the late Middle Ages, in some urban contexts, doctors and surgeons began to be involved, they did so only with particular functions (such as the prescription of medicines or the use of instruments), but the management of childbirth remained in the hands of women, be they midwives or practitioners (see Chapter 6).[2] Male figures specialised in childbirth assistance (man-midwife/accoucheur) would only spread, with different timescales, as we shall see, from the 17th to the 18th centuries, beginning in Northern Europe.

The second aspect, also related to this, concerned the close relationship of this event with death, a closeness certainly caused by the considerable risk to which women were exposed when giving birth, but also underlined by a view that linked the worlds of birth and death, as childbirth represented a link with the otherworldly reality from which the child came and to which a woman laid herself open by bringing him into the world.[3] Birth and death, which today's Western cultures represent as two irreconcilable and antithetical events, were seen in the past as close and connected, only separated by an uncertain and tenuous border, like a watershed line allowing two opposite sides to touch.[4] Birth was close to death and could easily turn into it, just like giving birth and *giving life* could mean *losing one's life*: "Every woman, when the moment of childbirth comes, has death at her door", people said in the Middle Ages (Lett 1998: 194).

Mother and child, the former by bringing into the world, the latter by coming into the world, were exposed to the risk of slipping into the opposite event. The poor standards of hygiene of the locations where it took place, especially in the countryside and in the mountains (so in most circumstances), the limited aids and instruments available to both midwives and men-midwives in cases of excessive bleeding, post-partum infections or eclampsia and the physical conditions of the women themselves, who were often affected by malnutrition and rickets, were all factors affecting the mortality rates of women in childbirth and of new mothers. Precise quantitative data is impossible to achieve about times when there were no statistical surveys, which were developed only during the 19th century.[5] Research conducted in the modern age, about limited contexts with often different environmental and social characteristics, must be considered with the caution all this entails; however, the data shows a mortality rate (calculated out of the total number of births) between 1% and 3%. According to Edward Shorter, before the 19th century, the childbirth mortality rate ranged 1.2% and 1.5%; according to Jacques Gélis, in France, it was between 1.1% and 3%; according to Irvine Loudon, in the 16th–17th centuries in England, it was around 127/10,000 births.[6] To get an idea of what this really meant in a woman's life in terms of risk, we need to multiply this figure by the number of pregnancies in her lifetime, fairly high on average (about 5–6 deliveries): this way, we get a figure between 5 and 15%,[7] which made childbirth one of the primary causes of death for women of childbearing age.

Pregnant women were well aware of this risk, as both material and written sources, the sayings and the evidence from a not-so-distant past clearly testify. Ex-votos, which represent an element of very long-term continuity in the Western world, bear witness to the extent and intensity of this concern. Stone, pottery or carved-wood statuettes depicting newborn babies in swaddling clothes have been found in the sanctuaries of various cities of the Roman Empire.[8] The same motif appears in the small repoussé bas-reliefs so frequently found in Christian sanctuaries, while votive tablets from the early modern age often reproduce birth scenes, even in very poor contexts.

All pregnant women must have felt this awareness, although it was not always expressed in written sources, especially where these were semi-formal: for example, in the many letters written by 50 princesses between 1560 and 1630 and collected by Eugénie Pascal,[9] what prevails and is expressed is rather their sense of responsibility and duty to ensure the continuation of their family bloodlines, while in less formal letters and more intimate writings, such as diaries, especially from the late 18th century, the feelings of fear of suffering and of death are also expressed. For example, on 20 March 1793, as childbirth approached, Venetian noblewoman Lucia Memmo Mocenigo wrote to her sister Paolina Memmo Martinengo:

> I also need to convey to you my fears, now that yours are over, of my impending childbirth; the pains I will have to face frighten me a great deal and I am aware of my cowardice and lassitude on such an occasion.
>
> *(ACBg, Memmo, 1, 1793)*[10]

"Perhaps this is the last time I shall be permitted to join with my earthly friends", Sarah Stearns noted in her diary in 1813, as childbirth approached (Shorter 1982: 69). It is therefore not surprising that in the early modern age, in some cities such as Venice, the habit of making a will in the last months of pregnancy was widespread. Notary records report stereotypical and recurrent formulas, which nevertheless still clearly express the women's awareness of the risk faced:

> I, Lucetta, daughter of the nobleman Schiavon [...] wife of Piero Greco da Lido, from S. Nicolò del Lido, healthy in mind, spirit and body, being pregnant and approaching childbirth, went personally to the house of the honourable F. Primadico, notary in the S. Fantino district [...] should my death occur.
>
> *(ASVe, Notarile, Testamenti, b.202, 1633)*

In 1592, even writer Moderata Fonte, born Modesta Pozzo de' Zorzi, author of *Il merito delle donne* (The merit of women), left a will before she died in childbirth, aged 37, while giving birth to her fourth child.

For this very real eventuality, in the Christian world, women approaching childbirth were required to go to confession, as some councils prescribed in the Middle Ages.[11] Even some 16th-century obstetrics manuals, such as the one by Scipione Mercurio, recommended that "pious and devout" midwives remind women to go to confession and take communion before their labour commenced: "for the obvious danger of death" (Mercurio [1596] 1713: 79) and, if possible, have masses or at least rosaries said for them.

As childbirth approached, the acts of devotion and prayers addressed to the deities overseeing it intensified: Artemis and Eileithyia in the Greek world; Diana and Juno Lucina in the Roman one, whose name perhaps referred to the coming of the child into the light. They were the main figures in a group of about thirty minor deities overseeing various aspects of labour: the nymph Egeria, who facilitated childbirth; Mater Matuta; the two Camenae (Antevorta and Postverta), divinities of birth presentations; the Dii Nixi, deities of contractions and pushing.[12] In the Christian world, the patron saints of pregnant women and of women in labour were above all Saint Margaret, as we have seen, as she had emerged unscathed from the mouth of a dragon; Saint Anne, as the mother of the Virgin Mary, and above all obviously the Virgin Mary herself, the epitome of motherhood and main intercessor with the Lord.[13] The prayers which became increasingly popular from the 16th century were addressed especially to her, such as The *Prayer of an Expectant Mother* of Saint Francis de Sales (see Chapter 1.8).

Her figure, often depicted as the Holy Mother, with the Holy Child in her arms, sometimes as *Mater Dolorosa* (Mother of Sorrows), recurred in birth ex-votos and is evidence of deep-rooted popular devotion.[14]

2 Preparing for the event

Preparation for childbirth was therefore primarily a religious preparation: a pregnant woman asked the gods to help her "fight" against the pains of childbirth (*pónos*),[15] or implored God to accept her suffering and to save the material and spiritual life of her child, as invocations in the Christian world often pleaded.

But everyday life recorded few changes, especially for the women of the lower classes, who continued to work without sparing themselves until the time of delivery in the countryside, in the shops and later, as we shall see, even in factories, even if, on the contrary, physicians recommended that they avoid efforts and increase rest.

In his *Gynaecia*, Soranus of Ephesus also recommended anointing the genitals and belly with oil and taking warm baths (*Gyn*. I, 56–57), which were also suggested in the Middle Ages and in early modern times, starting a few weeks before delivery (evidently a suggestion for the women of the *élites*, who could do it), together with soothing and aromatic herbal vaginal fumigations. Special perforated canisters and kettles had existed for this purpose since ancient times (Figure 3.1).

The realisation that labour was approaching depended once again on a woman's ability to read her body's signs, especially within a framework that considered the length of pregnancy to be variable and in the absence of any diagnostic tools. The sources are evidence of how careful women were to interpret them: "I have the body down, I feel the creature everywhere, but I usually feel it on the right-hand side, near the pit of my stomach", Roman noblewoman Eugenia Maidalchini wrote to her mother Maria Spada, for example, on 14 April 1657, aware of the importance of the position of the foetus for a successful delivery (D'Amelia 1997: 296).

Upon the onset of labour, a midwife was called, while the women prepared the woman in labour and the room. This preparation had ritual and symbolic aspects, as well as practical ones, which lasted over the centuries, despite differences in contexts and places.[16] First of all, all the belts and ties binding a woman's body would be undone: the bands holding her breast and belly, the laces of her

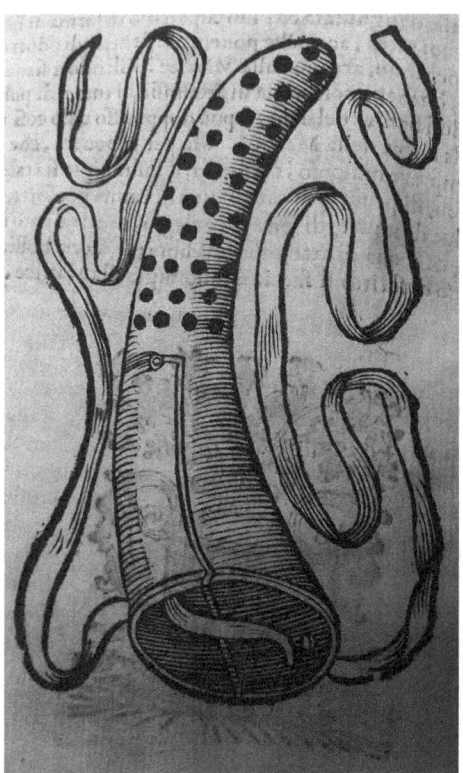

FIGURE 3.1 Tool for vaginal fumigations, from Scipione Mercurio (1618), *La Commare o riccoglitrice*, Milano: Giob. Bidelli, p. 294. Reproduced with permission of the Biblioteca Pinali antica (Padua).

shoes or sandals, the ribbons in her hair. In the bas-reliefs and statues from ancient Rome, women in labour are all depicted with their hair over their shoulders and untied shoes, as in the case of Cornelia, the famous exemplary mother of the Gracchi.[17] The act of undoing any laces had an analogical symbolic function: in the delivery, the knots that had sealed the womb at the time of conception had to be dissolved. Many expressions in the Greek language alluded to this: in the myth of Alcmena, Galanthis dissolved "the knots of labour", and, in Ovid's version, the protagonist herself declared that she had "loosened the bonds" and had "happily freed herself" (previously she could not give birth because Lucina kept her fingers and her legs crossed).[18]

Childbirth was therefore seen as a liberation, as the term still used today in some languages clearly indicates (e.g. the English *delivery*, from the Old French *delivrer*, itself from the Latin *de+liberare*), or as suggested by the Italian verb "*sgravarsi*", which means to rid oneself of a burden. This was certainly a liberation for the mother, but also for the child, who found the space inside the womb too narrow, almost a prison, and tried in every way to come out to the light.

The room was then prepared: windows and doors were closed, and crevices sealed, not only because cold and drafts were considered extremely dangerous, but also to keep out the evil spirits who threatened this delicate moment. A fire would be lit, not only to warm the room and heat the water, which was needed for many uses, but also for cooking, because a woman in labour was fed during labour and after the delivery. Fire also had a symbolic value and is also a recurring element in other cultures.[19]

Wherever it was, the room was then equipped with the necessary items; many in common use were adapted and used for childbirth: a basin of warm water to wash mother and baby, olive oil/grease for massages and internal examinations, pillows and sponges to mop up blood and fluids; rags for cleaning; woollen cloths to cover the woman in labour; invigorating drinks to revive her; scissors or similar tool to cut the umbilical cord; a thread to bind the umbilical cord; a pillow to place the baby and swaddling clothes to wrap him; aromatic herbs or spices to stimulate the woman in labour. The list Soranus made in his *Gynaecia* (*Gyn.* II, 2–3) was kept with few variations in the indications given by doctors to midwives for many centuries.

Various objects, which are outlined in great detail by Pliny in the Roman world and in the Middle Ages in the many books of *Secreta*, were also placed in the room or directly on the body of the woman in labour: they were minerals or plants, to which special powers were attributed, based on the rules of "sympathetic medicine".

One of these was the Rose of Jericho (also called "Resurrection Plant", as it can quickly sprout if watered after a long period of drought)[20]; another was the mandrake, whose roots resemble a human body and to which innumerable properties were ascribed. Some stones, such as agate, coral and above all the aetitis, were also believed to have special positive properties[21]: these precious objects were handed down from mother to daughter, and were sometimes lent by neighbours or brought by midwives.

In *De passionibus mulierum*, we read:

> It should be noted that there are certain physical remedies whose power is obscure to us, which are helpful when done by midwives. Therefore, let the patient hold a magnet in her right hand and it helps. Let her drink ivory shavings. Coral suspended from the neck is good.
>
> (*Trot.*,107, par. 118)

In the 19th century, in rural France, pregnant women also held some coarse salt in their hands (another substance with a strong symbolic value, also used in baptism), which was held tight as women pushed their babies out[22]; in this case, the symbolic aspect was combined with a practical-therapeutic function: as is well known, clenching one's fists helps to contract the muscles. As can be gathered from the text from the Salerno school of medicine mentioned earlier, doctors did not oppose these traditions right up to the 18th century, grasping their reassuring and certainly harmless function.

The objects also included one of the woman's husband's garments, as is widely attested in popular traditions all over Europe: this could be a sock or a hat, or a shirt, placed around the woman's shoulders or used to welcome the baby. The interpretation of this varies: some insist on the symbolic function of these objects, as evocative or as a substitute of a father's presence, some on their superstitious value.[23]

Other religious objects were added in the Christian West, a clear example of cultural syncretism: in addition to the relics of the Virgin's and saints' belts, scrolls of parchment with sacred images and prayers were also included; in the Middle Ages, the parchment with the prayers would sometimes even be eaten.[24] Saint Melania the Younger (4th century AD), according to her biography, when assisting a distressed woman in childbirth, stretched out a loose belt, the gift of a saint, on her belly, obtaining the immediate delivery of the child.[25] Scipione Mercurio praised the 16th-century tradition which existed in Lombardy to keep in churches, available to all pregnant women, "some relics of saints, arranged so as to be able to be carried, which they put on all women in labour" (Mercurio [1596] 1713: 79). During the first childbirth of Maria de' Medici (1601), wife of king Henry IV of France, the relics of Saint Margaret's belt were placed on a table in the room; in 1638, on the occasion of the birth of her son, the future king Louis XIV.[26] Anne of Austria had the relics of the Virgin Mary's belt brought over from the Puy-Notre-Dame sanctuary.[27]

In central and southern France, for a very long time and right up to the 20th century, the custom of a *sachet-accoucheur* was widespread: this contained miniatures and sacred texts and was similar to the "saints' bag" used in some regions up to the 19th century.[28] It was also customary to put an image of Saint Anne above the bed and light a candle to it.

3 The childbirth scene: places, people and practices

Labour was a journey, sometimes even a very long one (it could take a few days), which took place at home. The exact location varied a lot, depending on the pregnant woman's social class, but in the Western world (unlike in other cultures), it was always a domestic place, in the broadest sense of the term. Lying-in hospitals run by man-midwives only began to increase in number and spread throughout Europe, as we shall see, in the 18th century, and were initially just for unmarried and destitute mothers.

Soranus recommended that it be set up with two beds: a soft one to "rest on after delivery" and a harder one "for lying down during delivery" (*Gyn.* II, 3).[29] In the houses of the common folk, this location could be the bedroom, for those who had it, or, in winter, the kitchen, by the fireplace.[30] In the countryside and in the mountains, women often gave birth in the cow shed, where in fact families would also spend their evenings, because it was the warmest place. It should be noted that, in some rural contexts, both traditions lasted right up to the 20th century, as evidenced by some life stories.[31] After all, as Gélis observed, the Nativity scene itself, with Jesus Christ in a stable, between an ox and a donkey, had to ring familiar to the faithful: his worship reiterated the human nature of the son of God, his choice to share the condition of the poor.[32]

Around the woman, there were a number of female figures: family members, friends or neighbours, and especially a midwife, whose role was central.[33] But who were these women? The answer is related to different family structures, kinship systems and neighbourhood strategies. In peasant-extended families, where the patrilineal and patrivirilocal system prevailed (this system prescribed that, after her wedding, a woman moved in with her husband's family), the first person to be present at a birth was certainly her mother-in-law, assisted by her sisters-in-law. But in some aristocratic and upper-middle-class contexts, for instance, in southern France in the 17th century, women returned to their fathers' homes to give birth, especially for their first child.[34] In towns and cities, neighbours were very likely to lend assistance at a birth, in addition to mothers and sisters. These were not secondary variations: within extended families, not only was the relationship between mother-in-law and daughter-in-law strongly hierarchical, but was also characterised by conflicts and tensions that often came to the fore precisely during childbirths.[35] Helping a woman in labour was nevertheless considered a dutiful act of female solidarity: "Let the fire burn and run to the woman in labour", a popular proverb from the South of Italy said (Ranisio 1996: 72).

As for the midwife, we shall see later the precise social profile of this important figure and its transformations, bearing in mind that behind this name, there were in fact different figures, with different skills.

Husbands stood outside the door, in the wings; their presence at the event was replaced – as we have seen – by symbolic objects that evoked them. The image, shown by many films of the 1950s and 1960s, of fathers nervously pacing up and down while waiting for their children's birth, and trying to interpret sounds and cries coming from within the room, reflected a general situation that remained unchanged for centuries. A husband would be ready to intervene if there was a need: to call the midwife, the surgeon or the priest, to carry heavy objects or even support his wife if necessary, to perform special interventions (such as *concussio*), especially in a difficult birth.[36] However, in the early modern age, in some rare contexts, the presence of a husband is also attested during childbirth, to assist the midwife, especially if living in isolated settings. In the 18th century, this was confirmed by Frank, who, when commenting on some traditions of the American native populations, wrote:

> Even among us, fathers of families now and again render this service or they at least keep the woman giving birth on they lap, instead of letting their child be brought into the world in a labor chair and with the assistance of the first female neighbor who is available.
>
> (Frank [1779] 1976: 80)

Childbirth at court deserves a separate mention, as in this case the father's presence is well documented, as is the proximity of ministers and senior officials.

Given the importance of an heir's birth, linked to succession rights and even to political stability, childbirth took on a public connotation: it was ruled by precise ceremonials, followed by a large number of people and controlled by senior officials, whose task was to verify the identity and legitimacy of the newborn. A possible exchange or substitution at birth was one of the most frequent rumours running through the courts, especially in countries where the Salic law was in force. Beyond the differences that characterised the ceremonials of the various European courts, ministers and high officials generally waited for royal births in an adjacent room, while the king would often attend the birth itself. When Mary of Modena, wife of James II of England, began to feel the pains of labour, at the end of a very dubious pregnancy, "The messengers ran in all directions to call priests and doctors, council ministers and wardrobe ladies; and a few hours later, a large number of public officials and quality ladies were gathered" (Witkowski 1890: 17).[37]

A detailed description of childbirth at court has been left by Louise Bourgeois, midwife to Queen Maria de' Medici: a canopy with curtains had been installed in the room; underneath it, there were the labour bed, birthing chair and other chairs where the king, his sister and some ladies sat. The high court officials waited in an adjacent room.[38] For all 22 hours of her labour, the king remained by his wife's side, encouraging and comforting her, while the women prayed. Philip II, king of Spain, was also present at the miscarriages and premature births suffered by his unfortunate wife Elisabeth of Valois, if it is true that on the third such occasion, he handed her the medicine that Elizabeth's mother, Catherine de' Medici, had sent for her daughter.[39]

Helping a woman in labour meant, on the one hand, supporting, comforting and encouraging her, and, on the other, carrying out a series of practices where traditional medical and pharmacological knowledge was intertwined with decidedly symbolic gestures, creating complex rituals where even local traditions had a significant impact. The emotional and psychological aspects were just as important as the medical one: for this reason, doctors recommended that midwives be cheerful and brave.

Within a symbolically analogical representation that viewed the child as detaching himself from his mother like a fruit from the tree, practical help was primarily aimed at favouring this detachment with movement: a woman in labour had to move about, albeit supported by other women, and go up and down a few steps. Moderate movement in labour was recommended by doctors until the 18th century. In *De passionibus mulierum*, we find:

> Let the woman be led about at a slow pace through the house. And those men who assist her ought not look her in the face, because on account of this women are accustomed to be shamed by that during and after birth.
> (Trot., 101, par. 91–92)

Louise Bourgeois also recommended leaving a woman in labour free to move and reported feeling sorry for those who were forced to stay still, because this makes their pain twice as unbearable.[40]

According to this principle, in the most difficult births, a practice known as *concussio* had been used since ancient times, especially to expel a dead foetus: not unlike how a tree was shaken to bring down its fruit, the woman was placed on a sheet, which was then held by its four sides, and shaken by strong men (*Exc.* II, 1 c 3). Trotula's advice was:

> Let us place the patient on a linen sheet and let us have it held by four strong men at the four corners, the head of the patient a little bit elevated. We will make the sheet be pulled strongly this way and that at the opposite corners, and immediately she will give birth.
>
> *(Trot.,123, par.145)*

In the 17th century, English man-midwife obstetrician Percivall Willughby reported it in his *Observations in midwifery*, man-midwife upon its long-term survival.[41]

Since labour could last for a long time, a woman in labour was given nourishing and restorative food and drink, to keep up her strength. Doctor J. Panzani, from Venice, in the second half of the 18th century reported that midwives administered "light soups prepared with fresh eggs and very generous wines", for their restorative power, confirming what other sources have reported since the Middle Ages about the drinking of wine, for its euphoric and mildly anaesthetic effects (Panzani 1774: 253).

To encourage the cervix to dilate fully, midwives resorted to manual dilation, using their well-oiled hands, and hot steam vaginal fumigations with soothing herbs.[42] In condemning its excessive use, for fear of damaging the child, Hildegard of Bingen confirms its widespread use in the Middle Ages, which continued in the early modern age. Lukewarm baths, with the addition of aromatic herbs, were highly recommended by doctors, especially in difficult births: "A bath is an excellent remedy for a difficult birth", Scipione Mercurio wrote (Mercurio [1596] 1713: 162), although the practice was certainly not widespread.

Laxatives fulfilled a similar function of preparing and facilitating the baby's passage, while warm poultices placed on the woman's belly encouraged the movements of the child, who was given a central role in childbirth. To increase contractions, decoctions and substances such as pepper and vinegar were used to cause sneezing or vomiting. In the 18th century, ergot (or claviceps purpurea) was also used for this purpose.[43]

In the final stage, women would take different positions to deliver their babies; in Europe and in the Mediterranean area, five positions were the most frequently used: squatting, kneeling, standing, sitting and also lying on a bed. In 1743, Doctor Pierre Dionis wrote that certain women were used to giving birth standing up, others on a chair, others on their knees, others on a mattress near the fire and others in their beds.[44] This choice did not depend so much on a woman's wishes, but rather on the weight of long-lasting local traditions, as anthropologists and historians have highlighted: a woman, in fact, was not really free, but complied with the current customs, suggested by those who assisted her.

The squatting position was also used in Ancient Egypt, where the goddess Meskhenet, patron of childbirth, was depicted with a brick on her head. In addition to being physiologically effective, this posture allowed the infant, as soon as he was born, the immediate contact with the earth that many cultures considered as an indispensable moment of the ritual, before being "lifted" up. This position was widespread in various European regions, such as Bavaria, where it is documented right up to the mid-19th century. Nowadays, it is still found in various non-European countries, among the native tribes of North and Central America and in North Asia.[45]

In Rome, the kneeling position (which doctors advised especially in difficult births) must have been used frequently if the deities who presided over contractions and pushing, the *Dii Nixi*, were portrayed in a statue on Capitol Hill precisely in this position.[46] It also features in literary sources from ancient Greece: in Hesiod's Theogony, the goddess Rhea gave birth in this way, and so did Leto, according to mythology.[47] In early modern Europe, both these positions gradually disappeared, because they were considered too animal-like.

The other two positions, standing and sitting, were more common. In the former, a woman would generally cling onto something that allowed her to bear down: a beam, a stake or a ladder, as in some French regions.[48] Even in the early 20th century, with a certain pride and as a sign of strength, some Italian peasants reported having given birth standing up.[49]

The latter position is attested by a very long-standing tradition all over Europe: it is mentioned in the Talmud, and in Greek bas-reliefs, women in labour are mostly portrayed sitting down. They could sit on the knees of a stronger woman (as often happened in the countryside), or on a special chair. The *obstetricalis sella* (birthing chair/stool), as it was called in the Latin world, was a special chair, cut in a half-moon shape in the middle, so that the woman could not slide down, but at the same time the genitalia were not compressed and the midwife could work sitting in front of her, on a lower stool, as shown in some bas-reliefs and drawings (Figures 3.2 and 3.3).[50]

FIGURE 3.2 Birthing chair, from Jakob Rueff (1587), *De conceptu et generatione hominis*, Francofurti ad Moenum: P. Fabricium, c18r. Reproduced with permission of the Biblioteca Pinali antica (Padua).

Childbirth **87**

FIGURE 3.3 Childbirth scene, from Eucharius Rösslin [1513] (1910: ch. III). Reproduced with permission of the Ministero dei Beni e delle Attività Culturali e del Turismo – Biblioteca Nazionale Marciana (Venice).

The one described by Soranus must have had two round-shaped supports at the sides, to allow the woman to rest her hands on them during labour (*Gyn*, II, 3). In ancient times, it had no back: women in labour had to be supported from behind; for this reason, he recommended that a group of three women assist the midwife.[51]

Also used in the Middle Ages, from the 16th century, its use spread throughout Europe, especially in urban centres.[52] Even queens gave birth on this chair, perhaps one covered with crimson fabric, such as the one used by Maria de' Medici, as described by her midwife, Louise Bourgeois.[53] Percivall Willughby confirmed its popularity in London in the 17th century, while disapproving its use.[54] It almost became the symbol of the work of urban midwives and of their prestige: when Giovanni Grevembroch, in his collection of images of clothes worn by Venetians in the 18th century, showed a midwife, he portrayed her as a woman followed by a servant carrying a folded birthing chair on his shoulders[55] (see Figure 6.2, Chapter 6). It also features in various painted nativities and many examples are found in various museums.[56]

Its success was certainly due to its promotion by physicians and surgeons: in addition to ancient texts, all obstetrics books printed in the vernacular from the 16th century onwards, such as Jacob Rueff's, recommended a birthing chair and also showed images of it, because, as Scipione Mercurio wrote, "weight helps to easily find the way to bear down" (Mercurio [1596] 1713: 93). From this moment onwards, it progressively spread and was the object of constant modifications, such as the addition of backrests and particular armrests. Various obstetricians (and some educated midwives) tried to introduce variations of it, more or less successfully. In the 18th century, one of the most famous was the one developed by German surgeon Lorenz Heister, which had the advantage that it could be reclined, turning into a bed, to allow a woman to rest during labour; it was even recommended in some theological texts.[57] Beds were also used, as evidenced by the Greek word *lechói*, which means both bed and childbirth, or the Latin word *genitalis*, which, according to Curatolo, indicated this special bed.[58] Sixteenth-century manuals, such as Scipione Mercurio's, recommended its use especially in difficult births which required particular obstetrical or surgical interventions.[59]

To have a complete view of this birth scene, we must imagine it not only crowded with women, but full of voices and shouts: in Christian Europe, in the Middle Ages, prayers (*Carmina*) were also sung[60] and expressing pain was not repressed; rather, it was part of the ritual, not only culturally accepted, but even encouraged. In this case, too, the cultural reason is obvious: since the suffering of childbirth represented the punishment for the original sin and every woman had to accept it as atonement for that sin, those giving birth without suffering would have been suspicious, as they went against God's law.[61] Women in labour then screamed loudly and their cries were heard throughout the neighbourhood, on the one hand, stressing the semi-public nature of the event, and, on the other hand, perpetuating patterns of behaviour. This also explains the focus of some autobiographical accounts, where the drama also fulfilled the intent of conforming to the model of a *mater dolorosa* achieving merit and dignity precisely through suffering (Figure 3.4).

However, this dramatic way of expressing pain undoubtedly had another function, too, well known to midwives: that of expressing fear; in this sense, it could be positive and liberating. In his manual, Michele Savonarola advised women to shout loudly, taking up a suggestion by Avicenna. "And know, woman, that screaming loudly in such cases is very beneficial to you, in fact Avicenna says: *et clamet* [let her scream!]" (Savonarola [1460?] 1952: 121). With a touch of opportunism, he advised doing it even if the pain was slight, if only to encourage her family members to take care of her and support her adequately:

> and even if it does not hurt you so much, I still advise you to scream loudly, so that your pain is believed, and your husband and the others in the home, feeling sorry for you, try to put down such great fire with capons, sugared almonds and good wines.
>
> (Savonarola [1460?] 1952: 121)

FIGURE 3.4 Childbirth scene, from Jakob Rueff (1587), *De conceptu et generatione hominis*, Francofurti ad Moenum: P. Fabricium, 3r. Reproduced with permission of the Biblioteca Pinali antica (Padua).

In her memoirs, Louise Bourgeois reported: "The queen was about to give birth. I saw that she was holding back from shouting; I begged her not to hold back, fearing that her throat would swell up. The king said to her: My love, do what your midwife tells you: cry out so that your throat does not swell up!" (Cited by Witkowski, 1890: 150).

Even in the early 20th century, in the French countryside, old women used to say "she must shout very loudly, so that the whole village may hear her!" (Verdier 1979: 93).

This cultural feature, which characterised the European countries, was the cause of profound misunderstandings in the encounters with different cultures: when European colonialists saw that African women give birth silently, they wrongly thought that their delivery was painless; thus, it became a widespread opinion that it was easier for "primitive" tribes to give birth: "the females of the uncouth peoples – for example, Dr G. Nessi wrote in the 18th century – give birth without the help of a midwife or doctor" (Nessi 1797: 53).[62] Even in that case, however, the behaviour of women had adapted to cultural content, but in the opposite direction: African women from many tribes still repress their cries because they consider it shameful to express suffering and because they believe that this damages their babies, making them weaker, or that it disgraces their husbands.[63]

Finally, a mother's screams would be joined by her baby's crying, a tangible sign of his coming into the world, proof of his birth also from the legal point of view. In ancient Roman law (the foundation of many medieval and early modern legal systems), to inherit from his mother, a child had to be born alive, even if this life lasted but a few moments; otherwise, he would not have inherited and his mother's dowry, if she died, would have been returned to her family of origin.[64] To achieve a spiritual birth in the Christian world, as we shall see later, a baby also had to show signs of life and crying was considered an unequivocal proof. This was therefore not only expected, but greeted with joy, and sometimes prompted by midwives, in a tradition that lasted for a long time over the centuries.

But why do babies cry? Medicine today tells us that this is due to the change in breathing, as babies begin to breathe with their lungs. From the origins of the Christian world, however, this crying was connected to the uncertain situation of a newborn, suspended between the world of the living and that of the dead. It was believed that his ancestors called him to them.[65]

The absence of crying in a living newborn baby was interpreted as a sign of holiness: the birth of saints was often characterised by their silent coming into the world.

4 "Natural" versus "unnatural" childbirth: the doctors' discourse

Let us take a closer look at medical knowledge regarding childbirth and at the treatments and ethical principles surrounding it.

In the context of the naturalistic perspective mentioned earlier, even within scientific discourse, it was the child who, like a fruit, detached himself from its tree, causing labour to start, when, upon becoming mature, he could not find sufficient space and food in the womb. "By moving and jumping with its arms and legs", he would break the membranes that held him wrapped and forced open the narrow exit, looking for a way out (Hippocratic Corpus, *NE*, XXX, 1, 531).[66] The child was therefore seen as the true protagonist of childbirth; the mother had a more passive role.

Although not fully shared by some authors, such as Soranus of Ephesus, this view remained strongly rooted. This is why the birth of a girl was seen as a greater risk factor for her mother, as girls were less active and weaker than boys: many cases of childbirth complications described in the Hippocratic texts are linked to female births.[67]

In order to identify the laws of nature, ancient medicine had tried to define the rules that characterised childbirth, gathering them in a set of times and presentations: on the one hand, the baby's maturity (he was not supposed to be born prematurely); on the other, the position he took during labour (it was supposed to be cephalic). A birth was "natural" (or *legitimus*, from the Latin *lex* = law)[68] if it respected this set of times and presentations. In contrast, any other type of birth was defined as "unnatural" and "illegitimate" (that is to say, not compliant with the law).

Taking up a definition given in the Hippocratic texts, Soranus of Ephesus had written: "The natural presentation for birth is the head presentation; the arms of the fetus are stretched along its thighs and it is expelled directly", thereby distinguishing the *katà phýsin skhéma* (presentation according to nature) from the *parà phýsin skhéma* (presentation against nature) (*Gyn*. IIb, 3).[69] This distinction, subsequently taken up by Arabic and medieval medicines, would be developed in the 16th and 17th centuries, with some variations, becoming a fundamental category in the classification of childbirths (Figures 3.5 and 3.6).

Eucharius Rösslin, author of the first text written for midwives in the vernacular, *Der Swangern Frawen und Hebammen Rosengarten* (1513) (The rose garden of pregnant women and midwives), wrote: "A natural childbirth is the one taking place at the appropriate time and manner, with the fetus in the cephalic presentation" (Rösslin 1537: 6),[70] not unlike what Ambroise Paré underlined in his *De la Génération*: "enfantement naturel […] quand les enfants viennent à terme, qui est au neuvième mois, et sortent la tête la première" (A natural childbirth is […] when babies are born full term, that is, in the ninth month, and come out head first) (Paré [1573] 1664: 599).

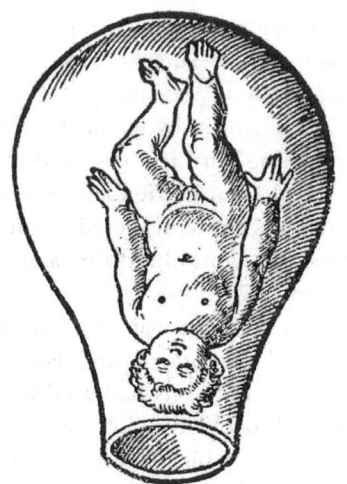

FIGURE 3.5 Foetus in cephalic ("natural") presentation, from Eucharius Rösslin [1513] (1910, p. 27). Reproduced with permission of the Ministero dei Beni e delle Attività Culturali e del Turismo – Biblioteca Nazionale Marciana (Venice).

FIGURE 3.6 Foetus in breech ("unnatural") presentation, from Eucharius Rösslin [1513] (1910, p. 30). Reproduced with permission of the Ministero dei Beni e delle Attività Culturali e del Turismo - Biblioteca Nazionale Marciana (Venice).

Scipione Mercurio, despite re-proposing this distinction, also introduced the new category of *preternatural birth*, drawn from Saint Thomas Aquinas' philosophy, to indicate phenomena that were outside the natural order, but could be explained according to the natural laws themselves.[71] Moreover, he also included in the category of natural childbirths the birth of a normal creature, "with all its limbs formed, and with human form" (Mercurio [1596] 1713: 6). His suggestions were accepted by several later authors, such as F. Mauriceau (*Traité des maladies des femmes grosses et des celles qui sont accouchées*, 1668).

This scientific view was influenced by elements of a deeper cultural nature, such as the idea that linked being born feet first to death and not to birth: since the ancient world, corpses had been carried feet first out of the house; consequently, being born feet first was also considered an ominous event: "It is in the natural order that one enters the world head first and goes out feet first", Pliny had written (cited by Belmont 1971: 135).

Natural did not mean easy in itself; even the ancients knew this very well. Even "natural" childbirths could be difficult and dangerous for the lives of both mother and child. The Hippocratic texts had used the term *dystokìa* (still used nowadays), which Soranus had specified did not express the pains of childbirth, but the difficulties that could arise, which could depend either on the mother (she was either too young or too old, showed uncontrolled emotions, was too fat, her birth canal was too narrow, her womb was diseased, etc.), or on the baby (too big, affected by deformity or monstrosity, the membranes had ruptured too early, the amniotic sac was too hard, death, etc.).

What is certain is that all malpresentations were considered intrinsically dangerous, even if breech presentations to a lesser degree: "all these presentations are bad and dangerous: to the extent that sometimes the fetus dies, sometimes the mother, sometimes both", Michele Savonarola had written ([1460?] 1952: 113). The lack of natural order was considered a harbinger of dangers that authors had tried to categorise according to its degree of complexity. This explains the meticulous attention paid by doctors when describing and listing the various presentations of the child in childbirth: from the 16th century onwards, printed midwifery manuals to be used by midwives were full of illustrations, showing the presentations of the child during childbirth (14 according to E. Rösslin, 15 according to J. Rueff).[72] I believe that the rough-and-ready quality they display is also due to their didactic purpose. In other words, with these images, doctors wanted to show midwives which "unnatural" presentations they could face during their work. According to L. Kassel, these representations played an important role in the construction of the hierarchically senior position of doctors compared to midwives.[73]

Some precise treatments, theorised in manuals and obstetrics texts for a very long time, originated from this representation of childbirth. They can be summarised in three fundamental points: a fundamental trust in the chances of success of a "natural birth", stemming from the basic idea that this happened, thanks to the forces of nature alone; the instruction to restore the natural order in unnatural childbirths; the sense of the precise limit of human intervention, which went hand-in-hand with the respect for the natural order.

In a "natural" birth, the role of those lending their assistance was considered marginal, as success could be achieved with the combined efforts of mother and child. All doctors agreed that, in this case, women did not need special help: "Childbirth – French obstetrician Paul Portal wrote – is accomplished by Nature itself. In this case, the child is brought into the world by his mother's efforts without the assistance of either a surgeon or a midwife" (Portal 1685: 1).

The recommendation was therefore to respect and let "Dame Nature" do the work, as Percivall Willughby wrote, not forcing its timings.[74] Medical ethics settled along the line of conforming to the natural processes, which could be supported, facilitated, stimulated, but never forced: doing it was considered dangerous and deplorable, a professional error where the sin of pride was implicit, a harbinger of negative consequences. The instructions "not to do violence to nature" were ubiquitous with doctors and represented a common element in the accusations they directed at midwives, at least until the second half of the 18th century, when, as we shall see, an opposite interventionist approach developed. W. Harvey (1578–1657) accused midwives of making childbirth unnatural with their hasty manoeuvres, as G.B. Morgagni reiterated (1682–1771).

On the contrary, in an "unnatural" childbirth, it was necessary to intervene to "help" nature itself, to "correct" it, as Scipione Mercurio wrote. It was then a matter of assisting the natural processes, of "imitating" them or of reproducing them, bringing anomalies back to a state of order. About unnatural childbirth, Morgagni wrote:

> Being nature too weak, first of all, as far as possible, it must be helped with suitable enemas and with anointing the belly; then, if this is not enough, it is necessary to resort to drinks of the same kind, more apt to imitate nature than to excite it with violence.
>
> *(Morgagni [1761] 1837: 90)*

The fundamental recommendation was to correct these malpresentations, bringing the foetus back to a cephalic presentation, through manual manoeuvres, the so-called internal "versions" (from the Latin *vertere* = to turn), which could even amount to a complete top-to-bottom turning in the womb. Soranus of Ephesus, in his *Gynaecia*, had written that "if the fetus is situated abnormally, one must make the position normal" (*Gyn.*, IIb, 8).[75]

All obstetrics manuals right up to the 18th century prescribed them, showing midwives how to carry them out depending on the different presentations of the foetus, thus recovering a very long-standing and traditionally female knowledge.

It was an intervention that was anything but simple and was very painful, as a midwife had to introduce her (well-oiled) hand inside the womb and gently turn the baby (with the risk of causing bleeding and lacerations). In some cases, these manoeuvres were effective and useful, even indispensable, and were prescribed right up to the 20th century. In others, such as in breech or face presentations, they were, however, totally unnecessary, real "errors", as A. Velpeau recognised in the 19th century:

> There is no doubt that the principles professed by the father of medicine led to serious errors in practice, prompting doctors to turn a fetus on its head when it presented differently, refusing to give childbirth the opportunity of occurring spontaneously when the child appeared in a breech presentation.
>
> *(Velpeau 1835: 44)*[76]

In short, it is obvious that the representation of childbirth not only guided its approach in terms of treatment, but also conditioned it to the point of causing errors of intervention, such as the forced adherence of the only presentation of the foetus considered "natural". This is an important aspect, which is not often highlighted in many histories of obstetrics.

Only in the 16th century, in addition to a cephalic version, the podalic one was also introduced, a manoeuvre carried out to extract a baby by its feet, which Celsus and Soranus had already described, but which had then fallen into disuse.[77] J. Rueff talked about it in *De conceptu et generatione hominis*, later followed by Scipione Mercurio, and especially Ambroise Paré in his *De géneration de l'homme* (1573), who sanctioned its use in the 16th century with the authority generally granted to him.

5 "Sacrificing the fruit to save the tree": the priority of a mother's life

The treatments and interventions suggested by traditional medicine, however, were completely useless in some situations, such as in cases of bleeding or of an extremely small pelvis (the widespread presence of rickets was a frequent cause of this). In these cases, mother and child would inevitably die with unnecessary and prolonged suffering. How should a midwife behave: let both of them die, or intervene to save at least one life? And which of the two should be saved: the mother or the child? This was an ethical problem that raised moral, social and religious questions.

For many centuries, from the ancient world to the Counter-Reformation, an approach shared by culture, medicine and religion favoured the mother's life over the child's. The greater importance of her existence compared to the foetus' was underpinned by the representation of the event itself: a mother was the "tree", a child the "fruit", with a still uncertain existence; it would have been absurd to tear down the tree to gather its fruit. Another factor to bear in mind is that, after a long and difficult labour, a child's viability and survival chances would be very uncertain. In short, there was a precise hierarchy of social significance between mother and child, which recognised the former as of greater value, putting her safety before her child's in high-risk pregnancies and childbirths. Soranus of Ephesus had written:

> If a manual extraction of the fetus fails because of its size or because it is dead or because it is somehow wedged, then it is necessary to resort to more energetic means: its extraction with instruments and an embryotomy. Even if these means actually kill the child, it is necessary to save the life of the mother.
>
> *(Gyn. IIb, 9)*[78]

It should also be emphasised that the child, in virtue of a scientific view that saw him as the protagonist of childbirth, was in a sense held responsible for the threat he presented to his mother's life, as if he were going to cause her death. A deeply rooted representation if, despite some changes, we still find it at times occurring in the 20th-century tradition: "He nearly killed his mother", says the protagonist of Hemingway's *A Farewell to Arms* in response to the doctor who shows him his son, born after a Caesarean section (Hemingway 1929: 347).

This ethical principle of the priority of the mother's life, present in the Greek and Roman worlds, was also accepted in the Christian one, despite the focus on the protection of life, resulting in their condemnation of abortion and infanticide, which distinguished Christians from pre-Christian religions. Tertullian (2nd–3rd centuries AD), for example, in his *De Anima*, Chapter 25, supported resorting to an embryotomy if a woman's life was at risk, based on the principle of legitimate defence, considering the foetus precisely as an aggressor to his mother's life, potentially guilty of "matricide": "Let the child be killed while still inside the womb, with cruelty which is necessary, as the one who is about to die is committing matricide" (cited by Filippini 1995: 258, 2010: 159).

During the Middle Ages, other theologians had reaffirmed the same principle: the suppression of the child's life during childbirth fell within the exceptions contemplated in the fifth commandment, as an act of legitimate defence on the part of the mother towards a being who put her life at risk: "an albeit involuntary aggressor", as Saint Antoninus of Florence called it (Filippini 1995: 257–258).

Despite the importance of the administration of baptism for the purposes of eternal salvation, no one was allowed to perform interventions that might compromise the life of the mother in order to save the child: in his *Summa Theologiae*, Saint Thomas Aquinas had clearly stated: "We should not do evil that there may come good. Therefore it is wrong to kill a mother so that her child may be baptized" (*Summa* III, 68, 3, 11).

In these cases, craniotomy or embryotomy operations were performed: the former were operations aimed at reducing the size of the foetus' head, to facilitate its extraction or expulsion; the latter aimed at reducing the size of its body. The first obstetrical instruments were therefore small knives, pincers or simple hooks, described in the Hippocratic *Excision of the foetus*. Soranus also gave an accurate description of an embryotomy (*Gyn.* IIb, 9), resumed in the Middle Ages by Guy de Chauliac.[79] The instruments available were increased and perfected over the centuries, particularly between the 17th and 18th centuries, with the invention of various craniotomes, perforators, cranioclasts and cephalotribes, with the aim of reducing the damage that might be caused to the mother, exposed both to lacerations and to infections, which could leave permanent damage.[80] With this precise aim, to avoid "very considerable violence" to women as well, French obstetrician François Mauriceau invented the *tire-tête*, a craniotome which he made readily available, "to contribute as much as I can – as he pointed out – to the public good" (Mauriceau [1668] 1681: 355).

These operations were originally performed by midwives, but, from the late Middle Ages, with the birth of the guilds, as we shall see later, they became the responsibility of the guilds of barber-surgeons, who were exclusively charged with the use of instruments, according to a distinction between treatments and practices codified at different times throughout Europe, combined with a progressive marginalisation of women in medicine and surgery. The function of surgeons in childbirth was as "angels of death",[81] in the sense that they intervened in cases where the death of the foetus had already occurred or to bring it about themselves. This did not mean that midwives did not continue to use these instruments illegally even in the early modern age; in fact, according to some historians, midwives were "prepared to use any instruments" (Shorter 1982: 88). As far back as 1767, a medical commission in the State of Milan, charged with an inquiry into the work of midwives, reported that they had found "such women sometimes equipped with iron tools and hooks of strange and rough workmanship" (Parma, 1984:103).

Instruments designed to extract a child who was still alive did not appear until the 17th–18th centuries, with the invention and use of the vectis forceps, the "iron hands" that promised to bring a child alive into the world, restoring the dignity of surgeons and assigning them an altogether new role.

During the Counter-Reformation, the Church began to condemn these interventions, if there were indications that the child was alive: embryotomies were considered lawful only in cases where the death of the child had been ascertained. This was a significant change, brought about by multiple factors: a greater empathy for the life of the child, the refusal of surgeons to continue to be the "angels of death" and, above all, in the context of the Counter-Reformation, the growing importance of the issue of the double death, that is to say spiritual, as well as physical death, in the absence of baptism. In Catholic countries, professional ethics increasingly rejected interventions described as *occisivi*, i.e. resulting in the death of the child and, in high-risk childbirths, when faced with the impossibility of saving both lives, advocated a doctor's duty to refuse to intervene, leaving nature to take its course, thereby leaving the decision to God.

This continued at least until the second half of the 18th century, when the practice of Caesarean sections on living women became established, with a further change of ethical perspectives and principles, as we shall see (Chapter 10.5).

6 The "second delivery": the placenta

Childbirth ends neither with the delivery of the baby nor with the cutting of his umbilical cord, no matter how important this moment is in signalling the separation of the newborn from his mother. It ends with the delivery of the placenta, an organ laden with symbolism in all world cultures. The very terms used to identify it in several languages underline this essential fact: in French, for example, the placenta is *la délivre* (from *délivrer* = to free), i.e. what marks the end of childbirth (but also *arrière-faix* [after-birth] or *enveloppe* [sheath]). In other languages, the term used refers to the time sequence: the placenta is what "comes after"; *afterbirth* in English; *Nachgeburt* in German; *seconda* and *secondina* (the second one) in Italian; it is known as "*il secondo parto*" (the second childbirth) in some Italian dialects.

The term placenta (from the Latin *placenta* = flat bread) makes its appearance in the 16th century, when a specific medical interest for this organ started to emerge, with Vesalius' anatomical studies, especially the lovely anatomical table he devoted to it in *De humani corporis fabrica* (ed. 1555). It is first used a few years later by Realdo Colombo in *De re anatomica* (1559).[82]

A complex set of beliefs surrounded this organ and its delivery represented a particularly significant moment, be it for medical reasons or for cultural and symbolic ones. It was seen as the set of roots that had connected the baby to his mother's body; it was, therefore, complementary to the baby's body, like the umbilical cord, and just as a plant could not be uprooted without its entire root system, the birth of a baby could not be considered complete before the delivery of the amniotic sac in the "second childbirth". By analogy, the placenta was symbolically joined to the newborn: it was believed to remain linked to the baby for the whole of his life through a "sympathetic, or analogical union", as beliefs and restrictions widespread in various parts of Europe underlined.[83] At the same time, it was seen as an ambiguous, liminal object, coming from the afterlife, not entirely belonging to the world of the living and endowed with special powers.[84] For this reason, being born wrapped in the placenta ("with your shirt on", according to an Italian proverb) was not only considered a good omen, but also possessing particular magic or healing powers, as in the case of the *benandanti* ("Good Walkers"), who in the early modern age were tasked with protecting villages and harvests from witches.[85]

Even medicine assigned great importance to the moment of its delivery, for different reasons, connected to the series of problems that could befall mothers following its difficult or late delivery: "Childbirth is a big thing – Louise Bourgeois wrote – but the *délivrance* is a different matter altogether" (Bourgeois ([1609] 1992: 78).

According to the theory which saw the womb as unstable and able to move around the body, if the placenta was not promptly delivered, it was believed that it might slide back up and inside the womb which, contracting and closing, would stop it from being delivered altogether. Not only this, but being liable to deteriorate and decay quickly, it would give off such vapours as to choke and make the woman insane, causing her death. In *La Comare*, Scipione Mercurio stated:

> very soon they decay if they remain in the matrix after the birth of the baby [...] and because of the vapours caused by their decay rising to her diaphragm and to her head, the woman becomes asthmatic, insane, and often choked by them, she dies.
>
> *(Mercurio [1596] 1713: 189)*

It should be noted that such a view was still found in several mountain regions even at the start of the 20th century, if it is true that a Swiss midwife would say to her patients, when the delivery of the placenta was late: "It's high time we go after it, otherwise it would have started to climb up" (Shorter 1982: 64).

For this reason, 16th-century obstetrics manuals recommended that midwives "use every device to deliver the afterbirth", keeping a good hold on the umbilical cord and making sure that it did not slip out of their hands, while they "admired the newborn, or moved about, or tended to the woman", advising them to tie it to the woman's thigh as a precaution (Mercurio [1596] 1713: 190).

If the placenta was not delivered spontaneously, it was necessary to encourage the womb with a series of remedies, many similar to the ones used for childbirth (massaging and pressing the abdomen, provoking sneezes, fumigations or exhalations). Even "remedies" based on analogical medicine were used: a wide range of potions made with emetic herbs and ointments, often made from animal placentas, had been recommended since ancient times, combined with symbolic objects. Their aim was to encourage the placenta to come out and open the womb, even using its presumed sensitivity to odours. Giovanni Marinello, like many others, recommended making the woman smell some foul thing to push the organ back down, in addition to applying scented vapours in the vagina, because the matrix "follows scented substances and flees from the foul and smelly ones" (Marinello [1563] 1574: 268).[86]

In extreme cases, a manual extraction would be necessary, "after oiling one's hands with sweet oil [..] attempts will be made to detach it gently", as Gerolamo Mercuriali wrote: *De morbis muliebribus* (1601) (cited by Nardi, 1954: 165); this procedure was anything but simple, since the placenta might have become attached to the side of the womb. Furthermore, there was a risk of rupturing it and leaving some pieces behind, which was extremely dangerous for the woman (Figure 3.7).

The anxiety and rush that many midwives showed in delivering the placenta, pulling on the cord so hard that they sometimes caused the womb to come out (as happened in several situations described, for example, by Louise Bourgeois or G. Mauquest de La Motte), was motivated by a system of long-standing medical opinions which emphasised the risks, suggesting hasty interventions. In some European contexts, such speed was even prescribed by the law: a German decree in the sovereign state of Wied-Runkel (1771) ordered midwives: "the afterbirth is never to be left to nature, but instead must immediately be retrieved by hand" (Shorter 1982: 65).

The umbilical cord was generally cut three to four inches from the navel, as doctors recommended, using a sharp implement. The objects used varied according to the context. In several regions, scissors, if possible kept in spirits (as in the

FIGURE 3.7 Manual extraction of the placenta, from Cosme Viardel (1748), *Observations sur la pratique des accouchemens naturels, contre nature et monstrueux*, Paris: chez d'Houry. Reproduced with permission of the Biblioteca Pinali antica (Padua).

French province of Languedoc), were used; elsewhere, a sharp piece of glass or pottery would be used; a knife was rarely used, as it was believed to have a negative influence on the child's personality: it might make him aggressive.[87] Often, the implement differed according to the gender of the newborn.

Because of the healing powers attributed to it, the placenta was used to revive the baby, in case of weakness or difficulty in breathing, by placing it directly on his body. Alternatively, it was used to relieve the mother's *post-partum* pains, by also placing it on her belly.[88]

Lastly, its disposal followed specific and varied rituals according to contexts and local traditions: whatever accident befell it would be reflected on the newborn, causing illnesses and death. In the West, it was a very common practice to bury the placenta in a field near the house; above it, a tree or bush would be planted, which would become the mirror image of the child: it was possible to derive predictions on the child's health by the plant's growth.[89] In other areas, however, such as in Sicily, it was instead entrusted to water; elsewhere, it was even dried out, together with the umbilical cord, and carefully preserved as an antidote against infertility and other illnesses, or to promote the child's development. It should not be thrown away with the waste, similarly to other parts of the child's body (such as the umbilical cord), both for symbolic reasons, as we have seen, and to ensure that nobody else could retrieve it and use it for magic or witchcraft: it was in fact already widely believed in the ancient world, and even more so in the medieval and early modern ages, that it was used in magic rituals, similarly to the remains of foetuses and stillborn babies.[90] During the witch-hunts of the 15th and 16th centuries, the Church ordered it be destroyed by fire; in 17th-century Venice, two synods, under the threat of excommunication, ordered midwives to burn the afterbirth immediately and not to sell it.[91]

Finally, it is notable that in many contexts, especially in rural areas, the task of removing this link between a mother and her child was appropriately entrusted to the father, who was in fact responsible for burying it. This custom was still recorded in some Italian provincial areas right up to the mid-20th century.[92]

Notes

1 Cantarella (1985); Loraux (1995); Yan (1992); Gourevitch, Danielle and Raepsaet-Charlier (2001); Sánchez Romero and Cid López (2018).
2 Park (2006, 2018); Foscati (2014, 2017); Blumenfeld-Kosinski (1990); Laurent (1989).
3 Magli (1978).
4 Aubert (1989: 440); Lett (1998); Mantegazza (2017).
5 It should also be noted that only in the last thirty years of the 19th century, the duty was imposed on doctors to indicate the cause of death, as Loudon has pointed out (Loudon 1992: 23).
6 Shorter (1982: 98); Gélis (1984a: 344); Loudon (1992).
7 As Catherine Rollet and Marie-France Morel have pointed out (2000: 52). Laget wrote 7% (Laget 1982: 281); Shorter stated 8% (Shorter 1982: 98); Jacques Gélis estimated it to be between 5 and 10% (Gélis 1984a: 344).

8 Curatolo (1901); Deyts (2004); Gourevich, Morini and Rouquet (2003). An important collection of these votive offerings is located in the museum of Villa Giulia in Rome and contains various terracotta objects depicting the uterus and also newborns in swaddling clothes (Curatolo 1901: ch. VII).
9 Pascal (2010: 139–166).
10 ACBg, Archivio Memmo, b. 1, Letter from Lucia Memmo Mocenigo to Paolina Memmo Martinengo, 20 March 1793 (I'm currently conducting research on this).
11 Laurent (1989: 223).
12 Belmont (1971); Bettini (2013); Aubert (2004).
13 Laget (1982); Gélis (1984a); Laurent (1989).
14 Warner (1976: ch. 14).
15 Loraux (1982).
16 About the ancient world, I have mainly consulted: Curatolo (1901); Bettini (2013); Gourevitch, Morini and Rouquet (2003); Fanos and Yurdakök (2010); Rubiera Cancelas (2015); Medina Quintana (2015). About the medieval world: Laurent (1989); Green (2008); Foscati (2014); Park (2018); Gislon Dopfel *et alii* (2019). About the early-modern age: Laget (1982); Pancino (1984); Gélis (1984a); Shorter (1982); Labouvie (1998); Schlumbohm, Duden, Gélis and Veit (1998). For a comparison between different cultures: Witkowski (1887); Speert (1973); Rollet and Morel (2000).
17 Corridori and Fanos (2010: 80).
18 Bettini (2013: ch. 1).
19 Rollet and Morel (2000: 40–41).
20 Gélis (1984a: 194); Baldini (1991: 56).
21 Dasen (2004b: 134–135); Foscati (2014: 313); Cavallo (2018).
22 Loux (1998: 129).
23 Vidossi (1960: 180–193); Laget (1982: 136); Baldini (1991: 58–62); Loux (1998: 134).
24 Oslan (1992: 138–139, 2018); Green (2009: 170); Foscati (2014: 316–319).
25 Rousselle (1992).
26 Witkowski (1890: 150).
27 Ibidem.
28 Berthiaud (2013: 56).
29 Temp.: 72.
30 This custom lasted in Venice until the early 20th century, as evidenced by Mariuccia Giacomini's research (Giacomini 1985: 129–140).
31 "We gave birth in the cowshed to have a bit of warmth – a peasant from Piedmont reported – lying on straw, over a clean sheet; I am surprised we never caught any infection" (Revelli 1985: 257). The Venetian midwives interviewed by Mariuccia Giacomini described giving birth on kitchen tables (Giacomini 1985).
32 Gélis (1984a: 171).
33 Park (2018); Laurent (1989).
34 Laget (1982: 131).
35 Farge (1976); Zanolla (1980).
36 Park (2018).
37 Translated from the French edition, like the following quotations from this text.
38 Witkowski (1890: 150–151).
39 Ibidem (33–37).
40 Bourgeois ([1609] 1992: 74).
41 Shorter (1982: ch. 5).
42 Gourevitch (1984: 171–172); Nardi (1954: 49).
43 Shorter (1982: 78).
44 Cited by Gélis (1984a: 200).
45 Speert (1973: 246).
46 Belmont (1971: 162).
47 Bettini (2013: ch. 3); Corridori and Fanos (2010: 79).

48 It was called a "palholada" childbirth, meaning "with the ladder" (Laget 1981: 151).
49 Revelli (1985: 227).
50 Corridori and Fanos (2010: 75–78); Curatolo (1901).
51 Gourevitch and Raepsaet-Charlier (2001: 134).
52 Park (2018); Shorter (1982: 56); Gélis (1984a: 209); Filippini (1993: 152–175).
53 Witkowski (1890: 150–151).
54 Shorter (1982: 58).
55 Grevembroch ([1754] 1981: 154).
56 The 18th-century Sicilian birthing chair was also foldable and can be found in the museum of the Welcome Institute (McTavish 2018).
57 Cangiamila (1775, table 1).
58 Curatolo (1901: 63).
59 Mercurio ([1596] 1713: 183–184).
60 Foscati (2014: 313–316).
61 Laget (1982: 160).
62 Translated from the Italian edition.
63 Also pointed out by Rollet and Morel (2000: 48).
64 As happened, for example, in medieval Florence (Chabot 2011).
65 Lett (1998: 67).
66 HPott.: 83.
67 Demand (1994: 6).
68 Rueff (1580: 9).
69 Temp.: 184–189.
70 I consulted the Latin translation done by his son, Eucharius Rösslin the Younger (Rösslin 1537). Further quotations are taken from this edition. Translated from this Latin edition, like the following quotations from this text.
71 Daston (1998, 2000); Daston and Pomata (2000).
72 Nardi (1954: 147).
73 Kassel (2018).
74 Shorter (1982: 62).
75 Temp.: 186.
76 Translated from the French edition.
77 Nardi (1954: 147); Darmon (1981: 179).
78 Temp.: 196.
79 Gourevitch (2004); Green (2008: 102); Foscati (2014: 325).
80 Speert (1973: 273–276); Hibbard (2000).
81 Blumenfeld Kosinski (1990: 104).
82 d'Yvoire (2000: 86).
83 Frazer (1922: I, ch. 3); Loux (1998); Rollet-Morel (2000: 59–64).
84 Ginzburg (1992: part III, ch. II).
85 Ginzburg (1983); Belmont (1971).
86 Traslated from the Italian edition.
87 Rollet-Morel (2000: 53–55).
88 Pancino (1984: 193–201).
89 De Gubernatis (1878: 121); Frazer (1922: I, ch. 3); Gélis (1984a: 285–286); Baldini (1991: 101–103); Rollet-Morel (2000: 61–62).
90 Auber (1989: 435).
91 Pancino (1984: 33).
92 Orrù, Putzolu (1994: 170).

4
BIRTH AND POST-NATAL PERIOD

1 The birth setting

The numerous paintings that, in the Christian West, depict the birth of the Virgin Mary, or of other saints, show scenes in many respects similar in their essential elements, with the details about the moments immediately following childbirth in the Western tradition: the new mother is lying in bed, well-covered by blankets, and some women are giving her something to eat and drink, usually a cup of broth with some bread. At the foot of the bed, other female figures are taking care of the child: the midwife, who generally stands out as the oldest woman, is holding him while she baths him in a basin, while another woman prepares the swaddling clothes in which he will be swaddled (Figures 4.1 and 4.2).[1]

On one side of the scene, therefore, the mother was portrayed, resting and being restored, and on the other side, the washed and swaddled child; the symbolic objects of this moment, representative for the woman of the end of her "great effort" and the beginning of her motherhood, for the infant of the beginning of his autonomous life outside his mother's body, were the bed and food for the former, water and the swaddling clothes for the latter.

But let us look more closely at these gestures, paying attention to how mother and child mirror each other.

Once labour was over, after being washed, dried and dressed, a woman was put to bed, taking care, as Scipione Mercurio suggested, to dim the light.[2] She was immediately fed, in order "to recover the strength lost in the great effort of labour and the large quantity of blood lost", as François Mauriceau warned ([1668] 1681: 368), with restorative food: generally broth with the addition of eggs and bread. She had to rest, but should absolutely not sleep for at least 3–4 hours, for the fear that death might surprise her in her sleep, so the women would busy themselves around her to keep her awake; this direction lasted until the early 18th century.

FIGURE 4.1 *Birth of the Virgin*, Venetian School (1589), oil painting on wood, in Venice, Church of Santa Maria Formosa. Reproduced with permission of the Curia Patriarcale of Venice, Ufficio Beni Culturali.

FIGURE 4.2 Tintoretto, *Birth of St John the Baptist* (about 1546–1548), oil on canvas, in Venice, Church of San Zaccaria (chapel of Sant'Attanasio). Reproduced with permission of the Curia Patriarcale of Venice, Ufficio Beni Culturali.

106 Giving birth and being born

As for the child, the first gestures a midwife performed in Greek and Roman times were placing him on the ground, announcing his gender and then lifting him up, if he was alive and healthy.[3] These were ritual gestures, recurrent in many cultures, which underlined on the one hand the parent–child relationship with Mother-Earth, the body which generated all beings, and on the other the child's separation from his mother.[4] Contact with the earth was also believed to make the child stronger. This tradition disappeared in Christian Europe, but neither quickly nor completely, if what Scipione Mercurio reported, when condemning it, that in the mid-16th century it still took place in some locations in Italy, is true.[5] The custom of lifting up the child, however, lasted even longer (as can be seen in the *De partu hominis*, title page, 1537) (Figure 4.3).[6]

Even bathing a newborn had a ritual character, in addition to the purpose of cleaning him by washing off the blood and greasy substance which covered his body. The precise features of this ritual varied according to contexts and times.

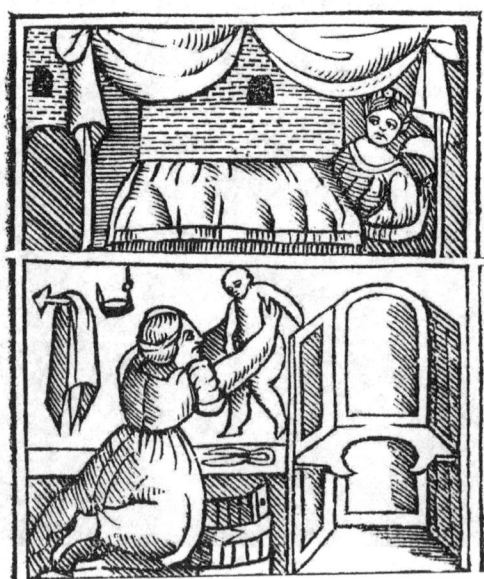

FIGURE 4.3 Title page of Eucharius Rösslin (Rodhion) (1537), *De partu hominis et quae circa ipsum accidunt libellus*, Venice, Bernardinum Bindonis, in Eucharius Rösslin [1513] (1910).

A very long medical tradition that lasted from ancient times to the 17th century, going from Soranus to Galen, to Avicenna, right up to Michele Savonarola and Scipione Mercurio, stated that the baby should be immersed in warm water to which some ingredients had been added, after – according to Soranus – gently rubbing his body with a mixture of salt, honey and mallow (*Gyn.* II, 13). The ingredients added to the bath varied: some, for example, as Scipione Mercurio himself pointed out, in a sort of historical list, added a little wine, oil and/or fragrant herbs (e.g. rose or sage).[7] The use of cold water to strengthen him was limited both to Spartan society in the classical era and to Aristotle's advice, although a long-standing legend, which appeared in many medical writings even in the early modern age, continued to attribute it to the peoples of the North, the Germans in particular.[8]

These initial contacts were particularly important: a midwife would also gently clean the child's eyes and clean and check every orifice, carefully examining his body, not only to check its integrity or for the presence of malformations or wounds, but also to gather signs and make predictions about his fate, similarly to what happened during the birth itself. Being born "with one's shirt on" (i.e. wrapped in the amniotic sac) was considered a good omen, as we have already seen, while being born "unnaturally", e.g. in a breech presentation, was a bad omen. This was the so-called Agripino birth (from the Latin *aegre partus* = to be born with effort), from which the name Agrippa derived, and it foretold a troubled life, as in the case of the famous Roman general Agrippa or other famous people, such as, for example, Rabbi Leone Modena (1571–1648), evidence of a long tradition that crossed religions and social classes.[9] Even sainthood could be foretold by being born with particular signs on one's body, such as Saint Roch, born with a red cross on his chest.

After washing and cleaning the infant, a midwife would perform a series of manipulations and manoeuvres designed to shape his head and body, compressing the bones of the skull and/or nose, pulling his arms and legs if they were of different lengths, correcting the position of his ears, cutting the frenulum under his tongue, manipulating his genitals, in short acting as she would with soft wax to "reshape" his body, as Savonarola wrote, in other words to give him a new and beautiful shape: "working out a beautiful shape" (Savonarola [1460?] 1952: 139).[10]

These practices, aimed at giving infants an appearance appropriate to the aesthetic canons of their cultural context (which were therefore not always the same), had been suggested by physicians since ancient times: Soranus wrote that it was necessary to bring the child back to his "natural" shape (*katà phýsin schema, Gyn.* II, 14), after the misshaping suffered by his body during childbirth.[11] But even when physicians distanced themselves from this practice, in the 18th century, it still continued in popular traditions, in some contexts until the end of the 19th century. In 19th-century Italy, the Austrian Government engaged in a tough battle, waged through many decrees, in order to combat these customs (see Chapter 10.9). In some areas of France, the practice of "faire une tête longue" (making the head long), by compressing and binding the head tightly, was still current at the end of the century.[12]

Even swaddling a baby's body, which lasted for an extraordinary length of time in Western culture, surviving, in some contexts and with rare exceptions, until the 1960s,[13] was carried out with corrective and/or preventive intent, to straighten the bones and prevent incorrect postures and/or malformations: as a seedling is tied to a stick to make it grow straight, so too was a baby tightly swaddled from head to toe, until he became a kind of cocoon, making sure that his arms were well stretched along his sides and his legs were well separated (as many paintings show). After two or three months, his right arm would be released first, to get him accustomed to using it, then his left one, but still leaving his legs swaddled at least until he was a year old, or even older.

Evidently, all these practices did not only have an aesthetic function, but were also a symbolic and ritualistic one, as markers of the separation from the mother: they were designed to humanise the child, purifying him from any foul traces and from his mother's blood, removing any residue of his life inside the womb, making him conform to the expected formal canons and accentuating his gender attributes, thus transforming the being born from his mother's entrails into a child ready to be welcomed by his family and his community. For this reason, the figure of the midwife acted as a linchpin between natural and social births: the person who had brought about the former, by extracting the child from the womb and lifting him towards the sky, prepared and covered his body to then return him to his mother and father in his new form, ready for the latter. Many representations of birth reproduced this second step: the return of a swaddled infant to his mother.

An observation by Scipione Mercurio also deserves to be remembered, as he recommended to midwives that this be done as soon as possible: "after a quarter of an hour has passed", they had to lay the child next to his mother, "so that he touches her side". He emphasised the beneficial effects of this physical closeness[14] that "would almost preserve him from endless diseases" (Mercurio [1596] 1713: 96). On the contrary, breastfeeding immediately after birth was considered very harmful and was forbidden, for a combination of medical and ritual reasons. On the one hand, colostrum (the first milk produced by mothers) was judged by physicians to be harmful to the child, precisely because "it was milk infected by the filth of menstrual blood" (Mercurio [1596] 1713: 362), in other words by lochia (the blood lost by mothers in childbirth): milk and lochia were considered incompatible. On the other hand, this prohibition emphasised the symbolic separation between mother and child after birth.[15]

Physicians advised not to feed newborns for several hours and then only with sweet and slightly laxative substances, to encourage them to expel the meconium (matter contained in the foetus' bowels). These varied according to the contexts: warm water and honey, as Soranus suggested (*Gyn*. II, 17); stewed apples, butter and sugar, according to Scipione Mercurio, who also suggested giving a little rhubarb syrup and chicory as laxatives; almond oil or honey, according to others.[16] In addition to these, Louise Bourgeois also suggested administering a little warm wine with honey, if the baby appeared weak, as she herself said she had done at the birth of Louis XIII, to revive him.[17]

The generally harmful effects of these practices should be emphasised: nowadays, we know, for example, that colostrum is useful and valuable to the health of a newborn.

2 Breastfeeding and wet nurses

According to the Hippocratic texts and Galen, breast milk was formed from blood, the primary element from which other bodily fluids (such as sperm) originated, according to the principle of haemogenesis.[18] After giving birth, as it was no longer required to feed the foetus in the womb, blood was believed to flow towards the breasts where, once cooked and turned white, it was transformed into new food for the child, according to the "extraordinary harmony" that connected the breasts and the womb both in reproduction and in sexuality.[19] For this reason, a mother's blood loss was considered incompatible with the production of healthy and nutritious milk. Mothers were not, therefore, allowed to breastfeed their babies for a few days and, when they started doing so, they had to abstain from sexual intercourse. In the economy of the circulation of bodily fluids, sexual intercourse, by attracting blood towards the womb, would impoverish the milk, making it watery, if not actually spoiling it, thus depriving babies of the food they needed. Furthermore, intercourse entailed the risk of a new pregnancy that would channel blood to the womb to feed the foetus, causing milk production to cease altogether.

Physicians therefore urged women to abstain from sexual intercourse: "I order all women who are nursing babies to abstain completely from sex relations. For menstruation is provoked by intercourse, and the milk no longer remains sweet" (*San.* I, 51, 21).[20]

This is surely one of the reasons behind the use of wet nurses, one of the most persistent customs in history, which clearly shows how the reproductive function was regulated since ancient times by cultural and social norms.[21] For millennia, women from the élites first, and later on from the urban popular classes, entrusted the task of breastfeeding their children to other women, often peasants, although some characteristics of the person were believed to be passed on through the milk, just as they did through blood. This happened despite the fact that breastfeeding was valued from the symbolic point of view: it was the only bodily aspect of motherhood to be extolled in goddesses and divinities as well, from Isis to Juno (who was supposed to have illuminated the heavens with her breast milk), to *Dea Nutrix*, to the Virgin Mary, often depicted as *Maria Lactans* (Breastfeeding Madonna).[22] In the Christian world, in artistic representations, it was also charged with symbolic meanings, as a symbol of charity.[23]

Clearly, husbands had no intention of depriving themselves of their sexual rights over their wives' bodies for long periods of time (breastfeeding could last more than a year), nor of their presence in social life, as Mary Wollstonecraft pointed out in 1792,[24] even if moralists pointed their fingers only at the lack of motherly love and vanity of women who were supposed to avoid breastfeeding so as not to ruin their breasts and to be able to go to parties. In the hierarchy of marital and family duties and of the socially expected behaviour of wives, breastfeeding was a long way down.

But other factors also contributed to this widespread custom, including an ambivalent view of breastfeeding, which on the one hand extolled it as a gesture of love, but on the other rejected it as a somewhat animalistic bodily behaviour, unworthy of high-society women and therefore to be provided by slaves, servants or women from the lower classes.

Also practised in the Greek world, wet nursing became particularly widespread in imperial Rome, where it was provided by the *nutrix lactaria* or *assa nutrix*, often slaves.[25]

In the Middle Ages, it was part of the feudal system of reciprocal services linking vassals to their peasants: breastfeeding the lord of the manor's children was one of the obligations of a peasant family, in an exchange that strengthened social relations and symbolic relationships.[26] In urban Europe, the children of upper-class families (especially daughters) were frequently sent to be wet nursed in the countryside, not only because it was cheaper than accommodating a wet nurse at home, but because the air of towns and cities was believed to be unhealthy, whereas the rural environment was considered healthier and wet nurses believed to provide more nutritious and healthier milk.[27] This choice often involved subjecting newborns to long and dangerous journeys; it also created a distance between mother and child which would last a few years and would affect their emotional relationship.

The practice of wet nursing developed further during the early modern age, extending to the urban middle classes and to the families of craftsmen and merchants. The reason, in this case, was related to the work of women in shops and workshops, to their need to be free to carry out an activity essential to their families' survival. It is no coincidence that wet nursing reached its maximum development between the 17th and 18th centuries, in manufacturing or commercial cities, such as London, Paris and Lyon, where silk processing was one of the main economic activities:

> In Paris, in 1780, in a population of between 800,000 and 900,000 inhabitants, out of 21,000 children born every year, fewer than 1,000 were breastfed by their mothers, 1,000 by wet nurses who lived in their employers' homes, and all the others, that is 19,000 newborns, were sent to be wetnursed in the suburbs or in the countryside.
>
> *(Bellavitis 2018: 137–138)*[28]

In the late modern age, due to the large numbers of abandoned babies, the foundling hospitals also sent more and more of them to external wet nurses, as the ones living in the hospitals were insufficient, thus giving peasant women an additional source of income.[29] This expansion in wet nursing fed a vast market, making the wet nurse (*balia* in Italy, *nodriza* in Spain, *nourrice* in France) one of the most widely spread female workers in European history, even though the particular nature of this job, where what was sold was produced by the workers' bodies, and was not a simple service, should not be forgotten.

Like all markets, even wet nursing had its own rules and tariffs, often sanctioned by contracts. Those stipulated in the 14th–16th centuries by the Florentine families studied by Christiane Klapisch-Zuber highlight the exclusive role of fathers in these agreements, which were in fact signed by the child's father and the wetnurse's husband (*balio*).[30]

But this was not the case everywhere: in fact, the women of the family would often be the ones to select the wet nurse and conduct the negotiations.[31] In some contexts, such as in France, wet nursing was regulated by law as early as the 14th century: a royal ordinance from 1350 fixed salaries and forms of intermediation valid for the whole kingdom. In early modern times, there were public wetnursing offices in some European cities, such as Paris, Stockholm and Hamburg.[32]

The practice lasted until the first half of the 20th century, despite the repeated invitations more or less forcefully addressed over the centuries by physicians to "pious and praiseworthy mothers" (Mercurio [1596] 1713: 251) to take on the task themselves, and despite the attacks waged by Enlightenment thinkers in the second half of the 18th century in support of breastfeeding.

Realising the uselessness of these recommendations, physicians focused their attention above all on identifying the characteristics of a good wet nurse, so as to allow families to make appropriate choices (Figure 4.4).

Michele Savonarola, in his book addressed to the women of Ferrara, recommended that she be young, but not excessively so (aged around 30), with

FIGURE 4.4 The wet nurse, from Giovanni Grevembroch [1754] (1981), vol. III, p. 155.

"good colouring", that is healthy and strong, neither fat nor thin, "of good and praiseworthy habits", with a calm and gentle personality, well-developed breasts, a recent mother (no longer than a month and a half), if possible the mother of a son (this was a sign of "purer, warmer and better" blood), accustomed to eating lightly (Savonarola [1460?] 1952: 197). They would obviously need to check that she was not pregnant. These directions were also repeated with few variations in later texts. In addition to this, physicians also taught how to recognise good quality milk, starting from an examination of her breasts. Sebastiano Melli, following Scipione Mercurio, reiterated in the early 18th century that they had to be "moderately swollen", with protruding nipples, not too turgid or thick, "so as not to trouble the infant's mouth or be too much effort for him". The milk should neither be too fatty nor too watery, be whitish in colour, with a pleasant smell and "a slightly sweet taste" (Melli 1721: 248–251). To assess its consistency and quality, it had to be allowed to run down the palm of their hands.

Physicians also gave directions on a wetnurse's lifestyle and on the food she should eat: she had to eat moderately, avoid excessively salty food which might alter the flavour of her milk, lead a life which was neither too sedentary, nor too tiring, avoid alterations of mood, be scrupulously clean and dress in a way which left her breasts free and unbound. One of her obligations, which was specified in the contracts, was to abstain from sexual relations.

From many points of view, therefore, their breast milk was a precious resource for peasant women and women from the working classes, and not having it or losing it was a real misfortune. For this reason, they did not hesitate to resort to many expedients, which varied according to the context: potions, superstitious objects, such as "milk stones", rubbed over their breasts because they were considered lactiferous, or the water from "milk springs", often to be found in limestone, or collected in "milk caves", where the presence of stalactites was reminiscent of drops of breast milk.[33] Resorting to the intercession of deities or saints was fundamental: ex-votos depicting breasts were found in various temples dedicated to Hera/Juno (such as the temple of Uni/Juno and Vei/Demeter in Vulci, whose artefacts are exhibited in the Museum of Villa Giulia in Rome). In the Christian world, the Breastfeeding Madonna was invoked above all, but also Saint Agatha, because of the features of her martyrdom (her breasts had been torn off with pincers) or Saint Mammes of Caesarea who had miraculously seen his breasts grow so that he could breastfeed an abandoned baby who was dying.[34]

If none of these devices worked, female solidarity was used: breastfeeding a newborn could be undertaken by relatives, friends or neighbours (the so-called "milk mothers"), which still happens today in many non-European cultures.[35] Finally, goat's milk was also used since ancient times and with bottles of different material and workmanship.[36]

3 Impurity: a period of time between life and death

The period following labour and childbirth was thought to be full of dangers and risks, for the lives of both the mother and the child: it was a particularly delicate phase, with both beings hanging in the balance. As we have seen, in the past, birth and death were believed to be near and concomitant events, similarly to what happens today in other cultures: mother and child, in giving birth and in being born, were exposed to the risk of dying. The condition of a new mother was compared by medicine to that of "a seriously injured person" and as such "easily at great risk of succumbing" (Frank [1779] 1825: 262),[37] according to an analogy present in many authors: excessive bleeding and puerperal fever, the origin of which was unknown, always lurked. This fear remained well rooted in the popular tradition until the 19th–20th centuries: "For forty days a woman who gives birth overlooks her open grave", said a Venetian proverb (Bernoni [1878] 1980: 21). "For forty days you'd always be on the edge of death", the peasant women from Verona said in the early 20th century (Filippini 1983: 75).

For similar reasons, the life of the child was also greatly at risk, due to the premature births, the prolonged labours, the instruments used, the low hygiene standards, the poor resuscitation techniques and the limited knowledge of neonatal diseases,[38] frequently recorded in Italy with the generic definition of "*spasimo*" (spasm) as we find in parish registers from the early modern period.[39]

Mortality was very high, although calculating the exact figures before the 19th century presents similar challenges to those found for maternal mortality, as data often referred to limited areas, with different socio-environmental characteristics, and was gathered from inconsistent sources and detection systems. According to some research, at the time of the Roman Empire, about 28%–30% of children died during their first year of life.[40] Working from the books of *Ricordanze* (Memories) of Florentine families between 1300 and 1550, C. Klapisch-Zuber calculated an average mortality of around 20% in a sample of 1,000 children aged between one and three, with significant annual fluctuations due to periods of plague and epidemics and with a greater incidence of female mortality, which suggests a "[gender] discrimination in relation to mortality", for social and cultural reasons to which we shall return (Klapisch-Zuber 1996: 167). Mortality was higher in the first year of life: comparing various European studies on the *ancien régime*, Jacqueline Hecht calculated it between 200/1,000 and 250/1,000[41] slightly lower than the figure recorded in Northern Italy, where it peaked at 313/1,000.[42] But in some cities, such as in Venice, it exceeded this figure, fluctuating (from the mid-17th to the mid-18th centuries) between 20% and 37% (up to 1 year of age).[43] In any case, these are shocking figures, which show that one child in three or four died in their first year, and especially in their early days.

This social reality combined, as we have said, with a cultural representation that saw birth as an event intimately connected with death: where did a newborn come from, if not from that "other" world where the spirits and souls of the dead dwelled? A long tradition interpreted the birth of a child as a replacement for the loss of a family member: it was considered normal, after the death of an elderly member of the family, for a newborn child to take his or her name, as if the two lives arrived and departed from the same otherworldly place.

A newborn was seen as precariously suspended between the world of the living and that of the dead, belonging to the former, but not yet completely separated from the latter, in communication with the spirits in a liminal condition which made him fragile, different and ambivalent: in the Middle Ages, they were considered symbols and representations of Christ, but at the same time prey to the devil, *enfant des miracles* and at the same time instruments of the devil.[44] They were believed to cry at night because the ancestors called them back to them, fighting for them with the living. Various protection rituals which involved mother and child had similarities with rituals for the dead. In Ancient Greece, the impurity of a woman who had given birth was considered equal to that of a corpse, as Theophrastus wrote: "Do not touch a grave, nor a dead body nor the bed of a new mother" (cited by Frank [1779] 1825: II, 231). In many contexts, newborns were placed in their cradles in closed rooms, and watched over by candlelight, just as the dead were kept vigil. Since ancient times, the women who brought children into the world also prepared the bodies of the dead,[45] a custom preserved in some contexts until the 20th century: in the village of Minot (Chatillon, France), the woman who "made children" also "made the dead", underlining with her gestures the intimate closeness of the two events.[46] In Sardinia, the figure of the midwife traditionally coincided with that of the *accabadora*, the woman who practised a form of euthanasia.[47]

Medieval culture had developed this closeness between birth and death, grasping the similarities between the two liminal states of life (early childhood and old age), along the lines of incapacity and the need for care.

Because of this alleged contact with the spiritual world, mother and child were considered impure. The representation of impurity after childbirth and birth appears as a very long-standing transcultural feature, which in the Western world took on various facets and meanings over the course of time.[48] In addition to contact with the afterlife world, impurity was also linked to bleeding: the blood lost during childbirth and in the following days (the lochia) was considered as impure and corrosive as menstrual blood, to the extent that, in ancient times, the women who had assisted in births had to undergo a purification rite for having stained their hands. Even at the beginning of the 18th century, the founder of occupational medicine, Bernardino Ramazzini, included the alleged corrosive power of the lochia with the main causes of midwives' occupational diseases, "caused by the post-partum flow falling onto their hands, and at times inflaming and ulcerating them because of its corrosive nature", made worse by their "noxious smells and fumes" (Ramazzini [1700] 2009: 145). A child's impurity, therefore, also stemmed from his contact with his mother's blood.

The Jewish religion made explicit reference to this, assimilating the loss of blood in the menstrual cycle to that in childbirth and in the post-natal period, and therefore the impurity of the former to the impurity of the latter: as the Book of *Leviticus* stated,

> If a woman have conceived seed, and born a man child: then she shall be unclean seven days; according to the days of the separation for her infirmity shall she be unclean [..] But if she bear a maid child, then she shall be unclean two weeks, as in her separation.
>
> (Lev. KJV, *12*, 2–5)[49]

The Christian religion inherited these contents and made them its own, combining them with some linked to the original sin. Words like "guilt" and "sin" recurred in novena and prayer books and even the term "devil" featured in some women's accounts from the 20th century: "We had the devil, when we gave birth we harboured sin" (Filippini 1983: 127).

Thus, impurity and sin overlapped in the Christian view, remarking upon a situation that exposed women to the devil's influence and temporarily excluded them from their community: a new mother had "the devil" and was in "sin", which some clearly defined as "original sin", as if the fusion with the body of the child, marked by the original sin, had spiritually contaminated the mother as well:

They said that we are like beasts ... that we have the original sin ... it needs to be erased and so we had to bless the mother. They said: "You must go and be blessed because otherwise you are not like the Christians, because you have the original sin" (Filippini 1983: 80).

The multiplicity and ambiguity of these contents are linked to a fact appropriately emphasised by Claudia Pancino[50]: the Christian Church had never officially defined the state of impurity or the prohibitions and rules surrounding the period of post-partum quarantine, limiting itself, after the Council of Trent, to issuing norms about the blessing ceremony for new mothers, including it in the *Rituale Romanum* ('De benedictione mulieris post partum', [1614] 1740: 142).[51] It was precisely this inclusion which reiterated, albeit implicitly, the state of impurity rooted in the previous pagan and Jewish traditions.

4 Beliefs and rules

Due to their supposed impurity, mother and child were at the same time in danger and dangerous, in need of protection on the one hand, and of being separated from the rest of their community on the other. They were therefore isolated and protected for a period of time which varied depending on the different cultures. In the Christian West, it had generally been fixed at 40 days for the mother (the so-called "quarantine" in the Italian tradition), taking the symbolic importance of the number from the Jewish tradition (40 were also the days Christ spent fasting in the desert), after which the purification ceremony took place. For the child, however, this period came to an end with the celebration of baptism.

This period of marginality, beyond the differences in terms of content, featured in all the rites of passage that in traditional societies articulated the fundamental changes in the life of individuals (birth, puberty, motherhood); it represented the first of the three invariable sequences that anthropologist Arnold Van Gennep identified as recurrent in all cultures: separation, liminality and incorporation.[52] The purpose of these rituals was to emphasise the change in role and status of a person within their family and community: for a woman, her becoming a mother (for the first time or again); for a child, his becoming a son, part of a family and a community. From this point of view, the separation could have a positive function not so much health-wise, as some of these rules were actually dangerous, but psychologically and socially: it was a length of time, defended and protected, which allowed a woman to work out her new role of mother, make contact with her child and redefine her relationship with her husband, in short to return to a normality characterised by new roles, duties and relationships.

During this period, mother and child had, first of all, to be defended from the evil spirits that roamed around them, be they the restless spirits of women who had died in childbirth (as people believed in the Veneto region), or devils, orcs or witches, who might take a baby away or switch it.[53] Popular traditions gathered in 19th-century Italy, for example, show a vast range of connotations and names attributed to these beings.[54] To prevent them from entering the house, doors and windows were tightly shut, plugging all cracks, as we have seen. Objects believed to have dissuasive powers were put before doors or above beds: for example, crossed knives, small lights, tinkling chains, crucifixes and blessed images, in a combination of sacred and profane. In addition, amulets and talismans were placed in the room, on the cradle and around the necks of both mother and child.[55] In this case, there were many local variations as well: a frequently recurrent element was salt, tied in a little bag around the necks of mother and newborn, or certain stones such amethyst, garnet or coral (which in many medieval and early modern paintings can be seen around the neck of the Baby Jesus); wolf teeth or red ribbons were also used, thanks to the apotropaic value attributed to this colour.[56] These objects, popular in a long-standing pagan tradition, were joined in the Christian West by other sacred objects, such as, for example, the rosary, which the women from Friuli wore around their necks throughout their quarantine, or, in Southern Italy, a small bag containing sacred images and prayers (the "little dress"), which was also tied around the child's neck.[57]

From the early Middle Ages until the 1950s and 1960s, in various parts of Europe, mothers were not allowed to leave their homes: they might see witches or spirits. In France, people avoided showing a child who was taken in a procession to be baptised.[58]

Sight played a decisive role in these taboos, to the extent that a woman was not even allowed to see her own reflected face: in some places, as in the Verona area, the mirrors in the house were covered with cloths.[59] In the Middle Ages, menstruating women were also forbidden from looking at mirrors. A similar prohibition was applied to the child: "The mirror causes throes and you must not put children in front of mirrors", people recommended in Venice.[60]

In an ambivalent way, however, the presence of a new mother was also dangerous to others: a new mother could bring misfortune to other people's homes, make plants wither and cause ailments. For this reason, she was exempted even from going to mass, although the Church never formally sanctioned this prohibition.

Inside the house, behaviour was regulated by strict rules and prohibitions, which varied depending on contexts and periods, according to deep-rooted local traditions which, in patriarchal and patrilocal families, saw mothers-in-law in charge of ensuring they were abided by, so once again fulfilling the roles of custodians and guarantors. For the first eight to ten days, a new mother was often not allowed to get out of bed, and in some Italian regions, the sheets could not be changed either, because the whiteness of the fabric was believed to attract blood. Hence, in Italy, a new mother was described as *"impagliolata"* or *"impagiolata"*, a term linked to the word for straw (*paglia*), of which mattresses were made (in other words, bedridden).[61] The traditional English term for maternity hospitals (lying-in hospital) also probably derives from the fact that women who have recently given birth, should normally lie in bed.

They had to be on a special diet, which generally consisted of broths made with hens or capons, often with the addition of eggs and bread, sometimes accompanied by a glass of wine.[62] The list of prohibitions and things to avoid was rather complex and diversified and involved, in addition to food, daily activities: women were not allowed to do certain jobs, put their hands in water or breathe in bad smells. Any infringement of these prohibitions could have serious consequences: any illness caught during the post-natal period would not be got over.

It should be emphasised, however, that both the details of the rules and their duration were very variable. In the countryside, women often resumed their work quickly, if the need was there:

> The robust new mothers from the countryside – J.P. Frank reported in the 18th century – let but a few days pass after giving birth, either they leave their beds and hasten, as if they were healthy, to take care of their domestic chores.
>
> *(Frank [1779] 1825, II: 262)*

Being unclean, a new mother did not participate in the baptism ceremony, which was held in the first few days after the birth, as the Council of Trent had ruled. This did not mean that she could not be visited inside her home: on the contrary, a tradition already very widespread in medieval and early modern times required friends and relatives to go and visit new mothers, to celebrate the birth. In many European regions, new mother's parties are attested on the day of the child's baptism. Frank himself wrote: "In many countries and even in the countryside it's practice to hold banquets with relatives and friends on the day when newborns are baptized and this custom is the second source of many ailments that befall new mothers" (Frank [1779] 1825, II: 264).

In 15th-century Florence, among noble families, friends and relatives would visit a new mother bringing *deschi da parto* (birth trays) full of food and richly decorated with scenes of triumph, alluding to the new mother's "victory".[63] In various places in Europe, for the occasion, noble palaces were decorated with silks and tapestries woven with gold and silver, and rich furnishings. In France, on the birth of Mary of Burgundy (1457), the room had been covered with *"damas vert et de soie verte"* (green damask and silk), a colour reserved for queens and noble princesses.[64] Francesco Sansovino, in his book *Venetia, città nobilissima et singolare* (Venice, noble and singular city) (1581), reported the custom of "richly setting the rooms, and in particular the one where the woman lies, with decorations such as paintings, carvings, gold and silver objects and other fine things" (cited by Molmenti 1973: II, 335); the luxury was such as to induce the Senate to intervene during the 16th century to limit such ostentation, in the context of sumptuary laws that also extended to baptisms.[65] At this time, the fashion of *tazze della puerpera* (new mother's cups) or *tazze della comare* (midwife's cups), broth bowls or cups in finely decorated ceramics, also developed; this custom soon reached other European states, in the name of the ostentation of luxury that conquered the European aristocratic classes in the early modern age.[66] In the 17th century, restrictive measures similar to those passed in Venice were also issued in some German States, going so far as to abolish the custom "of holding banquets during some women's post-partum period", fining husbands or godfathers, in an attempt not only to curb luxury, but also to protect the new mother's health, as the one issued by the county of Nassau-Katzenelnbogen (1615) explained:

> In order for women who have recently given birth to enjoy the peace they need, we ask that they not be tormented so many times a week by the visits of numerous friends and neighbours, nor that at such meetings banquets be held.
>
> *(Frank [1779] 1825, II: 274)*

5 Purification rituals

The period of marginality would end with a purification ritual which reintegrated the woman into her community and sanctioned her return to normality. In this case, too, the forms of these rituals were subject to variations as a consequence of the overlap of different religious and cultural traditions.

In Ancient Greece, the purification of the new mother seemed to have happened on the same day as the *Amphidromia*, a ceremonial feast celebrated within the first week of a child's life, which also signalled his social birth.[67] In Rome, five days after childbirth, everyone who had participated in it would make a sacrifice and purify their hands. The newborn would be placed on the home altar and handed over to his wet nurse by the midwife. A private celebration with gifts to both mother and child would follow.[68]

The Jewish religion required the woman to visit the temple, bringing the priest an offering of a lamb, a dove or a turtledove, after 40 days if a son had been born, and after 80 if a daughter, as prescribed in the Book of *Leviticus* (*Lev. KJV* 12, 1–8): a gender difference which highlighted the impurity caused by the birth of a girl as greater.

According to the Gospels, even Mary had undergone this purification after the birth of Jesus, at the same time as his presentation at the temple: in the liturgical calendar, this event is in fact called *Purificatio Beatae Mariae Virginis* (Purification of the Blessed Virgin Mary), or Candlemas, and is celebrated on the 2nd of February, exactly 40 days after Christmas.

Christianity kept this ritual, with some variations, erasing the different duration of impurity according to the newborn's gender, and taking the figure of Mary as a role model. There is, however, a contradiction in the construction of the image of the Madonna in Christian theological tradition: as we have seen, the Second Council of Constantinople, in the 6th century AD, had sanctioned Mary's virginity even after she had given birth to Jesus (see Chapter 1.9). What stain or sin was the Madonna supposed to have which needed cleansing? Not the sin of lust, having never slept with a man, nor the contamination with the original sin of the child that she carried in her womb, nor the spilling of blood during childbirth. The substantial discontinuity with the Jewish religion is clear, but the ritual was kept not only by the Catholic Church (and is attested as early as the late Middle Ages), but also by the Reformation, a sign of how deeply the cultural representation of the impurity of new mothers was rooted. The recurring interpretation in the commentaries referred to an act of humility by the Madonna who, despite being pure, "did not disdain being considered similar to other women", and "standing in the temple among the commonest women, as if she were one of them" (Riva 1860: 488),[69] as stated in *Novenas* and prayers to be said on the day of purification.

It is true that the Church never officially spoke of purification rituals, but always of a 'blessing' of the new mother, referring to the "pious and worthy custom", and framing this as an act of thanksgiving for having escaped a mortal danger ("give thanks to God for her deliverance"), as the *Rituale Romanum* (1614) reported under the heading *De benedictione mulieris post partum*: "If a new mother, immediately after childbirth, according to a pious and worthy custom, wishes to go to church to give thanks to God for her deliverance, and asks a priest for a blessing" (*Rituale Romanum* [1614] 1740: 142).

However, the articulation of this rite contradicts the content, as it has the features of a genuine purification ritual. The woman had to wait outside the door, holding a burning candle, until the priest invited her indoors. Once inside, before the Madonna's altar, he sprinkled her with holy water and recited a psalm. At the end of the ceremony, the woman made a donation to the church and returned home, where a small party often took place, sometimes in the presence of the midwife. In France, on this occasion, a *pain des relevailles* was offered, symbolising the afterbirth.[70]

This ceremony took on different names in Europe: in Italian, it was called "andare a farsi benedire" or "andare in santo", as in the English phrase *Churching of Women*. In French, it was called *relevailles*, a term connected to the rising from bed, so to the return to normal activity. In German, it was called "blessing of the new mother" (*Aussegnung der Wöchnerin*).[71] Although the ritual remained almost unchanged up until the 20th century, the timing tended to be brought forward in many contexts, to as little as 8–10 days from the birth.

It is important to highlight some analogies between this ritual and that of baptism, as we shall see: covering one's head and not being seen; the sense of precariousness and risk connected to the route; waiting for the priest outside the door: all details which, in both cases, indicate the situation of marginality concerning the community.

What consequence could these rituals have in the life experience of women, in their perception of motherhood, on their representation of themselves? It is difficult to say, especially for the more distant past. What emerges from anthropological research and oral history is their ambivalent character. On the one hand, in fact, they had a positive value: on the practical and social levels, they allowed the new mother to recover her physical and psychological strength after childbirth.[72] In this perspective, many 20th-century women attributed a positive value to the rules of the post-partum period, calling them "forms of respect" by relatives towards the woman who had given birth, in spite of a certain intolerance with excessive restrictions.[73]

On the other hand, however, these rules, by virtue of their contents, had negative consequences on the perception of the body, as they stressed the ambivalent value attributed to the bodily experience of motherhood, emphasising the unspeakable and shameful aspects. Some women indirectly touched upon this, covering with silence what someone had the courage to say, if only as a rhetorical question, expressing an uneasiness which retrospectively, in a changed context, could finally be put into words:

> But why 'of the devil'? Because we had a baby? Why, blessed child? What has this child I have given birth to, this son brought to me? That I am 'of the devil'? Was it not wrong?
>
> *(Filippini 1983: 82)*

The experience of motherhood appeared marked in the lives of women from a profound contradiction, suspended between pride and shame, strength and weakness, approval and rejection. By bringing a child into the world, the woman fulfilled her familial, social and religious duties, fulfilling her female identity and acquiring a new role in her family, but at the same time, she was exposed to risks which were not only to do with death, but with contact with spirits, experiencing the temporary exclusion from her community, and therefore the negativity that culture attributed to the female body in its maternal function, and internalising it. Precisely when she felt fulfilled as a mother, the woman perceived herself as 'dirty', weak and dangerous. The negative values attributed to the physical experience of motherhood undermined the life experience of it, introducing elements of weakness and negativity in a woman's self-representation.

The split between social/spiritual and physical motherhood transformed this into an ambivalent experience, contributing to a fragmented and contradictory identity.

6 Infanticide and abandonment

The killing of newborns was a very long-standing transcultural phenomenon, although present in different ways on the social scene. Its history belongs to the imaginary and cultural spheres no less than the social one; these two aspects were closely intertwined over time, with considerable variations in the representation of the phenomenon, the perception of its gravity, its lawfulness/illegality, the sanctions and surveillance systems, in a trend that is anything but linear or progressive.[74]

On the one hand, therefore, we have the unfolding of the history of a practice used for centuries both by families (to control or select births) and by unmarried mothers: it should be remembered that, in the course of the early modern age, motherhood outside marriage increasingly became a source of dishonour, with a reduction of the social acceptability of "illegitimate" children.[75] On the other hand, we have the unfolding of the history of an imagined tradition where the embodiment of ancestral ghosts and fears, collective obsessions and nightmares were the figures of a bad mother who destroys her children after giving birth to them, or of "enemies" who kidnap and kill them, be they different social groups or characters ambiguously connected with the forces of evil (witches). Equally recurrent was the association of infanticide with magic rituals, often linked to cannibalism, of which religious minorities were suspected: the first Christians in the Roman world were accused of this, and so were the Jews in the Christian world, as well as heretics and witches (often midwives), who were at the top of the list of those suspected of consorting with the devil.[76] It must be emphasised that this imaginary world was equally shared by the educated élites and the popular classes: Pliny the Elder talked about it in his *Naturalis historia*, as did the 15th-century inquisitors H. Krämer and J. Sprenger, and the educated and enlightened Pope Benedict XIV, who, in the 18th century, in his bull *Beatus Andreas* (1755), ultimately sanctioned the very existence of ritual infanticide. This obsession materialised and exploded socially in sudden attacks and violence against suspicious minorities (such as the *pogroms* against the Jews) or in planned repressions, as in the case of the witch hunts, macabre episodes dotting Western history.

On the legal level, we must first of all stress the profound fracture separating the ancient world from the Christian one, connected to the different representations of the foetus/infant on the one hand, and, on the other, of the figure who has power over his life. What has been said about abortion also applies to infanticide: the voluntary interruption of pregnancy and the killing or abandonment of infants were, after all, part of a range of similar and often not differentiated actions,[77] all gathered in the penal category of *parricide*. In the ancient world, as we have seen, the rejection of a newborn was considered legitimate and socially accepted, as indeed was abortion, on the condition that it be decided by the father, even if more often it manifested itself in the form of abandonment: so "letting die", rather than killing. In the Christian world, on the contrary, it was a serious infringement of the laws of God, "father" of all creatures and master of their existence: it was therefore a sin, for which the Penitentials of the high Middle Ages provided public penances. The perception of its gravity, however, underwent considerable variations over the centuries,[78] with more marked emphasis in the transition between the Middle Ages and the early modern period, with the shift from sin to crime which represents the turning point in the history of infanticide. At this point, attention became increasingly focused on the figure of the infant-killing mother, who emerged in the collective imagination as a woman managing a free, lustful sexuality, unhindered by conjugal bonds, while the child's father remained in the shadows and unaccountable. The criminalisation of sin by secular justice was part of a curbing process of female sexuality which, as we have already discussed, the political authorities took on progressively, thanks to the symbolic link between women's honour and the honour of their city.[79] Strict laws against infanticide, although articulated differently from state to state, were passed throughout Europe, from the Bamberg Criminal Code (1507) to the *Constitutio Criminalis Carolina* (1532), issued by Charles V, which formed the basis of justice systems until the 18th century, to the 1624 Infanticide Act passed during the reign of James I Stuart (1624), in an ever-worsening escalation: women were burnt to the stake, impaled and buried alive; they were often taken to the gallows with the corpse of the child (or a symbolic puppet), in a public spectacle of the event obviously intended as a deterrent.[80]

Nor were these laws disregarded, as research conducted in the judicial archives has shown, although it is difficult to have an overview of the phenomenon: the low number of trials and convictions (according to data available from the archives, especially in the German cities of Nuremberg, Gdansk and Frankfurt between the 16th and 18th centuries)[81] gives the impression that women more often managed to escape the clutches of justice, just as the authorities suspected, or that juries were reluctant to apply the harsh sentences provided for by the law (but this was the case in the 19th century)[82] and for this reason, they intensified the surveillance on single women and pregnant women considered "at risk".

From the trials, a rather precise social profile of infant-killers emerges: they were generally single, poor women, who lived off their own work, often servants or peasants, frequently orphan, who paid the price of casual relationships or rapes. Lucia Cremonini, the girl sent to death in Bologna in January 1710, whose story has been reconstructed by Prosperi (2005), perfectly fits this profile: an "honourable girl", fatherless and a maid, she had spent a Carnival evening in the company of a young priest. Even the various infant-killers who came from other Italian regions were mostly peasant women, servants and farm labourers, who often acted alone, or were helped by family members (especially by their mothers).[83]

This research, precisely because of the sources on which it is based, might suggest the wrong conclusion that infanticide only concerned unmarried mothers: it was not so, even though the force of justice was mainly directed against them. On the contrary, it remained a practice followed by families with great historical continuity, beyond religious and civil norms, "a form of birth control, routinely applied by peasants in hard times" (Hanlon 2003: 473). In this sense, historians speak of "mortality strategies" implemented by families across Europe, which included various behaviours: infanticide, child abandonment and child neglect within the household.[84] In some contexts, such as in Italy and especially in Tuscany, these phenomena were genderised, affecting girls in particular. Hanlon's research on the parish registers of a small village in Tuscany (Montefollonico) in the mid-17th century has revealed how families, at times of economic slump or prolonged famine, resorted to selective infanticide and on a rather considerable scale (up to 1/4 or even 1/3 of children born alive in difficult years), favouring boys over girls, thus confirming the view already put forward by C. Klapisch-Zuber (1985) and R. Trexler (1973).[85] A similar phenomenon occurs, albeit in different ways and for different reasons, even nowadays in some Asian countries, where there is a clear variation in the natural male/female ratio at birth.

Death was therefore hidden, or passed off as the spontaneous suffocation of infants in their parents' bed.[86] Aware of this, the Church had intervened to oppose this practice since the Middle Ages: starting with the Fourth Lateran Council (1215), various synods had forbidden parents from keeping newborns and babies under one year of age in their beds under penalty of excommunication, especially during the 16th and 17th centuries, when concerns over the child's spiritual fate intensified, and after the formalisation by the Council of Trent (Chapter 7, session XIV); the synods of Milan (1576), Chieti (1636) and Torcello (1676) made express reference to it.[87]

Parents were advised to use special care with their infants, for whose protection special gadgets had already been developed, such as the *"arcuccio"* (little arc), which held up the bed sheets,[88] but Cardinal Carlo Borromeo even imposed the use of a separate crib, the *"cunino"*. Although this prohibition was constantly reiterated, it was just as frequently ignored, and rarely enforced, as shown by the few police reports and convictions found in the archives.[89]

Although abandonment of newborns ("baby dropping") was not a conscious death strategy, it was no less lethal, as pointed out by Lynch, who described it as "tantamount to infanticide" (Lynch 2000: 147).

This is another social practice that took place over a very long time, and whose history is inscribed in myth and legend, and in fairy tales, involving the realms of the imaginary and symbolic, as well as that of social reality. See, for example, the many mythical or heroic figures saved by chance from abandonment (from Moses in the Bible, to Perseus, Oedipus in Greek mythology, to Romulus and Remus, the founders of Rome) or the many fairy tales about children of all ages abandoned in woods or on moors.[90]

In the ancient world, this practice was accepted: it was up to the father (or to the Ephori in Sparta) to decide whether to welcome a newborn child or reject it, as we shall see in the next chapter.

In Rome, the well-known *Columna Lactaria*, in the *Forum Olitorium*, was one of the customary places where infants were abandoned and where the presence of infant traffickers, the *nutricatores*, was also attested.[91]

Despite its condemnation by Christianity, even in this case, the phenomenon did not abate; in fact, it significantly increased during the Middle Ages and especially in the 16th century, when special foundling hospitals were created for abandoned children, starting in Italy, from Venice (1346) to Florence, which, with its hospital of the Innocents (1445), became a model for later institutions,[92] although a more precise idea of the phenomenon from a quantitative point of view was only possible in the 18th century.[93]

Historians have questioned the relationship between this increase and the moral condemnation directed at unmarried mothers: some have attributed the increase in abandonments in the Christian West to the moral sanction and loss of honour that followed a birth out of wedlock, especially in countries where honour was an essential prerequisite for the social existence of women.[94] Others have investigated the relationship between illegitimate births, abandonments and paternity searches, especially in the late modern age, when the possibilities of paternity searches were reduced (they were finally abolished by various 19th-century civil codes).[95] From the 13th to the 14th centuries, foundling hospitals were opened in various European cities, aiming to protect the lives of these children as much as possible, removing them from the dangers presented by the elements and by animals. They greatly developed in the 15th century, as part of the reform of hospitals intertwined with the commitment of confraternities and parishes to provide greater assistance, especially in Northern Europe.

The creation of specific foundling hospitals did not curb the phenomenon: in fact, according to some historians,[96] it indirectly caused an increase, in a kind of delegation of the responsibility for unwanted children to institutions and parishes, especially in the 18th–19th centuries. If it was not its cause, it certainly represented its "premise".[97]

This delegation was not only socially accepted, but in many countries incentivised and made "obligatory", in cases of illegitimate births, not only by families, but by the parish priests themselves, who thus aimed to remove from the parish the "scandal" of illegitimate births and the presence of children born out of wedlock[98] (see Chapter 2. 7). In the early 19th century, in a different political climate and within a project to combat child mortality, the Austrian Government, in an attempt to limit abandonments, issued a special circular addressed to parish priests, inviting them not to encourage single mothers to abandon their children at the foundling hospital.[99]

As in the case of infanticide, the phenomenon of abandonment was not limited to single mothers. On the contrary, the authorities knew very well that families also brought their legitimate children to foundling hospitals, especially during periods of famine, epidemics, wars and above all, between the late 18th and early 19th centuries, following the increase in the number of women working in factories, workshops and family businesses.[100] As Volker Hunecke has shown in his detailed research on the Milan foundling hospital, in the mid-19th century, more than half of the infants abandoned were legitimate: in 1842, 62.5% of the 2,706 foundlings were generally brought by poor but hard-working families, who could not manage without the work of mothers during the first year of a child's life.[101]

This happened despite the very high mortality recorded in these institutions, caused by overcrowding which favoured the spread of disease, the lack of live-in wet nurses, the living conditions and the often insufficient resources. The figures are merciless and give the impression of a real cull: in London's Foundling Hospital, between 1758 and 1760, 81% of the 7,290 abandoned children died; in Paris, at the *Hospice des Enfants-Trovés*, between 1773 and 1777, 4/5 of the 31,951 abandoned children died in the first year of life; in Florence, as many as 89%, in the period between 1792 and 1794.[102]

Faced with these figures, some historians have pointed their fingers at the insensitivity of mothers[103] and their scarce motherly love, underlining that this was also the result of a cultural construct.[104] This is obviously a simplistic explanation, which once again ends up blaming women, while not grasping the complexity of the phenomenon, its internal features, the weight of sexual morality, the forms of restriction and control over the female body, or the incidence of family survival strategies,[105] in historical periods when birth control methods were not yet known.

Notes

1. Morel (2010a).
2. Mercurio [1596] (1713: 96).
3. Curatolo (1901); Köves-Zulauf (1990); Corbier (1999); Fanos, Atzei and Corridori (2010); Corridori and Fanos (2010).
4. Rollet and Morel (2000: 52–53).
5. Mercurio ([1596] 1713: 92). Baldini (1991: 65).
6. Rösslin ('Rodhion Eucharius') (1537).
7. Mercurio ([1596] 1713: 94–95).
8. Pancino (2015: 51).
9. Curatolo (1901: 79); Belmont (1971: 67–79); Coulon (2004: 218).
10. Translated from Italian edition. See: Laget (1982: 186–191); Morel (2013).
11. Gourevitch and Raepsaet-Charlier (2001: 121).
12. Gélis (1984a: 434–457, 1984b).
13. Pancino (2015: 87); Morel (2007: 61–84).
14. This direction was only recently taken up by paediatricians.
15. Loux (1998: 136–137).
16. Mercurio ([1596] (1713: 96). Rollet and Morel (2000: 66–67); Pancino (2015: 119–121).
17. Witkowski (1890).
18. Sissa (1983); Gourevitch (1984); Dean-Jones (1994); Pomata (1995); Green (1998).
19. Bernardino Ramazzini spoke of "extraordinary harmony", in *De morbis artificum diatriba (The Diseases of Workers)* ([1700] 2009: 159): Pomata (1995: 45–47).
20. For the Latin text, I used: Galen, Claudius (1548) *De sanitate tuenda, libri sex, Thoma Linacro Anglo interprete,* Lugduni: Guliel. Rouillium (I, 51, 21). For the English translation: *A translation of Galen's Hygiene (de Sanitate tuenda)*, by Robert Montraville Green, Springfield: Charles Thomas publisher, 1951: 19.
21. Fildes (1988); Delahaye (1990); Maher (1992); Lett and Morel (2006); Thirion (2010: 232–241); Muzzarelli (2013: 3–45).
22. Thirion (2010: 232–233); Dasen (2004b: 125–144); Warner (1989: ch. 13).
23. Sperling (2013).
24. Fiume (1997: 93).

25 Gourevitch (1984: 234); Fildes (1988: ch. 1); Gourevitch and Raepsaet-Charlier (2001: 122–124); Testa and Tsotra (2010).
26 Knibiehler (2003: 11–33).
27 Lett and Morel (2006).
28 Gélis, Laget and Morel (1978: 157–158).
29 Fildes (1988: 72–74); Da Molin (1994); Reggiani (2014: 59–64).
30 Klapisch-Zuber (1980, 1985: ch. VIII).
31 D'Amelia (1999).
32 Gélis, Laget and Morel (1978: 163–165).
33 Thirion (2010: 236).
34 Baldini (1991: 150–155).
35 Maher (1992); Rollet and Morel (2000).
36 Rollet (1983: 81–91); Delahaye (1990).
37 Translated from the complete edition published in Italy in 1825 (see ch. 2, note 71).
38 Woods (2009).
39 Vanzan Marchin (1985: 21); Filippini (2018: 73).
40 Hopkins (1983: 225); Laubenheimer (2004: 295).
41 Hecht (1980: 29–84). The data presented by Julia for rural France in the second half of the 17th century is higher: 350/1,000 (Julia 1996: 232).
42 Between 1670 and 1800, Del Panta reported mortality in the first year of life as fluctuating between 256/1,000 and 313/1,000: Del Panta, Livi Bacci et alii (1996: 85–89).
43 Beltrami (1954: 161); Derosas (1999); Breschi, Derosas and Manfedini (2000).
44 Lett (1998); Gélis, Laget and Morel (1978).
45 Bruit Zaidman (1992).
46 Verdier (1979); Caforio (2002).
47 Bucarelli and Lubrano (2003); Potzolu (2006: 14).
48 Magli (1978); Laurent (1989: 209–218); Bruit Zaidman (1992: 369–370); Baldini (1991); Lett (1998); Loux (1998); Rollet and Morel (2000).
49 *Leviticus*, 12, 2 and 5. King James version. Taken from the online version: www.kingjamesbibleonline.org/Leviticus-Chapter-12/.
50 Pancino (2011: 56–66).
51 *Rituale Romanum* [1614] (1740). The *Rituale Romanum* is a set of books issued by the Catholic Church, containing precise provisions for the celebration of the sacraments (baptism, confirmation, marriage, confession, last rites). It was issued after the Council of Trent by Pope Paul V on 7 June 1614 (Constitution *Apostolicae Sedis*).
52 Van Gennep [1909] (2019).
53 Magli (1978).
54 Have dealt in particular with this: De Gubernatis (1878); Zanetti (1892); Tassoni (1973); Bernoni (1980); Ranisio (1996); Baldini (1991); Casagrande (1994); Amalfi (2005); Pancino and Pillon (1985); Pancino (1984); Pirovano (1985).
55 Fanos, Corridori and Cataldi (2003); Gregorio and Cataldi (2010).
56 Pancino (2015: 24–29).
57 Baldini (1991: 138–147).
58 Gélis (1984a: 525).
59 Tassoni (1973); Filippini (1983: 79).
60 Bernoni (1980: 30).
61 Baldini (1991: 72).
62 Laurent (1989: 207); Pancino (1984: 201–205).
63 Jacobson-Schutte (1980: 474–496); Colucci (2005: 285–357); Park (2018).
64 Laurent (1989: 211).
65 Davanzo Poli (1985: 64).
66 Rigon (1985: 80–82).
67 Bruit Zaidman (1992: 367); Fanos and Corridori (2010: 44–46).
68 Köves-Zulauf (1990); Curatolo (1901); Corbier (1999); Gourevitch, Morini and Rouquet (2003).

69 Translated from Italian edition.
70 Gélis (1984a: 295).
71 Pancino (2010).
72 Rollet and Morel (2000: 95).
73 Filippini (1983: 81).
74 Da Molin and Stella (1984); Rose (1986); Lynch (2000); Jackson (2002); Prosperi (2005).
75 Laslett (1977); Stone (1977); Cavallo and Cerutti (1980, 1990); Fiume (1989); Lombardi (1997).
76 Prosperi (2005: part. I, ch. 2).
77 Lynch (2000: 133–134).
78 As pointed out by Laubenheimer (2004: 296).
79 Muller (2012).
80 Prosperi (2005: 57–65); Hoffer and Hull (1981).
81 In Geneva, only 31 women were accused of infanticide between 1595 and 1712, 25 of whom were sentenced to death. In Essex, 33 were sentenced to death between 1580 and 1709. In Frankfurt, 18 women were sentenced to death out of 43 accused between 1562 and 1696. In Nürnberg, 67 were sentenced to death between 1503 and 1743. In Gdansk, 62 were sentenced to death between 1558 and 1713 (Prosperi 2005: 63–64).
82 Donovan (1991); Van der Lugt (2018).
83 Povolo (1979); Prosperi (2005); Ferrario (2008).
84 Lynch (2000: 134); Shorter (1975).
85 But this discrimination does not exist in other European contexts, as Lynch has pointed out in a comparative analysis (Lynch 2000: 144). A similar phenomenon occurs, albeit in different ways and for different reasons, even nowadays in some Asian countries, where there is a clear variation in the natural male/female ratio at birth (Meldolesi 2011).
86 Flandrin (1973).
87 Pedrini-Dubbini (2018).
88 Pancino (2015: 349).
89 Recent research carried out by Pedrini and Dubbini on the diocese of Jesi (Italy), between 1566 and 1602, revealed only 22 reports of death by suffocation in the parents' bed (Pedrini and Dubbini 2018).
90 Becchi (1994: ch. 4); Borgeaud (2004: 114–123).
91 Curatolo (1901: 66–67); Gourevitch (1984: 212).
92 Da Molin (1993); Grandi (1997); Hunecke (1987); Terpstra (2005).
93 As pointed out by Hunecke (1991: 32).
94 Laslett *et alii* (1980), Kertzer (1993); Fiume (1989).
95 Rose (1986); Cavallo and Cerutti (1980, 1990); Lombardi (1997); Bartoloni and Lombardi (2018).
96 Laslett (1977).
97 Hunecke (1991: 32).
98 Da Molin (1981).
99 Filippini (1985, 2018).
100 Hunecke (1994).
101 Hunecke (1987: ch. 5.1).
102 Hunecke (1991: 148–149).
103 Shorter (1975); Langer (1973).
104 Badinter (1980).
105 Appropriately stressed by Lynch (2000); Frandrin (1976); Hunecke (1987).

5
SOCIAL BIRTH

1 Rites of passage

In all cultures, the physical birth is followed by another kind of birth, the social one, which, by means of a ritual, signals the newborns' entry into their family and their community, and their recognition as members of both. The ways in which this rite of passage[1] took place explain the cultural representations of birth, family roles, kinship systems, the link between family, community and state, and the values attributed to newborns in a gender and class perspective.

Some aspects of this ritual, beyond the differences between the different contexts, above all between the ancient world and Christian society, stand out as significant precisely because they are recurrent: on the one hand, the incidence of gender difference, and on the other, the role played by fathers (and generally by men as a group) and the irrelevance of mothers.

While the physical birth was brought about by the mother, assisted by women as a group, the social birth was often performed by the father, sometimes accompanied by other male figures: the father celebrated the ritual, brought the newborn to the synagogue (in the Jewish religion) or attended the celebration officiated in church by a priest (in the Christian religion). The mother's absence emphasised the difference between the two births, physical and social, and the different role played in them by the two parents.

As for the sex of newborns, it always determined significant variations, more or less marked depending on the religion, but always aimed at highlighting hierarchies. The greater importance of the birth of a boy was expressed either by a clear differentiation (as in the Jewish religion), with a distinction in timing and gestures (as in ancient Greek and Roman societies), or with certain details in the traditional rituals (such as in christening processions in the Christian religion).

The midwife – as we have seen – acted as mediator between the former and the latter: she witnessed the physical birth, delivered newborns to their father and went with them and their father to their christening. She therefore represented continuity and connection between physical and social births and at the same time acted as a link between mother and father.

2 In the ancient world

In the ancient world, the birth ritual expressed, in addition to the family's patrilineal structure, the father's power: he decided whether to accept or reject the newborn and took on a central role in the rite. There were strong elements of continuity between the ancient Greek and Roman worlds: in both, the ritual of purification was celebrated within the family and the father was its priest and magistrate.

In Athens, it consisted of two distinct moments: a private and a public one. Between seven and eight days after a birth, the *Amphidromia* was held, a family ritual celebration to purify the hands of the women who had participated in the birth; the child was carried, run around the hearth and finally laid on the ground. This was the crucial moment of the rite, with a strongly symbolic connotation: he was introduced into the sacred space of *Hestía*, symbol of the house and of civilisation. The father thus broke the baby's bond with his mother, recognising the newborn as his offspring son and naming him. A sacrifice to the gods and gifts from relatives and friends would follow.[2]

The official presentation to the city took place in the public celebration of the *Apatourìa*, which lasted three days, when the baby's introduction to society was carried out with the full definition of the baby's name, a crucial moment of recognition of individual identity and inclusion in the family network in all cultures. In ancient Greece, the name of the male family line was added to the baby's first name: his father's name (the patronymic), the name of his *démos*, his paternal grandfather's name and finally his mother's and her ancestry's.[3]

In Sparta, the ritual took on particular features and contents, as Spartan children did not belong exclusively to their families. The public magistrates known as the Ephors were tasked with welcoming newborns and deciding on their social birth. If a newborn appeared deformed or was judged too weak, his abandonment was decreed and he would be exposed on the slopes of Mount Taygetus; otherwise, the child was returned to his father to be raised until the age of seven, when this task was taken on directly by the State.

The Roman ritual took up many elements of Greek culture, with an emphasis on the decision-making role of the *pater familias*: his *ius vitae necisque* (the right of life and death over family members) was exercised from the moment of birth, in his choice whether to accept or reject the newborn that the midwife laid at his feet on the ground. Some historians have argued that this decision was expressed in the symbolic gesture, carried out directly by the father or by someone else on his orders, to pick the child up and hold it in his arms (*tollere*); on the contrary, leaving the child on the ground signalled his wish he be abandoned.[4] However, this interpretation has been questioned by some research, according to which the verb *tollere* should be understood more metaphorically as "to bring up".[5]

The newborn's sex also affected the date of the public celebration of the *Dies lustricus*, when the purification ritual took place: eight days after the birth of a girl, but nine for a boy. After the ritual bath (*lustratio*) and the invocation of the *Fata*, the baby was named: three names for a boy: *prenomen* (personal name), *nomen* (name of his *gens*) and *cognomen* (identifying his parents' branch of the family); two for a girl: in addition to a personal name, that of her *gens*, in its feminine form. A small gold or leather ball (*bulla*) was placed around the child's neck; the banquet followed.[6] These are the main elements of a celebration of which few details are known, as it was a private ritual. Newborns, who were not recognised by their fathers, were abandoned.

The Jewish ritual (*Brit Milah*) was characterised by its marked gender differentiation and its strong symbolic and religious values. On the eighth day after birth, during daylight hours, baby boys were often taken to the synagogue to be circumcised. According to the Bible, the practice was ordered by God to Abraham as a sign of His covenant with the Jewish people: "This is my covenant, which ye shall keep, between me and you and thy seed after thee. Every man child among you shall be circumcised. And ye shall circumcise the flesh of your foreskin; and it shall be a token of the covenant betwixt me and you" (*Genesis KJV*, 17, 10–11).

The ritual thus expressed the dual content of being a social birth and also of belonging to the Jewish people, reiterated by the explicit exclusion in the event of default: "And the uncircumcised man child whose flesh of his foreskin is not circumcised, that soul shall be cut off from his people; he hath broken my covenant" (*Genesis KJV*, 17, 14).

In this case, too, as in ancient Greek and Roman rituals, the baby's father officiated the rite when the child would be named, but an expert replacement could however be delegated: the *Mohel*. The rite was divided into three acts: the *Milah*, that is the cutting of the foreskin itself; the *Periah*, the turning of the underlying mucosa and the *Metzitzah*, the oral suction of the spilled blood. The ceremony, which was attended by relatives and friends, was followed by a ceremonial lunch. Even Jesus, according to the Gospel of Luke, was circumcised on the eighth day after his birth. Males therefore bear the mark of belonging to the Jewish people on their own bodies.

No ritual was planned following the birth of daughters: a private celebration took place (*Zeved Ha Bat*), during which they would be named.

3 In the Christian world

Despite some elements of continuity (purification, naming, celebration), Christianity brought forth a profound rupture in relation to these rituals, at the same time an expression of the new idea of birth (and rebirth) and of the values of religion.

Social birth was sanctioned by the sacrament of baptism, through which the creature (a term that recalls the work of the Creator), conceived and born with the original sin, was purified, received divine grace and became part of the community of believers, that is to say of the Church. The ritual therefore signalled a dual distinction between physical and spiritual births, between the flesh and the spirit, and accomplished at the same time the spiritual and social birth. Whoever was baptised acquired a dual citizenship: both the earthly and the heavenly one.[7]

This representation of baptism as a new birth was underlined in the theological language by metaphors and similarities played on the assimilation of the Church to the mother, who "conceived" and gave life to the new Christian, causing him to be re-born into the new family. Various aspects of the ritual underlined this rebirth, a social replica of the birth from the body of the Church: the baptismal basin recalling the maternal womb, the water recalling the amniotic fluid, where the newborn was immersed, to then be "raised up high" by the priest, who performed gestures similar to the midwife's and father's in the ancient world.[8]

In the early church, this sacrament was reserved for adults, who were administered it after a long process of preparation, called catechumenate, when they were accompanied by two sponsors (*sponsores*), in a community still threatened by persecution. The practice of baptising children (paedobaptism) slowly increased in line with the spread of Christianity and the proliferation of Christian families, from the 5th to the 6th centuries and in a profoundly different context, both politically and theologically, compared to the origins, with the Christian Church becoming the dominant religion after the Edict of Theodosius (380 AD).[9] This was also influenced by the establishment of Saint Augustine's view that the sacrament was essential to achieve spiritual salvation, sanctioned by the Council of Carthage (418 AD). In this perspective, the death of a newborn without the sacrament became a double bereavement, depriving the infant of both earthly and eternal lives. For this reason, from the 7th century onwards, severe sanctions were prescribed in Church Penitentials for parents who allowed a child to die without having him baptised, even though immediate paedobaptism did not become established in the Christian West until the late Middle Ages.[10]

The aspects and features of the rite reflected the fundamental principles of the new religion, whose characters, revolutionary at the time, are even more obvious in a comparison with the ancient world: first of all, the sacredness and respect for life and the substantial equality of each human being before God. All children had full access to baptism, whether they were legitimate or illegitimate, slaves or aristocrats, male or female, healthy or sick: everyone was guaranteed a spiritual rebirth and social acceptance. No longer did the ritual take place in the home, but in the baptistery, which in medieval cities was "the symbolic place of collective belonging" (Prosperi, 2005: 153). It was celebrated by a priest, a central figure in the religious and civil community, the representative on Earth of a God who was the Father of all creatures.

Like all rites of passage, this was also divided into the three phases of separation, liminality and incorporation.[11] The child was taken to the baptistery in a festive procession with friends, relatives and above all godparents (replacing the ancient *sponsores*), who responded in the rite on behalf of the child. The priest welcomed him outside the baptistry door, where exorcisms would be performed; the child was then brought to the baptismal font, where the Apostle's Creed would be said, followed by the anointing and immersion in water, while the priest pronounced the words of the rite ("In the name of the Father, of the Son and of the Holy Spirit"): in Greek, the word baptism itself meant "immersion"; baptism by aspersion began to spread from the 9th century.[12] At the end of the rite, the child would be dressed in a white robe, symbolising the resurrection. The ceremony ended with the imposition of the stole in the shape of the cross, the reading of a passage from the Gospel and the exhortation to godparents about their responsibilities. The ringing of bells finally announced to all the admission of a new Christian to the community.[13]

Mothers clearly had no role, nor did they participate in the rite, as they were considered impure[14]; fathers attended the ceremony, but as spectators; parents were joined (and symbolically replaced) by new spiritual fathers and mothers: godfathers and godmothers ("*compare* and *comare*") who undertook to be guarantors of the children's spiritual growth (Figure 5.1).[15]

Starting from the 7th century, several synods expressly forbade parents to act as godparents to their children (Council of Mainz, 813 AD).[16]

The father's role, which had been so central in the ancient world, was greatly reduced, replaced on the one hand by the priest celebrating the rite, and on the other by godfather and godmother.

During the 13th century, even the choice of name, the relevance of which we have already stressed, was transferred to the Church, through a dispute with families which usually preferred the names of their relatives, to underline family continuity and belonging. The outcome of this conflict was a mediation that saw the name of a saint, often the one remembered on the day of the baptism, imposed by the Church, joining the name chosen by the parents.[17]

The name of the child was immediately entered in the register of baptisms, kept at the church, as the Council of Trent had sanctioned. These new elements codifying the rite marked an important turning point in giving the clergy control of the rites of passage in human life, starting precisely with birth, and further accentuated the fracture between physical and social births, setting out spiritual and natural parenting, spiritual and natural kinship in opposition; the relevance of the spiritual elements was reiterated by obligations, prohibitions and duties, which underlined the symbolic significance of the spiritual relationship.[18]

According to ecclesiastical rules, there could only be one godparent, either male or female, as the Council of Metz (893 AD) had decreed ("one [is] God, one is baptism, one the person who receives it from the font, [one] must be the [spiritual] father or mother of the child") (Alfani 2006: 45), but the presence of a godmother, with other people as well, is attested as early as the 8th century. In fact, in the various social contexts, there was a varyingly extensive proliferation in the number of godparents, a kind of multiple godparenthood, particularly in

FIGURE 5.1 Pietro Longhi, *The Baptism* (1745), oil painting. In the background, a female figure is hiding; many critics think this is the mother, who could not attend the baptism because she was considered impure. Reproduced with permission of the Querini Stampalia Foundation of Venice.

Central and Southern Europe, despite the Church's numerous but vain attempts to curb it: in some regions and social classes, the number could reach several dozens, and even a hundred as in 15th–16th-century Venice.[19] In fact, spiritual kinship was significant from the social point of view: it was the basis of relationship networks, of client relationships and of paternalistic links between different social classes (noble godparents would attend the baptism of poor children and vice versa).

As a further break with the ancient world, the presence of women in the social birth rite, both as godmothers and midwives, needs to be highlighted. Their admission to the sacrament not only as companions, but also as spiritual mothers, represented an enhancement of the female gender, which would perhaps deserve a more careful assessment. Women were thus admitted to the sacred sphere and – as spiritual mothers – participated in the sacrament; at the same time, because of the double meaning of spiritual and social birth, they were invested with a significant social role in the community, of guarantors of a child's spiritual growth. The fact that their numbers were lower compared to males, and that in some contexts they were either rarer or absent altogether, does not reduce the symbolic meaning of this, especially since in other areas, they held greater value than godfathers: it was believed that only a godmother could give birth to a Christian.[20]

A female presence next to the male one finally prevailed after the Council of Trent, with the establishment of the binary model (only two godparents, usually one male and one female.

As for the midwife, she acted as a mediating figure between the physical and the social-spiritual births, accompanying the child to the holy font and the cleansing of his soul, after being the first to cleanse his body. In many contexts, she would be the one carrying him in her arms to the church, or playing an important role in the baptism procession. Her function as mediation between the first and second births was symbolically reiterated by the objects she held in her hands during the procession: a vase or a jug, symbols of purification.[21]

In many contexts, such as in various Italian regions, midwives also took on the role of spiritual mothers, becoming godmothers, as shown by some research on the baptism registers from the second half of the 16th century, for example in Venice, where they were registered with the double name of *"comadre-comare"* (co-mother – godmother).[22] On the other hand, the very name used in some regions to identify midwives, *"comare"*, was revealing of a symbolic closeness between godmother and midwife which was strongly felt by the communities. The combination of the two roles made the midwife the godmother and *comare* par excellence, the "mystical mother" of the whole country.

Alongside this, it should also be remembered that she was given the important responsibility of administering baptism "conditionally", in the event of the baby's life being in danger during childbirth: various synods required it, such as the Council of Trier, especially from the 12th century onwards, when real anxiety about death without baptism became increasingly common[23]; this task emphasised the importance of her figure, with the recognition of a responsibility that "in essence is a Priestly faculty", as the priest Girolamo Baruffaldi, author of an instruction manual on the administration of baptism, remarked in the 18th century.[24] If the child survived, he had to be taken to church to complete the ceremony; otherwise, he was at least ensured eternal life.

4 Baptism between the Reformation and the Counter-Reformation

During the 16th century, baptism was at the centre of a profound theological and dogmatic reworking, within the rift between the Protestant and the Catholic religions: the different meaning attributed to grace, and the substantially negative view of the effects of the original sin that Luther had taken from Saint Augustine, made it one of the central elements of differentiation between the Church of Rome and the Protestant ones, which were divided not only on the concrete aspects of the ritual, or on the subject of the baptism of newborns, but on the value to be attributed to the sacrament itself.

In general, we can say that this divergence led the Protestant religion to stress its character as birth within the Christian community, while the Catholic religion confirmed, in addition to this, its power of salvation, as A. Prosperi pointed out.[25]

Luther, intervening several times on the subject, starting with the publication of *A sermon on the holy and most venerable sacrament of Baptism* (1520) recognised baptism as a sacrament and kept it, but giving it the meaning of a child's entrance into the community of believers, rather than of a resolutive event for the purposes of salvation. For Calvin, the rite had the value of a commitment that the family and the community made towards a newborn. The Anabaptists, on the contrary, denied the validity of the baptism of children and accepted only that of adults. Such views had significant implications for the ideas of salvation and of the fate of the souls of children who died without baptism: with predestination, the administration of the sacrament was not the exclusive gateway to eternal life.

The ritual was also modified by Luther, with a simplification that reduced exorcisms and prayers, while the spiritual kinship became less important. Similar provisions were also established by the Church of England with the *Book of Common Prayer* (1549).[26]

As regards the choice of name, the abolition of the cult of saints implied the abandonment of the imposition of the name of the saint celebrated on the day of baptism and the increased use of names taken from the Bible: it was a significant change that showed the religious affiliation even in people's names.

The Council of Trent reiterated the crucial value of the sacrament of baptism for the purpose of erasing the original sin, reaffirming its efficacy in the transmission of grace and therefore eternal salvation (decree of 17 June 1546). The ritual was more rigorously codified through a series of detailed norms aimed not only at fighting abuses, but also at disciplining behaviours that by then had become indications of belonging to the Church of Rome. The practice became one of the crucial points of the Church's theological and dogmatic counteroffensive. The rules, established by Pope Paul V in the *Rituale Romanum* (1614), reiterated the fundamental principles of the sacrament: the duty to baptise early, to keep baptismal records, the importance of spiritual parenting (even with the reduced number of godparents), as well as aspects in the ritual that had been codified over the centuries.[27] The outcome was, for parents, the explicit prohibition to delay the ceremony, to baptise at home (except when newborns were at risk of dying), to celebrate the ceremony with pomp, and, for parish priests, the duty to monitor compliance with the rules and to instruct midwives.

The timing of baptism, left rather vague in the Council's indications (*quam primum*, "as soon as possible"), materialised in the norms issued by various Catholic

Synods which fixed it, in a diversified but strict manner, in the time between the day of birth itself (Autumn 1712) up to the following eight days (Sens 1658)[28]; with an average, in practice, of two to three days after birth[29]; in some Italian regions, this timing lasted up to the first half of the 19th century.[30]

The speed with which these norms spread in the social reality testifies as to the determination of the Church of Rome's commitment to their application, establishing instruments of control and monitoring on the territory (from pastoral visits to diocesan synods), combined with strict sanctions: repressive tools alongside educational tools, aimed at training godparents and midwives.[31] At the same time, however, this also highlighted to what extent the population, especially in Catholic countries, had internalised fears and anxieties about the fate of children who died without baptism.[32] The fear of eternal death, in a context marked by high infant mortality, ended up being even stronger than the fear of physical death, which was considered a likely occurrence, as documented by the high number of "conditional baptisms" administered, as reported in the parish registers: 1 out of 15, according to surveys conducted by Laget about some French parishes in the Hérault (Languedoc-Roussillon region) between 1700 and 1750[33]; 1 out of 20 in 1786, according to research I carried out in a Venetian parish.[34]

The combination of these aspects related to doctrine, ritual and identity, and the symbolic value taken on by the practice produced a profound differentiation in the European religious landscape, which would deepen in the following years, to the extent that a kind of baptism fury developed in Catholic countries and even further afield, among the indigenous populations in the New World (with mass baptisms of adults and children). It even extended to abortions (as we shall see in Chapter 10) and to the Jews (with forced baptisms often practised by lay people).[35]

5 The dual death and the construction of Limbo

In the Christian world, a dual birth was mirrored by a dual death, of the body and of the spirit, with the deprivation of eternal life. Newborns who died without baptism tragically experienced them both, even though they had not committed any sins, precisely because of the original sin: not having gone through the second birth, they could not be part of the community of believers and could not access that of the blessed, the Kingdom of Heaven, not even on the day of the Last Judgment. This view, strongly supported by Saint Augustine in the *Enchiridion*, gained more ground in the following centuries, until it was sanctioned by the Church.

Such exclusion from the Kingdom of Heaven was symbolically reiterated by forbidding burials in consecrated ground, places where the bodies of the believers were waiting for the Day of Judgment, when the souls would resume their original bodies: "If he was found dead and could not be baptised, he should not be buried in a sacred place", the *Rituale Romanum* ordered ('De baptizandis parvulis') ([1614] 1740: 7).

The construction of Limbo as a place in its own right, even within the Underworld, occurred during the 12th century, within the theological elaboration of the celestial landscape which expanded the intermediate places, primarily Purgatory; this points to a society undergoing a profound transformation and expressing the need to rethink the forms of divine justice less as dichotomies.[36] Limbo was imagined precisely as a place where all the souls who had not committed any sins but were still marked by the original sin could be located, either because they had been born before Jesus' coming (such as the righteous men from ancient times, or the patriarchs), or because they had died without being baptised, such as newborn babies (*Limbus puerorum*).[37] This place therefore included various sections, such as the Limbo of children and that of the patriarchs, for example, but its location in the Underworld remained uncertain. In his *Divine Comedy*, Dante located it in the first circle of Hell, where Virgil himself dwelled. Others, such as Saint Thomas Aquinas, located the Limbo of children under that of the patriarchs and above Purgatory. It should be noted, however, that its existence was never sanctioned by dogma and in the landscape of the Underworld remained the least defined place.

Even more open was the discussion about the punishment infants would receive. Saint Augustine, in confirming their damnation, underlined its lightness, speaking of an "extremely light sentence". This view was later taken up by many theologians, especially in the 13th century: they extended the distinction between the original and personal sins, linking it to the difference between physical torment and torment of the soul, reserved for infants. The Council of Trent addressed the question, decreeing: "For, unless a man be born again of water and the Holy Ghost, he cannot enter into the kingdom of God" (session V. 4).[38]

However, the controversy over Limbo and over punishment was rekindled in the 18th century, within a contrast between different theological stances, but in 1794, Pope Pius VI reiterated the existence of the Limbo of children as part of the netherworld. Only in 1912, however, did Pope Pius X place it in a separate location, stating that children who died without being baptised went to Limbo, where there is neither reward nor punishment: as they were marked by the original sin, they did not deserve Paradise, but neither did they deserve Hell or Purgatory.

It took until contemporary times, 19 April 2007, to finally see Limbo reduced to a mere theological hypothesis: a document drawn up by an International Theological Commission (*The hope of salvation for infants who die without being baptised*) and approved by Pope Benedict XVI expressed, on the basis of "serious theological and liturgical bases", the "hope that children who have died without being baptised will be saved and enjoy the beatific vision".[39]

6 Rituals which replaced baptism

In the Christian West, the fate of children who died without being baptised therefore appeared very tragic from many points of view: in an attempt to combine justice and rigour, the theory of the original sin and the importance of grace, the Church ended up denying salvation to the very creatures who had not yet begun their lives and had not committed any sin, while granting it, for example, to repentant murderers or the so-called "savages" of the New World. Locked in Limbo for eternity, without even being named, from the 12th century, they were buried outside cemeteries. About their fate, a very long-standing popular tradition imagined them suffering from an everlasting and ominous restlessness, similarly to other souls, such as suicides. Their tormented spirits would wander around the places where they were born, in search of water as they were perpetually thirsty, to underline their initial deprivation of the sacred source.[40] According to a belief attested since the 15th century, they were part of that "raging army" who enjoyed tormenting the living with night-time ambushes. To fight off these negative forces, in the Middle Ages, the corpses of newborns who had died without baptism would be impaled.[41]

Against this backdrop, combining the exclusion from Paradise, the absence of a sacred burial and eternal restlessness, it is not surprising that the death of an unbaptised newborn was considered the most tragic of possibilities, affecting not only the parents, but also the community as a whole.[42] Furthermore, this loss was often associated with sins and divine punishment.

The testimonies collected in the archives attest to these feelings and to the fear felt by women in labour that the child might die before being born and baptised even 'conditionally'.[43] How could this tragic fate be avoided? How could they be brought back into the Christian community, granting them eternal salvation at least? During the Middle Ages and the early modern age, popular piety had come up with multiple "corrective rituals", aimed at evading the rigour of a norm that was unacceptable in its harshness.[44]

In Mediterranean countries, these rituals often meant baptising the child whilst still in the womb by baptising the mother's body, by virtue of the intimate connection between the two bodies. In Portugal, this was called *bautismo anticipado*. Elsewhere, people believed that the foetus could be purified by its own mother, by taking Communion: according to some theologians, in fact, children could be saved by their parents' intentions. The so-called "baptism for the dead" (*baptismo pro mortuis* or *super mortuos*) was much older and had been practised on both children and adults since the early days of Christianity. It meant baptising a dead person, while a living person "answered" for him. Although it was condemned by the Third Council of Carthage (397 AD), it continued to be practised for centuries.[45]

But the most widespread ritual in Central and Northern Europe (from the Alps to the English Channel) was the "temporary resurrection".[46] People believed that, thanks to a miracle, a dead child could come back to life for the short time necessary to be baptised. In the late Middle Ages, this belief was consolidated by the building of real sanctuaries, generally dedicated to the Virgin Mary and called in France sanctuaries à *répit* (i.e. of the sigh), devoted to this practice. The bodies of dead babies would be taken there, often by theirs fathers and the midwives, after journeys lasting several days and connotated as atonement pilgrimages. Having placed the dead babies on the altar, in the heat of the candles, the people would wait for the bodies to

show some signs of life (loss of fluids or blood, sighs, etc.), before proceeding to baptise and bury them in consecrated ground, thus giving the children a name, a worthy burial and, above all, the guarantee of eternal life.

The popularity of these rituals, already attested in the 12th century, reached its peak after the Council of Florence (1438–1439) and especially after the Council of Trent (1545–1563). To have an idea of the size of the phenomenon, we can simply look at the figures provided by J. Gélis: in France alone, the sanctuaries *à répit* he catalogued were as many as 279 and in a single sanctuary (in Ursberg, near Augusta, in Bavaria), over 34 years (1686–1720), there were 24,000 cases of temporary resurrection.[47]

The Church charged its bishops with regulating this practice, even though many synods between the 15th and 16th centuries declared it illegal. The Reformation sharply criticised this ritual and tried to remove it, not always successfully.

During the Counter-Reformation, the Church continued to tolerate it, using the miraculous event as an instrument of pastoral care. Only from the 18th century, in a context characterised by greater rigour, there was a decisive turnaround: various pronouncements by the Holy Office forbade resorting to the *répit*, right up to its definitive condemnation by Pope Benedict XIV (*De Synodo Diocesana*, 2nd edition, 1755). However, just like other replacement rituals, it continued to be practised in secret right up to the issue of the Napoleonic and other similar European civil codes of law: the new norms on burials, with their compulsory medical certification of death, caused this ritual to disappear forever, erasing from the social and spiritual landscapes the extraordinary recurrence of the "miraculous" resurrections of stillborn children.[48]

7 Post-mortem Caesarean sections

In the medieval landscape, characterised by the importance of baptism and by the spread of sacrament-related anxiety (but also by the emergence of dissections in medical practice), the practice of post-mortem Caesarean section, carried after the death of the woman, emerged and developed. Its previous history is inscribed in myth and legend: it was part of the "extraordinary births" of gods and heroes who, when being born, shunned the natural ways of men.[49] Thus, in the Greek myth, were born Dionysus and Adonis, whereas the god of medicine, Asclepius, was extracted from his mother's belly by his father, Apollo.[50] When, in the Middle Ages, the figure of Julius Caesar took on mythical traits, even the great Roman general was said to have been born in this way, as a sign of distinction, as can be seen from many miniatures; in fact, Isidore of Seville, interpreting a passage by Pliny the Elder, even linked the etymology of the general's name to it: "Caesar ab utero caeso" ("from the cut womb").[51] In the Roman world, there was apparently a law attributed to Numa Pompilius (8th–7th centuries BC), the

Lex Regia, which forbade the burial of a pregnant woman before the foetus was extracted; it was reported by the Digest, in Justinian's *Corpus iuris civilis* (533 AD). But none of the doctors who dealt with obstetrics (Soranus of Ephesus, Galen, Celsus) described this intervention (nor is there any trace of it in Hippocrates' writings) and the research conducted so far has not found any evidence of its application, to the extent that several scholars have suggested that it was an invention by the same Justinian, aimed at legitimising an intervention that Christianity intended to promote. As for Julius Caesar, it is certain that his mother died during his campaign in Gaul; therefore, she definitely could not have died when giving birth to him.[52]

The operation was first promoted by theologians in the late Middle Ages, with the aim of saving the soul of a child who had not managed to be born due to his mother's death before or during labour: "If, however, the mother die while the child lives yet in her womb, she should be opened that the child may be baptized" (*Summa*, III, 68, 11), wrote Saint Thomas Aquinas in the *Summa Theologiae*, forbidding at the same time the carrying out of Caesarean sections on living women (see Chapter 3.5).

Various Councils, between the 13th and 14th centuries, imposed the obligation of post-mortem Caesareans: they took place in Canterbury (1236), Cologne (1280), Ravenna (1311) and Langres (1404), in parallel with the establishment of dissections.[53] In some cases, the method of execution was also indicated, with the recommendation to keep the dead mother's mouth open to allow the child to breathe[54] and midwives were ordered to carry out this operation, and in fact it is documented as having taken place in the 16th century.[55]

Various civil legislations also resumed this rule, as a duty imposed first on midwives, then on surgeons, but in actual fact, there are still considerable doubts on the application of these rules and on the actual practice in the Middle Ages. The Council of Trent definitively sanctioned it throughout the Catholic world: the *Rituale Romanum* (1614) established that a Caesarean section should be performed immediately after the death of the woman in order to extract the child and baptise him: "If a pregnant woman is dead, the foetus shall be taken from her as soon as possible with great care and, if alive, shall be baptized" (*Rituale Romanum* [1614] 1740: 7).[56]

Despite this, the operation was rarely carried out, both for cultural and medical reasons. In the first place, it was considered almost impossible, in the light of medical beliefs, for a child to be extracted alive from his mother's body. Thus, the indispensable condition for the administration of baptism was missing ("*si vivus fuerit*"). Secondly, the chance these children might survive was considered so unlikely that their name was accompanied by the definition "*nonnati*" (not born), a term that reaffirmed both the anomaly of a birth that took place outside the order of nature and the miraculous nature of their survival. This was the nickname given to Saint Raymond of Peñafort (1175–1275), patron saint of women in labour, Saint Paul of Merida and the legendary Scottish hero Macduff, in Shakespeare's Macbeth, who is described as "none of woman born".

A birth presumed being born of one's mother, that is to say a baby being "pushed into the light by nature", as priest Girolamo Baruffaldi wrote in the mid-18th century in an instruction manual for midwives on how to baptise: *La mammana istruita per validamente amministrare il Santo Sacramento del battesimo* (The instructed midwife to validly administer the Holy Sacrament of baptism).[57]

For these reasons, midwives and doctors preferred to resort to other devices to ensure that a child was baptised during labour: if there was a risk the mother might die, they used empirical tools (sponges, syringes, pumps) to try and reach the unborn baby and baptise him "conditionally". François Mauriceau in his *Traité des maladies des femmes grosses* describes these baptisms in detail, referring to the use of special syringes, one of which is even included in his obstetric instruments table.[58]

It must be said, however, that the validity of this baptism was considered dubious by various theologians, both for material and conceptual reasons: because it was not possible to check whether the child was still alive; because the baby has not formally been "born" into the light (and birth was an essential condition for rebirth); finally because it was not possible to ascertain the human nature of what was being born: as we have said, it could be a monster or worse still a mole.

Notes

1. van Gennep [1909] (2019).
2. Bruit Zaidman (1992); Gourevitch, Morini and Rouquet (2003); Fanos, Atzei and Corridori (2010).
3. Mitterauer (1993).
4. Fanos and Corridori (2010: 82–87).
5. Köves-Zulauf (1990); Corbier (1999).
6. Curatolo (1901: 73); Gourevitch and Raepsaet-Charlier (2001: 118).
7. Prosperi (2005: 150–174, 2006).
8. Laget (1982: 311–312); Fine (1994).
9. Corblet (1881–1882); Alfani, Castagnetti and Gourdon (2009); Lett (1998).
10. Lett (1998: 205).
11. van Gennep ([1909] 2019).
12. Gélis (1984a: 531).
13. Laget (1982: 307–320); Pancino (2010: 423–430).
14. Only the reform introduced by the Second Vatican Council, with the codification of the Rite of children's baptism (applied as from 1970), recommended the mother's presence during the administration of the sacrament, thus contributing to lengthening the period of time between birth and baptism.
15. Fine (1994); Alfani (2006); Alfani, Gourdon and Robin (2015).
16. Alfani (2006).
17. Mitterauer (1993).
18. Prosperi (2005: 150–174, 2006).
19. Molmenti (1928, II: 336–338); Chauvard (2012).
20. Palumbo (1991).
21. Gélis (1984a: 521–536).
22. Chauvard (2012: 181–196).
23. Shorter (1982: 41); Lett (1998: 208).
24. Baruffaldi (1746: XIII).
25. Prosperi (2005: 188–189).

26 Villani (2006: 551–571).
27 *Rituale Romanum* [1614] (1740: 7–8, 'De Baptizandis Parvulis').
28 Gélis (1984a: 521–522).
29 Pancino (2015: 358).
30 Munno (2015: 438).
31 Caffiero (2004).
32 Filippini (1993: 58).
33 Laget (1982: 284–288). For a comparison, a century later: Gourdon, Georges and Labéjof (2004).
34 Filippini (1993: 173, note 45).
35 Caffiero (2004).
36 Le Goff (1984).
37 Corblet (1881–1882); Lett (1998: 215–220) and (1997: 81–83); Franceschini (2017).
38 The Council of Trent, *The canons and decrees of the sacred and oecumenical Council of Trent*, ed. and trans. by J. Waterworth, London: Dolman, 1848: 23. Taken from the online version https://history.hanover.edu/texts/trent/ct05.html. See Filippini (1995: 64–70).
39 International Theological Commission, *The hope of salvation for infants who die without being baptised*. Taken from the online version: www.vatican.va/roman_curia/congregations/cfaith/cti_documents/rc_con_cfaith_doc_20070419_un-baptised-infants_en.html.
40 Schmitt (1994); Lett (1998: 215–216).
41 Foscati (2014: 329).
42 Flandrin (1973); Julia (1996: 236).
43 Filippini (1993: 158); Foscati (2014: 329).
44 Seidel Menchi (2000: 139–158); Cavazza (1982: 551–582).
45 Gélis (2006: 305–323).
46 Fornasa (2018). This recent research has further extended the area in Italy where this ritual took place to the hills around Vicenza, so beyond the Alps, previously considered the southern limit.
47 Gélis (2006: 195).
48 Gourdon and Sage Pranchère (2018: 41–64).
49 Bernheim (2010: 42–43); Filippini (1995: ch. 1.1).
50 Crainz (1986).
51 Blumenfeld-Kosinski (1990: 48–90); Bettini (2015: 119–144).
52 As pointed out by Gourevitch (2004: 244–245).
53 Pundel (1969); Blumenfeld-Kosinski (1990); Baskett (2017).
54 Foscati (2019).
55 Niccoli (2005: 154).
56 Filippini (2010: 151).
57 Baruffaldi (1746).
58 Mauriceau ([1668] 1681: 354); Fazzari (2013: 671–677).

6
THE MIDWIFE

1 Features and skills

Let us take a closer look at this figure, who played a central role in childbirth and birth, both in the ancient world and in the Christian West.

Some essential traits of her social and professional profile were outlined by Plato in the famous passage from the *Theaetetus* in which Socrates assimilates his philosophical method (*maieutics*) to that of his mother Phaenarete, a *maîa*, i.e. a midwife:

> Just take into consideration the whole business of the midwives, and you will understand more easily what I mean. For you know, I suppose, that no one of them attends other women while she is still capable of conceiving and bearing but only those do so who have become too old to bear [..] And furthermore, the midwives, by means of drugs and incantations, are able to arouse the pangs of labor and, if they wish, to make them milder, and to cause those to bear who have difficulty in bearing; and they cause miscarriages if they think them desirable [..] Well, have you noticed this also about them, that they are the most skillful of matchmakers, since they are very wise in knowing what union of man and woman will produce the best possible children?
>
> *(Theae.Fow., 149b, c, d)*

A midwife was first and foremost a *gennaìa* (noble) woman, i.e. respected and valued by her community, with direct experience of motherhood from being a mother herself, already advanced in years, who knew about sexuality as well as childbirth, and was also a clever matchmaker. Thanks to her skills, she could help a woman give birth, by bringing on her labour pains or by lessening their intensity with the help of drugs and spells; she was also able to procure abortions.[1]

These basic traits characterised this figure in the long run, especially from the late Middle Ages to the 18th century, beyond the significant differences affecting it in different times and contexts. Both in the cities and in the countryside, midwives were generally mature women, married or widowed, although there were examples of unmarried midwives since the ancient world.[2] A direct experience of motherhood was believed to be the first and fundamental requirement of a competence that had its roots not only in the acquisition of knowledge and practices, but in personal experience. Soranus attested to this precisely as he criticised it (*Gyn.* I, 4), as did later sources. Scipione Mercurio, in the 16th century, wrote that a midwife was "almost like a mother" (Mercurio [1596] 1713: 77) both because of her age, and because, as a mother, she advised, comforted and helped. In France, she was referred to as *bonne mère* (lit. 'good mother') (Figure 6.1).[3]

FIGURE 6.1 The midwife ("counsellor"), from Jakob Rueff (1587), *De conceptu et generatione hominis*, Francofurti ad Moenum: P. Fabricium: c 17r. Reproduced with permission of the Biblioteca Pinali antica (Padua).

The story of Agnodice, the mythical figure of a Greek young woman who had dressed up as a boy so as to be admitted to Herophilus' school, become a doctor and assist women in childbirth, thus safeguarding their privacy, has no historical foundation: it is a legend which in the course of history has been variously interpreted.[4]

Being advanced in years made midwives freer from the domestic tasks of caring for their children, for a profession that required availability at any time and freedom of movement; it also allowed them to move about more freely without compromising their honour. The Registers of Midwives, held in some European cities from the 16th to the 17th centuries onwards, confirms their status as married or widowed, their advanced average age and long professional experience. In the Italian countryside, as various surveys have confirmed, in the 18th century, midwives were "all women of advanced age, seeming to them [to the population] that the greatest skill is derived from their age" (Parma 1981: 117).

Their art was often handed down within their families, from mother to daughter or granddaughter; their husbands also frequently practised a medical profession, as surgeons or apothecaries, according to the sharing of crafts that characterised artisan families in Europe.[5] Louise Bourgeois, French midwife to Queen Maria de' Medici, was the wife of a military surgeon who had trained with Ambroise Paré,[6] as were the Dutch Catharina Schrader, active at the turn of the 17th and 18th centuries,[7] and the English Elizabeth Nihell, author of the *Treatise on the Art of Midwifery* (1760).[8] Louise Bourgeois' daughter followed in her mother's footsteps. Angélique Marguerite Le Boursier du Coudray also came from a well-known family of doctors (or surgeons) and her son-in-law worked with her.[9] Even in Italy, this family tradition is widely attested by the pleas presented to the health courts, especially during the 18th century (generally to ask for exemptions from the current regulations), where many midwives declared that they had been "instructed in this profession by their aforementioned mother" many years before (Filippini 1993: 155).

Like all crafts, midwifery required a long apprenticeship, which took place by accompanying a midwife in her work: the sources often report the presence of other helpers and assistants working with midwives. Soranus himself suggested that a team of women, with different functions, should attend childbirths (*Gyn.* II, 5). These helpers were generally more concerned with the mother than with the child: they supported her, fed her, comforted her before and after childbirth and helped the midwife with preparing a bath and with swaddling the baby. In the ancient world, these women were called *huperétides* or *adsestrices* (or *assestrices*) or *ministrae*.[10] In late-medieval Florence, they were called *guardadonne* (women-watchers), precisely because they dealt specifically with the mothers, while midwives concentrated on the babies.[11]

A midwife's area of expertise was not limited to assistance with pregnancy and childbirth. Plato attested to a wider knowledge in the field of sexuality which has been confirmed in various contexts even in medieval and early modern times. The ecclesiastical and civil authorities resorted to midwives, for example, to ascertain a woman's virginity: it should be remembered that, by order of the Inquisition, Joan of Arc was examined by two midwives during her trial, both in Poitiers and in Rouen.[12] In some countries, such as Italy, France and Germany, in early modern times, they were called upon in trials for "rape" or "deflowering with promise of marriage" (i.e. to ascertain a girl's virginity), or to verify the woman's physical inability for sexual intercourse, or to establish the causes of newborns' death when suffocation was suspected.[13] Midwives were also consulted, especially by people from the lower classes, about issues to do with the menstrual cycle and with breastfeeding and in cases of sterility.[14]

Assistance during childbirth, however, was the core activity of an art that centred on great manual dexterity: the main tools of the job were in fact their hands, which midwives used to recognise, during their examinations, the state of pregnancy or the beginning of labour, the level of dilation of the cervix and a child's presentation; they could rub and press when needed, dilate and pull, gently stimulate or act with energy depending on the case: a knowledge of what to do without seeing that reached the highest level of skill when the internal manual versions practised in cases of "unnatural" presentations needed to be carried out. This is why Soranus recommended that midwives have "long and slim fingers", "short nails" and "soft" hands (*Gyn*. I, 3).[15]

An important aid used by midwives was the birthing chair, as we have seen (Chapter 3.3). Used in cities since ancient times and very popular in early modern European cities, it almost became a symbol of the profession, so much so that in Venice, in 1624, the *Magistrato alla sanità* (Magistrate for Health), in an attempt to oppose the abusive practising of the profession, issued a circular which forbade women who were not licenced to practise from "bringing in or leaving such chairs in the houses" (Filippini 1993: 155) (Figure 6.2).

Midwives asked women to sit on it and would sit in front of them but a little lower down in order to examine them, manually dilate their cervix and pull the child during the final stage of childbirth, taking care not to look at women in the face, as obstetrics manuals recommended, so as not to offend their modesty, as shown in the bas-relief of the tomb of Scribonia Attice (140 AD).[16] From this position, the Latin word *obstetrix*, meaning "the one placed in front" (from *ob* + *stare* = to be placed in front), is derived, and from which the name given to midwives in Italy in the 19th century (*ostetrica*) is, in turn, also derived.

In cases of malpresentations, as we have said, they resorted to internal versions, with the woman lying on a bed: it is no coincidence that German historian Sibylla Flügge has highlighted these manoeuvres almost as a symbol of their skills.[17] In extreme situations, the use of rudimentary instruments, such as hooks and knives to carry out embryotomies, is attested in many contexts, as we have said (Chapter 3.5), even after the late Middle Ages, when this skill had been entrusted by the rules to the guilds of barber-surgeons.[18]

It was a difficult and heavy job, which required strength: "for she takes a double task upon herself during the hardship of her professional visits", as Soranus pointed out (*Gyn,* I, 4),[19] because labour could last many hours;

FIGURE 6.2 A midwife with her servant carrying a birthing chair, from Giovanni Grevembroch [1754] (1981, vol. III, p. 55). Reproduced with permission of the Ministero dei Beni e delle Attività Culturali e del Turismo - Biblioteca Nazionale Marciana (Venice).

courage and a cool head, because childbirth could present sudden difficulties; calm and optimism, to encourage the woman in labour not to lose heart. In the 16th century, Mercurio Scipione wrote: "a midwife should be affable, cheerful, graceful, jokey, brave, she should always cheer pregnant women up by promising they will give birth to a boy safely and without feeling much pain" (Mercurio [1596] 1713: 79).

Evidence of how hard their work was is also contained in medical sources. The founder of occupational medicine, Bernardino Ramazzini, in *De morbis artificum* (The Diseases of Workers) (1700) wrote in chapter 19 (Diseases of Midwiwes): "they exhaust themselves to such an extent (in particular when assisting the wives of the wealthy and when labour is particularly difficult) that, when it is over, they return home exhausted and worn out, cursing their profession" (Ramazzini [1700] 2009: 146).

Discretion and reserve were also required, because by entering people's homes, they learned private secrets they were not to divulge; and charity, because they had to assist not only rich women, but also poor ones, and be prepared to lend their assistance sometimes even for free.

To these attributes, Christian society added that a midwife had to be "pious and devout"; in other words, a believer and of good morals, precisely because she was responsible for the spiritual salvation of newborns, if there was a risk that they might die during or shortly after birth. This is the reason why Jewish midwives were forbidden to attend Christian women in childbirth, just as Christian women were forbidden to assist Jewish women in labour, except in cases of extreme urgency.[20]

It must be said that it was a job that granted recognition and an important social role, in the countryside as in cities: midwives were valued and respected by their communities. Some of the words from European languages used to identify them in the early modern age allude to this prestige, which placed them in an important social position. In English and French, the recurring terms were *wise woman* and *sage-femme* (wise woman), *bonne mère* or *matrone*, similar to the Spanish *madrona*; these terms indicated respect and set them apart, making them so special that in certain contexts, such as Spain, their husbands, rather than with their own names, were identified as "the husband of the *madrona*", a rare event in the history of women.[21]

In Italian, in addition to *mammana*, the term *comare levatrice* (godmother midwife) was used, because in many places, as we have seen, a midwife was traditionally chosen as a godmother, taking on a role that reiterated the importance attributed to her position. In other cases, the words used alluded to crucial functions in their profession: the terms *raccoglitrice* (gatherer) and *levatrice* (raiser) (used in Italy) highlighted two symbolic moments in her role: that of gathering the child and of raising him to the sky; *levatrice* comes from *levare*, to raise, as in German *Hebamme* (from *heben* = to lift).

2 The "midwife-witch"

As we have seen, according to Plato, midwives were able to help women not only to give birth, but also to abort, and used both medical practices and spells, dealing also with sexuality.

That midwives knew how to induce abortions with potions (*pharmakia*) is evidenced by the sources: Soranus indicated methods and procedures that also recurred in other texts (*Gyn.* I, 60–61). On the other hand, it is important to remember that abortion was not forbidden in the ancient world. As for spells, we have no direct evidence, but it is very likely that they were practised, because medicine and magic did not belong to separate spheres, and the art of healing made use of many magical tricks with a long tradition: formulas, rituals and amulets, as we have seen. In *De morbis muliebribus* (1587), Girolamo Mercuriale wrote that women performed *incantamenta* (spells),[22] and Giovanni Marinello reported examples of magical rites performed by them in his book.[23]

For all of these features, midwives appeared to the male gaze as ambiguous figures, participating in the sphere of life, but also in that of death, possessed of ambivalent powers, able to be very respectable, but also potentially dangerous. There are not many ancient authors accusing them of deceit and wickedness, ranging from the exchange of newborns (mentioned by Aristophanes) to the dismemberment of aborted foetuses and to the use of menstrual blood to make potions and spells (*piacula*). Many accused them of practising witchcraft, such as Pliny, who used contemptuous words against them (*Nat. H.*, XXVIII, 70).

Midwives therefore in many respects might appear similar to witches. This is an important element to underline, which links the ancient world to the medieval and early modern ones and arises from the suspicion that men felt towards a world of knowledge and practices from which they were excluded, from their fear for an autonomously female sphere of action which, as such, was potentially threatening.[24]

However, it must be emphasised that in the early modern age, this gaze was also shared by some educated midwives, who tried to set themselves apart from the others. Louise Bourgeois, in her *Instructions to my daughter* (her apprentice), stressed the "marvellous importance" of her work, but warned her about the ambivalence of a craft that offered divergent paths: one to save oneself, the other to be damned (Bourgeois [1606] 1992: 176).

3 The control of the Church

The ambivalence that characterised the figure of midwives meant that over time different attitudes to them prevailed, ranging from suspicion, to contempt, to appreciation. In the Christian Middle Ages, the first two prevailed above all: the condemnation of abortion and infanticide, a phobia towards sex and a horror of the female body widespread among the clergy cast a dark shadow over this figure, which came increasingly to coincide with that of the witch, behind whose power the shadow of the devil appeared. Every midwife was considered a potential witch because of the aspects that characterised her profession: being an elderly woman, often alone, aware of the powers of herbs, knowledgeable about female secrets, in contact with the impure bodies of mothers and newborns and also for their proximity to the world of spirits that were thought to hover around births.[25]

In the *Malleus maleficarum* (The Hammer of Witches) (1486), the Dominican inquisitors Krämer (Henricus Institoris) and Jacob Sprenger wrote that nobody harms the Catholic faith more than midwives.[26]

The ancient accusations of exchanging newborns, of trading in placentas, of spells with menstrual blood went hand in hand with the more serious suspicions of carrying out abortions and ritual infanticides with the intention of offering the soul of the child to the devil. With the women tried and tortured for witchcraft, in the sad episode in European history of the witch hunt, there were numerous *obstetrices*, to the extent that in Alsace, the term *exenhebamm* (midwife-witch) had been coined.[27] In 1587, in the German city of Dillingen, a midwife was accused of causing the death of 40 newborns with witchcraft.[28]

The repressive action, which the Church put in place with particular vigour in the 14th and 16th centuries, was fuelled by a true obsession with abortions and infanticides, but it also responded to a more complex set of objectives linking the struggle against the magical practices widespread in the social reality and the attempts to control female sexuality (in particular outside marriage, as we have seen), which could not leave out the figure of the midwife.

This offensive was combined with an educational action, through which the Church aimed to control midwives and make them an instrument in its fight against pagan worship and heresies. The role they played in their communities made them an important pawn in the process to Christianise society, especially after the Protestant Reformation, by virtue of the symbolic significance of different belonging taken on by baptism, "a frontier between warring states", between the Catholic and Protestant religions (Prosperi 2005: 192).

Starting precisely from the fact that midwives were allowed to baptise "conditionally" in the childbirths at risk, in the second half of the 16th century, various episcopal synods, such as the one wanted in Milan by Carlo Borromeo (1580), imposed on parish priests the obligation to instruct midwives in administering the sacrament, also requesting they keep a register of the midwives examined.[29] These directions were codified and extended to the whole of the Catholic world with the *Rituale Romanum*, which regulated the administration of the sacraments in line with the decisions of the Council of Trent. Parish priests had to ascertain the morality and good conduct of each midwife, the absence of any suspicion of witchcraft, their profession of faith and ability to baptise correctly. Their names were entered in the registers of baptisms. Monitoring was carried out by bishops during their periodic pastoral visits, and in fact, in the ample documentation related to them, the attention to the work of the midwives is ubiquitous.[30] In the 17th century, in Rome, these checks were implemented by the Cardinal Vicar.[31]

Access to the profession was thus controlled directly by the parish priests, who in some contexts, especially in country parishes, personally appointed midwives, communicating their names to the faithful.[32] In the cities, where the mobility of the population made control more complex and where civil regulations often existed, this endorsement took place indirectly, through the release of faith certificates, indispensable for practising the profession, and keeping registers of the midwives approved by parish priests, as happened in Venice.[33]

The "political" aspect of the legislation was more obvious in countries with mixed religion, where the Church engaged in a real battle to prevent Protestant midwives from practising the profession, in agreement with the political authority, as happened in France in several instances over the 17th century (ordinances in 1680, 1698 and 1724).[34] It is no coincidence that the first Italian manual of obstetrics addressed to midwives, *La Comare o ricoglitrice*, was written at the end of the 16th century by Scipione Mercurio, a doctor trained in Bologna at Aranzio's school, but also a Dominican friar (Girolamo), attentive to sacramental matters, as reflected in many directions in his book, where midwives are entrusted not only with the physical, but also the spiritual care of women: for example, midwives were instructed to encourage women in labour to confess and take communion before giving birth and "to persuade relatives, that even when the child is well, they must have him immediately baptised by a priest" (Mercurio [1596] 1713: 107).

4 Control and regulation of political institutions

The ecclesiastical institutions were not the only ones to pay special attention to midwives: between the 15th and 16th centuries, although at different times depending on the context, many political institutions also issued regulations aimed at controlling the activity of midwives, defining on the one hand the rules to practise their profession, and on the other the duties and limits of their intervention.

These public initiatives were part of deeper transformation processes that had to do with the consolidation of the city guilds, with the reorganisation of the various health authorities and also with the control over female sexuality that the city authorities were beginning to exercise, in synergy with the ecclesiastical institutions, as we have seen. From this, in a context of greater attention to the health of citizens, arose both the figure of the municipal midwife, chosen and remunerated by the city government, and the first forms of assistance to poor women in labour.

These processes were accompanied by a limitation to the midwives' sphere of competence and by a progressive marginalisation of women in the practice of medicine, according to a tendency that affected all female professions at that time.[35] In the case of midwives, however, this tendency is even more striking, precisely due to the absence of alternative male childbirth professionals, at least until the 18th century. This was an important turning point, which started on the one hand a process of control and professionalisation, but on the other a progressive curbing of competence, with the issue of increasingly restrictive rules that subjected their work to the control of doctors.[36]

The first public rules were issued in some Southern German cities and in Rhineland: in 1452, in Regensburg, a *Hebammenordung* (ordinance on midwives) established that municipal midwives would be chosen by a commission of "honourable" women and that Christian midwives could not attend Jewish women. Another one, in Heilbronn, forbade midwives from performing post-mortem embryotomies or Caesarean sections without first consulting a physician; similarly, a provision issued in Freiburg in 1510 imposed the obligation to consult a doctor in all cases when the child presented in childbirth in an "unnatural" presentation. The Nuremberg regulations established rules related to the apprenticeship and practice of the profession, which only widows and for the first time explicitly even unmarried women were allowed to practise.[37] During the 16th century, similar laws were also passed in other European cities: in Flanders (Bruges 1551), Switzerland (Zurich 1554) and France (Lille and Paris in 1550 and

1560): everywhere, midwives were required to take a public oath before joining the profession.[38]

During the 17th century, the procedures and requirements to access the profession became more complex and the professional hierarchy that subjected midwives to doctors became more marked, with midwives needing their approval to practise the profession, a rule that had already been imposed in Spain much earlier, since the end of the 15th century. In Paris, the 1580 statute and subsequent 1587 ordinance imposed on aspiring midwives a two-year apprenticeship with a practising one, an examination before a medical commission and a public oath, with a restriction of their responsibilities.[39] In 1692, a royal edict, then extended to the whole country, subsequently extended the rules: after a three-year apprenticeship period, they had to take two examinations before a commission of surgeons chaired by a doctor; if they passed, they had to take an oath. Their competence was therefore assessed by doctors, even though this examination must have been a formal one, given that doctors had a purely theoretical knowledge of childbirth.

In the Republic of Venice, the *Capitoli circa il medicare e comporre medicamenti* (Chapters on the treatment and composition of medication) (1603), which reorganised the practice of health care, entrusted the experienced doctors and surgeons with carrying out post-mortem Caesarean sections. A subsequent deliberation (1624) imposed on those who wanted to practise the profession "*d'allevaressa o comare*" (of midwife) the need to take an examination before a medical commission and to be enrolled in a special register, providing penalties for unregistered midwives. Another ruling (1689) recorded a further increase in the pre-requisites to be allowed to take the exam: being able to read, bringing a "sworn confirmation" by their anatomy teacher certifying that they had attended dissections, in addition to a certificate of at least two years' apprenticeship with a registered midwife.[40] In Bologna, from 1686, midwives had to be examined by the College of Physicians (Protomedicato) and take an oath swearing not to give medications or perform bleedings.[41]

The relationship between political and ecclesiastical institutions in the control of midwives was often marked by exchanges and collaboration: especially in Catholic countries, governments resorted to the Church in their fight against any illegal practice of the profession, contributing to religious control in exchange. In Venice, for example, a 1689 deliberation by the *Provveditori alla Sanità* (Health Magistrates) imposed on parish priests the obligation to disclose the names of the registered midwives and to report illegal ones, while a subsequent one, dated 1719, included with the mandatory requirements for State registration, in addition to a certificate of baptism, another certificate issued by the parish priest on the ability to administer it.[42]

As for the practice, midwives were progressively forbidden from administering medication by mouth (the responsibility of physicians) and from using instruments (the prerogative of surgeons); moreover, they had to consult doctors in cases of difficult childbirths.

In some advanced urban contexts, this distinction in skills between midwives, doctors and surgeons during pregnancy and childbirth had already been established in the social reality since the 15th century: in Florence and Milan, as we have said, doctors cared for the reproductive life of the women of the élites and were consulted during labour, as was the case with Lucrezia Borgia or Bianca Maria Visconti. Even the dissections began to be practised in some families to discover the causes of death, as with the death of Fiammetta Adimari, wife of Filippo Strozzi (1477).[43] The situation in villages and especially in the countryside was very different, either because of the actual difficulty in finding surgeons or doctors when needed, or because the population was not very keen to consult them.

5 A variety of figures

So far, we have talked only about midwives; in fact, research has shown that since the ancient world, there were different figures of birth attendants, characterised by different knowledge and skills (educated midwives and simple birth attendants with different skill levels).

In Greece, next to the *maîa*, there was the *iatròs gynaikeîos* (female doctor) or the *maîa kai iatròs* (midwife and doctor)[44] and, in Rome, too, some *obstetrix* was also called *medicus*.[45] It is clear that, despite being excluded from medical studies since the 5th century, in Greece, many women participated in the renewal of the discipline brought about by the Cos school and were educated.

The existence of an exchange of information and knowledge between doctors and midwives is proven and even declared by various authors, such as Galen and Pliny, who quoted opinions and discussed prescriptions and medication used by them; Galen dedicated his treatise *On the Anatomy of the Uterus* to a midwife.[46] Furthermore, we have already seen how many midwives were wives of surgeons-barbers. On the other hand, how could physicians obtain information on the physiology and pathologies of pregnancy and childbirth, if not through the mediation of those who had direct working experience of them? For this reason, Soranus maintained that the best midwife (*arίste*) should also have, in addition to a solid experience, general theoretical knowledge of medicine and surgery, since she had to suggest diets, prescribe medications or use instruments if needed (*Gyn*. I, 4). In addition to these figures, at the lowest level, there were the *sagae*, who were at the same time midwives, matchmakers and sorceresses and sometimes practised obstetrics.[47]

Some historians maintain that the fall of the Roman Empire marked a discontinuity compared to the ancient world, with the loss of theoretical knowledge and a progressive disappearance of educated midwives.[48] But already in the 12th century, various sources documented the presence of female professionals in childbirth (ventrières, sages-femmes, obstetrics),[49] which differed from other figures devoted to the care: in France, they were called *fisiciennes, chirurgiennes, barbierès* and *guérisseuses*.[50]

In the early modern age, this differentiation was present in the social reality, which saw the presence of educated midwives and healers alongside that of mere practitioners, depending on the contexts and the affluence of the customer base. In some German cities, for example, between the 15th and 16th centuries, the *ehrbaren Frauen* (respectable women) worked, who were consulted, in addition to midwives, during childbirth, when there were complications, and who also prescribed medication.[51] This differentiation widened during the 16th–17th centuries and continued even beyond the foundation of the schools of obstetrics, enduring in certain European regions until the early 20th century.[52]

The first printed obstetrics manuals, written in the vernacular by doctors during the 16th century and addressed to midwives, presumed, after all, a fairly educated public, able to read, even if unfamiliar with the *latino sermone* which represented the language of the scientific community and of physicians: "My midwife does not understand Latin", Scipione Mercurio wrote (Mercurio [1596] 1713: *Prefatione*). The first such manual, dedicated to Duchess Katharina of Braunschweig-Lüneburg, was published in 1513 by German surgeon Eucharius Rösslin (Rodhion) with the metaphoric title *Der Swangern Frawen und Hebammen Rosengarten* (Rosegarden for pregnant Women and Midwives),[53] and was subsequently translated into Latin by the author's son Eucharius Junior (*De partu hominis*, 1532).[54] The second was published in Spain a few decades later by Damian Carbón, with the title *Libro del arte de las Comadres o Madrinas y regimiento de las preñadas y paridas y de los niños* (1541).[55] In Italy, the first texts to be published were the book by Giovanni Marinello, *Le medicine partenenti alle infermità delle donne* (The cures for women's diseases) (1563),[56] dedicated to "genteel and honest women", which included his educated daughter Lucrezia, then, at the end of the century, *La Comare o ricoglitrice* (The Midwife) by Scipione Mercurio,[57] reprinted several times, but more than a century elapsed before the next book was published: Sebastiano Melli's *La Comare levatrice* (The Midwife) (1721).[58]

Educated midwives were not just the readers of these works: some of them were also authors of texts where they reported observations and interventions derived from their experience.[59] Some of these were extensively "looted" by doctors, who drew information and techniques from them, which they then inserted in their own manuals, without however crediting their sources.[60] The most famous female authors and works include the French Louise Bourgeois and her *Observations diverses sur la stérilité, perte de fruits, fécondité, accouchements* (1609)[61]; the Dutch Catharina Schrader, with her *Memory-Boek* (written between 1693 and 1740)[62]; the German Justine Siegemund, the author of *Die Chur-Brandenburgische Hoff-Wehe-Mutter* (1690),[63] where she described a manual technique which has gone down in the history of obstetrics with her name (the so-called "hand-turn", used to extract a breech foetus). In the 18th century, we should mention the English Sarah Stone, the author of *A Complete Practice of Midwifery* (1737),[64] and Elizabeth Nihell, with *A Treatise on the Art of Midwifery* (1760),[65] the French Angélique Marguerite Le Boursier du Coudray, with the handbook for her courses (*Abrégé de l'Art des accouchements*, 1759),[66] Marie-Louise Lachapelle (1769–1821), sage femme en chef in the new maternity clinic in Paris, author of the *Pratique des accouchements ou Mémoires et observations choisies* (1821)[67] and Marie Gillain Boivin (1773–1841).[68] In Italy, the first obstetrics manual written by a woman was published in Naples by Teresa Ployant, a Frenchwoman working in Italy, obstetrics teacher at the Ospedale degli Incurabili and titled *Breve compendio dell'arte ostetricia* (1787).[69]

Thus, as we can see, between the 16th and 18th centuries, some educated midwives took on a mediating role between high and popular cultures, in turn instructing the uneducated practitioners, passing on their techniques and experiences in the form of observations and/or memoirs.[70]

As far as practical activity and social role are concerned, it must be said that the development of cities in the Middle Ages, with the organisation of health and welfare structures, offered midwives new employment opportunities. We have already seen how, from the 15th century onwards, in some European cities, municipal midwives were established, who were also consulted about medical-legal matters in rape, abortion and infanticide trials. In Paris, the Hôtel-Dieu Hospital had already had a special ward for poor women in childbirth since 1348; in Lille, a similar ward was also created in 1431, at the Saint-Jacques Hospital, where *ventrières* and *sages-femmes* worked.[71]

In various cities, midwives welcomed unmarried pregnant women in their homes, assisting at childbirths destined to remain secret and taking newborns to foundling hospitals. Salaried, employed midwives thus joined those working independently, who, in turn, varied in terms of their education and training. Being midwives in the countryside or in small villages was not the same thing as working in a big city, where the opportunities of information and cultural exchanges, and therefore of updating one's knowledge, were greater. Furthermore, working in the poor neighbourhoods of the cities was certainly different from working in the rich ones, which provided a more select customer base. A midwife serving the aristocracy could get to court and have the honour (and glory) of assisting the queen, as in the case of Louise Bourgeois, *sage-femme de la Reine*, as she herself loved to introduce herself.[72]

It is true that those who worked in small towns may have had less competition and greater freedom to practise, as evidenced by the long career of the Dutch Catharina Schrader, who assisted as many as 3,000 childbirths, as shown by her extraordinary book of memoirs.[73]

It must also be said that the process designed to professionalise midwives ended up bringing out in an increasingly distinct way the new category of "illegal" midwives: those who continued to practise without a licence or registration, as their ancestors had done for centuries.

Notes

1 Bettini (2013: ch. 12).
2 As pointed out by H. King (1998) and I. Marland (1993).
3 Gélis (1984a: 177).
4 As H. King has pointed out (1998: 181–184).

5 Cavallo (2007).
6 Perkins (1996).
7 Schrader [1693] (1987).
8 Cody (2005).
9 Gelbart (1998).
10 Bettini (2013: ch. 1); Gourevitch and Raepsaet-Charlier (2001: 134).
11 Park (2006: ch. 3).
12 Gélis (1984a: 38).
13 Filippini (1993: 155–156); Hacke (2004: 158–162); Pedrini and Dubbini (2018).
14 In Venice, for example, in the 18th century, this was customary among the popular classes (Filippini 1993: 155–156). According to Park, this did not happen in the Middle Ages (Park 2006, 2018).
15 Temp.: 5–7.
16 Curatolo (1901).
17 Flügge (1998).
18 Shorter (1982); Pancino (1984); Parma (1984); Foscati (2017). On the other hand, the practice of episiotomy, mentioned by K. Park (2018), is not documented in sources from the medieval and early modern ages.
19 Temp.: 5.
20 Harris-Stoertz (2017: 40).
21 Ortiz (1993: 97).
22 Mercuriale (1587).
23 Mercuriale (1587); Marinello (1574).
24 Ehrenreich-English (1973).
25 Forbes (1966); Ehrenreich-English (1973).
26 Mackay (2009: ch. 13, 'The method by which midwives sorceresses inflict greater losses when they either kill babies or offer them to demons by dedicating them with a curse').
27 Gélis (1988: 50).
28 Levack (1987: 134).
29 Pancino (1984: 29–30).
30 Evenden (1993); Harley (1993); Ortiz (1993).
31 Fiocca (1983: 147).
32 Parma (1984: 92).
33 Filippini (1985: 132, 1993: 157–159).
34 Gélis (1988: 53–54).
35 Bellavitis (2018).
36 Donnison (1988); Blumenfeld-Kosinski (1990); Flügge (1998). On the roots of this process and the rise of male authority in pre-modern gynaecology, see Green (2008).
37 Flügge (1998); Shorter (1982: ch. 3).
38 Darmon (1981: 183–184).
39 Darmon (1981: 183–185); Olive (1992: 7–15). The 1580 statute in 24 articles is published in Ibidem (1992, 12–14).
40 Vanzan Marchini (1985: 23–24).
41 Pomata (1994a: 139).
42 Filippini (1985: 152).
43 Park (2006: 121 and 320, note 38).
44 King (1998: 179); Bettini (2013: ch. 12).
45 Gourevitch (1984: 224–225).
46 King (1998: 276).
47 Bettini (2013: ch. 12).
48 Green (2008: 34–36); Park (2018).
49 Harris-Stoertz (2012, 2017).
50 Blumenfeld-Kosinski (1990: 98).

51 Flügge (1998).
52 Shorter (1982: ch.3); Caforio (2002: ch. 7).
53 Rösslin Eucharius [1513] (1910).
54 Rösslin, Eucharius ('Rodhion') (1537).
55 Carbón (1541).
56 Marinello [1563] (1574).
57 Mercurio [1596] (1713).
58 Melli (1721).
59 Witkowski (1891).
60 As W. Pulz has shown (1996: 593–617).
61 Bourgeois [1609] (1992).
62 Schrader [1693] (1987).
63 Siegemund ([1690] 2005); see Pulz (1998).
64 Stone (1737); see Grundy (1994) and Woods and Gallery (2014).
65 Nihell (1760); see Cody (2005).
66 du Coudray ([1759] 1976); see Gelbart (1998).
67 Lachapelle (1821); see Sage- Pranchère (2017).
68 Boivin (1827); see Carol (2011).
69 Ployant [1787] (1803).
70 Pulz (1996).
71 Beauvalet-Boutouyrie (1999: ch. 1).
72 Bourgeois [1609] (1992); see Olive (1992).
73 Schrader [1693] (1987).

PART III
The 18th-century juncture

Foreword

The 18th century represents a profound turning point in the history of birth, one of those phases of sudden acceleration in the processes of transformation that sometimes occur over the *longue durée*. The change involved the whole birth scene, with the people, places and therapeutic practices involved: the figure of the "man-midwife" became established, introducing new obstetric instruments and operations; lying-in hospitals opened up, imposing different rituals and interventions; midwifery schools spread; a new model of midwife was defined; in short, the medicalisation process that would unfold more widely in the following century had begun. These were significant social transformations, derived from deeper cultural changes and centred on the representation of childbirth and birth themselves: the image of the female body in its reproductive function was being entirely revised, also in the light of a new representation of the foetus that redefined the concept of birth.

At the root of these changes was a complex set of political, scientific and cultural factors: from the emergence of a specific interest in population as an "object" to be managed, combined with pressures for demographic growth, to the emergence of a new view of the body and of a changed sensitivity towards the foetus, against the background of the discoveries promoted by the scientific revolution of the second half of the 17th century. These are multiple and different factors, but it would be misleading to try and establish hierarchies of priorities between them, whereas it is important to consider them in their interconnections instead. The birth of biopolitics, i.e. of the political control of bodies and management of lives, according to Foucault's well-known definition[1] took place at a lively historical juncture, at the intersection of larger and more complex processes.

As happened with analogous processes of transformation, this one also developed in a way that was anything but homogeneous and linear, with different methods and at different times in the various European countries, as a consequence of economic, social and religious factors: the difference between Protestant and Catholic areas was a significant variation, interwoven with those linked to economic context, social class and urban or rural environment. There were also resistance and conflicts not only between midwives and men-midwives (an aspect which may have been stressed too much), but also between these representatives of medical science and the population, in many cases reluctant to accept innovations and public standards. Even the medical world was affected by contrasts reflecting schools and therapeutic and ethical guidelines so different between them that, in some cases, they even led to criminal complaints, especially on particularly burning issues from an ethical point of view, such as Caesarean section on live women.

Finally, the resumption of a strong ecclesiastical initiative around baptism should be pointed out, in the light of the new discoveries in embryology, which started a real campaign to promote the practice of post-mortem Caesarean sections and baptism of embryos. It was the first step in a redefinition of Church policy in the field of reproduction, in response to state initiatives. The development of biopower in an area traditionally controlled by ecclesiastical institutions in fact implied a reworking of the relationship between State and Church which was full of contrasts, all the more because it took place against the background of a process of secularisation of science, prompted by the Enlightenment and then by positivism. From this very battleground in the 19th century, the Church would re-launch its counter-attack to regain a dominance centred precisely on the defence of the life of the foetus.

Note

1 Foucault (1973 and 2008).

7
THE INSTITUTIONALISATION OF MIDWIVES

1 Childbirth: public and political interests

During the 18th century, childbirth was at the centre of very important interests: they became public and political affairs on which the attention of government men, doctors, scientists and philosophers was concentrated. This transformation first started from a new idea of the State that fully asserted itself with the Enlightenment: that of a "social body" whose stability and international prestige were correlated, first of all, to the number of inhabitants.[1] However, the premises to this view can already be found in the thought and reasoning of some philosophers and doctors from the second half of the 17th century.[2] This fundamental coincidence between population and State made health and its pursuit a political objective: "The purpose and duty of any wise government clearly are population and work", Voltaire had written (cited by Filippini 1995: 111).

An enlightened sovereign was tasked with combatting mortality and disease to guarantee good standards of living and health for his citizens, in short with taking care of the social body, ensuring its growth and improvement. Duty and political power were thus redesigned, with a clear shift from the sphere of death to that of life, both real and symbolic: biopower replaced "the old power of death, where the symbolic essence of sovereign power was concentrated, with the careful administration of bodies and management of life" (Forti and Guaraldo 2006: 59).

The fight against mortality and to encourage population growth was thus inscribed as one of the first political objectives, and in order to accomplish them, a special sector of the art of government was set up: the so-called "medical police", which, in its 18th-century meaning, indicated "a strategy for the elimination of the causes, moral and physical, of de-population", a prerequisite for demographic development (Panseri 1981: 192). The intervention of the State was no longer limited to extraordinary initiatives, aimed at coping with epidemics, but materialised in the creation of comprehensive projects that invested in institutions, health practitioners and citizens.[3]

In this context, the sphere of reproduction was suddenly charged with political values.[4] Birth was seen as the moment when the social body was renewed, and losses were reinstated; consequently, maternal and infant mortality, as well as a private loss, represented a threat to the public interest, all the more so as each child, in view of his life potential, represented "a whole exploitable capital". Consequently, "a careful attention to saving men from the moment of their birth means securing subjects for the State, individuals for society and good for the human species", as Professor Sebastiano Rizzo wrote in 1776, when inaugurating Venice's midwifery school.[5] It is significant that at that time and in that new theoretical perspective, even the terms and definitions changed, as reflected by these quotations where the term "capital" is used: the ancient term "generation" was gradually replaced by "reproduction", borrowed from the fledgling capitalism, as pointed out by Hopwood.[6]

The female body in its reproductive function was therefore placed in a liminal position between the private and public spheres, with a consequent reduction in marital power: "The pregnant woman – the founder of social medicine and public health Johann Peter Frank observed – is not only the wife of an individual citizen, but also the hope of the State, whose protection she now has to enjoy" (Frank [1779] 1976: 74), intervening, if necessary, even to curb private power, as well as to remove the obstacles which may threaten her life and that of the child that is about to be born, a new "citizen" and a member of a modern nation-state.

This resulted in an ambivalent public enhancement of motherhood: on the one hand, in fact, women's reproductive function was extolled and protected; on the other, as we shall see, it was charged with responsibility and subjected to new forms of discipline. Frank expressed it in the following terms:

> The female sex deserves veneration and all possible consideration in a condition through which the whole is maintained by the daily replenishment of new world citizens, the development of all states promoted and individual families perpetuated. A good police, thus, must be watchful for the sake of this most necessary class of persons, maintain them in their good state and respect and protect them. The police must use all possibilities to see that all matters, evident and even unobtrusive, are vigorously removed through which the great work of procreating our posterity, and thus our population, may be weakened or even smothered. Therefore, the police must use real paternal care to avert the dangers which threaten mother or child, or both together, so that every woman in her blessed state may attain her aim joyfully and in comforting security.
>
> *(Frank [1779] 1976: 70)*

However, it would be simplistic to read these transformations solely in terms of biopower or biopolitics, thus implying the domination over the fertile female body[7]:

an attention to birth, a desire for the survival and well-being of individuals were shared by a wide swathe of public opinion: in short, political interest combined with more widespread instances of rejection of death that had already emerged from the 16th to the 17th centuries, but which quickly gained ground in large sections of the population during the 17th and 18th centuries.[8] It is no coincidence that the term "happiness" ran through the century as a leitmotif, ideally linking philosophical texts, private lives and collective movements: we find it articulated in different ways in elopements, in letters between parents and children, in philosophy books and even in the United States *Declaration of Independence* (1776). When the Italian philosopher Ludovico Antonio Muratori wrote *Della pubblica felicità oggetto de' buoni prìncipi* (About public happiness as the objective of good princes), he had a very earthly goal in mind that he set as objective for a good sovereign.[9]

In this perspective, death in childbirth was seen as an unacceptable loss, an aberration to be fought and prevented, as shown by the life stories that archival research has brought to light, which are evidence of a rejection of suffering and death that turned into an active search for remedies. The story of Venetian noblewoman Lucia Memmo Mocenigo, who, at the end of the 18th century and after various miscarriages, was willing to go through her pregnancy and childbirth away from her family, in Vienna, to be assisted by a trusted obstetrician in the hope of finally having a baby, appears emblematic in this sense.[10] But similar stories (in spirit if not in the actual facts) can be found in the notebooks of the *accoucheurs* or in hospital notes, as evidence of an active and transversal attitude with respect to the various social classes.

In short, the political initiative interpreted a widespread tension, taking root all the more because it was in tune with a more extensive social need that demanded improvements and solutions to a humanly distressing problem that struck individuals, but emerged from the sphere of individuality to become a social problem.

2 Midwives on trial

In this perspective, maternal and infant mortality, as well as a human tragedy, became a problem for the community and the State. Population surveys, promoted in various countries by the emerging discipline of statistics, collected and analysed losses also in terms of forecasts: descriptive statistics were replaced by a kind of "political arithmetic" that fed the collective fear of depopulation and degeneration of the human race which, having emerged at this time, spiralled during the 19th century.[11]

In the search for the causes of this mortality, the traditional forms of childbirth assistance, and consequently midwives, were put on trial. If already during the 17th century, they had sometimes been accused of negligence and ignorance, in the 18th century, they were the objects of a true smear campaign which identified in their incompetence and crudeness the cause of the loss of so many lives. Doctors, politicians and scholars wrote pamphlets and appeals against them, using a range of derogatory terms: "idiots", "crude", "murderers" and "sadists" (Pancino 1984: 81–84). Country midwives and practitioners were especially targeted, but the disgrace was ultimately extended to the entire category.

Their lack of scientific knowledge was questioned above all, as well as their lack of visual experience gathered from the human dissections carried out by doctors. Against the backdrop of the Enlightenment, their traditional knowledge, based on manual skills and oral tradition, was devalued: the emphasis on scientific progress confined it to the sphere of obscurantism, marking it as dangerous. If in the Middle Ages and in the early modern age, the suspicion that weighed upon midwives was above all linked to magical practices and to a relationship with the devil, in the century of the Enlightenment, it arose instead from their lack of medical training and illiteracy.[12]

Elements of cultural distance combined with gender hierarchies, accentuating the inferiority of midwives, portrayed as "very brazen and abominable young girls", "gossips", as Venetian doctor Cesare Musatti described them in the following century:

> But finally what is a midwife, nine times out of ten? A woman, sometimes even passably good looking, always a gossip, who with or without the consent of the Mayor, having willingly brought up 5 or 6 individuals into the society, has therefore given herself to common midwifery: and only because she was the mother of numerous children, she passes for one of the seven wise men from Ancient Greece in matters of gynaecology.
>
> *(Cited by Vanzan Marchini 1985: 46)*

In actual fact, this smear campaign also arose from an obvious professional conflict: the aspiration of surgeons to practise midwifery, and to break up a very long-standing female monopoly; in short, it was functional to their promotion onto the birth scene and to the acquisition of social credit by public institutions. The midwives themselves were well aware of it: Neapolitan Maddalena De Marinis, for example, wrote in 1838:

> it was a matter of expelling [from the profession] the people who practised it; nothing was therefore more suspicious than whatever evil, horror or death was attributed to the incompetence of midwives; pronounced by those who had a clear interest that they should not exist.
>
> *(Cited by Guidi 1986: 117)*

They certainly did not remain silent: those who could write reacted, revealing on the one hand the implicit aims in these accusations, and on the other disputing the presumed superiority of medical knowledge, i.e. the theoretical basis of the smear campaign: a controversy and a clash arose which would continue even into the following century.[13] Justine Siegemund, at the end of the 17th century, discussing the use of the *speculum matricis*, had already emphasised that the "being able to see" boasted by surgeons did not mean "being able to do" and that a theoretical knowledge did not necessarily translate into the practical ability to help a woman in labour, which required manual skills instead:

> You suggest to me the use of the *speculum* [...] even if this involves more pain. Now even when I have seen for a long time what presentation the baby is in, I cannot however help him with my eyes ... And if an inexperienced midwife sees the baby's presentation, but does not know what she must do in this case, what good is seeing to her? [...] my hands, my fingers had reached the natural feeling or the knowledge; I could feel and discern as precisely as if I had baby's presentation under my eyes. This is why using the *speculum* is in my opinion an unnecessary torment.
> *(Cited by Pulz 1996: 599)*

This fact was reiterated in all texts written by midwives, where manual skill is highlighted as a crucial aspect of their profession: the hand thus takes on symbolic importance, as opposed to the surgeon's instruments, within an oppositional framework that contrasted touching with seeing, a living body with a dead one, the oral tradition with the written one, empathy with detachment (Figure 7.1).

FIGURE 7.1   Manual midwife operation in a difficult birth, from Scipione Mercurio (1618), *La Commare o riccoglitrice*, Milano: Giob. Bidelli, p. 176. Reproduced with permission of the Biblioteca Pinali antica (Padua).

The fact that this was "a hand of a gender not different" (from that of the woman in labour), to underline at the same time manual skill and gender identity, is one of the topics that midwife Benedetta Fedeli Trevisan included in her plea to Venice's Health Court to be allowed to continue to legally practise, as we shall see (Chapter 8, par. 5), the traditional manual versions.[14]

3 "The light of knowledge": the creation of midwifery schools

Imparting knowledge to midwives appeared in this context of public offensive as the first step to modify the traditional forms of assistance to which childbirth mortality was attributed. If midwives were ignorant and crude, why not instruct them? – Ludovico Antonio Muratori asked – becoming the voice of a widespread opinion, which reflected the Enlightenment trust in progress based precisely on the acquisition of scientific knowledge.[15]

Following this belief, in the second half of the 18th century, training initiatives aimed at midwives took place in many European countries: courses and midwifery schools aimed primarily at women, and then also at surgeons. These were very different initiatives, but they were characterised by some common elements: the fact that they were almost always taught by surgeons, that the courses for student midwives were different from those for surgeons and that the teaching aimed not only to teach anatomy and physiology, but also to train in the broadest sense of the term, instilling standards of behaviour and the respect for professional hierarchies, and so were essentially aimed at redesigning a new model of midwife.

In many cases, the initiative was taken by surgeons or man-midwives who started private courses, making their own resources and instruments available, such as William Smellie in London (1740), who also opened an infirmary for the poor mothers, where clinical training took place, and who held 280 courses in 10 years (over 900 male practitioners and an unknown number of "female pupils").[16] In Paris, a similar initiative was started by accoucheur André Levret (1703–1780), whose school became a reference point for Italian surgeons, too. In Italy, in Bologna, as early as 1753, Giovanni Antonio Galli, before being charged with this task by the Senate, held in his own home a private midwifery school for surgeons and midwives, for which he had put together a precious *supellex ostetricia*[17]; in Verona, Antonio Piccoli used his own home, with an anatomical museum attached to it, for the training of country midwives.[18]

Private initiative often preceded and prompted the public one: very soon, in fact, in most European countries (except for Great Britain), public institutions supported these schools, with the aim of "addressing the incompetence of midwives" and protecting "as many fertile mothers as possible to the State", as stated in the decree of the founding Senate of the midwifery school of Venice (cited by Cappelletto and Filippini 1982). In Italy, between 1757 and 1779, 13 midwifery schools were opened, mostly concentrated in the northern and central states, such as in Turin (1732), Bologna (1757), Milan (1767), Venice (1770), Padua (1774), Modena (1776) and Macerata (1779).[19]

In the 1770s, similar institutions were created in Germany, the Netherlands, Switzerland and Spain. In the German states, Jena (1771), Bruchsal, Detmold (1774) and Dresden (1775) were the first cities to implement these initiatives. In Switzerland, a midwifery school was first opened in Basel in 1771; in Belgium, in 1775.[20] With some delay and some difference compared to the other European states, in Spain, the schools for midwives were opened in the last decade of the century: in 1795, the Barcelona school was born on the initiative of the College of surgeons. In 1787, a 'chair of childbirths' (*Càtedra de partos*) for the instruction of surgeons was created at the Madrid College of Surgery.[21]

A separate case is represented by France, where a midwife, Angélique Marguerite Le Boursier du Coudray, requested and obtained, in 1759, a royal patent which authorised her to hold midwifery courses throughout the kingdom. Thus began an extraordinary tour that brought her, over 25 years of activity (from 1759 to 1783), all over France to train thousands of midwives.[22] In subsequent years, she was followed, however, by male trainers, the *démonstrateurs*, as her proposal to train other midwives-teachers (*démonstratrices*) had been rejected, right up to the opening of the first national midwifery school in Paris, at the lying-in hospitals, on 22 December 1802.[23] Duration, organisation and methodologies were obviously different: the courses could be intensive and last for a few weeks as they did in France, or last longer, even two years, with weekly lessons, as in Venice. In some cases, the school was attached to a hospital and worked as a boarding school, with an adjoining dormitory for students during their courses. This model prevailed at the end of the century, coinciding with the spread of lying-in hospitals throughout Europe. For practical training (even where lying-in hospitals existed), models made of wax, terracotta or leather, which also reproduced a pregnant pelvis and womb, were also used. For this purpose, Giovanni Antonio Galli had invented two dummies representing women about to give birth, with glass wombs, so as to be able to check from the outside the correctness of the manoeuvres performed by students. Madame du Coudray had also devised a *machine à démontrer*, a life-size dummy made of fabric and leather, with the dummy of a newborn incorporated, to demonstrate the process of birth.[24]

Anatomical wax dummies were particularly common in Italy: the ones produced in Bologna in the mid-18th century by the Manzolinis, a couple working with Galli, were famous for their excellent quality. It should be noted that Anna Morandi Manzolini was awarded the title of "wax modeller for the chair of anatomy" (1756) and lecturer, thus becoming the first woman in Italy to obtain similar academic status, followed, at the end of the century, by Maria Dalle Donne, the first woman to graduate in medicine (1799), who was appointed the director of Bologna's midwifery school in 1804.[25]

Considerable educational importance was attributed in Italy to dissections, in particular to the "displaying" of a womb, which students had to attend; in fact, one of the certificates they had to produce for their exams was issued by the anatomist. At the end of their courses, they had to pass an exam in front of a commission of surgeons and doctors, which issued their diploma, qualifying them to practise.[26]

4 A new model of midwife

These schools marked a profound discontinuity compared to the past: an apprenticeship based on experience, on the transmission of a midwife's "know-how", was replaced by training based on puppets and machines, which implied a reductive view of childbirth, focused on the final stage, with a loss of the overview of an event that involved the whole person and where emotional reactions are no less important to its success. The break was even more obvious when the boarding-school model became more widespread, replacing the traditional apprenticeship with a working midwife.[27]

Even more radical was the transformation that these schools introduced in the characterisation of the figure of the midwife. After an initial stage, in fact, they opened not only to widowed or married women, but also to young and unmarried women. The case of Milan's school of midwifery is emblematic in this sense: if in 1767, it mostly welcomed married women (with their husbands' consent), in 1791, it admitted single girls.[28] Sixty years later, the school lowered its minimum age for admission to 18, setting its maximum at 30.[29] In Madame du Coudray's courses, students were also selected on the basis of their age, preferably younger than 40. Older women were excluded, as happened in Milan, where an elderly midwife, although well established in her practice, tried in vain to gain admission in order to legalise her position. A survey conducted in France in 1786 highlighted this change: one in two midwives was under 50; one in five younger than 40.[30] A profession that for centuries had been based on maturity and direct experience became a profession open to young women, certainly easier to mould and readier to absorb new models and professional hierarchies.

In fact, the training also aimed to redefine the tasks and the scope of midwives' intervention as compared to surgeons', with a reduction in their skills and spaces of action and an intensification of the control over their work in the community. In Spain, for example, midwives had to take a solemn oath to call a doctor or surgeon in difficult childbirths and not to give any medication.[31] In Piedmont, the Regulation issued in 1732, in addition to setting the rules for the running of the school, also defined the rules for practising the profession, forbidding the use of instruments by midwives and requiring the display of a sign outside their homes.[32] In Venice, a 1786 law forbade the use of instruments, in addition to the traditional prohibition of giving oral medication; this prohibition was reiterated over the century in many European states.[33]

Nineteenth-century regulations expanded these rules into strict sets of duties and prohibitions that the midwifery schools taught: together with their licence-to-practise certificates, specific instructions were also handed to the students. In their working practice, in many contexts, they were subject to the control of a doctor: the first Health Code issued in the Lombardy-Veneto region (1858) entrusted doctors with the task of supervising midwives, reminding them of their duties and reporting them to the authorities if they infringed the laws.[34] At the beginning of the 19th century, the "midwifery bags" began to be sold, containing the necessary equipment for their job; this useful tool would later become almost symbolic of the profession, but its implicit regulatory implication is clear.[35]

The impact of these training initiatives varied considerably from state to state, from region to region, with a clear distinction between city and countryside, and between north and south. In many countries, such as in France, they were supported by local administrations and by the clergy, who sometimes contributed to organising them even on the financial level; in others, such as in Germany, after an initial delay, they spread rapidly in many cities; in others still, especially in southern Europe, they found it more difficult to become established, so much so that large areas were excluded until the second half of the 19th century.

The reasons for this delay were many: especially in southern Europe, few families were prepared to deprive themselves of valuable labour for long periods; many husbands were unwilling to allow their wives to go to school as they considered it dishonourable; many women were reluctant to leave their villages; there was a strong distrust of these initiatives and the conviction of their substantial uselessness was well rooted. Furthermore, illiteracy was widespread in many contexts, limiting the access of women to schools; finally, there were the economic factors linked to the scarce resources of many Municipalities and/or Universities and their uneven distribution.

Moreover, the clergy, in some Catholic countries, proved to be uncooperative, perhaps for fear of losing their monopoly of control over midwives.[36] Even in a very lively city from a cultural point of view such as Venice, the midwifery school attracted limited enrolments. The professor of midwifery in 1794 wrote that the students were "few in number and few were faithful and constant" (cited by Filippini 1985a: 156); this was an optimistic statement, in the light of only 5 registered students. The Provincial Congregation admitted that "in the external Municipalities, where the need is greater, there are very few women who can read and write and there is then a general horror at the prospect of leaving one's village".[37] To overcome this problem, some girls from the foundling hospitals were sent to the school, as the French government had arranged in Milan (1808).

The number of registered midwives remained insufficient in Italy for a long time, often even where midwifery schools existed: an investigation started in the Duchy of Milan in 1790 revealed that in the countryside illegal midwives were more than double the number of registered ones (132 against 62 over 21 parishes). Another survey, promoted by the Provincial Congregation of Venice 35 years later, revealed that many Municipalities were completely without qualified midwives.[38]

For this reason, unqualified midwives were allowed to practise, in the knowledge that their work was irreplaceable. The Austrians in the Lombardy-Veneto region explained this line of conduct, by distinguishing midwives into three categories: the *approvate* (registered), the *abusive* (illegal) and the "*tollerate*" (tolerated), i.e. those who "were active in areas that were otherwise completely lacking in assistance", while underlining the "purely provisional character of this tolerance" (Filippini 1985b: 34–35). In reality, this "temporary" situation lasted from government to government until the end of the 19th century. Only Crispi's law on the protection of public health and safety (1888) would really lay the foundations of welfare in Italy, making the establishment of municipal midwives mandatory and assistance to the poor free.[39] Two years later, the *Regolamento speciale con istruzioni per l'esercizio ostetrico nei comuni del Regno* (special Rules with instructions for midwifery practice in the Municipalities of the Kingdom) confirmed the rules and limits of the profession, rigorously setting out the treatment midwives could provide and their obligations: assistance at natural deliveries only, the obligation to keep a special bag with the necessary equipment for this purpose, the prohibition to use surgical instruments or manual versions, registration of childbirths, the obligation to call a doctor in case of unnatural birth. The results of the *Inchiesta sulle condizioni igieniche e sanitarie dei Comuni del Regno* (Inquiry into the health and welfare conditions of the Municipalities of the Kingdom) (1886) highlighted that 40% of them did not have any without authorised midwives and in many others, despite the appointment of a local midwife, the work was carried out by practitioners, especially in mountain areas and in the south.[40]

This situation, particularly widespread in Italy, existed in other European countries, too, albeit with some differences and peculiarities. The existence of unqualified practitioners alongside registered midwives is documented throughout the continent during the 19th–20th centuries. In mid-19th-century Germany, the women of the popular classes were still predominantly assisted by practitioners, *Wickelfrauen*, so called by the action of swaddling the newborn (*wickeln* = to swaddle).[41]

Also, in Königsberg, Prussia, right up to the 20th century, more than half of the childbirths in the countryside were attended by practitioners. In Brittany, Northern France, midwives lived mostly in the cities; in the countryside, peasants turned to practitioners.[42]

In many rural areas, childbirth was attended by the *femme-qui-aide*.[43] In Great Britain, even at the beginning of the 20th century, three types of midwives still existed: *trained midwives*, with a certificate; *bona fide midwives*, allowed *ope legis* and recognised as able to practise; and *uncertified midwives*, without certificate or approval, who continued to practise illegally.[44]

5 Qualified versus unlicenced midwives: an age-old competition

The creation of midwifery schools opened up a far deeper rift in the world of midwives than the one which had long existed between registered and illegal ones. Many, especially the educated ones, supported the need for education and promoted it, seeing in this path the only chance to regain social prestige and maintain a central role on the birth scene. In the age of Enlightenment, professionalising their work was the only way to counter the invasion of man-midwives, the "fatal turn of events", as Teresa Ployant wrote:

> They are already indifferently abandoning mothers in the hands of men in France and England and threatening the same in the rest of Europe. Let us

then be quick to stem this fatal turn of events and through tireless study make the public realise that we are the ones that can bring childbirth to a happy outcome, and at the same time save women's modesty.

(Ployant [1797] 1803: 6)[45]

They therefore reclaimed the female tradition of the profession in the name of defending modesty, but within a new professional identity that required scientific knowledge, theoretical preparation and study, not just the acquisition of manual skills. Precisely in order not to become mere "childbirth nurses", they aimed at a professionalisation that would guarantee employment and recognition by institutions and doctors.

Thus, in various contexts, a strong conflict arose between traditional practitioners, who had on their side the prestige enjoyed with the population, the support in many cases of parish priests and local doctors, and the young midwives educated in midwifery schools, proud of their certificates and with precise job expectations. It was these young women who denounced the old midwives first, whose competition deprived them of the promised work, engaging them in a war of complaints and appeals to the authorities.

This dispute ended up involving in many cases the population, reflecting the importance of the social turning point of this juncture: in many places, especially in rural areas, people sided with the old midwives, rejecting a figure that did not fit with the tradition in their characteristics and practices. In Lombardy, for example, in the small village of Pieve di Binasco, in 1769,

everyone in one voice said that this woman [the old midwife] behaves very well in the practice of midwifery and that all women absolutely intend to use her, therefore excluding any other, even though they are approved by the Medical Commission.

(Parma 1984: 126)

Similar episodes were recorded all over France, from Auvergne to Alsace, with the population often siding with the old midwives and against the new *sages femmes*.[46]

These disputes continued until the end of the 19th century, evidence of the progressive distance that tended to separate the old midwives from the new, increasingly critical and aggressive towards competitors, accused of unfair competition and of discrediting the profession. In Italy, in 1893, some registered midwives from Naples went so far as to file an appeal with the State Council for "violation of rights and of just interests affecting registered midwives" (Basso 2015: 166–167), thus obtaining in 1893 the suspension of any further extension of amnesty against illegal midwives. At the end of the 19th century, they would resort to the same terms used by 18th-century physicians to discredit illegal midwives, accusing them of being "ignorant, immoral, dishonest, superstitious women" (Vitiello 2006: 481), as reported in the 1894 Naples *Bollettino delle levatrici* (Bulletin of midwives).

It should be further emphasised that, in the name of professional accreditation, many registered midwives came to accept their professional subordination to doctors, their duty of "passive obedience", as stated in the 1894 *Giornale delle levatrici* (Journal of midwives),[47] recognising the hierarchy underlying the medicalisation process. In actual fact, however, this subordination, although formally accepted, continued to be poorly tolerated in practice, as reflected in the autobiographical accounts of many Italian midwives from the early 20th century.[48]

Notes

1 Cole (2000); Blum (2002); Rusnock (2018).
2 As has been shown by Kreager (2018).
3 Rusnock (2002, 2018).
4 Gélis (1988); Blum (2002); Cody (2005); Filippini (1997, 2002).
5 Rizzo (1776: 3).
6 Hopwood (2018a).
7 Foucault (2008).
8 As highlighted by Gélis (1988: 326–327).
9 Venturi (1969).
10 The story has been reconstructed and told in a narrative form by Robilant (2008).
11 Dupaquier (1985); Brian (1994); Schweber (2006); Rusnock (1999, 2002).
12 Pulz (1996); Pardo-Tomàs and Martinez-Vidal (2007).
13 Donnison (1977); Marland and Rafferty (1997); Chamberlain (2007); Cicatiello (2018).
14 Filippini (1984, 1985a: 168).
15 Pancino (1984: 85).
16 Wilson (1995: 124); Donnison (1988); Woods and Gallery (2014).
17 It is now kept partly in the Obstetrics Clinic of the Ospedale Sant'Orsola (Bologna), and partly in the city's Istituto delle Scienze, in Palazzo Poggi (Bologna).
18 Pancino (1984).
19 Pancino (1984: 224, table); Franchetti (2012: 53–57).
20 Siebold (1991, vol. 2: 493–494); Gélis (1988: 183).
21 Ortiz (1993: 100–101).
22 Gelbart (1998).
23 Beauvalet-Boutouyrie (1999: ch. 8); Sage-Pranchère (2017).
24 Benozio, Beugnot, Demoy et alii (2004).
25 Cavazza (1997, 2003).
26 Filippini (1985a).
27 Betri (2010).
28 Parma (1984: 151–152).
29 Franchetti (2013: 378–379).
30 Gélis (1988: 200).
31 Ortiz (1993: 101).
32 Pancino (1984: 94–95).
33 Pillon (1981); Vanzan-Marchini (1985); Wilson (1995).
34 Filippini (1985b: 35).
35 Gissi (2006b: 79–96).
36 Pardo-Tomàs and Martinez-Vidal (2007).
37 ASVe, Imperial Regio Governo, LXX, 3/1, Provincial Congregation, 11 June 1825.
38 Parma (1984: 148).
39 Vicarelli (1997).
40 Basso (2015: 55).

41 Shorter (1982: 142).
42 Shorter (1982: 46).
43 Verdier (1979); Caforio (2002).
44 Etzioni (1969); Spina (2009: 53–54); Marland and Rafferty (1997: 1–13).
45 Translated from the Italian edition, like the following quotations.
46 Gélis (1988: 210).
47 Pancino (1984: 175).
48 Lanzardo (1985).

8
MAN-MIDWIVES ON THE CHILDBIRTH SCENE

1 The establishment of man-midwives

The public pleas to protect the population, which, as we have seen, gained ground during the 18th century, led to an enhancement of obstetrics as a branch of surgery and to the establishment of the figure of the man-midwife, i.e. a surgeon specialised in childbirth assistance (called *accoucheur* in French, *chirurgo-ostetricante* in Italian and *Geburtshelfer* in German). What for centuries had been a marginal sector gradually became "an important part of surgery",[1] on which public and private hopes and expectations were pinned. This enhancement directly involved the guild of surgeons, as obstetrics traditionally was a branch of surgery, representing for them an opportunity for social and professional advancements (Figure 8.1).

So let us look more closely at this figure and at the features which brought them strength and prestige at that particular time. In the first place, there was their scientific knowledge (of both anatomy and physiology), on which Enlightenment society based its expectations of social progress[2]; it is no coincidence that the most famous obstetricians of the time had themselves portrayed holding a book, either writing it, as J-L. Baudelocque did, or leafing through it, as W. Hunter did, or even with an entire library in the background, as in the case of P. Rodin.[3]

On the academic level, obstetrics acquired its own independent content at the university level, with the creation of dedicated chairs: the first one was founded in Padua in 1761 and named *De morbis mulierum, puerorum et artificum*, later changed to *Ad artem ostetriciam, ad morbos mulierum*.[4] But, above all, in the second half of the 18th century, it was affected by the profound revolution involving the whole of medicine, radically transforming the forms on which its knowledge was based, thanks to the clinical observation that Foucault considered the basis of contemporary medicine.[5]

FIGURE 8.1 Title page of Cosme Viardel's (1748), *Observations sur la pratique des accouchemens naturels, contre nature et monstrueux*, Paris: chez d'Houry. The caption says: "*Non impar Lucianae*" ("not inferior to Lucina", the Roman goddess of childbirth). Reproduced with permission of the Biblioteca Pinali antica (Padua).

Lying-in hospitals, supported in many countries by public funding, were opened in all major European cities, with the primary aim of providing man-midwives not only with theoretical knowledge or the opportunity to witness human dissections, but also the chance to observe childbirths and receive the kind of training that was otherwise difficult to access in practice. Great Britain and France were at the forefront of this innovation, with the Strasbourg Lying-in Hospital, established by Fried in 1728, and the one set up by William Smellie in London, which attracted students from all over Europe, but especially Germany, Austria and Italy.[6]

When the Grand Duke of Tuscany decided to institute the teaching of midwifery in Florence, he sent Giuseppe Vespa to Paris, whereas Lucas Boër was sent by Holy Roman Emperor Joseph II on a real European midwifery tour, even spending a few months in London, after visits in Belgium, Holland and France.[7]

This new clinical approach brought important results in terms of knowledge (especially regarding the mechanism of childbirth and the configuration of the pelvis), extensively reported in medical journals, where midwifery was becoming increasingly important. This culminated, at the end of the century, in the publication of the first specialist journals: the *Archiv für die Geburtshilfe*, published in Jena in 1787; the *Journal für Geburtshelfer* and the *Lucina oder Magazin für Geburtshelfer*, printed in Frankfurt and Marburg in 1787. In Italy, the first journal was published in Bologna in 1788 with the title *Dell'arte ostetricia: fogli periodici con rami colorati* (Of the obstetric art: periodical sheets with coloured branches).

The spread of midwifery courses and schools also fed a rich production of manuals, a further element of promotion and income for man-midwives. Historian Jacques Gélis counted 245 of them, published between 1668 and 1815 in 13 European countries, mainly in Germany, France and Great Britain[8]; Claudia Pancino recorded 25 published in Italy in the 18th century, which almost doubled in the early 19th century, reaching 40 titles.[9] Some were addressed to midwives and were written in simple language, with questions and answers, so as to be understood even by "idiot midwives", as the title of Vincenzo Malacarne's manual significantly states.[10] Sometimes, the same author produced two versions, one for doctors and the other for midwives, as in the case of Jean-Louis Baudelocque, who wrote both the manual for surgeons *L'art des accouchemens*, and the simpler *Principes sur l'art des accouchemens, par demandes et réponses, en faveur des sages-femmes de la campagne*.[11]

2 Forceps and vectis: the "iron hands", symbols of the new midwifery

The production of midwifery aids also experienced a rapid increase, with the invention of a variety of instruments: to the ancient hooks used in embryotomies, new devices for the extraction of live foetuses were added, such as forceps and vectis. This was the revolutionary gamble of man-midwives: to save not only the mother, but also the child, or rather save the mother without sacrificing the child. Forceps acquired an emblematic value in this sense: the "iron hands" developed by man-midwives promised to achieve what a midwife's human hands were powerless to do: extract a living child in difficult childbirths. It is no coincidence that the instrument appears in some portraits of famous man-midwives as a symbol of their new specialisation: Giovanni Antonio Galli is portrayed in Bologna holding a set of forceps.[12]

This promise appealed to the new social sensitivities and expectations: extraction tools, boasted about by surgeons in previous centuries (crotchets; craniotomes, etc.), now appeared to many as "criminal and barbarous resources", especially since many theologians had spoken against them. As early as in 1648, the Parisian doctors of theology had condemned embryotomies, as Levret recalled in 1761: "A man-midwife who has human feelings must almost always look with horror at the other instrumental methods used in several cases; especially since today they are considered reprehensible before God and men" (cited by Nardi 1954, II: 263).

The advent of forceps therefore represented, in the eyes of many, a fundamental milestone in the history of midwifery: the start of the "most brilliant" era of this "art", as Baudelocque wrote,[13] the symbol of progress and of the defeat of death.

Its invention is credited, according to historians of obstetrics, to several people of different nationalities: by some to Flemish Jan Palfijn (or Jean Palfyn), who in 1717 presented to the Paris *Académie des Sciences* a tool designed to extract the head of a foetus wedged in the pelvis (but its reception by top surgeons was not favourable), by others to the Chamberlens, a French Huguenot family, who had fled to England in 1569, during religious persecutions. Both had developed an instrument consisting of two spoon-shaped branches that were inserted into the womb separately, fastened together and pulled jointly from the outside.[14] The Chamberlens managed to keep their invention (the actual inventor was probably Peter the Elder, a barber-surgeon and son of the founder, William) a secret for 4 generations because of their greed, as they used it in their activity, boasting that they were able to save women in labour, "without any prejudice for them and for the infants", as Hugh Chamberlen wrote in his preface to Mauriceau's treatise (cited by Nardi 1954: 225). However, a public demonstration held by Hugh Chamberlen in Paris in 1670 on a woman with rickets in the presence of Mauriceau had a disastrous outcome for both mother and baby, thus strengthening the great French obstetrician's opposition and marking the failure of the attempt to sell and market the instrument. The sale, however, appears to have been partly successful in the Netherlands, with the purchase by Endrich Van Roonhuyzen of a set of forceps, or possibly just half of one, a kind of vectis. The Chamberlen tool-bag was hidden by Dr Peter Chamberlen at Woodham Mortimer, near Maldon, under the floorboards of the country house where he lived and where it was found in 1813, after his death.[15]

These early forceps, however, were predominantly straight, and so ill-suited to use. Towards the middle of the 18th century, French André Levret and Scottish William Smellie almost simultaneously modified the forceps, introducing a curving of the metal branches which suited the shape of the pelvis, thus making the instrument much more effective in extracting a baby when there was lack of progress through the birth canal (Figure 8.2).[16]

As a symbol of the new midwifery, the instrument experienced an extraordinary success and spread rapidly, with the development of innumerable variants. At the beginning of the 19th century, French Alfred Velpeau had counted more than a hundred types, 33 of which were introduced in 1833 alone. Half-way through the century, H.F. Kilian listed 130, with minimal changes in curvature, length and handle grip.[17]

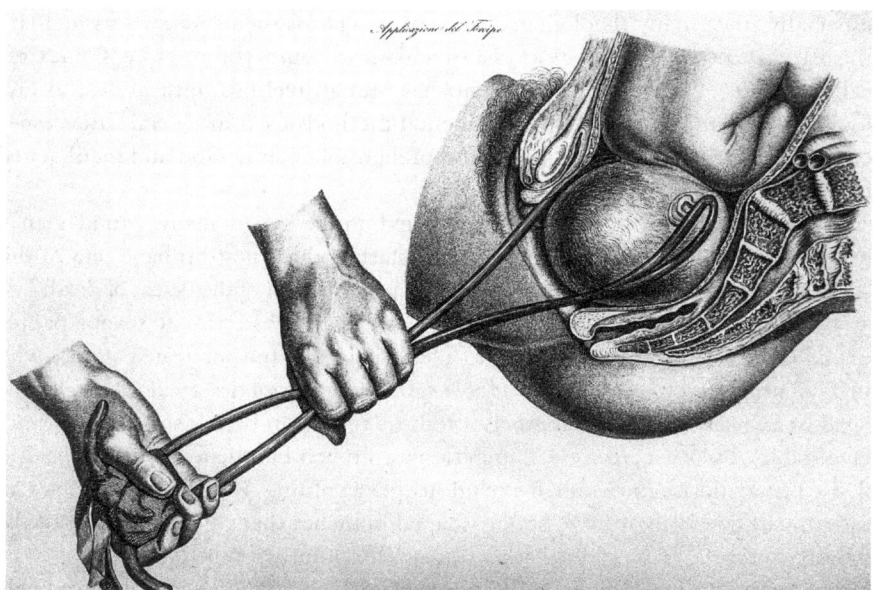

FIGURE 8.2 Deployment of forceps, from Giovanni Raffaele (1841), *Ostetricia teorico-pratica. Atlante.* Reproduced with permission of the Ministero dei Beni e delle Attività Culturali e del Turismo - Biblioteca Nazionale Marciana (Venice).

The enthusiasm generated by this instrument caused an "operational" craze that at the end of the century reached absurd proportions, with a use close to 50% of childbirths in some lying-in hospitals and with completely contradictory results compared to its stated purpose. As evidence of the trust in and the spread of the instrument, it is significant that, in 1817, when Princess Charlotte Augusta, daughter of princess Caroline and George, prince of Wales, died after a prolonged labour, the man-midwife was accused of not using forceps.[18]

Using it correctly, however, that is to say in the right way and at the right time, required long training; otherwise, serious damage could be caused to both mother and child, with lacerations and ruptures of the womb and compression of the skull of the unborn child. Midwifery historian Alfonso Corradi, also using data collected by Tarnier and other doctors, calculated a rate of mortality due to the use of forceps in Paris hospitals of 28% for mothers and 46% for foetuses.[19] These figures are certainly very different from those recorded in other regions of Europe, such as Fulda and Hesse, where, according to Shorter, in the 1830s maternal mortality had dropped to 3–4%.[20] These problems lasted until the first half of the 20th century so much so that, despite the lowering of mortality rates, the specific diagnosis of *failed forceps outside* (FFO) was devised.

In addition to forceps, the introduction of vectis should also be mentioned: this was used to correct the position of the foetus in childbirth and force its exit.

Used by Dutchman Van Roonhuyzen in the 17th century, its use spread in the following century, especially in Holland, Belgium and France.

Two other instruments had a decisive impact in midwifery practice and imagination: the pelvimeter and the stethoscope. The former, devised by Baudelocque, was a kind of compass made up by two prongs moving at one end along a sliding scale, thus making it possible to work out the measurement of the pelvis diameters. By measuring the external conjugate diameter, it was believed that the internal one, the anteroposterior diameter of the pelvic inlet, subsequently named "Baudelocque's diameter", could be calculated. This allowed a scale of difficulty in childbirth to be set out, marked by precise numerical values, which also set the limit (below 2.5 inches) beyond which birth through the natural route was impossible, as in the cases of pelvis deformed by rickets. In actual fact, Baudelocque's best known contribution contained an error that was to hinder obstetric practice for the next century and a half.[21] But this was still unknown: the discovery was enormously successful and contributed to increasing the prestige of this man-midwife, because it reinforced the image of midwifery as an exact science, based on mathematically irrefutable measurements.

The other instrument, the stethoscope, developed by René Laennec and presented to the Paris *Académie des Sciences* in 1818, was a simple hollowed wooden tube that, resting on a woman's belly, allowed the heartbeat of a foetus at an advanced stage of development to be heard, confirming that it was alive: what happened inside the womb was thus removed from the intimate perception of women, becoming something ascertainable from the outside.

This was a phase of intense experimentation of various obstetric operations, some of which, after their initial success, were abandoned, as they were shown to be useless or harmful. This is the case, for example, with symphysiotomy, the cutting of the pubic cartilage to widen a woman's pelvic opening in cases of extreme narrowness. Proposed by Jean-René Sigault, it was performed for the first time on a living woman in Paris on 2nd October 1777, with the assistance of Alphonse Leroy. It provoked such enthusiasm that the two inventors were awarded silver medals by the Paris Faculty of Medicine, while "a symphysiotomy epidemic" spread in France, and also in Holland and Spain. In Italy, it was promoted by Girolamo Personé in his *Trattato della sezione della sinfisi del pube e del taglio cesareo* (Treatise on symphysiotomy and on Caesarean section), from 1781.[22] The continuation of this experiment showed how misplaced this trust was and how dangerous and debilitating the intervention was for women: out of 42 women who had undergone the procedure, 15 died in Paris in the next few years and others were permanently disabled.[23]

Another operation which became more popular, in conjunction with the use of forceps, was episiotomy, the lateral surgical incision of the tissue at the base of the vagina, the so-called perineum, to widen its opening. Designed to facilitate both the insertion of the instrument and difficult births, it was subsequently used as a preventive measure even in natural childbirths, especially in the 20th century, to avoid possible lacerations of the perineum.[24]

Even "artificial premature labours", caused by puncturing the membranes to save the mothers in cases of extremely narrow pelvis, first attempted by Macaulay in 1756, became officially part of midwifery practice after Thomas Denman presented it at a meeting of man-midwives in London, beginning to use it in 1785.[25] And in the second half of the 18th century, as we shall see, the practice of Caesarean sections on living women also gained ground.

3 Active versus waiting obstetrician: a conflict of perspectives and practices

The use of these instruments and interventions varied considerably in midwifery practice, with a differentiation that ran across Europe, with two schools of thought strongly divided on the role of man-midwives in childbirths: between "active or operative" and "waiting" midwifery.[26] As suggested by these terms, given by medicine historians, the former supported a greater role by the man-midwife in childbirth, the latter greater prudence and patience, in line with ancient tradition. In the mid-18th century, these two schools consolidated the former in France with André Levret, the latter in Great Britain with William Hunter (1718–1783),[27] with the other national schools gravitating around this polarisation, from the German school, which favoured the active role, to the Austrian one led by Johann Lucas Boër (1751–1835), which followed the waiting approach. In this midwifery landscape, the Italian States were divided.

Both these schools were based on an overall idea of childbirth, from which the approach to treatment was derived. Active midwifery was rooted in Descartes' mechanistic view, which during the 17th and 18th centuries had been developed in medicine, from anatomy to physiology. The body was described as a set of pieces, threads and wheels, according to Hobbes' well-known representation.[28] The physiological processes were also reproduced within this analogy, as Harvey did with the blood system and as Philippe Hécquet also did, even more comprehensively, in the 18th century. Towards the middle of the century, this approach had also affected midwifery, especially in France, thanks to the writings of Levret and Astruc.[29]

The title of André Levret's manual was symbolic of this new medical-philosophical approach: *L'art des accouchemens démontré par des principes de physique et méchanique* (The art of childbirth demonstrated by principles of physics and mechanics) (1753). According to a definition destined to become famous, childbirth was presented as a "natural, mechanical operation, which may be demonstrated by geometry" (Levret [1753] (1761: 80). Jean Astruc came to describe it exactly in terms of a geometric problem, of a volume that had to be extracted from a given cavity: "From an extensible cavity of a given capacity, pull a flexible body, of given length and size, through a dilatable opening up to a certain point" (Astruc [1766] 1771: LXXJ).[30] Baudelocque also speaks of a "mechanical operation" in the preface of his manual: "The art of childbirths is a practical art, where all the principles are certain and all the operations can almost lead to geometric certainty: is childbirth not simply a mechanical operation subject to the laws of motion?" (Baudelocque 1781: VIII).[31]

Childbirth was thus reduced to a mathematical problem, the solution of which essentially depended on the relationships between volume and forces, between the numerical values of the container (the pelvic bones) and the content (the measurements of the baby's head), as well as on the types and forms of its presentation: for this reason, this school of thought was called "anatomic-mathematical".[32]

Such a view had important repercussions in terms of research: in this process of "geometrical reproduction of childbirth", part of a broader landscape of "geometrical reproduction of nature", it decisively advocated both the recording of measurements and the study of presentations and positions of the full-term foetus (meaning for the former the identification of the part that presented first in the upper part of the pelvis; for the latter, the relationships between this presented part and the different points of upper pelvis area). This field of research, started by François Solayrès, was followed in particular by his student Baudelocque, who classified as many as 16 presentations and 94 positions of the full-term foetus, with a complex taxonomy, clearly inspired by the natural sciences, which later obstetricians, such as Joseph Capuron and Franz Naegele, tried to simplify. In this process of geometrical reproduction of childbirth, by using a pelvimeter, he "mathematically" demonstrated the existence of "impossible" childbirths through the natural route, as mentioned earlier.

The application of Mechanism to midwifery thus gradually contributed to removing from the event its sacred aura, in a process linked to a wider depreciation of nature, whose objective limitations were being proven: not only could nature follow unusual routes, but could also be a cruel stepmother, setting lethal mechanisms in motion; the positive value of science and technology was thus emphasised as a means to correct its limitations.

The "waiting" school of thought was rooted in the organicistic view of nature, reworked in light of Newton's new theories. His dynamic view of matter, when applied to the sciences of life, had led to a revival in the representation of nature as a fruitful organism, endowed with autonomous and mysterious power.[33] In the medical-scientific context, this revival had been fully developed in Vitalism, based in France at the University of Montpellier, where Joseph Barthez was active, but taken up more widely in Europe, especially in Britain, where Hunter's influence was decisive.[34]

This view reworked the ancient metaphors of women as "field and land" and of the child as "fruit", in the name of an admiring and respectful gaze towards nature and its mechanisms, where the hand of God could be gleaned. Nature and God are terms that occur together in the works of Vitalists, since nature was the mirror and expression of His power. Out of all the natural functions, childbirth appeared as the ultimate expression, "the great spectacle of Nature", as Jean-François Sacombe, a pupil of Barthez, called it (cited by Filippini 2003: 268).[35] In this school of thought, scientific observation was joined by admiration, and research had physiology rather than pathology as its primary objective, supported by the belief that there could not be any intrinsic impediments to the natural state and that nature could overcome the obstacles that stood in its way, as long as "art works with it rather than against it" (Sacombe 1798a: 103).[36] "Nature left to herself will seldom fail to accomplish her own work", John Harvie wrote in 1767 (cited by Shorter 1985: 383).

According to the Vitalists, human error or alterations in the state of nature produced by society were the causes of any serious dystocia and death in childbirth. In Sacombe's view, midwifery was "the art of overcoming the obstacles that the vices of our physical education and the corruption of customs [...] are continually opposing to Nature in the most important of its functions" (Sacombe 1792: ch. VIII). This perspective was clearly applying Rousseau's philosophical principles, popular at the end of the 18th century, to midwifery.

The theoretical clash between the two opposing views had important repercussions on the treatment front: for the formers, man-midwives had to have an active role in childbirth and intervene promptly with instruments and/or interventions to avoid possible risks to the mother and/or the baby; for the latters, he had to let nature work, respecting its times and ways.

The world of European midwifery was thus profoundly divided both in theory and in practice: in some contexts, the use of forceps reached shocking rates; in others, it remained extremely limited, similarly to other obstetric interventions. German man-midwife Friedrich Osiander, in Göttingen, boasted about using instruments in 40% of childbirths, while Viennese Johann Boër, on the contrary, was proud of having intervened with instruments only once in 200 childbirths and in only two out of 1,000 with surgical interventions, with the use of forceps limited to 0.4% of cases.[37] And if for the followers of the anatomic-mathematical school, this instrument marked the beginning of progress in midwifery, for the supporters of waiting midwifery; on the contrary, it marked the beginning of an inauspicious and "degenerate" age.[38]

W. Hunter went as far as to say that it would have been better if they had never been invented, since "where they save one, they murder twenty" (Shorter 1982: 85).

This difference animated complex polemics, intertwined with different deontological views on the priority of the life of the mother over that of the child or with oppositions between corporations where not only midwives were involved, but sometimes even physicians, critical of man-midwives and in some cases eager to carve out their own space in this new professional field, as in the case of Sacombe, who was a physician.

In England, midwife Elizabeth Nihell strongly attacked man-midwives, particularly Smellie, accusing them of using the instruments excessively and causing serious damage, as the title of her book suggested: *A Treatise of the Art of Midwifery setting for various Abuses therein, especially as to the practice with instruments* (1760), a real accusation against the violence used to Nature, where she reiterated that: "Nothing can be more important to well-doing of the patient than for non violence to be used to Nature, who loves to go her own full time, without disturbance or molestation" (cited by Shorter 1985: 383).[39]

Teresa Ployant also pointed her finger against the "horrible instruments of cruelty" in her manual *Breve compendio dell'arte ostetricia* (Ployant [1797] (1803: 4), while Maddalena De Marinis accused man-midwives of making "the cradle of life an arsenal of death because of the hooks, knives, forceps and vectis introduced" (Guidi, 1984: 116).

No less harsh was the criticism of "waiting" physicians and man-midwives: in 1751, an anonymous pamphlet, *The Petition of the Unborn Babies*, attributed to anatomist Frank Nicholls, was presented at the Royal College of Medicine in London. In it, the unborn babies themselves voiced a denunciation of the tortures and deaths caused by the "cruel instruments", implicitly alluding to Smellie's activity.[40]

The clash was particularly fierce in France, where Sacombe even founded a midwifery school against the anatomic-mathematical view: the *École anti-symphyso-césarienne* (1798), with the aim of not only opposing the rival school of thought, but also freeing "the fairer sex from the thousand painful and useless manoeuvres, giving back to this art its ancient splendour and trying to bring it back to the path of nature" (Sacombe 1798b: 32). By suing Baudelocque for the death of a woman in childbirth, he even tried to use the legal route. His defeat (and subsequent conviction for defamation of character) marked the end of this school of thought and with it also the attempt to extend the practice of midwifery to physicians, henceforth firmly secured in the hands of surgeons.

4 European differences

The establishment of man-midwives on the childbirth scene in Europe occurred in very different ways and at different times, but substantially with a clear division between north and south: in Great Britain, Northern France and the Netherlands between the end of the 17th and the beginning of the 18th centuries, there were already various man-midwives or *accoucheurs* who attended normal as well as difficult childbirths, with larger and smaller sets of patients.[41] Guillaume Mauquest de La Motte is one of the better known, also because he left a precious account of his activity in the *Traité des accouchemens naturels, non naturels et contre nature*.[42] Active in northern Cotentin between the end of the 17th and the beginning of the 18th centuries, he attended on average up to two childbirths a day, assisting women of all social classes. Paul Portal, who worked in Paris at the same time, reported the increasing practice of being assisted by an *accoucheur*. In the first half of the 18th century, in London, William Giffard assisted on average with 50 childbirths per year, of women of all social classes, mostly difficult ones.[43]

Even in Great Britain, their establishment was rapid towards the mid-18th century (1720–1770),[44] although initially there were some mistrust and resistance: man-midwives were initially regarded with suspicion and made the subject of satire by sections of the public opinion and even by doctors: by doing a traditionally female job and entering a female scene, they were putting their masculinity at risk; consequently, they were looked upon as "half women", discredited and ridiculed.[45] Even the cover of John Blunt's (pseud. of S. W. Fores.) famous book, *Man-Midwifery Dissected* (1793), presented an ironic play on words: a *man mid wife*.[46] Significantly, some of the first man-midwives were not English, but Scottish, like William Smellie; therefore, outsiders were more willing to risk in their search for professional space and advancement.[47]

In France, in the traditional histories of midwifery, the spread of this figure is related to some court events: in 1663, the Sun King, Louis XIV, had called man-midwife J. Clément to attend to the childbirth of his mistress, Louise de La Vallière, thus launching the fashion of the *accoucheur*. Although the models imposed by the dominant social classes should not be underestimated, the phenomenon is more complex and the example of de La Vallière's childbirth is rather the sign of a confidence that was emerging throughout society, starting from the aristocratic classes. If in the 1730s, in Paris, many women still refused the *accoucheur*, fifty years later, in 1786, their percentage was significantly lower. Even in other cities, such as in Reims, between 1770 and 1797, an *accoucheur* like Pierre Robin had a very intense activity, with an average of 183 childbirths per year and a varied clientele, as evidenced by his valuable *carnets*.[48] So, man-midwives were active not only in the capitals, but also in smaller cities and towns, and they assisted women of all social classes, both in difficult and natural childbirths.

This trend was consolidated during the 19th century. In 1831, a doctor from Landau (Germany) wrote: "It is striking how the midwives are used less and less each. Now that women have gotten over their previous prejudices about modesty, the man-midwife has become fashionable for simple, natural deliveries" (Shorter 1982: 142). The same happened in Berlin: "Prosperous mothers almost always call a man-midwife to attend them; the less well-off content themselves with a midwife or a so-called handy-woman *Wickelfrau*" (Ibidem). In Great Britain, according to a survey carried out on a sample of rural localities, in 1895, three-quarters of all new mothers were assisted by a doctor.[49]

The social reality of southern Europe was very different: there, childbirth assistance remained firmly in the hands of midwives not only in the 18th century, but throughout the 19th and the first half of the 20th centuries as well.

The presence of man-midwives remained limited to difficult childbirths, according to the division established by law. But they found it difficult to intervene even in these cases, and not only in small towns, but also in important cities such as Venice: as late as 1800, the College of Physicians and Surgeons complained that "women in labour love to be assisted by women and those who agree without disgust or fear to be handled by the men of this art are rare" (Filippini, 1985a: 179, note 70).

This great differentiation was mainly due to cultural reasons: in this area, large sectors of public opinion considered it "indecent" for women to be visited by a man, even for health reasons: it was still a case of exhibiting those parts of the body that were significantly called "shameful" and this deeply clashed with their sense of decency and propriety. Some doctors also fully or partly shared this view, such as the Italian Vincenzo Malacarne and Giuseppe Moscati, or the French Philippe Hécquet, author of the pamphlet *De indécence aux hommes d'accoucher les femmes* (1705), where he maintained that it was "in the order of things that it be a woman to assist another woman in childbirth" (cited by Pancino 1984: 87). Italian philosopher Ludovico Antonio Muratori considered it "more decent" for the profession to be practised by women. Still in the name of female modesty, midwife Teresa Ployant invited women to educate themselves, to stem the encroachment of man-midwives on the childbirth scene.[50]

Another factor was linked to the confidence that the population had in midwives: Bolognese surgeon Giovanni Antonio Galli admitted that "here in Italy women in labour have the custom of only resorting to the help of midwives and of trusting only a midwife's skill" (cited by Pancino 1984: 99). In Naples, man-midwives did not have a proper title: they were called with the masculine form of the term *mammana* (female midwife): *vammanoni* (i.e. *mammanoni*), a custom which highlights the priority of the female figure in the collective imagination.[51]

This was also intertwined with the midwives' resistance to call a surgeon even in difficult deliveries, both so as not to have to admit to their professional defeat, and not to upset the family, sometimes reluctant maybe also for economic reasons. The important role played by the Catholic Church must also be emphasised: it is no coincidence that, if we try to trace the boundaries of the establishment of *accoucheurs*, we discover that they follow fairly the area of dominance of the Protestant faith. In these countries, a new body ethics that broke the ancient barriers of modesty in the name of survival and health[52] became established earlier. In Catholic countries, this seems to have been hindered not only by the persistence of a form of fatalism in the face of death, but also by the enduring values and symbols of maternal sacrifice embodied by the figure of the Virgin Mary (at the centre of a theological elaboration that clearly separated the two religions).[53] On the symbolism of which she is an expression, the Church founded its power of control over female sexuality, defending its monopoly against the intrusions of science and State.[54] Between the 18th and 19th centuries, a difficult phase of negotiation between ecclesiastical and political institutions, and between science and religion, began, not without tensions and conflicts, but also characterised by new alliances and synergies that still condition the laws of some Catholic countries, such as Italy and Ireland.

5 Midwives and man-midwives: the issue of manual interventions

This process of establishment of the figure of man-midwives was often accompanied – as we have seen (Chapter 7) – by legislation and norms that entrusted the assistance in difficult childbirths and the use of all midwifery instruments exclusively to them. In practice, the two different roles were thus officially and definitely separated: midwives assisted in natural childbirths, man-midwives in cases of dystocia, applying the interventions, both surgical and instrumental, that these involved. The caricature on the title page of John Blunt's book, *Man-Midwifery Dissected* (1793),[55] lends itself to being interpreted in this sense, with the image of a human figure vertically cut in two: on one side, a midwife shows her hand and has a basin nearby; on the other, a man-midwife holds the forceps in his hand and has a shelf of instruments in the background (Figure 8.3).

Enacted with the aim of fighting maternal and neonatal mortalities, this legislation was actually contradictory in its purpose, because it did not take into account the particular characteristics of childbirth: the difficulty in diagnosing dystocia, its often sudden onset during labour, the urgency of the intervention. If it could work in lying-in hospitals, or in some urban contexts, it certainly was significantly problematic to apply in rural or mountain areas, where finding a man-midwife could take too long or be almost impossible.

To overcome these drawbacks, midwives might have been trained in the use of forceps or vectis, while limiting it to special situations, in the absence of a man-midwife, as indeed some suggested (e.g. in Italy, some surgeons such as Giuseppe Moscati and Orazio Valota had expressed their opinion in this sense[56]), but this possibility clashed with the interests of the corporation of surgeons and with the symbolic value taken on by these midwifery instruments.

Not only did this not happen, but midwives were even forbidden from practising those internal manual manoeuvres that were part of their traditional art and that they could perform very well, as some man-midwives explicitly admitted (such as Edmund Chapman in 1735).[57] Manual versions performed inside the womb were then recognised as "surgical operations" and the responsibility of man-midwives. Venice's Medical-Surgical College, in line with other European medical colleges, specified this in 1802, supporting this principle with etymological arguments: "Let manual midwifery be part of surgery, as the etymological meaning of the word '*chirurgia*' (surgery), from the Greek '*chiron*' and '*jon*' (work and hand), states it without any doubt" (Filippini 1985a: 163). Other laws passed in the Kingdom of Italy in the second half of the 19th century confirmed it: "A midwife is forbidden from using surgical instruments or performing manual interventions on the fetus in the womb", art. V of the *Regolamento speciale con istruzioni per l'esercizio ostetrico delle levatrici dei Comuni del Regno d'Italia* (special Regulation with instructions for the midwifery practice by midwives of the Municipalities of the Kingdom of Italy) (1890) specified (Figure 8.4).[58]

This prohibition clearly deprived midwives of any chance to act at the onset of difficulties in childbirth, putting her in a critical situation both from a professional and moral point of view, as, in many instances, they were forced to choose between abiding by the law (which decreed they should not intervene) and saving mother and child (who suggested that they do it). This is what midwife Benedetta Fedeli Trevisan clearly denounced in 1800, in a petition addressed to Venice's *Regio Supremo Tribunale di Sanità* (Royal Supreme Health Court):

In fact, it is already proven that, in the encounter with a laborious childbirth, every moment, every delay is absolutely decisive and dangerous; it is therefore appropriate for a midwife not to delay and be perplexed [..] unfortunately there

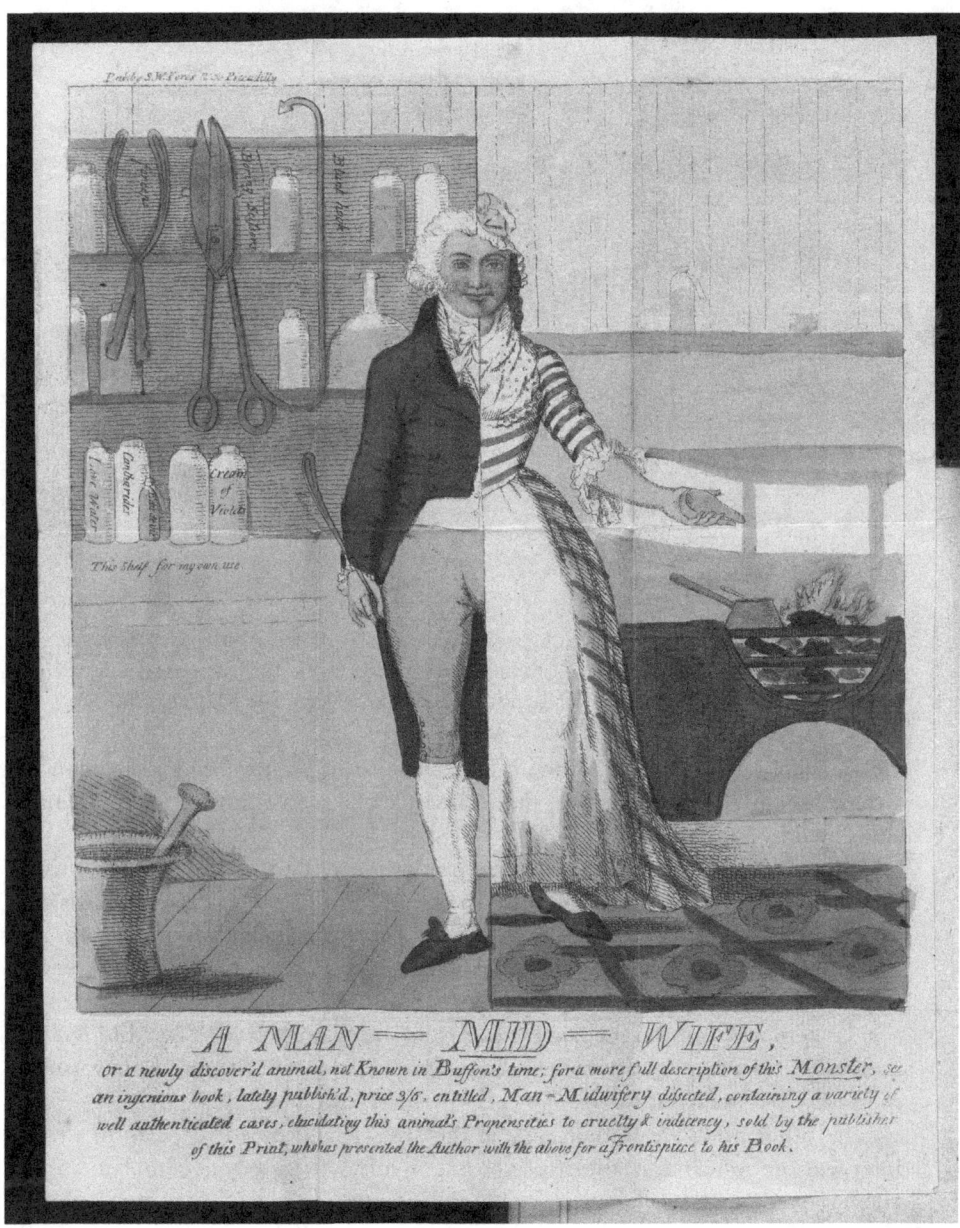

FIGURE 8.3 Title page of John Blunt's book (1793), *Man-Midwifery Dissected*. The book has the licence: Creative Commons Attribution (CC BY 4.0).

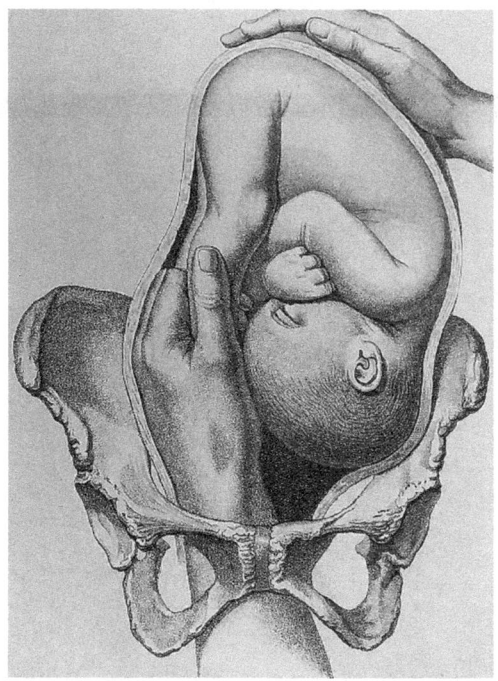

FIGURE 8.4 Versions and extraction, from Giovanni Raffaele (1841), *Ostetricia teorico-pratica. Atlante*. Reproduced with permission of the Ministero dei Beni e delle Attività Culturali e del Turismo - Biblioteca Nazionale Marciana (Venice).

are frequent cases when a midwife either has to break the law or abandon a woman in childbirth to her fate, in the absence of a man-midwife readily available (cited by Filippini 1984: 167).[59]

To remedy this situation and the "burdensome state of uncertainty", this Venetian midwife asked to be allowed to obtain a minor surgery diploma, which would allow her to continue to legally perform these manual interventions, as indeed happened. But hers was a very particular career path, undertaken by very few educated and combative women, such as Dutch sisters Elisabeth and Neeltje Van Putten, who around the same time passed the examination to be admitted to the guild of surgeons and achieved the title of *vroedmeestere*, the feminine version of *vroedmeester* (man-midwife).[60]

The other midwives either applied the law, or continued to perform these interventions ignoring it, thereby exposing themselves to formal complaints and convictions.

Even Teresa Ployant acknowledged in her manual that she had performed these manoeuvres, citing a specific incident that had taken place at the Naples' lying-in hospital: "On that occasion I disobeyed the orders for the sole purpose of making it known that I, too, know full well how to extract the foetuses in any position they may be, and possess the light of knowledge of which others have tried to deprive me" (Ployant [1797] 1803: 102).

Similar claims occur in other testimonies, such as that of a German midwife who, brought to court for this reason, claimed to have practised as many as 24 manoeuvres.[61] Just as it is well known that in Paris' lying-in hospital, Marie-Louise Lachapelle, by virtue of her authority and the power that derived from it, not only practised these versions, but also applied the forceps, as she herself wrote in her manual *Pratique des accouchements* (1821), with a level of autonomy that was unmatched in Europe.[62]

More than a century later, oral testimonies highlighted not only the inner drama expressed by Benedetta Trevisan, but even more the risk to which women in labour were exposed precisely because of this rule. A midwife from Friuli said:

> Once the afterbirth did not appear, a very serious thing, and I could not intervene, even if the woman was losing blood: that is, I could do it at my own risk, because if the woman died I would be in trouble. I had to help women to deliver it, but if it went well, it was well done! But if the woman died, I would go to jail. But if the woman died without me doing anything, nothing would happen, while if I helped her I would go to jail! This was the law. These are a doctor's work: if I invade the field, I'm wrong.
>
> (Lanzardo 1985: 18)

One may wonder why man-midwives had wanted to claim for themselves interventions that belonged to the manual tradition of midwives and that surely at the time they were mostly ill-prepared to perform. The fact is that the responsibility for these interventions was of crucial importance for the roles of the two figures in childbirth: at a time when instrumental practice was still limited, forbidding midwives from carrying out these manual manoeuvres meant making them completely dependent on their assistance, in need of a figure behind them, in short, simple "nurses" of childbirth. On the contrary, in many southern states, assigning them to man-midwives meant securing a much broader right of presence, and bypassing what they themselves recognised as the greatest obstacle to their presence: the aversion of women in labour. In other words, the real goal was full control of childbirth, including assistance to natural childbirths, as someone openly hoped: "It would be useful for humanity- Dr Michele Frari wrote in 1886- that the wise custom of other countries be admitted among us as well, that even regular childbirths, i.e. all childbirths be assisted by man-midwives" (cited by Vanzan Marchini 1985: 47).

The preferred option was therefore to introduce legislation that clashed with common sense and put the lives of women in labour at risk, but served to promote the figure of the man-midwife and a medicalisation of childbirth that struggled to impose itself in the social reality.

Notes

1 As the Venetian Senate wrote in the founding decree of the Venice School of Midwifery in 1773 (Filippini 1985a: 155).
2 Fissel (2018).

3 Speert (1973: 168 and 219).
4 Premuda (1958).
5 Foucault (1973).
6 Donnison (1977); Wilson (1995); Moscucci (1990); Woods and Gallery (2014).
7 Witkowski (1891); Corradi (1874–1877); Fasbender (1906); Siebold (1891); Nardi (1954).
8 Gélis (1988: 330–331).
9 Pancino (1984: 59–60).
10 Malacarne (1808).
11 Baudelocque (1787).
12 It is now in the Museum of Palazzo Poggi of the University of Bologna, which presents a rich collection of instruments of the 18th-century Bolognese obstetrical school: https://sma.unibo.it/it/il-sistema-museale/museo-di-palazzo-poggi/collezioni/gallery.
13 As J.-L. Baudelocque wrote in *L'art des accouchemens* (1781, vol. 1: X). The expression was taken up by Italian man-midwife Pasquale Leonardi Cattolica, who edited the third Italian edition of the *Dell'arte ostetricia* (Baudelocque 1833: XII).
14 Aveling (1882); Siebold (1891–1892); Fasbender (1906); Gall (1939); Nardi (1954: 218–228); Hibbard (2000).
15 Aveling (1882); Wilson (1995: 65–78); Rundi Hutter (2010). These instruments (the four pairs of forceps, three levers, three crotchets and three fillets) are now held by the Royal College of Obstetricians and Gynaecologists in London.
16 Hibbard (2000).
17 Nardi (1954, II: 262); Speert (1973: 282–284).
18 Randi Hutter (2010).
19 Corradi (1874–1877: 988).
20 Shorter (1982: 98).
21 Speert (1973: 212).
22 Personé (1781).
23 Gélis (1987, 1988: 376).
24 According to Park, episiotomies were already carried out by midwives in medieval and early modern times (Park 2018), but I did not find any confirmation of this in my research, nor elsewhere in other studies. Some midwifery historians have attributed its introduction to G. A. Michaelis (Fasbender (1906); others to F. Ould who suggested it in 1742 (Shorter 1982).
25 Betta (2006: 154).
26 Nardi (1954: 300–305).
27 Bynum and Porter (1985).
28 Ehrard (1963); Daston and Pomata (2003); Cavarero (1995: 187–195).
29 Filippini (2003a).
30 Translated from the French edition.
31 Translated from the French edition.
32 Nardi (1954, II: 266–272).
33 Merchant (1980).
34 Ehrard 1963 (ch. IV.3); Duchesneau (1985); Daston and Pomata (2003).
35 A full and exhaustive reconstruction of the figure of Jean-François Sacombe, to whom I have devoted some essays (Filippini 1992, 1995 (II part, ch. 1) and 2003a), has never been carried out. Ignored or defamed by midwifery historians (for example, Dumont and Morel (1968); Pundel (1969)), or mistaken for an advocate of symphysiotomies (Gall 1922), he was revalued in the 1970s and 1980s by followers of the "natural childbirth" movement, such as B. This (1982).
36 Translated from the French edition, like the following citations.
37 Siebold (1891–1892, II: 237–240); Nardi (1954: 270); Schlumbohm (2001: 72).

38 As Luigi A. Colla wrote in his manual (Colla 1798). The author had trained at Boer's school, translating some of his works into Italian.
39 On these allegations and querelles, see Vasset (2013).
40 Cody Forman (2005: 181).
41 As pointed out by Wilson (1985, 1995).
42 La Motte, Guillaume Mauquest de ([1715] 1989).
43 But in the calendar year 1730, he recorded 72 childbirths (Wilson 1995: 94).
44 Fissel (2018).
45 Cody Forman (2005).
46 Blunt (pseud. of Fores) (1793).
47 Cody Forman (2005); Woods and Galley (2014).
48 Gélis (1988: 312–313).
49 Shorter (1982: 142–143).
50 Ployant (1803: 5–6).
51 Guidi (1996: 118).
52 Gélis (1988: part. III, ch. 3). I discussed it in Filippini (1990).
53 Accati (1998).
54 Pelaja-Scaraffia (2008).
55 Blunt (pseud. of Fores) (1793).
56 Parma (1984: 121).
57 Shorter (1982: 83).
58 Basso (2015: 72).
59 Translated from the Italian edition.
60 Marland (1993: 201).
61 Shorter (1982: 83).
62 Sage-Pranchère (2017: ch. 3).

9
LYING-IN HOSPITALS

1 Unmarried and poor mothers in the service of training

During the 18th century, lying-in hospitals were established throughout Europe. Their establishment marks a crucial stage in the history of birth and of midwifery; on the one hand, because it laid the foundations for the process of hospitalisation of childbirth which would develop in the 20th century; on the other hand, because the practices and treatment models established in these institutions would later spread throughout the countries; moreover, the clinical experimentation which would have such a profound effect on the history of midwifery was carried out precisely in the lying-in hospitals.

Of all the 18th-century innovations, this is perhaps the one that most fully represents the set of goals put forward by political institutions in the field of birth, as it combined the multiple objectives that substantiated them: demographic, scientific and welfare. These hospitals were in fact functional to the training of man-midwives and midwives, but the aim was also to provide illegitimate and/ or destitute mothers with a secret shelter, in order to protect their honour, prevent infanticide and counter the extremely high mortality of foundlings.

The different relevance of these objectives produced variously marked differences, which characterised the various European institutions: in some, as in German lying-in hospitals, which were all university hospitals, the aim of training man-midwives, first and foremost, prevailed[1]; in others, as was the case in Catholic and Orthodox countries, the primary aim was the reception of unmarried mothers[2]; in yet others (in Great Britain, for example), the aim was, above all, the support for married but destitute mothers.[3] They were, however, united by some basic features: with the exception of Great Britain, they were mostly financed by the State or by other public institutions and placed under the management of a man-midwife, who was also the head-teacher in the school, and were reserved for two groups of women: unmarried mothers ("illegitimate") and married but destitute ones ("legitimate").

The formers were then divided into fee-paying and non-paying. In exchange for their free accommodation and treatment, destitute mothers were expected to agree to being examined during clinical training, with a distinction between pupils: married women participated in the training of man-midwives, unmarried ones in the training of midwives; this distinction was aimed at safeguarding the girls' modesty as much as possible. "Illegitimate pregnant women" had a right to anonymity: they could keep their names secret and cover their faces with veils.[4] In Catholic countries, they would usually leave their children in foundling hospitals, participating for some time in the breastfeeding of these babies.[5]

This opportunity, which marks a clear differentiation between Catholic and Protestant countries (where mothers were required to take their children with them when they left the hospital), is linked to different cultural and social factors: the sense of female and family honour; an illegitimate child's different status; the laws regarding the paternity searches; the role of the Church. The scandal arising from bearing an illegitimate child was considered very serious, especially at a time when the limits of social acceptance of illegitimate motherhood were narrowing, even before the civil codes forbade paternity, at the turn of the 19th century. The formalising of this principle in the Napoleonic Code and in other European codes of law marks a significant turning point in the history of women: unmarried mothers were left without any legal protection and unable to exercise the types of pressure to which they had resorted in the past, if only to force fathers to support their children financially (see Chapter 2.7).[6]

In various places, the parish priests themselves pushed women, who had become "mothers through illegitimate intercourse", to take refuge in lying-in hospitals and then abandon their babies, to avoid the serious scandal between their parishioners and such bad examples of "immorality". To counter the phenomenon, in the Lombardy-Veneto region, the Austrian government was forced to issue a special circular: *Sopra l'obbligo ai parroci di non suggerire alle madri di passare i parti illegittimi agli esposti* (On the obligation for parish priests not to suggest that mothers put their illegitimate babies into foundling hospitals) (27 luglio 1832).[7]

The establishment of lying-in hospitals also marks a significant innovation in terms of the fight against infanticide, by emphasising prevention rather than repression. The fact that an unmarried pregnant girl could be admitted in an institution often far from her village in good time allowed her to preserve the honour whose loss was indicated as one of the main causes of many infanticides. At the inauguration of Prague's lying-in hospital, in 1789, Joseph II said:

> The lack of shelter and the fear of shame will no longer serve as excuses for mothers to kill their children. A shelter for pregnant and unlucky women exists and they are invited to come here. They will neither be questioned about their religion nor about their social position.
>
> *(Le Fort 1866: 141)*[8]

The same aims had inspired the reform of both Vienna's and Milan's lying-in hospitals, standardising the institutions in the Austro-Hungarian Empire.

The proximity of lying-in and foundling hospitals established the symbolic link between the two institutions, in a trend prevailing between the late 18th and early 19th centuries when, during the reorganisation of different types of hospitals, lying-in hospitals were separated and located in independent buildings. In Milan, for example, the new lying-in hospital, established in 1780 in the former convent of *Santa Caterina alla Ruota*, also included the foundling hospital.[9] In Paris, the *Office des Accouchées* of the *Hôtel-Dieu* was transferred during the Revolution (1795) to the new lying-in hospital housed in the rooms of the former convent of Port Royal, with an adjoining foundling hospital.[10] This proximity, which took place even in smaller hospitals, avoided the problems of transporting infants, contributing to their protection.

The women admitted were actually largely unmarried, as has been established by research on entry registers, in a percentage ranging between 70% and 80% in the first decades of the 19th century (in Paris, the *filles-mères* reached a percentage of 82.8%; 69% in Göttingen; 72.5% in Turin). Most of them were girls belonging to the poorest section of the population: domestic servants, peasants and seamstresses.[11] The first two categories were the most frequently represented: young peasant women, sent to the cities to serve in the houses of the nobility and middle class, were particularly exposed to their own masters' advances or aggressions. As they very often lived in the latter's homes, they were most likely to find themselves having to rely on lying-in hospitals.

Moreover, despite what the regulations stated, many pregnant women were taken to lying-in hospitals and forcibly locked up by family members, or by the police; a minority of them were prostitutes. As I said, a considerable role was played, in this step, by the figure of parish priests who, according to the rules, were responsible for drawing up the certificates of poverty necessary to be admitted.

Married women or widows (which also included various "illegitimate" ones) were also, for the most part, victims of violence, "abandoned or pushed out of their homes by brutal husbands, or widows forced to leave their children in the hands of other people", as Scipione Giordano, director of Turin's lying-in hospital, wrote in the mid-19th century (Giordano 1876: 21).[12]

In most lying-in hospitals, the rules allowed unmarried women to be admitted a few months before the birth, when the pregnancy became obvious: in Turin, in the mid-19th century, most were admitted between the 7th and 8th months of pregnancy; the same happened in Venice, with admissions lasting 62 days. In Göttingen, between 1791 and 1829, an average admission lasted 46 days.[13] The right to anonymity was guaranteed with varying degrees of diligence and in different ways: in some lying-in hospitals, women wrote their names on tickets that the consultant opened only if necessary; in others (such as in Göttingen or Turin), their identity was shown on the secret entry registers; elsewhere (such as in Turin), they were also given a "hospital" name. They could also cover their faces with a veil, but this right seems to have been rarely exercised. Scipione Giordano reported:

I had made the veil available to those women who wanted to use it; few though, I confess, used it. Having taken the first step, having crossed the threshold of the hospital, and having already been recognised by their companions in misfortune and by the attendants, many cared very little about being recognised by those who surrounded them for the purpose of giving midwifery assistance (Giordano 1876: 24).

There were few paying patients; the regulations allowed them not to participate in the clinical training, to be housed in separate rooms and even to have a maid (in Turin, their percentage was around 8%).[14] They certainly continued to prefer the houses of midwives, as in the past, despite many laws forbidding it.

Life inside the hospitals was based on a strict, "cloister or prison" (Giordano 1876: 22) discipline based on a clear separation from the outside, on a rigid allocation of the time devoted to work, religious practice and medical examinations, which gave these institutions a hybrid and in many ways ambivalent appearance, halfway between the prisons of the *ancien régime* and modern hospitals, where medical assistance went hand in hand with moral re-education.[15] Pregnant women were required to work for the benefit of the hospital (spinning, sewing or laundering), do the cleaning, go to confession and pray. They could spend some time during allocated hours with a family member in the parlour, but under strict surveillance. In some lying-in hospitals, such as in Russia, they had to assist other women in childbirth. The nurses and midwives were required to "watch over that pregnant women behave with calm and composure, that they attend modestly to divine service", and even "to closely guard them to prevent their escape".[16] Some patients, in fact, tried to escape, as if from a prison, even putting their lives at risk, as Turin's obstetrician Scipione Giordano reported:

> I mention one fact: one of these women, nine-months pregnant, using sheets cut into large strips, lowered herself from the height of the second floor into the street; the rope was not long enough; she fell and fractured her femur. This example can give an idea of the state of prostration affecting many of the patients, who did not have such energy.
>
> (Giordano 1876: 28)

All patients had to participate in the clinical training: they were visited in special rooms by a man-midwife, in the presence of groups of students who practised, in turn, especially during childbirths.

It is clear that women tried to avoid this exhibition of themselves, concealing their labour as long as they could, as the doctors themselves testified. Luigi Cazzani, a man-midwife in the lying-in hospital in Pavia, reported in his 1862 annual report about a woman who,

> in the hope of keeping her childbirth concealed from the practising students in the hospital, was able to silently manage her pain to the point where, after the membranes of the egg broken and a large amount of water fallen on the ground, could no longer conceal her condition.
>
> (Cazzani 1863: 24)

Even Edoardo Porro, a man-midwife in Milan's lying-in hospital, in 1872 wrote that "Most pregnant women conceal the first pains of labour as far as possible in order to reduce the time during which they are forced to remain under surveillance or assistance in the delivery room" (cited by Pomata 1980: 500).

This requirement, in exchange for free admission, was criticised by a section of the public opinion, which considered this exchange as a kind of legalised prostitution. As late as the beginning of the 20th century, in Verona, the lying-in hospital was reported to be "widely considered almost a branch of the city's brothels for the pregnant women admitted there" (Ibidem: 502).

This reservation was also shared by some doctors: in 1866, Dr Ferdinando Palasciano opposed the establishment of the lying-in hospital in Naples in the name of female modesty, stating that all the patients should have been "warned first about what was demanded of them" and given their "full consent" (cited by Guidi 1986: 123).

For this reason, in the larger and better-organised hospitals, unmarried patients were housed on separate floors or wards from married ones, so as to be able to identify the ones destined to the training of midwives and man-midwives, trying at the same time to shelter the girls as much as possible from male contact and gaze. Other precautions to guard the patients' modesty included codifying the training according to rigid rules that ensured, for example, not only the presence of a teaching midwife, but that the woman in labour would be covered, with her face veiled, or turned so she would not face the doctor.

After childbirth, they spent on average two further weeks in the hospital and had to be available to breastfeed the foundlings for a few months, unless they paid a fee.

British lying-in hospitals deserve a separate mention, as they differed from the European ones both in terms of practice and in their patients: they were in fact supported by charity donations and depended on the philanthropic associations that regulated the admissions and appointed both doctors and midwives, who had to be either unmarried or widows. Each member had the right to have a certain number of women admitted, depending on the amount of money paid. It was a system destined to consolidate relationships of patronage, where women played an important role. Another distinctive feature consisted in the fact that in general, only poor married mothers were admitted, who could not subsequently abandon their children.[17] The first lying-in hospital founded in London in 1749, specified it in the name itself: The Lying-in Hospital for Married Women, later renamed British Lying-in Hospital. The City of London Lying-in Hospital, opened in 1750, was also for poor, married women. Only a few lying-in hospitals, such as the General Lying-in Hospital, founded in Westminster in 1752, did not reject illegitimate mothers.[18] In Dublin, Ireland, the first Lying-in Hospital (the Rotunda) was founded by man-midwife Bartholomew Mosse in 1745.[19]

It is clear that this was influenced by a profound cultural difference in the understanding of the concept of charity, which separated Catholic from Protestant countries, for which moral judgement was the basic criterion for selection. Unmarried mothers gave birth to their children in workhouses' lying-in hospital wards.[20] We must also remember that, in the England, throughout the 18th century and until the 1834 Poor Law (Bastardy Clause), fathers were required to support their illegitimate children, under penalty of imprisonment if they refused.[21]

2 New midwifery rituals and practices

The distribution of European lying-in hospitals varied a great deal. They were concentrated mostly in cities and in the North, and varied in size, too: alongside the large institutions in Paris, Vienna, St. Petersburg and Moscow, which in the mid-19th century exceeded 1,500 deliveries per year, they were more modest structures, averaging a few hundred deliveries per year (e.g. London, Bremen, Berlin, Frankfurt). In Italy, they were primarily located in the cities of the North and Centre, often in modestly sized buildings. With the exception of the larger ones in Milan, Turin and Naples (around 400–500 deliveries per year), the others admitted only a few hundred pregnant women, even though, during the 19th century, they grew steadily.

They were managed by a man-midwife, the director of the midwifery school, who supervised the entire staff, ensured midwifery lessons took place and prepared official reports. A head-midwife also had an important role: she welcomed the incoming patients, guaranteed order in the wards, followed the natural deliveries, took care of the transport of newborns to the foundling hospital (if this took place) and assisted the director in non-natural deliveries as the only "female authority", as stated in the regulations of the Padua lying-in hospital.[22] In Catholic countries, there was another figure who played an important role: a priest, who was in charge of moral education, religious practices and the baptism of newborns. The good functioning of the hospital largely depended on the relationships between these three figures, set by the regulations, but in practice was determined above all by agreements and alliances influenced by long-standing traditions and cultural and/or religious orientations. In 19th-century Italy, there were sometimes strong conflicts between medical and ecclesiastical personnel, which also led to dismissals and/or resignations.

In Milan, for example, the charity nuns, whom the management had decided to bring to *Santa Caterina alla Ruota* in 1846, were forced to leave after four years due to conflicts with the director, who objected to their excessively rigid discipline, their "too sensational solemnity in the administration of the last comforts of religion (i.e. the extreme unction) to pregnant women undergoing operations or dangerously ill", with counterproductive effects on the patients' health (Griffini 1868: 558). Also in Turin, man-midwife Scipione Giordano lamented the excessive influence of the priest who intervened in the life of the wards, creating a climate of guilt among the patients: "religion, designed to support and console [is] often an instrument of terror" (Giordano 1876: 22). This conflict ended with Giordano's resignation in 1863.

In many European hospitals (from France to Italy and Austria), the head-midwife had significant power. In Paris, between the 18th and 19th centuries, in the Port-Royal lying-in hospital, Marie-Louise Lachapelle's role of *sage-femme en chef* was even more emphasised by the scarce presence of Baudelocque, *accoucheur* of many ladies from the European nobility, caught up in an intense web of commitments with its external clients. This also explains the low number of obstetric operations recorded at the hospital (equal to 1.3% of cases between 1798 and 1809), also affected – according to Scarlett Beauvalet-Boutouyrie – by a change of direction by Baudelocque himself, towards a more "waiting" approach to midwifery, consolidated by his successor Antoine Dubois.[23] On the contrary, in Göttingen, the figure of the *Geburtshelfer* was dominant and his presence very powerful: Friedrich Benjamin Osiander, man-midwife between 1792 and 1822, supported the absolute priority of clinical practice and considered the women hospitalised "as living manikins" to be used for the sake of the teaching institution.[24] Assisted by his students, he intervened in 46% of childbirths, applying the forceps in 40% cases.

It is clear that these hospitals, precisely because of their training function, imposed treatment models and practices destined to become established even beyond the hospital walls in the local practice, thus consolidating the process of medicalisation of birth.[25] The position of women during childbirth fitted with these models and practices: the traditional variety of positions was replaced by a fixed one, and the bed replaced the birthing chair. The most frequent reason given by man-midwives was that the chair hastened the delivery and could cause lacerations. In actual fact, the lying-down position was more comfortable and dignified for the man-midwife; it was more practical for training purposes and lent itself to the use of instruments. In lying-in hospitals, therefore, a special bed was used, placed in a delivery room, in front of a fireplace (Figure 9.1). Man-midwives also imposed it in their private practices: giving birth in bed then became the fashion in the privileged classes, who resorted more frequently to a man-midwife.

On this choice (chair or bed), a debate opened up that transcended the medical world and involved women, with conflicting positions. In 1793, Venetian noblewoman Lucia Mocenigo gave birth to her first child in her bed, assisted by man-midwife Giuseppe Vespa, and discussed it heatedly, first in her letters to her sister Paolina, who, on the contrary, continued to prefer a birthing chair:

> I cannot help answering an item from the letter you wrote me last week: you do not approve for yourself of the less dangerous way of giving birth in bed: what do you believe is the cause of your troublesome and prolonged [blood] loss? Precisely from a delivery on the birthing chair; it is only natural that the efforts made in that position should bring more consequences than those which such an event in an almost horizontal position, that is to say on a bed, requires: Vespa told me that he would be very pleased to talk to you about this matter.
>
> (ACBg, Memmo's Archive, b. 1)[26]

In lying-in hospitals, discipline protocols were also established which, despite being typical of all hospital institutions, were strengthened by the weakness and social marginalisation of the pregnant women. The extremely bad treatments they were subjected to remained a persistent feature in many lying-in hospitals, particularly in Southern Europe, until the second half of the 20th century, when the range of people using them began to change. It should, in fact, be emphasised that, since the second half of the 19th century, there had been a steady growth

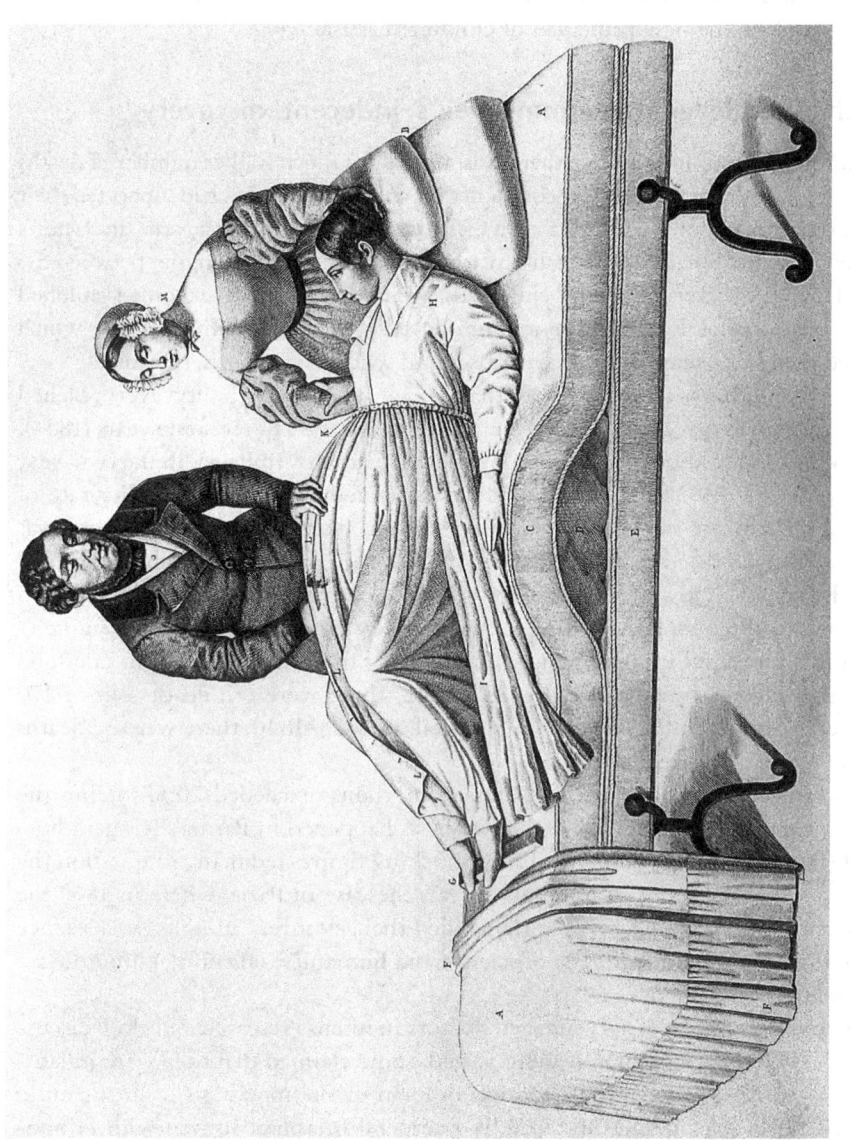

FIGURE 9.1 Obstetric examination by a man-midwife, from Giovanni Raffaele (1841), *Ostetricia teorico-pratica. Atlante*. Reproduced with permission of the Ministero dei Beni e delle Attività Culturali e del Turismo - Biblioteca Nazionale Marciana (Venice).

in the number of poor, married women who resorted to hospitals in the most desperate situations, sometimes after days of labour, in an attempt to save their own lives. To cope with situations like these, in some hospitals, an emergency midwifery service was created, to provide home care to poor pregnant women. They would help to secure the establishment of hospitals in local areas, thus further spreading the new principles of childbirth assistance.

3 Childbed fever and Semmelweis's 'indecent' discovery

In European lying-in hospitals, there was generally a much higher number of deaths than in home deliveries. In clear contradiction with the aims that had supported their creation, in many of the institutions which aimed to be *machines à guérir* (in Tenon's famous words),[27] maternal mortality reached staggering levels, ranging between 5% and 11%. In the days following childbirth, women caught a fever, called childbed fever, or puerperal fever (a definition introduced by Thomas Willis in 1676), which caused their body temperature to increase until, within a few days, they died.[28]

In Milan, Italy, in the decade 1834–1843, overall morbidity even reached 39%, with an average mortality of 7.2%, and peaks of 22.8% in some years (1834), when the disease affected more than half of the patients. In Pavia, in the two-year period of 1829–1830, one third of the patients fell ill, with a mortality rate of 11%. In Turin, in 1859, in the married-women ward alone, the mortality was 6%.[29] This was discouraging data compared to the mortality in home deliveries, which was much lower: in Paris, it was 0.6%, compared to 8.2% in the lying-in hospitals in 1861–1862, according to the report by Interior Minister Malgaigne.[30] Maternal mortality in some lying-in hospitals in the UK was lower: in London's Lying-in Hospital in the decade 1833–1842, there were ten deaths out of 170 deliveries and in Dublin's Lying-in Hospital, in 1833–1840, there were 32 deaths out of 1,881 deliveries.[31]

In some periods, in Italy and France, mortality exceeded 20%, forcing the authorities to temporarily close the wards, as happened in Parma's lying-in hospital (1868) or in Paris (1866).[32] These shocking figures led many to question the very existence of lying-in hospitals, as was the case in Paris, where in 1869 the *Societé médicale des Hôpitaux* even demanded their closure, "au nom de la science et de l'humanité" (in the name of science and humanity) (Beauvalet-Boutouyrie 1999: 309).

The search for the causes engaged doctors in intense research and close discussions.[33] The theories branded about varied: some claimed that they were inflammatory processes due to the retention of lochi or the metastasis of breast milk; others spoke of epidemics induced by puerperal miasmas, in line with Hippocrates' theories; others pointed their fingers at the "moral suffering" affecting the hospitalised women, thus identifying the causes in their social and psychological suffering. Political institutions were also involved in resolving what appeared to be a social as well as a health issue. In 1864, the French government sent Dr Léon Le Fort on a tour of major European lying-in hospitals to carry out a comparative investigation; the data he gathered still represent a valuable source of information for the study of motherhood, even if he did not succeed in identifying the medical causes of such high mortality.[34]

The merit of guessing the true cause of mortality is ascribed to a young Hungarian doctor, one of Škoda's pupils, an assistant at the first midwifery clinic in Vienna's General Hospital (*Allgemeines Krankenhaus der Stadt Wien*), directed by Professor Klein: Ignác Semmelweis (1818–1865).[35]

Since the clinic was divided into two parts, one for female student-midwives and the other for male surgery students, Semmelweis had tried to understand why, in the section attended by male students, mortality was much higher than in the other, a fact which was well known to patients, who begged to be admitted to the latter. For example, in 1833, the annual maternal mortality rate in the first clinic (for male students of surgery) was 527/10,000 deliveries; in the second clinic (for female student-midwives), it was 226/10,000.[36]

When he analysed the autopsy report of a doctor, a friend of his, who had died of an infection contracted from blood during a dissection, he realised with amazement that the infection was very similar to that found on women who had died of childbed fever. He thus deduced that the infection caused by corpses and childbed fever had the same origin and that man-midwives and male students were the carriers of the infection, as they moved from the anatomy room to the delivery room without taking any precautions. It should be remembered that, following Klein's orders, they had to perform several post-mortems in the morning, before entering the obstetrics ward.

In 1847, Semmelweis therefore required all staff to wash their *hands* with *chlorinated lime solutions*, achieving a dramatic drop in mortality (to 127/10,000).[37] Despite this, he was strongly opposed, and his theory rejected by large part of the academic world, first of all by Klein: few doctors were willing to accept the inconvenient truth that attributed to their hands the responsibility of the high mortality among mothers and babies.

Regardless of Škoda's support, Semmelweis' contract was not renewed and he decided to leave Vienna and move to Budapest, where he continued to apply his *Lehre* first at the Szent Rókus Hospital, then at the university hospital. But he experienced hostility and resistance from many colleagues and health personnel even there. The difficult working conditions and, above all, the criticism and silence directed at the book he finally published in 1861, *Die Ätiologie, der Begriff und die Prophylaxis des Kindbettfiebers* (The Etiology, Concept and Prophylaxis of Childbed Fever),[38] caused him to develop an aggressive and obsessive attitude which became increasingly worse. He began to show signs of obvious madness; for this reason, he was committed to the Vienna asylum in 1865, where he died a few weeks later, in a cruel twist of fate, of sepsis, caused by a cut he had received in the hospital.

Thirteen years later, Louis Pasteur, after isolating the streptococcus bacterium from the blood of a dead mother, irrefutably proved the correctness of his theory in a memorable lecture at the *Académie de Médecine* in Paris, which marked the birth of modern microbiology and the beginning of a new chapter for lying-in hospitals. Following his theories, English surgeon Joseph Lister adopted similar measures, requiring all personnel to wash their hands with carbolic acid (phenolic acid), thus succeeding in reducing mortality. French and German practitioners implemented Lister's ideas in 1874; in the early 1880s, these antiseptic measures were adopted in all European lying-in hospitals, with good results.[39]

The battle for antisepsis (against the spreading of germs) was soon joined with that for asepsis: to prevent infections, rubber gloves, masks and above all the boiling of instruments were introduced at the end of the 19th century. In France, S. E. Tarnier and A. Pinard were pioneers in this battle, reorganising the lying-in hospital, named after Baudelocque, according to the new principles: ventilation and daily washing of the rooms with antiseptic liquid, washbasins in every room, rigid separation of the sick from the healthy, washing of women in childbirth and new mothers with antiseptic fluid. They thus succeeded in lowering mortality from 1.2% (1891) to 0.43% (1899).[40] So, the war against puerperal fever recorded its first significant victories, even though it was only towards the mid-1930s that it could be said to have been definitively won, when the advent of sulphonamides (the early antibiotics) made it possible not only to prevent, but also to cure and heal infections, opening a new era in social and health history.[41]

4 Puerperal insanity and infanticide: new medical, legal and social perspectives

Another disease, in some way related to childbed fever due to its onset in the postpartum period, was the focus of attention of doctors between the 18th and 19th centuries. It did not affect the body, but the mind, causing – according to their descriptions – conditions of alienation so profound as to make women dangerous to themselves and others, especially to their babies, against whom they exhibited aggressive behaviour that could lead to infanticide. Its symptoms were initial irritability and sadness, making these women complain incessantly; being affected by insomnia and lack of appetite; and increasingly intense agitation, which finally precipitated into full-blown madness.

The women most often affected were unmarried and poor mothers, who crowded the majority of the rooms in the new hospitals opened, thanks to the reorganisation of the late 18th century, but even women from the privileged classes were afflicted by it. Doctors treated them by forcing them into straight-jackets, isolating them and keeping them in the dark, sedating them with opium, chloroform, ether or ammonia or applying leeches to their temples and genitals. Women often recovered within a few weeks.[42]

As in the case of childbed fever, doctors analysed the symptoms and progress of the illness, wondering about its possible causes. In this respect, traditional medicine provided the usual explanation linked to an imbalance in the humours, the so-called "hysterical suffocation": that is to say an invasion of putrid humours, a stagnation of their lochi rising from the uterus and spreading through their bodies, or a stagnation of their breast milk that, failing to escape from their breasts, spread through their bodies until it flooded their brains, as Dr Nicolas Puzos wrote in his *Traité des accouchemens, contenant des observations importantes sur la pratique de cet art [..] et sur les dépôts laiteux* (1759): "When breast milk settles in the brain it produces dementia or madness" (cited by Fiume 1995: 86).[43] Puerperal mania was, in short, "directly linked to the act of giving birth" (Marland 2004: 113).

The first psychiatrists of the late 18th century, however, distanced themselves from these explanations, focusing on the incidence of what they referred to as "moral causes", i.e. psychological and social factors. It was clear to them, as would be for psychoanalysts, that the triggering factors had to be sought, in addition to the physiological imbalance produced by pregnancy and childbirth, also in the psychological and social discomfort experienced above all by unmarried mothers in a society where the mother figure was extolled, but only within a legitimate family, whereas the so-called "illegitimate pregnant women" were terribly marginalised, all the more so within the new bourgeois morality. Bound by laws forbidding paternity searches, rejected by their families, greatly oppressed by their poverty, many caved in under the weight of loneliness and dishonour. Admission to lying-in hospital, although it allowed some to conceal their guilt, was often just the umpteenth stage in an ordeal of suffering.[44] A 22-year-old weaver admitted to the Salpêtrière Hospital in May 1857, with "an altered figure, a restless gaze, limbs agitated by convulsive quivering, completely alien to what happened around her and plunged in a kind of ecstasy" (Fiume 1995: 98–99), was a girl whose lover had beaten and abandoned her as soon as he became aware of her pregnancy, threatening to kill her and the child.

But puerperal insanity did not only affect "illegitimate" mothers: it was an expression of other forms of hardship that mothers, especially poor ones, experienced, exposed as they were to repeated, unwanted pregnancies, subjected to heavy daily work, sometimes victims of domestic violence, or abandoned by their husbands, powerless against their abject poverty and unable to support their children: in the mid-19th century, the majority of women admitted with this diagnosis to the Royal Edinburgh asylum (whose archive was studied by H. Marland) "were married to labourers, tradesmen and artisans, farmers and farmer servants" (Marland 2004: 107). It was this "social aetiology" that the doctors in the first asylums, from P. Pinel to J.E. Esquirol in France, to William Tuke in Great Britain, saw much more clearly than many doctors of the second half of the 19th century, who would attempt again to find organic causes to the disease, even departing from traditional explanations.

The focus of medical attention on puerperal fever first and on puerperal insanity later had important repercussions both on scientific research and case law.

At this time, in fact, medicine "discovered" puerperium as a specific stage: through the study of postpartum pathologies, "medicine included the puerperium within its knowledge", initially as a pathological condition, then as a physiological one (Arena 2015: 964). The physician Robert Gooch was the first to use the term "puerperal insanity" in its influential treatise *Observations on puerperal insanity* (1820). During the 19th century, the terms lochi and *quarantine* were progressively replaced, precisely by the terms "puerperal condition" or "puerperium", beginning to describe in detail its duration (from the first hours after childbirth until the resumption of menstruation) and bodily transformations: the return of her genital organs to their initial size, the first production of breast milk, etc., in a kind of physiological regression that sees a newly delivered woman (a *puerpera* in Italian) progressively resume her physical condition prior to her pregnancy, while a psychological process that transforms her into a mother begins. In midwifery manuals, biological motherhood was thus distinguished into the three stages of pregnancy, childbirth and puerperium, characterised by physiological, pathological, but also psychological peculiarities.

The focus of puerperal insanity, as a mental illness included with the specific diseases of the puerperium (before it was named postpartum psychosis), fuelled a new perception and sensitivity towards infanticides and the figure of infant-murderers. In many countries, both public opinion and the law were increasingly oriented towards considering this crime, especially if committed by an unmarried woman, as a gesture of momentary madness, an irrepressible and unconscious impulse in the delicate phase following childbirth.[45]

The law dealt with this new medical approach within a review that considered psychosis as a possible pathology specific of the puerperium. From the legal point of view, dishonour was a mitigating factor, as it was able to alter the "fragile mental balance" of a new mother.[46] Law expert G.B. Impallomeni in his book on the Italian Penal Code (1891) wrote that "in this case, the murder is caused by the extraordinary nervous excitement and the pathological condition experienced" (cited by Selmini 1987: 49). On the other hand, the court statistics themselves showed by then that infant-murderers were largely precisely unmarried and poor girls: a survey conducted by the French Ministry of Justice (1880) pointed out that 66% of the women tried were unmarried and 83% were poor and illiterate.[47]

The tendency towards mitigating their sentences, which had already begun in the early 19th century in some European legislations, such as the Austrian one (which since 1803 envisaged extenuating circumstances for reasons of honour), spread in the second half of the century to most European codes, which distinguished between infanticide of an illegitimate child and infanticide of a legitimate one and recognised the *honoris cause* as the first extenuating circumstance. This crime was thus transformed, from being classed as heinous to an "excused" murder. In the new Zanardelli Penal Code of the Kingdom of Italy (1889), the penalty was considerably reduced compared to the capital punishment prescribed by its predecessor, the Sardinian Code (1859): from 3 to 10 years' imprisonment, if the crime had been committed in the first five days after the child's birth to protect the honour; this mitigating factor was also included in the later Rocco Code (and also extended to family members involved in the crime).[48]

In infanticide trials celebrated between the late 19th and early 20th centuries, acquittals became increasingly frequent: in French and English courts, they reached the rate of 37 % (as pointed out by Fiume 1995: 108 and Rose 1986: 70 ff). In Italy, too, unmarried defendants were almost always acquitted, either because it was impossible to ascertain that the child had been alive at birth, or thanks to the extenuating circumstances of "irresistible force" or the reasons of honour. The evidence given by women underlined these aspects (obviously also as part of their defensive strategy): their initial unawareness of their pregnancy, sometimes of the birth itself, their terrible shame and/or the upheaval following the birth. A girl from Imola, for example, told the judge in 1886:

> To conceal my mistake, finding myself in the throes of delirium [...] I took the child in my arms and with my left hand I clenched her throat with all my strength, until it no longer gave any sign of life [...]. I ask God's forgiveness for the crime committed. I will add only, to my justification that I was in a state of unspeakable anxiety.
>
> *(Cited by Selmini 1987: 98)*

This was a profound change in perspective that, at the end of the century, concerned not only the theory and practice of the law, but more broadly the representation of infant-murderers, increasingly overlapping and coinciding with that of young unmarried mothers and looked on with a more compassionate gaze, which captured the suffering of unmarried mothers, the bias of norms and the immunity of seducers, all resonating within newspapers, magazines and novels.[49] Rather than a monster and a murderer, an infant-killer was increasingly frequently seen as an unfortunate, seduced and abandoned girl, who suffered from a "temporary deficiency in maternal feeling", in a process of "pathologising the crime" that would progressively be extended, during the 20th century, also to married women.[50]

It should be noted that the women's emancipation movement led a specific battle in favour of unmarried mothers, emphasising their sad condition and calling for the abolition of the ban on paternity searches. In 1896, in Milan, Italy, a propaganda committee for the reform of art. 189 of the Civil Code was set up, chaired by Dr Edoardo Porro, which also called for the introduction of sanctions for men who avoided their responsibilities as fathers.[51] In the Unites States, the Legitimation League, fighting for the rights of illegitimate mothers, was established in 1890.[52]

Notes

1 Schlumbohm (2007, 2012); Metz-Becker (1997).
2 Preussler (1985); Filippini (1992, 2002a).
3 Wilson (1995); Cody Forman (2004).
4 Preussler (1985); Filippini (2002a); Schlumbohm (2018).
5 Zocchi (1999); Reggiani (2008).
6 Cavallo and Cerutti (1990); Amato Vincenzi (1988); Phan (1989); Bartoloni and Lombardi (2018).
7 Steffani (1839).
8 Translated from the French edition.
9 Zocchi (1999); Reggiani (2008).

10 Beauvalet-Boutouyrie (1999); Sage-Pranchère (2017).
11 Beauvalet-Boutouyrie (1999: 143 and 147–148); Schlumbohm (2007: 3–36, and 1998: 170–191); Filippini (2002a: 181).
12 Translated from the Italian edition, as the following quotations.
13 Schlumbohm (2001: 65).
14 Filippini (2002a).
15 Campbell Ross (1986).
16 As reported in the rules of the lying-in hospital in Padua: *Prescrizioni per le infermiere alla clinica ostetrica*, 2 august 1924, art. 17 (ASVe, I.R. Governo, 1825–1829, LXX, ½).
17 On the importance of moral judgement in charity in Protestant countries, see Woolf (1986).
18 Wilson (1995: 145–158).
19 Campbell Ross (1986).
20 Rose (1986: 22).
21 Rose (1986: ch. 4).
22 ASVe, *Istruzioni d'Ufficio per la ostetrica superiore alla Clinica ostetrica*, I. Regio Governo, 1825–1829, LXX, ½.
23 Beauvalet-Boutouyrie (1999: 157–164).
24 Schlumbohm (2001: 73).
25 Metz-Becker (1997); Cody Forman (2004).
26 *Lettera di Lucia Memmo Mocenigo a Paolina Memmo Martinengo* (Letter from Lucia Memmo Mocenigo to Pauline Memmo Martinengo), Vienna, 22 December 1792.
27 Foucault et *alii* (1976).
28 Loudon (2000: 14).
29 Filippini (2002a: 179).
30 Beauvalet-Boutouyrie (1995: 69, table).
31 Loudon (2000: table 5.1 'Deliveries and maternal mortality rates in certain lying-in hospitals in the UK and the Continent of Europe during the late eighteenth and first half of the nineteenth century'). Average for the period: 587/10,000 deliveries in London's Lying-in Hospital and 172/10,000 deliveries in Dublin's Lying-in Hospital. See also: DeLacy (1989).
32 Pancino (1992: 346–347).
33 Corradi (1874, 1877: ch. 42); Almaviva (1999).
34 Le Fort (1866).
35 Nuland (2003); Carter and Carter (2017). Writer Louis-Ferdinand Celine had written his thesis about him in 1924 (Celine 1937).
36 Loudon (2000: 94, table 7.2).
37 In 1848, annual maternal mortality rates in the first clinic: 127/10,000; in the second: 133/10,000 (Loudon 2000: 95, table 7.4); see also Nuland (2003).
38 Semmelweis [1861] (1983).
39 Shorter (1882: 132).
40 Beauvalet-Boutouyrie (1999: 353); Sage Pranchère (2017).
41 As pointed out by Loudon (1992).
42 Fiume (1995); Marland (2004).
43 See Arena (2016: 139).
44 Casarini (1983).
45 Guarnieri (2005).
46 Selmini (1987); Montani (1995).
47 Fiume (1993: 108).
48 Guarnieri (2005).
49 Rose (1986).
50 Selmini (1987: 150).
51 Gorni and Pellegrini (1974: 58); Dickmann (2013); Bartoloni (2018); Gazzetta (2018).
52 Hall (2018).

10
THE "FOETUS-AS-CITIZEN"

1 New theories about generation

A real revolution, destined to have profound repercussions beyond medicine, had swept through the field of reproduction in the last decades of the 17th century, bringing new theories to the fore. In the wake of the Scientific Revolution, free from the ideological boundaries of ancient authors and also thanks to the new optical lenses, scientists had finally "seen" what not even dissections had allowed to fully grasp until that moment, namely that a woman's body was not a reversed mirror image of a man's: the ovaries were not the internal "testicles" and, above all, they produced eggs (hence their new name).[1] There followed the intuition that these eggs might play a central role in reproduction, as physician William Harvey strongly suggested (*ex ovo omnia*).[2] The ancient Hippocratic-Aristotelian theories of generation that had lasted for thousands of years, going through different philosophical and scientific approaches, began to be questioned in an atmosphere of heated debates, new scientific theories and experiments carried out on animals which included vivisections, in order to discover the secrets of human reproduction.[3]

This intense research activity involved physicians, biologists and naturalists and, at the end of the century, led to the formulation of two new important theories: *ovism* and *animalculism*, both deeply influenced by the belief – encouraged by the increasingly widespread use of optical lenses – that the human eye could see but a small part of reality. The former was supported by Dutch biologist Régnier De Graaf (1672), the latter by naturalist Antony van Leeuwenhoek (1677), a fellow Dutchman, who, when observing semen through a microscope, had seen some moving corpuscles which he called *animalculi*: the term sperm would come into use only in the 1870s.[4]

Both theories subscribed to "preformationism", that is to say they were based on the idea that foetuses, with all their parts reduced in size (*preformed*, in fact), were contained either in the ovaries (according to ovists) or in the small animals present in semen (according to animalculists): they were viewed precisely as "miniature men".[5] The act of conception – it was believed – set off their development, which consisted essentially of the unfolding and enlargement of their compressed parts. There was also a third preformationist theory, put forward by Jan Swammerdam (1669) and Nicolas Malebranche (1674) in an attempt to reconcile new scientific discoveries with religious faith: that of the "pre-existence of germs", not produced by the bodies of individuals, but all created *ab initio* by God.[6]

The three theories were at the centre of an intense debate, but at the end of the 17th century, ovism gathered the widest consensus in the scientific field, gaining the support of authoritative scientists and physicians such as M. Malpighi, G.B. Morgagni, F. M. Nigrisoli, Thomas and Caspar Bartholin, F. Ruysch and Ch. Drelincourt.

In the 18th century, the success of this theory had significant consequences not only in scientific terms, but also in terms of culture and gender. For the first time, women acquired a major role in conception: they did not simply provide the matter, as Aristotle had claimed, nor were they a mere container for embryos, but they produced themselves the eggs which contained the germ. Men's contribution to generation was somewhat reduced: the male seed was not the noble substance imagined by the ancients, but a liquid full of tiny little animals; no longer was a father the *arché tes genéseos* (the principle of generation), but rather the one who, during sexual intercourse, could activate the development of what a woman already contained in her body.[7] This change helped to emphasise the mother's figure and role, supporting the biological determinism which became established at the end of the 18th century, redesigning the cultural representation of women.[8]

Research aimed at supporting the ovist approach became frantic throughout Europe. In Italy, Lazzaro Spallanzani conducted his first experiments on amphibians, fertilising numerous frog eggs with the seed of male specimens (*Saggio di osservazioni microscopiche*, 1765 (Essay on microscopic observations)). He even went so far as carrying out the first conception in a mammal (a dog), without however identifying the basic error of preformationism, a victim himself, as many others were "of the dominant role that theoretical formulations had [even] over experimental practice" (Bernardi 1986: 340).

2 The birth of embryology and the personification of the foetus

The emergence of preformationist theories also entailed a profound revision of the theories on the development of embryos. The previously supported view, organogenesis, which assumed a development of the foetus in distinct phases, no longer fitted with the idea of a preformed germ already present in the ovaries. In the second half of the 18th century, research was therefore also focused in this direction, thus marking the birth of modern embryology and of a new cultural representation of the foetus.[9]

In 1741, one of the first books published in Europe on this topic came out in Turin: *De naturali in humano corpore vitiosa morbosaque generatione Historia* by anatomist Giovanni Battista Bianchi (1741).[10] He had gathered together a true "museum of abortions", having for years collected embryos and foetuses at different stages of development, from the first days of conception onwards, and classified them in chronological order. His research overcame the fragmentation of the previous investigations, presenting a complete, albeit brief sequence of development (Figure 10.1).[11]

A similar, more refined sequential investigation was published at the end of the century by Samuel Thomas Sömmering, in Frankfurt, the *Icones embryonum humanorum* (1799).[12] In the meantime, William Hunter had also published his important work *Anatomia uteri humani gravidi tabulis illustrata* (1774) (The Anatomy of the Human Gravid Uterus Exhibited in Figures), with 34 detailed tables and copper-plate illustrations engraved by Jan van Rymsdyk, depicting embryos and foetuses at various stages of development.[13]

The outcome of this early research revolutionised not only the ancient organogenetic theories, but also the representation of the foetus that was connected to it: it was now presented with the characteristics of an individual, a small adult, from the very beginning, in a process of personification which was emphasised by its visual representations: in fact, it was often drawn in a vertical position, outside the womb, with strongly humanised features from the first months of pregnancy, in the act of smiling or playing such as the two-and-a-half-months foetus in Bianchi's table (Figure 10.2).[14]

These images conveyed contents that had no scientific basis, but expressed new ideological beliefs and attitudes: the perspective of autonomy, beauty and peculiarity used by the burgeoning embryology to look at the foetus.

In fact, the analysis of embryonic development prompted Giovanni Battista Bianchi to formulate a more general view of the concept of life, distinguishing a first phase inside the womb ("first life") and a second phase outside the womb ("second life [...] when the child emerges to the light"), seamlessly combined (Bianchi 1741: 66).

The autonomy of the foetus from its mother's body was not, therefore, just a figurative choice: it outlined the perspective followed by scientific research. It increasingly took shape during the 18th century, leading to the criticism of imaginationism and of the belief in maternal "cravings".[15]

After J. B. Winslow's and L. Heister's studies, many Hippocratic theories had become decidedly outdated; it had been shown that the foetus had its own heart and blood circulation. According to many physicians, this physiological autonomy was matched by an emotional independence that isolated it from maternal emotions, as an egg was independent from the hen, to use the effective image by naturalist G.-L. Leclerc De Buffon: "the foetus is as independent from its mother who is carrying it as an egg from the hen that is hatching it" (cited by Filippini 1997: 116).

Englishman James Blondel, in his book *The strength of imagination in pregnant women examined...* (1727),[16] and Frenchman Isaac Bellet in a book the title of which was already a manifesto (*Letters, on the force of imagination in pregnant women. Wherein it is proved, by incontestible arguments, drawn from both reason and experience,*

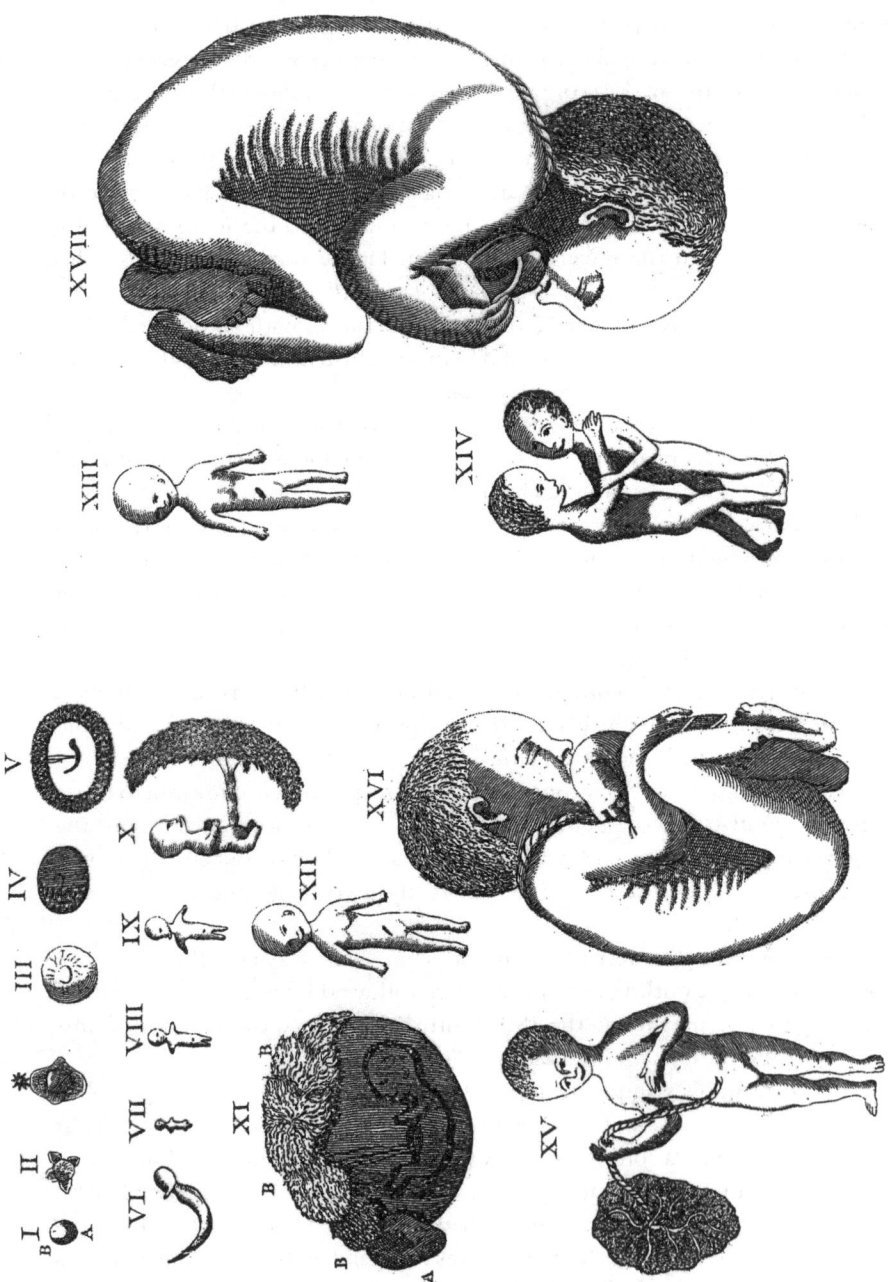

FIGURE 10.1 Table of embryological development by anatomist Gian Battista Bianchi, revised by theologian Francesco E. Cangiamila, from Cangiamila (1775). Reproduced from my collection.

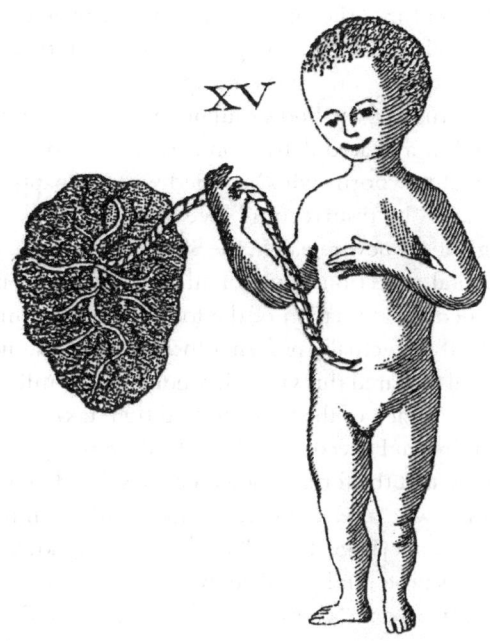

FIGURE 10.2 Detail of the illustration, figure XV: a foetus at 2.5 months. Reproduced from my collection.

that it is a ridiculous prejudice to suppose it possible for a pregnant woman to mark her child with the figure of any object she has longed for)[17] vehemently challenged the modelling strength of mothers which had been recognised for centuries, by linking the spots and malformations in newborns to problems in foetal development. Their views prompted a heated debate between imaginationists and anti-imaginationists which would last for decades and would end with such a clear victory for the latter that the ancient theory was ostracised from science and relegated to the context of superstition and folklore.[18] Thus, while on the one hand the new scientific theories gave mothers new importance in terms of conception, on the other hand, by stressing the autonomy of the foetus, they reduced their strength and the influence of their bodies in pregnancy.

3 Theologian F. E. Cangiamila and the campaign for post-mortem Caesarean sections

Almost four years after the publication of Giovanni Battista Bianchi's book on embryology, a book with an emblematic title destined to have great influence in Europe was published in Italy, in Palermo: *Embriologia Sacra, ovvero dell'uffizio de' sacerdoti, medici e superiori circa l'eterna salute de' bambini racchiusi nell'utero* (1745) (Sacred Embryology, or of the office of priests, doctors and superiors concerning the eternal salvation of children in the womb).[19] Its author, Francesco Emanuele Cangiamila, a Sicilian Jesuit priest, was an educated reformer and the director of studies of Palermo's seminary.[20]

In the mid-18th century, the interest in matters related to generation and birth, always very lively among theologians, was strengthened by the revolutionary scientific discoveries, due to their implications for the theories about the ensoulment of the foetus and the body/soul nexus. The different religious movements were involved in a heated debate on this issue, and were also divided on the fate of the souls of newborns who had died without baptism, on the validity of baptisms *in utero* and "by resurrection" (see Chapters 5–7).

Taking advantage of the new research, the Sicilian theologian developed original theological and pastoral reflections. First of all, in light of the new preformationist theories, the immediate animation of the foetus, at the moment of conception, seemed highly likely, if not actually proven; other theologians, such as, for example, Alfonso de' Liguori, also shared this view. Secondly, Cangiamila reworked the definition of birth in clear breach of the previous tradition: taking up Bianchi's distinction, he advocated a first and a second birth: a "birth in the womb" and one "out of the womb", specifying that the former should be considered more important, "since in the second birth he, who already existed, only manifests himself by coming out into the light" (Cangiamila [1745] 1751: 208).[21] Above all, however, the representation of the embryo was profoundly marked by a new perspective: from the first few days of life, it was configured as "a little boy", "an unborn child", as well as a creature beloved by Christ, worthy of the greatest compassion in view of its being helpless and defenceless, vulnerable to a dual death, both earthly and eternal.[22]

In light of this new sensibility, Cangiamila launched a real campaign for the preservation of foetal life, which took the form of a series of articulated proposals: from the traditional control over unmarried mothers to the creation of lying-in hospitals for destitute mothers, to the training of midwives. The practice of Caesarean sections post mortem became particularly important: the Jesuit priest from Palermo, in a departure from the past, promoted and encouraged it as the means to achieve a foetus' earthly and spiritual salvation. He suggested it be carried out not only on women who had died in childbirth (as the Council of Trent had decreed), but on all women who died during pregnancy, even those in the early months of gestation.[23]

His book was a huge success: it was approved by Pope Benedict XIV, translated into Latin and into many European languages,[24] imposed by bishops to parishes and seminaries. Jansenist Joseph Antoine Toussaint Dinouart, his French translator, in presenting the book, wrote: "Cangiamila has constructed a monument that will hand his name down to posterity" (Dinouart 1775: IV).

The popularity of the text prompted a widespread campaign to defend embryos and promote Caesarean sections on women who died during pregnancy, initially centred in Italy, but which was soon extended to the whole of Europe and even to some South American countries.

After various edicts were issued by the Catholic Synod, the political authorities also imposed the practice: in 1749, a special law was enacted in Sicily, the *Nuova Prammatica siciliana del taglio cesareo e dell'aborto* (New Sicilian Rules about Caesarean sections and abortions), directly inspired by Cangiamila, later extended by Charles III to Spain (1761) and to its colonies in America: it prescribed the intervention be carried out at any time during the pregnancy, setting harsh punishments for families and doctors who did not comply.[25]

In Sicily, a special panel of magistrates, chaired by Cangiamila himself, the *Deputazione dei Projetti*, was charged with overseeing the implementation of the law. The first figures were published in a report that was a kind of spiritual statement of the work done: the magistrates reported that in three years (1760–1762), 225 post-mortem Caesareans had been carried out, 1,011 miscarried foetuses had been baptised and various abortions had been prevented, for a total of 1,729 souls saved and granted eternal life.[26]

4 The protection of "unborn citizens"

Religious circles were not the only contexts to be affected by a new sensitivity towards the foetus: particular attention was also being paid to it by the secular world, particularly in medical circles imbued with the Enlightenment, active in the fight against mortality and in the defence of citizenship. As a newborn was to all intents and purposes a citizen, in this perspective, a foetus appeared as an "unborn citizen". This concept was developed by Johann Peter Frank. In his famous work *System einer vollständingen medicinischen Polizey* (1779–1788), Frank repeatedly stated that the embryo is in every respect a "citizen", although unborn.[27]

In this perspective, the foetus was configured as a sprout or branch, whose care was no less precious than that of the maternal "seedbed/spindle" which produced it, to use his metaphors, giving new forms to the ancient naturalistic analogies of the female body as the earth and the baby as a seedling ("tender trunks in the human tree nursery that are the budding objects of the hopeful country") (Frank [1779] 1976: 76).

If the body of a pregnant mother was "almost the property of the state", so was the tender embryo, "hoped-for citizen", which was developing in her, a seed which the state, rather than the parents, must seek to protect up to the moment of its perfect maturity ("also the hope of the state whose protection she now has to enjoy") (Ibidem).

This resulted in new duties of protection for doctors and public administrators, who should not limit themselves to checking the birth, but the entire journey leading to it: the entire process of pregnancy. The perspective of the fight against abortions was overcome in a perspective of prevention aimed at removing the causes of disease and miscarriages. Ahead of his times, Frank proposed the creation of a "Public List of Pregnancies", whose usefulness was also stressed in terms of prospective demographic calculations, to measure the potential development and "annual loss of hoped-for citizens" (Frank [1779] 1976: 77) and to analyse the causes of their deaths in more detail His proposal was not implemented, but it already showed the path that medicine would follow in later centuries, extending its attention to the entire reproductive process, in a project of overall medicalisation of procreation.

In a section of the second book, with other initiatives aimed at protecting the life of the foetus, Frank also dealt with the practice of Caesarean sections: *Of the section of pregnant women who have died before giving birth and of the preservation of the foetus*.[28]

As theologian Cangiamila had done, Frank also advocated it, but only if aimed at the birth of a "viable" foetus (that is, able to live independently at birth): in other words, only performed in the second half of pregnancy and after ascertaining the mother's death. Without these pre-conditions, the operation seemed to him a real barbarity, and he used very harsh tones against the "excessive zeal" of certain priests, the risk of "murders", when a mother's death was only apparent, talking about real "slaughters" taking place in the social reality. His position would be taken up and codified by 19th-century legal medicine.

These different religious and secular perspectives emerged clearly in the post-mortem Caesarean laws enacted in Europe in the second half of the 18th century. In Catholic countries where the influence of the Church of Rome was stronger, the practice was made compulsory at any stage of pregnancy, entrusted either to a man-midwife or, if necessary, to other people, regardless of the will of the families and with harsh punishments in cases of non-compliance. This was the case, for example, with the *Prammatica siciliana*, with Spanish law and also with the law of the Duchy of Milan (1764). In other Catholic States which were more independent of the Church of Rome, the decision was left to surgeons, as happened in the Republic of Venice, where, in 1760, an older law from 1608 had been reinstated. It should be noted that in France, no law codified the practice, despite the pressure exerted by the Jansenists.

In Protestant countries, where a lay purpose prevailed, the decision on whether or not to carry out the intervention was remitted to a doctor's judgement and to the will of the family, without any constraint, as evidenced by the laws of the towns of Ulm (1740) and Frankfurt (1786), and of the counties of Hesse-Kassel (1787) and Lippe-Detmold (1788). In some contexts, the practice was explicitly limited to the advanced stage of pregnancy, after ascertaining the woman's death, as in Württemberg (1775), in Lippe-Detmold, in Prussia (1811) and in Nassau (1818).[29]

Despite these rules, the practice of post-mortem Caesarean section continued to encounter strong resistance not only with the population, but also in medical circles, especially when, at the end of the century, a new idea of death as a process, rather than an instantaneous passing, emerged; this made it even more problematic to intervene quickly, as the aim of saving the child required. This change in perspective increasingly fuelled the fears of apparent deaths, very widespread at this time,[30] especially among surgeons and man-midwives, who feared sinking their scalpels in bodies that were not actually dead. As Catholic Luigi Pastorello observed,

> Opening a belly and getting into the innards of a woman who might still be alive, [maybe] for the only faint hope of being able to baptise the foetus and nothing more, was an idea that rightly tormented the minds of the most conscientious obstetricians, even those most loyal to Christianity.
>
> *(Pastorello 1854: 297)*

The statistics gathered in the 19th century, especially in some Central European countries, also revealed discouraging figures, far from Cangiamila's optimistic forecasts: the child's survival rates fluctuated on average between 1.3% and 5%.[31]

Added to this, there was the widespread hostility of families, for whom intervening on the body of a woman who had long suffered in childbirth was considered truly barbaric.[32] In the second half of the 19th century, the medical world was unanimous in supporting the lawfulness of the intervention only for health reasons and following a medical assessment, as some medical academies officially sanctioned (e.g. the *Académie Impériale de Médecine* of Paris, in 1860).

Situations of confrontation on the practice between doctors and parish priests were recorded in various Catholic contexts. In Italy, in 1849, the local physician doctor in Malamocco, one of Venice's islands, was denounced by the parish priest for refusing to perform the intervention on a pregnant woman who had died of cholera.[33]

In France, in 1846, a priest, following Cangiamila's and his follower, Bishop Jean Baptiste Bouvier's instructions, having tried in vain to persuade a surgeon to perform the section on a woman who had died in the fifth month of her pregnancy, had the surgery performed by a blacksmith.[34]

The resonance of similar events in the public opinion, which also fuelled waves of anti-clericalism, led the Catholic Church, at the end of the century, to adopt a more prudent attitude, which essentially remitted the practice to the judgement of doctors. In 1899, in response to a question, the Holy Office decreed that priests should not interfere in asking for the said section and much less in doing so, extending to the whole Catholic world a pronouncement already addressed to the missions. The battle to save the child was now carried out entirely on the bodies of living women.

5 Caesarean sections on living women

It is in this context, in the second half of the 18th century, that the practice of Caesarean section on living women also began, promoted by the interaction of the transformations we have so far outlined: a new sensitivity towards the foetus, the weakening of traditional hierarchies of social relevance between mother and child, the post-Enlightenment trust in the saving power of medicine and the emergence of a secular and mechanistic view of the body open to experimentation. A Caesarean section, in fact, implied the more or less conscious choice to privilege the life of the child compared to that of the mother, and to open the womb, giving a surgeon a power unthinkable before that time.

The profound rupture that this entailed can be fully grasped precisely in the light of history: for centuries, from the ancient world to the second half of the 16th century, such an operation had not even been conceived by medicine, precisely because it was completely foreign to the cultural and scientific horizons. Moral and ethical reasons, rather than technical-operative ones, made it inconceivable: it meant interfering with a natural process and opening an organ full of symbolic meanings, considered, as we have seen from the organicist tradition, almost like the "sanctuary of Nature". The operation was beyond the boundaries of what was lawful; it belonged to the sphere of wickedness and sacrilege: man could not decide to "change the order of nature", as, in the 17th century, *accoucheur* François Mauriceau wrote in his *Traité des maladies des femmes grosses*.[35]

Alongside this, it is important to underline the important technical-operative problems that an operation of this kind presented, with which medicine was not able to cope (heavy bleeding, septicaemia, suturing) and which almost certainly led to the mother's death; so, a Caesarean was in practice the equivalent of a murder. For this reason, in the Middle Ages, even the Church, precisely when promoting post-mortem Caesareans, had specified the boundaries of action along the line of the mother's death, as if to prevent the excessive zeal of some priests (see Chapters 3.5 and 5.7).

The first signs of a change in perspective came in the second half of the 16th century, within the new counter-reformist movements and the renewed focus on baptism. In 1581, physician François Rousset published a book in which he declared the possible success for both the mother and the child of an operation carried out on a living woman, specifying directions and techniques: *Traitté nouveau de l'hystérotomotokie ou enfantement caesarien*.[36] In this sense, he can be considered the "father" of Caesarean sections,[37] or its "inventor", despite the fact that he never performed any, but simply because he included them within the possible boundaries of medicine.[38]

At this point, a phase of scientific debate was started in 1598 by surgeon Jacques Marchant, which would last for several decades, with some tentative experimentation: Ambroise Paré, for example, allowed his pupil Jacques Guillemeau to practise it at the Hôtel-Dieu in Paris, assisting in person. The failure of the operation, followed by the death of the woman, contributed to confirming his opposition and the widespread condemnation of the medical world, which united the most authoritative physicians and surgeons of the time: from W. Harvey to P. Dionis to F. Mauriceau. The latter went as far as dividing the supporters of the operation into "dreamers" and "impostors", invoking laws against what he considered real murders (Figure 10.3).[39]

By the mid-18th century, this approach had changed considerably: in the new cultural and scientific climate, the practice began to be revived and supported by various physicians and man-midwives. This change was particularly evident in the French school: in 1743, J.F. Simon published an essay in the journal *Mémoires de l'Académie Royale de Chirurgie* in Paris where, based on the evidence of new cases he had gathered, he claimed that the operation may not necessarily be fatal for the mother.[40] His views were taken up by J.-L. Baudelocque, professor of obstetrics and head man-midwife at the new lying-in hospital in Port-Royale. Moving away from the previous approach followed by the French school, in the brochure *Recherches et réflexions sur l'opération césarienne* (1798), he argued for a doctor's moral duty to perform a Caesarean section in cases where a natural delivery was "impossible" and this impossibility had been verified with a pelvimeter: "instead of preventing it, other laws should make it mandatory, if it can be shown that it is the only way to keep the child alive without it being necessarily fatal for the mother" (Baudelocque 1798: 35). The consequence was one

FIGURE 10.3 Caesarean section on living woman, from Scipione Mercurio (1618), *La Commare o riccoglitrice*, Milano: Giob. Bidelli, p. 269. Mercurio was a supporter of the Caesarean section, although he had never performed it. Reproduced with permission of the Biblioteca Pinali antica (Padua).

of the most heated battles in the history of obstetrics. In Paris, in opposition to J.-L. Baudelocque, J.-F. Sacombe founded the *École anti-symphyso-césarienne* (see Chapter 8.3), whereas in London, W. Simmons reiterated in similar tones that "Life is in the hands of God", as he wrote in his work *Reflections on the Propriety of Performing the Caesarean operations* (1798),[41] later attacked by J. Hull (*Observations on Mr. Simmons's Detection* (Manchester, 1799).[42]

This change was clearly affected by secular and religious factors, as emerges from the debate. The rejection of craniotomy and embryotomy operations was one of the most important aspects: Baudelocque defined them as real murders, describing "the child's painful moans", the "scattered and palpitating limbs" (Baudeloque 1798: 36). For the same reason, he also rejected other interventions, such as induced premature births, which, although not fatal in themselves, were still adverse to the life of the foetus, on which his attention was concentrated. It is in this perspective, where the child was the priority, that Baudelocque came to define a Caesarean section as "the gentlest and safest of all the methods we can use to bring childbirth to completion" (Baudelocque 1781: 351).

The refusal to carry out interventions harmful to the unborn child was obviously linked to an active view of the man-midwife's role, who could not remain a mere passive spectator to the loss of two lives. In short, the choice was between the death of the foetus and that of the mother, in a war of figures attempting to show either operation as "possible" or certainly not fatal.

Another factor promoting the practice was related to the increase of post-mortem Caesareans, and to the spiritual aspects connected to them. In his book, F. E. Cangiamila had already declared the appropriateness of attempting Caesarean sections on living women, precisely because they also offered greater guarantees for the administration of baptism to the newborn baby.

Despite the limited technical innovations compared to the past and the persistent harmful direction not to suture the womb, but only the abdomen, between the late 18th and early 19th centuries, the operation began to be practised both in local contexts and in lying-in hospitals, with the inevitable outcome of extremely high maternal mortality, mostly due to blood loss or septicaemia. Medical historian Alfonso Corradi calculated the rate rounding it down to 67% of deaths, with peaks of 90% in hospitals: a real massacre![43] In the 131 Caesareans performed in Great Britain up to 1880, 108 women had died, according to the figures gathered by Thomas Radford in 1880.[44] In England, in 1842, out of 27 women operated on, only two survived.[45]

It should also be remembered that surgeons operated with their bare hands and without any knowledge of the ways to prevent and fight infections.

This marked a breach of a centuries-old ethical principle, a change in the hierarchies of social importance that divided the 19th-century world of obstetrics into two factions: a *maternal sect*, in favour of the mother's life (and therefore supportive of embryotomy operations) and a *foetal sect*, favouring saving the foetus (and therefore Caesarean sections); the former was mainly British and Protestant, and the latter mainly French and Catholic, according to William Tyler Smith, the second President of the Obstetrical Society,[46] and reiterated by historian J.H. Young himself: "The majority of British practitioners preferred craniotomy to Caesarean section. The final argument is the mother's inalienable right to be rescued, even if that involves the sacrifice of her child" (Young 1944: 84).

In actual fact, the option in favour of the child's life stemmed from religious principles, but also from secular demographic and eugenic reasons, or from a combination of both. This option led to the devaluing of women who, due to anatomical defects (mainly due to rickets), were unable to fulfil what was considered their family and social "duty". In the choice between saving their lives or delivering a potentially healthy child, the latter would prevail, as it was more useful to society, as Italian man-midwife Luigi Pastorello wrote: "I do not know therefore whether society cares more about a healthy and well-shaped child, such as usually can be saved by Caesarean section, or about a woman unsuited to such purpose" (Pastorello 1838: 81–82). Some doctors even went as far as to produce quantitative forecast figures to work out the lower demographic loss that would be suffered by the State.[47] In short, demographic and eugenic criteria, sometimes entangled with moral considerations, guided man-midwives in cases where the choice was left in their hands, making the role they were increasingly playing in the new social context even more explicit.

Even on the religious side, in many sectors, a clear shift was taking place compared to the old tradition. Whilst some theologians continued to uphold the right of the mother to defend her existence, considering the foetus as an albeit involuntary "*aggressor*", in the course of the 17th and 18th centuries, a new stance emerged which asserted the child's right as a priority and the mother's duty to sacrifice herself for her child's material and spiritual salvation. In 1733, the theologians from the Sorbonne stated it clearly, in response to a question asked by doctors: in at-risk deliveries, "the life of the child must be put before that of the mother and although the latter may put herself first without injustice, she cannot do it without failing in charity" (cited by Cangiamila 1775: 473–474). This judgement was widely referred to in the theological debates that continued throughout the 18th–19th centuries, until the Church of Rome intervened at the end of the century, as we shall see, with an explicit pronouncement by the Holy Office.

6 Saving the mother or the child?

"Sauvez d'abord la mère" (Save the mother first of all) was the recommendation that, on 20th March, 1811, Napoleon Bonaparte made to *accoucheur* Antoine Dubois who assisted Marie Louise of Austria in a rather difficult childbirth.[48] The choice between the two lives was one of the most dramatic occurrences arising in childbirth in a long historical phase that lasted until the second half of the 20th century, placing all those involved in an extremely painful, conflictual and controversial situation from the human and ethical points of view. The evidence highlights the desperate condition of women, the dismay of their family members, their husbands and their doctors. The man-midwives themselves spoke of "a painful crossroads", of "torture for their conscience" (Pastorello 1838: 78), caught between the duty of not letting two lives perish and that of carrying out an operation that favoured only one. In the 19th century, the medical academies were involved in a heated debate on this issue which at times took on the characteristics of a real head-on collision, exacerbated by ideologies and/or opposing corporate interests (as in the case of Sacombe and Baudelocque). Italian doctors put the issue on the agenda of the 1842 Congress of Scientists; in 1852, French ones debated it at the Paris *Académie de Medécine*, whilst addressing the issue of therapeutic abortion and of induced premature deliveries in at-risk pregnancies. The discussion was not focused exclusively on the choice between embryotomy and Caesarean section, but on other interventions as well, such as therapeutic abortions and premature induced labours, which midwifery had proposed in order to save the mother's life (and for this reason approved by the Paris *Académie de Medécine*).[49] It was discussed for the first time in London at the Medical Society in 1769, at William Cooper's suggestion, and spread in the second half of the century.[50] Another controversial point concerned the person authorised to decide: should it be the husband, the man-midwife or the woman herself? These questions anticipated some current issues in bioethics. For some, the choice had to be made by the husbands, for others by the doctors themselves, in their role as judges, as well as being *super partes*; for others, this was a matter on which the Church had to take a decision. There were very few people who envisaged a choice made by women, recognising them as subjects of a decision that concerned their existence: they almost always remained at the receiving end of conflicting views and powers. Even on their right to be informed, opinions were divided between those who claimed it was superfluous to make them aware of the possible outcomes of a Caesarean section and those who considered it unacceptable to keep them in the dark about the mortal risk they were facing.

No less intense was the debate among theologians, divided between those who, in order to support Caesareans, recalled the sins of Eve; those who highlighted the "natural" propensity of women for maternal sacrifice; those who reaffirmed their right to protect their own lives, even at the expense of the foetus and finally those who made subtle distinctions between a directly fatal operation and the one which was not necessarily so, in short, between killing and letting die.

Beyond the theoretical debate, the sources actually show how factors related to social class were decisive in directing this choice. A man-midwife paid by the family would rarely act without their consent, as conversely happened in lying-in hospitals or at home, when the women in childbirth were poor. It is no coincidence that, in the 158 Italian Caesarean sections carried out between 1780 and 1876 and analysed by Alfonso Corradi, the women in labour largely belonged to the lower classes, as confirmed by the place where the operations were performed, in most cases a lying-in hospital (62% of cases).[51]

In any case, these were disastrous deliveries, where the choice came at the end of a true ordeal, after various unsuccessful interventions, when the condition of the woman was by then desperate. The woman operated on by Michelangelo Asson at home in Venice, in 1846, had been

> in labour for 36 hours. Several man-midwives had unsuccessfully attempted to use the ordinary forceps, the cephalotribe and the crotchet. A version only managed to extract an arm up to the shoulder, which, like the woman's genital area, was exceedingly swollen.
>
> *(Asson 1846: 14)*

Women from the upper classes, more closely followed during their pregnancies, could prevent similar situations by resorting in time to therapeutic abortions or to induced premature labours, carried out precisely in cases of restricted pelvis, but which required prior planning.

Shocked by the massacre caused by Caesareans, in 1876, Edoardo Porro, a consultant at the Pavia's lying-in hospital, decided to try a new and drastic intervention: the simultaneous removal of womb and ovaries during the surgery on a pregnant woman with rachitis (Giulia Cavallini). What would subsequently be called the "Porro Operation", after the name of its creator and widespread in Europe and in the United States, succeeded in reducing maternal mortality to 24%.[52] However, it was condemned by part of the clergy, because it made women sterile, thus altering nature and preventing procreation, which was the purpose of marriage, until the bishop of Pavia, Lucido Maria Parocchi, an authoritative theologian, did not intervene on the matter declaring such operation legitimate.[53]

Five years later, A. Kehrer first (1881), and then M. Sänger (1882) devised a way to suture the uterine wall, correcting the "fatal error" that medicine had consistently repeated, and thereby laying the foundations of the classic, conservative Caesarean section: the 135 sections performed up to 1888 lowered maternal mortality to 26% and child mortality to 8%.[54] But it was above all the application of the principles of prevention of and fight against sepsis that, during the 20th century, inaugurated the new age of Caesarean sections, making them safe and finally "also" saving the lives of mothers.

7 Defending (the foetus') life: the verdict of the Holy Office

Despite the heated debate and the various requests addressed to the Holy Office, until the 1880s, the Catholic Church had always refrained from intervening on the matter of the choice between embryotomy and Caesarean section, believing that it did not have sufficient medical knowledge to express a moral judgement. Even in 1852, faced with a request presented by a canon of the University of Louvain, it had decided not to answer ("*nihil esse respondendum*", there is no answer).[55] Rather than setting general principles, it had preferred to assess each case individually, thus leaving room for interpretations which took the different circumstances into account.

This position totally changed at the end of the century when, in a series of successive pronouncements (1884, 1889, 1895, 1902), the Holy Office defined the limits of obstetric intervention in detail, declaring the illegitimacy of any operation potentially causing death whether directly or indirectly, thus clearly, albeit indirectly supporting the priority of its protection, emphasised by the popularity of the theory of immediate animation.[56]

In a crucial turning point in its policy, the Church of Rome prioritised defending the life of the foetus. From that moment onwards, in a crescendo of stances, the protection of fledgling life, with a subtle semantic shift, became, by definition, the "defence of life", as pointed out by Barbara Duden.[57] The result was the condemnation of all forms of abortion, including therapeutic ones. This remained a fundamental principle, reiterated by the Church even in the 1970s, in the midst of feminist demonstrations calling for the legalisation of terminations of pregnancy, and still valid nowadays. Speaking on the problem of abortion in cases of rape, in 2004, Cardinal Javier Lozano Barragán, the Vatican's health minister, stated: "therapeutic abortion does not exist. It's just abortion. And it is reprehensible" (cited by Politi 2008: 4).

What caused such a radical change in Church policy? In a context still marred by a very high maternal mortality rate following Caesarean sections, the decision appears to have been influenced by multiple factors, attributable not only to the birth scene, but also to the social and political transformations that more broadly characterised the second half of the 19th century, threatening ecclesiastical power: the establishment of Positivism and Marxism, the spread of Malthusian theories, the emancipation of women, the loss of temporal power. It was important to signal a firm counteroffensive, "to defend a principle against the invasion of the increasingly materialistic doctrines of our time", as Roman theologians wrote in 1866, following a case of embryotomy (Pennacchi 1884: 48–49). It was also necessary to ensure clear deontological guidance in the teaching of medicine, especially in the new Catholic universities that were being founded. In short, the time had come for the Church to fully regain its supremacy in the field of sexual morality through the declaration of a universal norm, valid both for science and the people. The intransigent defence of the life of the foetus, with its unprecedented formal rigour, stood both as a reaction to the ongoing processes of modernisation, and as a reaffirmation of the crucial role in controlling (primarily women's) sexuality which the Church had always played.[58] The codification of mandatory rules in matters of birth preceded those on contraception, which the Church of Rome defined with the same rigour in Pope Leo XIII's encyclical *Arcanum divinae sapientiae* (1880) and Pope Pius XI's *Casti Connubii* (1930), thus restating its leading role in this area.[59]

The value of sacrifice as an attribute linked to the maternal role was also restated as an implicit moral imperative in more recent times, through the "politics of sanctity": in 2004, Pope John Paul II canonised a young paediatrician, Gianna Beretta Molla, who, when diagnosed with a tumour in her womb in 1961, had refused to terminate her pregnancy, choosing to sacrifice her own life to allow her child to be born. She was presented to the world by Milan's Archbishop Carlo Maria Martini as an exemplary wife, mother and medical professional, as the engraving on the back of her canonisation medal stated (24 April 1994).

Thus, the exemplary female behaviour was also sanctioned from the symbolic point of view: the female oblative and sacrificial model that has also been re-proposed and extolled, albeit with some clear innovations, in recent Church stances: from Pope John Paul II's *Mulieris dignitatem* (1988) to Pope Benedict XVI's *Letter to the Bishops of the Catholic Church on the collaboration of men and women in the Church and in the world* (31–7–2004),[60] where living "for the other" is indicated as an ontological feature of women, a specific element of their difference.

8 Breastfeeding and new forms of childcare

"With infinite pleasure, I am writing to you from my bed, confirming to you the best news about myself and my son" – Venetian noblewoman Lucia Memmo Mocenigo wrote to her sister after her first childbirth in 1793 – "I have not yet had the consolation of beginning to breastfeed him, but I hope that in a short while this will happen". And, after a few days, she joyfully confirmed: "Dear Sister, I am breastfeeding my Alvisetto myself and I am very happy about it".[61]

Even a philosopher of the Enlightenment such as Pietro Verri had enthusiastically described his wife's breastfeeding by addressing his daughter directly:

> Seeing you at your mother's breast, my heart is full of the most tender and noble emotions [...] sweet nature, noble feelings [...] We make an interesting group, Marietta sitting on the bed, displaying sweetness and grace on her face, you at her breast, I kneeling beside, helping her to support you and gazing sometimes at her, sometimes at you.
>
> *(Cited by Fiume 1997: 93)*

The "interesting group" Verri talked about was the image of the new bourgeois family, nuclear and emotionally cohesive, and at the same time it was the sign of a new attention towards childhood involving not only mothers, but also fathers, and manifesting itself through new care practices. Breastfeeding was no longer just a moral obligation or an implicit completion of childbirth, as moralists and physicians instructed, but a "natural duty", an expression of motherhood assigned by Nature to women, as such, a pleasant and gratifying experience in itself, a fundamental moment to form lasting bonds of affection and transform the family.[62]

In clear breach of a centuries-old tradition which considered it unbecoming for women of the upper classes to breastfeed their children, this practice became fashionable among the educated *élites* of the enlightened aristocracy and bourgeoisie, supported by a real campaign promoted by doctors, philosophers and scientists that made it a flagship of the return to Nature on which the political project of a wider social and political regeneration was based. In his book *Émile ou De l'éducation* (1762), Rousseau invited mothers to raise their children themselves, as the basis of an improvement in customs and a repopulation of the state:

> But when mothers design to nurse their own children, there will be a reform in morals; natural feeling will revive in every heart; there will be no lack of citizens for the state; this first step by itself will restore mutual affection.
>
> *(Rousseau, Emile or Education, ch. 1)*[63]

Johann Peter Frank devoted an entire chapter of his monumental work to breastfeeding, even calling for measures against mothers who refused to do it ("the police should task all doctors, man-midwives and midwives with strongly recommending that new mothers carry out such a duty and with reporting to the magistrate those who comply and those who refuse") (Frank [1779] 1825, II: 295). In this perspective, breastfeeding went hand in hand with not wearing corsets during pregnancy and with banning swaddling clothes that prevented any movement in children's first months of life. "When the child draws his first breath do not confine him in tight wrappings. No cap, nor bandages, nor swaddling clothes" – Rousseau recommended – "Loose and flowing flannel wrappers, which leave his limbs free and are not too heavy to check his movements, nor too warm to prevent his feeling the air" (Ibidem).[64]

In actual fact, the French philosopher was but the supreme communicator of a new medical perspective which, taking children as a specific subject of research, redesigned their characteristics, physiology and particular illnesses, in breach of the previous tradition.[65] The English Walter Harris, George Armstrong and William Cadogan (*An Essay upon Nursing and the Management of Children from Their Birth to Three Years of Age*, 1748); the French Jean Astruc (*Traité des maladies des enfants*) and Jean-Charles Desessartz (*Traité de l'éducation corporelle des enfants en bas âge*, 1760); and the Italian Pietro Moscati and Gian Battista Palletta were the forerunners of this new branch of medicine. But the role of ferryman between the old medicine for children and modern paediatrics has been attributed in particular to Swede Nils Rosén von Rosenstein, with his book *The diseases of children, and their remedies*, first published in Swedish in 1764 and translated into various European languages.[66] The term paediatrics – derived from the Greek words *país* (child) and *iatreía* (cure) – was first used in the late 19th century. The discipline acquired its own academic identity in the last two decades of the 19th century: it was first taught in a university in Padua in 1882.[67]

Many traditional beliefs and practices were challenged by paediatricians: from the harmfulness of colostrum, finally recognised as an excellent natural laxative for newborns, to the use of swaddling clothes, the limiting of baths and the practice of wet nursing. Some of these practices were in fact identified as contributing factors to the high mortality; it was therefore believed that they should be opposed and uprooted. In his *Dissertation* on *les causes principales de la mort d'un aussi grand nombre d'enfants* (1775), Swiss doctor J. Ballexserd listed the use of wet nurses, the practice of swaddling and early weaning as the top three.[68]

A real campaign aimed at promoting breastfeeding and daily baths and against swaddling bands was encouraged throughout Europe by the intense production of manuals, hygiene books and almanacs, which contributed to codifying modern and "enlightened" behaviour and rules of child care, based on the new principles of hygiene. Directly addressed to women (another significant aspect), they were the signs of a special relationship that was established between mothers and doctors and that made the latter, especially in the positivist approach of the 19th century, the new "lay priest", the codifier of new behavioural patterns in the name of science and progress.[69] In the age of Revolution and liberalism, the rejection of swaddling bands almost took on the symbolic value of liberating the individual from the constraints and chains imposed by society: in the speeches of Democrats, it was linked to reclaiming civil and political freedom.

Midwives were directly affected by these innovations and invited to disseminate them throughout the population: "advising all mothers to breastfeed their offspring" was one of the duties included in the rules for student midwives admitted to Milan's midwifery school in 1825, in addition to "eschewing any harmful prejudice, abuse, spell, and other bad practices and habits involving pregnant women, women in childbirth, new mothers and their offspring".[70]

These care practices actually spread very unevenly through the different European contexts and social classes: the enlightened bourgeoisie and aristocracy, especially in Northern Europe, promoted them, as evidenced by the private writings of various noblewomen who, between the 18th and 19th centuries, extolled the delights of motherhood long before Paolo Mantegazza theorised them in his *Fisiologia del piacere* (The physiology of pleasure) (1854).[71] In the 1770s, in London, it had become fashionable among upper-class mothers to suckle their own children, although this fashion was certainly limited to a very narrow élite.[72]

On the contrary, the conservative aristocracy and the bourgeoisie, as well as the popular and above all the peasant classes, especially in southern Europe, were reluctant and slow to adopt these new trends, both in terms of hygiene and clothing. Even in the mid-20th century, as we have said, the use of swaddling bands was documented in many areas, especially rural ones, also because it allowed the child to be carried and moved more easily when working.[73]

Between the 18th and 19th centuries, wet nursing even intensified in some contexts, spreading in the urban proletariat wherever economic development implied the widespread use of female labour and a growing separation between home and workplace. In the mid-19th century, in Milan, fewer than 50% of poor women breastfed.[74] Similar figures are available for other major European manufacturing cities, such as Lyon, famous for its textile factories, and Paris, where in 1780, 19,000 newborns out of 21,000 were sent to be wet nursed and even at the end of the 19th century, about 1/3 of children were wet nursed[75] (see Chapter 4.2). Even in England, "wet nursing reached its height in the seventeenth and early-eighteenth centuries" (Fildes 1988: 79). The *baby-farming* system was also widespread among women from the poorer classes, with wet nurses taking on several children at a time, often in very bad conditions.[76]

As early as 1721, Italian surgeon man-midwife Sebastiano Melli had observed this phenomenon, noting in his manual *La Comare levatrice istruita nel suo Uffizio*:

> Not just princesses, but even the lowliest female now refuses to lose the beauty of their breasts [...] the situation has reached such a level of abuse that beggars look for a more destitute female than they are to give her their own babies to be breastfed.
>
> (Melli 1721: 243)

And at the end of the 18th century, Venetian G. A. Costantini, in his invective against the evils of the century, noted: "Fashion has decided [...] By now only the wives of porters and villains still breastfeed their children" (cited by Fiume 1997: 91).

These accusations are clearly marked by strong class prejudice, which above all stigmatised the imitation of the fashions of the *élites* by the popular classes, but they have the merit of highlighting the extension of the phenomenon to the lower classes. In actual fact, when the use of wet nurses really spread among less well-off women, it was mainly for different reasons from those identified by the authors: practical needs prompted by the industrialisation of the 18th–19th centuries and linked to the increased use of female labour in factories or in places which were different and/or away from home. Breastfeeding was incompatible with these new jobs. Similar reasons caused the increase in the number of legitimate children being abandoned, a phenomenon that reached shocking figures in the 19th century: in 1842, in Milan, almost half of all poor children were abandoned to the hospice of foundlings.[77]

In the aristocratic and bourgeois families where wet nursing persisted, the habit of having live-in wet nurses became widespread in the second half of the 18th century. This allowed mothers to have daily contact with their children, as well as to keep a close eye on the wet nurses:

> There are thousands of them here [in Venice], each better than the next – Giovanni Grevembroch wrote in the mid-18th century – The Matrons almost without distinction look over their children with jealous eyes, in such a way that wet nurses are barely able to leave the rooms.
> (Grevembroch [1754] 1981: III, 55)

The contradictions created by this custom, which remained popular in Italy until the 1940s and 1950s, are glaring: motherly love, which drove the women of the *élites* to house wet nurses in their palaces for many months, separated these poor peasant new mothers from their own newborns, forcing them into a prolonged separation that uprooted them from their families and their environments, with serious repercussions on their lives.[78]

In the second half of the 19th century, philanthropic initiatives to help poor mothers, such as the creation of paediatric clinics and of nurseries for infants, contributed more than anything else to disseminating the new principles of child care and assistance to the lower classes. Women from the liberal aristocracy and bourgeoisie took charge of this, investing both economic and human resources in this activity.[79]

9 Reforms and laws in defence of newborns

With greater or lesser commitment, many enlightened governments supported these medical campaigns aimed at reducing infant mortality by enacting laws and regulations aimed at protecting the lives of the new citizens.[80]

While criminal codes considered infanticide as a crime against the person, imposing harsh punishments, new rules on the registration of births were introduced, with the establishment of state registers of births. According to the Napoleonic Code, newborns had to be taken to the municipal offices within three days of their birth by their fathers, doctors or midwives, in the presence of two witnesses, for the drafting of the appropriate act.[81] Extended to the French empire, this reform was resumed, with various articulations, by many governments of the Restoration. In Austrian legislation, which also applied to the Lombardy-Veneto region, according to the 1816 provisions, parish priests dealt with the registration, thus taking on the role of civil officers.[82] Like births, deaths were also more rigidly scrutinised, in an attempt to prevent infanticide. Some laws, such as the Napoleonic and Austrian ones, imposed the requirement of a medical certificate for the burial of newborns and stillborns, in an attempt to counter the habit of burying them without any official check.[83]

The reforming intent also involved foundling institutions, which were real "death factories", with mortality rates that even in the 19th century exceeded 50%. The regulations of the time tried to reduce it with various reforms: the imposition of the wheel, commissioned by the Napoleonic government in 1811 (with a decree dated 19 January), was one of the first reforms. Placed in the opening of a window and open onto the street on the one side and onto an internal room of the institution on the other side, this rotating cylindrical device mitigated the consequences of abandoning foundlings in doorways, exposed to harsh weather and attacks by animals. Vaccination, aimed at eradicating the terrible smallpox epidemics, was also the object of a great campaign in the 19th century: it became mandatory for children in many European countries, such as in Norway (1810), Sweden (1815), the United Kingdom (1853 and 1867), Germany (1874) and Italy (1888), despite objections and resistance from the population.[84]

Nineteenth-century legislation was also characterised by the emergence of more precise rules aimed at eradicating harmful traditional practices from the population, such as cutting the frenulum of newborns' tongues and administering opiates [poppy seeds decoctions] to children to induce sleep, referred to in an article of the Austrian criminal code, or "neglecting (the) appropriate monitoring" of children.[85] A similar law was passed in the United Kingdom much later, in 1920, the Dangerous Drugs Act, which made opiates available only with doctors' prescriptions.[86]

The way in which baptism was administered was also criticised by doctors, who pointed out the risks of exposing babies to the cold in the winter months, of long journeys and of using cold water in the ceremony: these were all contributing factors to ill-health and mortality, exacerbated by the fact that the sacrament was administered in the first days of a child's life, as reported by Italian Giovanni Verardo Zeviani (*Su le numerose morti dei bambini* [On the numerous deaths of children], 1775), followed by Giuseppe Toaldo and Francesco Trevisan, the author of *Della preservazione dei bambini* (On the protection of children) (1823).[87]

To address these requests, already at the end of the 18th century, the prince-bishop of Würzburg had ordered parish priests to baptise babies in their homes during the winter (1790), while in the Kingdom of Italy, an innovative circular by the Ministry of Worship (1806), addressed to the bishops, urged the use of warm water in the winter months, for "the protection and health of the newborns who come to the holy font", highlighting their delicate constitution (Filippini 2018: 78–79). In 1846, this direction was taken up in a circular issued in the Lombardy-Veneto region "On the use of warm water in baptisms", which also suggested the use of special boxes to carry babies to the church. In fact, in the 19th century, various types of wooden "baptismal arks" with glass windows and metal handles began to be used.

Germany, Austria and Austrian Italy were at the forefront of these initiatives, which other countries implemented within a few decades. In France, for example, in the second half of the 19th century, a real battle against early baptisms and civil registrations was fought by hygienists such as Charles Monot, the author of *De la mortalité excessive des enfants pendant la prémière année de leur existence* (Of the excessive mortality of children in the first year of life) (1872), which caused a heated debate. Only in 1912–1914, however, did the Congregation of Sacraments and that of Rites partly accept their proposals, issuing two decrees that allowed home baptisms.[88]

At the end of the century (1896), the first international congress for the protection of children was held in Paris, while attention towards newborns and stillborn babies began to grow not only in the medical, but also in the legal and social fields.[89] This medical, social and institutional offensive, combined with new discoveries and techniques for newborn resuscitation and with the albeit slow and uneven improvements in living conditions, led to a progressive decrease in infant mortality over the 19th century, starting in Northern Europe (Great Britain and France), and followed by other European countries in the second half of the 19th century. In 1880–1884, in London, infant mortality in the first year of life reached 152/1,000 live births; in Paris, it was 172/1,000, and in Rome, 179/1,000.[90] In Italy, the "irreversible moment of the infant mortality trend happened around 1875–1880, when it fell below the 200/1,000 threshold" (Del Panta *et alii* 1996: 153). Twenty years later, in 1900–1904, it went down even further, to 144/1,000, in London, 111/1,000 in Paris and 131/1,000 in Rome (Derosas 1999: 42, table 2).

Notes

1. Laqueur (1990); Schiebinger (1993).
2. Ehkolm (2018).
3. Bernardi (1980); Darmon (1981); Roger (1997); Pinto-Correia (1997).
4. Vienne (2018).
5. Pinto-Correia (1997).
6. Roger (1997).
7. Pomata (2002: 168–171).
8. Schiebinger (1989, 1995); Moscucci (1990).
9. Duden, Schlumbohm, Veit (2002); Pancino and d'Yvoire (2006); Dasen (2007); Frydman *et alii* (2009); Leperchery (2010).
10. Bianchi (1741).
11. Filippini (1997: 113–117; 2002: 100–102).
12. Sömmering (1799). See Duden (2002: 36–41); Enke (2002).
13. Hunter (1774). See Rifkin, Ackerman and Folkenberg (2006: 195–218).
14. Bianchi (1741, table I, fig. XI).
15. Pancino (1996).
16. Blondel (1727). The book has had four English editions, two translations into French, one into Italian and one into German.

17 Bellet (1765). The book has had three French editions, one English translation and one Italian translation.
18 Pancino (1996: 15).
19 Cangiamila [1745] (1751).
20 Condorelli (1975).
21 Translated from the Italian edition, like the following quotes.
22 Cangiamila [1745] (1751: 2); Filippini (2002b: 110–111).
23 Laget (1979: 182).
24 Filippini (1995: 62, table).
25 Sanchez Arcàs (1950); De Demerson (1976); Rigau-Pérez (1995). Contrary to what has been claimed by Sanchez Arcàs (1950), De Demerson has shown that this law was actually enacted in Spain and in its colonies. The text of the law is published in Cangiamila (1775: 312–322).
26 Filippini (1995: 147, table).
27 Frank ([1779] 1976: 75).
28 Frank ([1779] 1825, II: 186 seq.).
29 Filippini (1995: 140–145).
30 Milanesi (1989).
31 Fasbender (1906: 983–984); Young (1944: 226–230).
32 Zocchi (2003).
33 Filippini (1995: 324).
34 Fredj (2009).
35 Mauriceau [1668] (1681: 344–345).
36 Rousset (1581).
37 As Pundel called him (Pundel 1969: 125).
38 Baskett (2017).
39 Mauriceau [1668] (1681: 344–345).
40 Simon (1743: 210–254).
41 Simmons (1798).
42 Young (1944: 58–63).
43 Corradi (1874–1877: 1042–1168); Filippini (2010: 161, table).
44 Pundel (1969: 201).
45 Loudon (1992 135).
46 Moscucci (1990: 141).
47 Filippini (1995: 255–256 and table).
48 Witkowski (1890: 367).
49 Le Naour and Valenti (2003: 28).
50 Betta (2006: 152); Loudon (1992: 133).
51 Corradi (1874–1877: 1122–1123).
52 Gall (1922); Mazzarello (2015).
53 Mazzarello (2015: ch. 8).
54 Gall (1922: 54–59); Nardi (1952: 318); Lurie (2013); Baskett (2017).
55 Betta (2006: 266).
56 Betta (2002, 2006: ch. 5).
57 Duden (1991).
58 Pelaja-Scaraffia (2008: 15–217, 256–258).
59 Betta (2010).
60 Available online at: www.documentacatholicaomnia.eu/03d/1966-2004,_CDF,_Acta,_IT_EN_GE_ES_PT_FR_PL.pdf.
61 ACBg, Archivio Memmo, b. 1, *Lettere di Lucia Memmo Mocenigo a Paolina Memmo Martinengo*, 2 and 24 April 1793.
62 Knibiehler and Fouquet (1982: 48–58 and 1983: ch. 4); d'Amelia (2005); Badinter (1980, ch. 3.1); Lett and Morel (2006); Hanafi (2017).
63 Rousseau, Jean-Jacques, *Emile or Education*, transl. By Barbara Foxley, London & Toronto: J.M. Dent and Sons, 1921, ch. 1. Taken from the online version: https://oll.libertyfund.org/titles/2256#Rousseau_1499_66.

64 Ibidem: ch. 1 (https://oll.libertyfund.org/titles/2256#Rousseau_1499_139).
65 Rollet (1996); Corsini and Sandri (1999); Pancino (2015).
66 Rosen von Rosenstein (1776); Lett and Morel (2006); Morel (2010).
67 Pancino 2015: 326).
68 Morel (2010b: 177).
69 D'Amelia (2005: ch. 3.5); Guarnieri (1999); Arena (2016: 131 et seq.).
70 ASVe, Miscellanea legislativa, b. XX (*Regolamento Scuola ostetrica di Milano, Formula di giuramento*, art. 10 and 11).
71 D'Amelia (2005: ch. 3.5); Fildes (1988); Knibiehler (2003); Hanafi (2017).
72 Stone (1977: 431); Fildes (1988: 118–122).
73 Pancino (2015: 87).
74 Hunecke (1987: ch. 6.2).
75 Gélis, Laget and Morel (1978: 158); Rollet (1978: 1198).
76 Rose (1986: ch. 11).
77 Hunecke (1987: ch. 5.2).
78 Perco (1984, 1999); Dadà (2002).
79 Guarnieri (2001a and 2001b).
80 Della Peruta (1979); Rollet (2001, ch. 7); Becchi and Julia (1996, vol. 2); Filippini (1985b); Gijswijt-Hofstra and Marland (2003).
81 Gourdon and Pranchère (2018: 49); Gourdon (2014).
82 ASVe, *Biblioteca Legislativa*, b. 493, *Istruzioni e discipline da osservarsi pegli atti di nascita, matrimoni e morte*, 19 gennaio 1816.
83 Gourdon and Rollet (2009); Gourdon and Sage-Pranchère (2018: 49–57); Filippini (2018: 76–80).
84 Assael (1995: 55); Rollet (2001: 188–194); Durbach (2004).
85 *Codice penale universale austriaco* (1815): art. 376–379. Filippini (1985b: 38–40).
86 Rose (1986: 12).
87 Toaldo (1787); Zeviani (1775); Trevisan (1823); Gourdon (2003, 2009); Bigatto (2000).
88 Gourdon (2009: 120–123).
89 Rollet (1990); Corsini (1996: 264); Charrier, Clavandier, Gourdon *et alii* (2018: 9–22).
90 Derosas (1999: 42, table 2). On the figures concerning the reduction in infant mortality in the second half of the 19th century, I also consulted: Corsini and Viazzo (1993); Corsini (1996: 250–281); Del Panta, Livi Bacci, Pinto and Sonnino (1996); Del Panta (1994: 45–60). See also: Breschi, Derosas and Manfedini (2000: 457–488); Pozzi and Barona (2012: 11–21). For the Italian context only: Pasi (1995).

PART IV
The contemporary age

11
THE MANY REVOLUTIONS OF THE 20TH CENTURY

1 Maternity protection

The economic and social transformations of the 19th century had introduced radical changes in the way many women from the lower classes lived their pregnancies and childbirths: the Industrial Revolution, which over the course of the century also involved the Southern European countries, had pushed millions of mostly young women to work in unhealthy factories, in very heavy working conditions and without any form of insurance or protection: no leave from work or reduction in working hours was granted because of maternity, before or after the birth. Disease, miscarriages and early labours induced by harmful working conditions significantly increased, as doctors soon reported, when, in agreement with the socialist parties and the emancipationist movement, they strongly denounced the phenomenon. In 1871, while researching osteomalacia[1] at Milan's maternity hospital, Dr Gaetano Casati highlighted how the incidence of the disease, linked to serious obstetric problems, was connected to the poor working conditions of female workers in the textile factories of the area, where tuberculosis was also rife.[2] In 1877, a survey by economist Giuseppe Toniolo revealed a high percentage of miscarriages among tobacco factory female workers, caused by noxious fumes, which also affected fertility.[3] In 1901, at the Nantes Congress of Obstetrics, Dr Adolphe Pinard called for the introduction of at least three months' leave from work for new mothers. After childbirth, in fact, workers returned to work immediately, leaving their newborns with their neighbours, in improvised and destitute nurseries where they were precociously weaned, with the consequent increase in infant mortality, as Dr Cesare Musatti, founder of the journal *Igiene infantile* (Child Health), denounced at a conference at the Ateneo Veneto of Venice (1877).[4] It was a social reality in stark contrast with the extolling of the maternal role and with the new models of care emerging at the time.

It is not surprising that, in this context, the female emancipation movement used the theme of motherhood as leverage not only to obtain political but also social rights, making its protection an essential objective on which there was a broad agreement between liberals, Catholics and socialists in a common "maternalist feminism" that aimed at the recognition by the State of motherhood as a social function.[5] The introduction of maternity leave for female workers was requested in all national and international women's congresses held in Paris: from that of 1878 to that of 1892 (the first to be defined as feminist), to that of 1896, where Léonie Rouzade first talked of the "social function" of motherhood,[6] right up to that of 1900, where the right to remuneration was expressly requested.[7] In Italy, the first plan to set up maternity funds was presented in 1894 in Milan by Paolina Schiff.[8] In 1912, in the US, some women's associations founded the Children's Bureau, an organisation supporting the rights of mothers and children.[9]

In the wake of this female mobilisation, shared by large sectors of the public opinion, between the end of the 19th and the first decades of the 20th centuries, laws were enacted to protect working mothers (which included maternity leave), matched by laws for the protection of children: in Switzerland first (1877), and then in Germany (1878), Austria (1888), Great Britain (1890), Portugal (1891), Sweden (1900) and Italy (1902).[10]

This maternity leave, initially unpaid and limited to the first few weeks after childbirth, was later extended to the last months of pregnancy, with a gradual inclusion of salary: the maternity fund, the first welfare state provision, was set up in Italy in 1910, three years earlier than in France.[11] Although restricted to a few categories of workers and limited in their application, these laws represent an important milestone in women's history, as they recognised motherhood as a social function.

This legislative commitment was accompanied, and in many cases preceded, by a large number of philanthropic initiatives with women from the elites at the forefront, often assisted by doctors, with a new synergy aimed at supporting poor working mothers, fighting mortality and disseminating the principles of hygiene and the new care models. In 1887, in Milan, on the initiative of some hospital doctors, including Luigi Mangiagalli, a new midwifery emergency service for poor women in labour and new mothers was set up, supported by emancipationists Alessandrina Ravizza and Ersilia Majno, according to a model later implemented in other cities.[12] Towards the middle of the 19th century, starting in France, the first nursery schools had also been created: in 1844, Firmin Marbeau opened the first crèche (he also wrote *Instruction de la crèche pour les mères de famille*), soon imitated by European philanthropists.[13] In Italy, the first "presepe" (crib) (as these nurseries were called) was opened in Milan in 1850 by Giuseppe Sacchi and Laura Solera Mantegazza, a doctor and an emancipationist respectively. The Venice one was similarly founded in 1877 by Elisabetta Michiel Giustinian with the help of Cesare Musatti, who took over its medical direction, making it a model at the national level.[14] Like the other "cribs", it was for working mothers only, who were allowed to take their children from the age of 40 days, on condition they went to nurse them 4–5 times a day. The nurseries' life was regulated according to the new principles of paediatrics, which included daily bathing and weighing, weaning with sterilised cow's milk, periodic measuring and the gathering of statistics. In these philanthropic institutions, support for working mothers and the promotion of breastfeeding were closely linked: in 1878, the *Société de l'allaitement maternel*, founded by Marie Bequet, had also been created in France for this purpose.[15] New forms of organisation were also offered to wet nurses: so as to ensure at least a safe and medically controlled service, special agencies were set up, such as the *Provvidenza baliatica* in Milan (1884), awarded a prize at the first National Congress for the Health of Mercenary Breastfeeding, held in Milan in 1899.

Another important service, which saw the light in the 1990s, was the establishment of health clinics for mothers, such as the *Goutte de lait* in France, where sterilised, low-priced milk was distributed, medical examinations were carried out and advice was given on breastfeeding and child care. Fifteen years later, in 1905, the first international congress of institutions operating in this sector was held in Paris.[16] It was a significant turning point: for the first time in history, it was not doctors who went to the mothers' homes, but the latter who went to a medical centre to be assisted and above all educated to be mothers, according to the principles of paediatrics. Breastfeeding, just like first care, would no longer be left to maternal instinct or tradition (not even that of more ancient medical directions): mothers needed education and teaching by doctors, who founded specific journals, such as *L'Igiene infantile. Monitore delle madri* (Child Health. A Mothers' Monitor), by Cesare Musatti (1878), or compiled manuals for mothers, such as the *Manuel pratique d'allaitement*, by Pierre Budin (1905).[17] In his 1913 report, as the Chief Medical Officer to the Board of Education, Newman stressed that the main influence [in causing infant mortality] was the ignorance of the mother and that it was necessary to educate her.[18]

These institutions had clearly set themselves multiple social, health and education goals: helping poor mothers, offering doctors a wide-ranging scientific observatory and disseminating the new principles of breastfeeding and hygiene in the proletarian classes, in order to prevent disease and fight mortality.[19]

2 Maternity and nationalism: the Italian case

Between the 1920s and 1930s, political initiatives in the field of birth were resumed throughout Europe, with interventions ranging from control to repression, from education to training, with the onset of assistance, care and prevention programmes paying special attention precisely to birth.

This phenomenon was affected by various factors: on the one hand, the proliferation of Malthusian theories and of forms of birth control in large sections of the population; on the other, emerging nationalist ideologies and authoritarian governments in various European states.[20] It should be remembered that various Neo-Malthusian Leagues had already been established in many Northern European countries in the last decades of the 19th century, starting with Great Britain (1878), Holland (1882) and France (1896).[21] The first international congresses were also held at the turn of the century, beginning with the Paris one in 1900.[22] Some women doctors, such as Aletta Jacobs, Emma Goldmann and Marie Stopes, had played a very active role in this movement and in the promotion of "birth control", a term that would later be coined by Margareth Sanger, who in 1921 founded the American Birth Control League.[23]

The proliferation of new sexual behaviours, linked to the spread of contraceptive methods (from the pessary to the condom, to *coitus interruptus*), had led to a progressive reduction in the birth rate, from the upper-middle-class families initially to the petty bourgeoisie and the urban proletariat, starting from Northern Europe. France was ahead, with a birth rate of 21/1,000 in 1900, while in Great Britain, Norway and Sweden, the rate fluctuated between 27 and 29/1,000; in Italy, it was 33/1,000, with a tendency, however, to a constant decrease.[24]

This decline in births, emphasised by statistics, had rekindled the fears of demographic decline that had already emerged in the 18th century, joined by concerns about economic and military crises. The disastrous French defeat in Sedan in 1870, during the Franco-Prussian war, was linked precisely to the notable demographic decline that had hit France, compared to a "young" nation such as Germany, causing a wave of fear in the French public opinion (but elsewhere, too). In this climate, the demographic question was back at the centre of public attention and political interest. In many European countries, laws were passed to support maternity and children: in addition to the Scandinavian countries and France (which first organised the *Mutualité maternelle*), Great Britain (1918), Belgium (1919) and Germany (1922) also issued measures aimed above all at defending poor and abandoned children. In the US, the *Sheppard Towner Maternity and Infancy Act* (1921) was passed, the first federal programme for the promotion of mothers' and children's health.[25]

The rise of nationalistic regimes in the 1920s–1930s further enhanced the demographic question, making it a priority for political intervention, resuming many of the themes from the second half of the 18th century: we can say that biopower then reached one of its most pervasive applications. Mussolini was profoundly convinced that the state was only as strong as the number of its citizens (as had been asserted during the Enlightenment); the number as power was a leitmotif of his politics: "So as to count for anything, Italy must face the threshold of the second half of the century with a population of no fewer than sixty million people […] the destiny of nations is linked to their demographic power", he stated in his famous Ascension Day Speech of 26 May 1927 (cited by Meldini 1975: 141) (Figure 11.1).

Demographic increase was intended as a premise for the development of a country which had industrialised late and was in need of cheap labour, and also for the colonial expansion required by the imperialist aims of the regime. In this perspective, protection laws were not enough: it was necessary to increase the birth rate, which the Duce set out to do in 1927, launching his demographic

FIGURE 11.1 'Number is power! Celebration of mother-and-child's day', article from fascist journal *Il Popolo di Romagna*, 17 December 1938, XVII. Reproduced with permission of the Gambalunga Library (Rimini).

campaign, or rather his demographic "battle", in fact, a term that metaphorically stressed the connection between imperialism and birth increase. However, one of the objectives was certainly also the desire for "the normalisation of sexuality",[26] which in the views of the regime meant imposing a return to traditional gender models, after the upheavals caused by the First World War. The traditional metaphor of birth and war (see Chapter 1.7) was thus resumed and represented, to exemplify the fundamental gender characteristics: "war is to man as motherhood is to woman" was another of Mussolini's postulates (cited by Meldini 1975: 35).

As in all battles, it was guided by a careful strategy of propaganda, control and education carried out by an army of employees, officials and party members, with the help of Fascist volunteers and patronesses. Repressive laws targeted anti-natalist behaviour more heavily than liberal conservative governments had already done: contraceptive propaganda and information were banned (1926), a bachelors' tax was introduced (1926) and the fight against homosexuality and abortion, defined in the new Rocco Criminal Code (1930) as a crime against the race, was intensified; fatherhood and the number of children became preferential career requirements.

In this perspective, motherhood was a "patriotic" duty: "In fascist Italy, the most fascist thing women can do is 'to pilot' many children", the Duce wrote to the prefect of Bologna, disapproving of an initiative to train female pilots (cited by De Grazia 1992: 76). Thus, there was a reductive articulation of motherhood in the sense of mere bodily production, which clashed with the expectations of enhanced social value expressed by the women's movement. In schools and in the media, intense propaganda extolled the model of the "Roman woman", strong and fertile, opposing it to foreign emancipated women, "women-in-crisis", thin and nervous. And as soldiers were granted public rewards, a recognition was set up for mothers, to emphasise the public and political importance of motherhood: on the Day of Mothers and Children, created in 1933, the most prolific women in the Italian provinces were invited to Rome and rewarded as benefactors of their motherland. A similar celebration had been set up in France in 1918, the *Fête des mères*.[27]

The demographic-increase project also included an articulated plan to assist unmarried and poor mothers: a reform in this area was more urgent than ever, after the abolition of foundling wheels, implemented in many cities as far back as 1870–1880, and after the ban on maternity searches was revoked (DR 11 February 1923, n. 336): this implied the requirement to identify a foundling's mother, thus depriving unmarried mothers of their right to anonymity. The obvious intention was to force them to recognise their children and take charge of them, guaranteeing in exchange assistance that could no longer be left only to charitable institutions or to the women's associations that had been founded in some Italian cities, such as Rome (the *Opera Assistenza materna*, in 1917), Venice (the *Istituto Casa-Famiglia*, in 1910) and Turin (the *Casse di maternità*).

On the Belgian model of the Oeuvre (1919), much appreciated in Europe, in 1925, the ONMI, *Ente Nazionale Maternità e Infanzia* (National Agency for Maternity and Infancy), supported by public, state and municipal funds, was established.[28] Its remit was to provide subsidies and free assistance to unmarried mothers, arrange their admission to maternity wards and provide financial support to their children. These activities were accompanied by social endeavours aimed at legalising irregular relationships and persuading mothers to keep and breastfeed their children: in short, at "raising the moral standards" of motherhood, a task which involved many fascist volunteers, who were thus indirectly able to keep a close check on the social reality.

The ONMI intervention extended to the creation of "Case della madre e del Bambino" (Homes for mothers and children), nurseries, obstetric and paediatric clinics and hygiene courses for mothers. A great deal of effort was therefore invested in the dissemination of new childcare practices and in the medicalisation of pregnancy and childbirth, but with clear differences between North, Centre and South (in 1939, 81 homes in the North, 43 in the Centre, 31 in the South and seven in Sicily and Sardinia).[29] Other legislative initiatives aimed at increasing the protection of working mothers were also introduced: in 1934, mandatory maternity leave (one month before the birth and six weeks after) and a two-hour breastfeeding break per day. Activities were advertised in the journal *Maternità e Infanzia* (Maternity and Childhood), created in 1926 as a further educational and propaganda tool.

As in the past, the figure of the midwife was also given special attention by the government, as an important pawn in its attempts at demographic enhancement, both in its fight against mortality and in the dissemination in society of care models and of the political objectives related to them: "[Midwives] must be considered as front-line fighters against morbidity, infant and maternal mortality, but also against the threats to the strength and power of our country, Italy", Professor Giuliano Perondi declared in 1929 (cited by Gissi 2006a: 108). The government aimed at greater professionalisation, discipline and involvement in family policies. In the reorganisation of corporations, the Fascist Midwives' Union and the national register were established; the union journal *"Lucina"* was published. The community midwife was now a professional, a symbol of innovation and modernisation. The distance between this figure and that of the traditional midwife was skilfully outlined by Pirandello in his novel *Donna Mimma* (1917) in the character of the young "Piedmontese" girl, fresh out of school, who arrives bold and confident in the Sicilian village, as a young "man in a skirt", to replace the old midwife, wrapped in her black shawl and in the safety of her traditional practices.[30] In 1937, the traditional term *"levatrice"* was replaced by *"ostetrica"* (from the Latin *obstetrix*): the feminine form of the title given to doctors (*ostetrico*, obstetrician): the word was a symbol of their new status and of the subordination to a doctor that this implied.[31] In practice, despite the propaganda, the number of community midwives increased by a mere 2% at the national level, leaving many areas still without this service.

Fascism increased its repression against midwives who avoided the obligations and prohibitions of the laws, both in terms of contraception and abortion. The Rocco Code also increased penalties, providing for imprisonment from 2 to 5 years.[32] The government resorted to repressive and arbitrary measures, such as internal exile, which could be imposed without evidence of guilt: 236 mostly qualified midwives were sent to internal exile on the basis of mere suspicions, charged with causing serious "harm to the national interests".[33] They were the only professional group affected by similar measures during Fascism.

The outcomes of the protection initiatives were positive in terms of infant mortality, which decreased by 19% between 1924–1925 and 1934–1935, although still remaining rather high when compared to the rest of Europe (99 out of 1,000 births in the first year of age, against the 57 of England and Wales and the 72 of France). As for maternal mortality, in the same years, between 1920 and 1930, it settled to around 2.5–3 out of 1,000 childbirths, with a downward trend recorded in all Western countries.[34]

Where the regime completely failed, however, was in terms of the increase in the number of births, which continued to decline over the 1930s in both the Northern and the Southern regions, despite a pro-natalist campaign: the birth rate went from 29.9/1,000 in 1921–1925 to 19.9/1,000 in 1941–1945.[35] The laws against contraception clearly did nothing but increase back-street abortions used as birth control, with the serious risks to women's health they entailed.

Italian fascist policies were not an exception in Europe, but were the best example of an authoritarian and repressive trend recorded in this area in various countries, supported by the emergence of clerical, irrationalist and racist tendencies. Similar initiatives to the Italian ones, although with different emphases and nuances, were also undertaken in France, where a 1920 law forbade contraception and another law, three years later, increased the sentences against abortion, in Belgium (1923), in Spain (1928) and in Ireland (1929).[36] Even homosexuality was more intensely and systematically repressed, in an attempt to build the image of the "new fascist man", the very symbol of the nation.[37]

3 Eugenics, sterilisation and forced abortions

Another spectre was haunting Western countries: the fear of "race degeneration", understood as a qualitative deterioration of the physical and mental characteristics of the population. It strongly emerged between the end of the 19th and the beginning of the 20th centuries, in the wake of Charles Darwin's and Cesare Lombroso's theories and in the context of mass migratory movements which characterised this period.[38] The theory according to which a hierarchy existed between races, given scientific credit by misleading anthropological, medical and psychological investigations, had also involved, in addition to the established belief in the superiority of the white race, a parallel fear of its likely corruption (compounded by its numerical inferiority), with the social, economic and political consequences that could arise from it. The body of the nation, understood as a set of racially homogeneous citizens, thus needed to be preserved in its integrity and purity, precisely in order to maintain its original identity and superiority, hence the need to defend the superior race from external contamination, first of all by avoiding mixed marriages, in a perspective of untainted reproduction.

In 1910, Julia Green Scott, president of the DAR (Daughters of the American Revolution), an American conservative association founded at the end of the 19th century, using metaphoric language alluding to the Holy Grail, declared:

> We must not only cherish and keep as a treasure the cup from which the current of human life flows; we must also keep the ingredients that are poured into the cup. We must also protect this fountain from pollution [...] We must also preserve the sources of our race in the Anglo-Saxon lineage, the mother of freedom and self-government in the modern world.
> *(cited by Moriani 1999: 54)*

It is no coincidence that the first theories of eugenics emerged in conservative American circles, where both emigration and the fear of contamination of the dominant, white, Anglo-Saxon, Protestant race (WASP) were the strongest. The first eugenic centres, such as the Eugenetics Record Office (ERO), which also supported policies to contain immigration and the prohibition of mixed marriages, were also founded in the US.[39] But eugenic movement and policies are also strong in colonial areas.[40]

The very next stage of this eugenics project was to act against "internal contamination", the propagation of "infected and degenerate protoplasm", preventing anyone with hereditary defects from procreating, limiting the "multiplication of organically weak people", so as to strengthen the race. The project was inspired by the new insemination techniques used in animal husbandry, with the aim of applying the successes achieved on farms in the selection of breeding animals to the human population. Hence, the proposal to subject anyone affected by mental illness to forced sterilisation translated into law in as many as 33 US states between 1909 and 1933 with the approval of the Supreme Court, which judged such laws as consistent with federal plans for a social as well as medical vaccination. It has been calculated that over 8,000 people were sterilised between 1928 and 1933.[41]

Several countries of the old world were inspired by these principles, especially in Scandinavia, where eugenic centres and societies also sprang up and where, in the 1930s, similar laws of forced sterilisation were approved. But it was certainly Hitler's Germany which implemented the consequences implicit in these aberrant theories most determinedly and brutally, from the prohibition of mixed marriages to sterilisation and forced abortions. Thus, there was a very significant shift in state policies: from the fight against mortality to the qualitative control of births, beyond the wishes of families and individuals, to underline the primacy of the State over the spheres of life.[42]

In 1933, the year Hitler came to power, the Interior Minister introduced the first law of forced eugenic sterilisation (law on the prevention of unworthy life). The decision was devolved to special courts (250 were established), which included jurists, geneticists, anthropologists and doctors, and could resort to the police to enforce their decisions: 400,000 people were sterilised in the following ten years, half of which were women.[43] A further law allowed abortions for eugenic reasons up to the sixth month of pregnancy, particularly in women affected by mental illness. Never before had a state gone so far as to implement such anti-natalist interventions. Once the right of the State to intervene in the biological destiny of people in terms of reproduction beyond their will was affirmed, the next step was to extend this principle even beyond the initial moment of reproduction. The prevention of birth "without value" opened the door to the "suppression of life considered *without value*" (i.e. of the disabled, the terminally ill, etc.); the first victims of this planned massacre were handicapped children under the age of 3.[44] The subsequent and extreme expression of the principle of protection of the race implemented by Nazi Germany was – as we know – the discrimination of Jews: in 1935, the law for the protection of German blood and honour forbade both marriages and sexual relations between Germans and Jews (later extended to people of colour and gypsies), a decisive step towards the special laws that would lead to the Shoah.

It should be emphasised that the laws related to forced sterilisation for eugenic reasons remained in force in some democratic countries (such as the US and Sweden) until the 1970s and that the vast majority of Danish, Norwegian and Swedish citizens sterilised from 1934 to 1976 were women.

4 The Catholic Church and the Protestant Churches

The first years of the 20th century were particularly hard for women, precisely in terms of regulating and controlling fertility, which markedly intensified. The Catholic Church also intervened by making a firm stand, but it could not fail to do so, in a reality marked by the spread of Malthusian practices and eugenic initiatives, against the backdrop of the revolutionary changes introduced even in terms of sexuality by the Russian Revolution, which first legalised abortions in 1920.[45] For some time, the Catholic world had been mobilised against what was defined as immorality and pornography: leagues for public morality and against pornography had been founded between the end of the 19th and early 20th centuries in various Italian cities, as part of a battle also supported by the *"Civiltà Cattolica"* journal.[46] The Church was also concerned about the encroachment of political intervention in an area of its competence, an action which it perceived as dangerous.

As an answer to all this, a very tough encyclical was published, destined to affect the following decades as well: Pius XI's *Casti Connubii* (31 December 1930). Taking up some pronouncements by the Holy Office also contained in a previous encyclical, Leo XIII's *Arcanum divinae sapientiae* (1880), in reaffirming the sacramental nature of marriage, its indissolubility and reproductive purpose, the Pope declared that he was worried about the "pernicious abuses" of the time, "the exaggerated physiological education by means of which, in these times of ours, some reformers of married life make pretense of helping those joined in wedlock" (*Casti Connubii*, par. 108),[47] firmly condemning every form of birth control:

> Any use whatsoever of matrimony exercised in such a way that the act is deliberately frustrated in its natural power to generate life is an offense against the law of God and of nature, and those who indulge in such are branded with the guilt of a grave sin.
>
> *(Casti Connubii, par. 56)*[48]

The only mild concession to married couples wishing to limit the number of births was periodic abstinence based on the assessment of fertile days. Without mentioning it, the reference to the studies on female fertility and to the method that Drs Kyusaku Ogino and Hermann Knaus, in different ways, had popularised in the 1920s was obvious. The encyclical reiterated the condemnation of all forms of abortion, even on medical and therapeutic advice, bringing abortion and eugenics into a single discourse, despite expressing pity for mothers: "we may pity the mother whose health and even life is gravely imperiled in the performance of the duty allotted to her by nature" (*Casti Connubii*, par. 64).

The position taken by the Pope also aimed to stress the authority of the Church in this matter, denouncing what was considered as interference by the state by advocating the superiority of natural juridical law. The ecclesiastic institution had to show the State the direction of its legislative interventions and of its social action, as the last part of the encyclical clearly stated. One year after the signing of the 1929 Lateran Treaty, the profound synergy with fascist birth policies was absolutely clear.

All the subsequent pronouncements by the Catholic Church followed this line, from Pius XII's, who called an "immoral attack" any action aimed at "preventing" the procreation of new life (*Discorso alle ostetriche*, 1951 [Address to the participants of the Congress of the Italian Catholic Midwives Union]),[49] to John XXIII's in his encyclical *Mater et Magistra* (1961), right up to *Humanae Vitae*, issued by Pope Paul VI in 1968, at the end of the discussions of the Pope's Commission on Population, Family and Births, whose institution had given rise to so much expectation of openness in civil society.

On this issue, there was a further split with the Protestant world, which, in a series of pronouncements by various Churches between the 1950s and the 1970s, on the contrary declared birth control legitimate, in light of the principle of a married couple's responsibility.[50] This was the principle inspiring the position taken by the bishops of the Anglican Communion in their report following the 1958 Lambeth Conference, entitled The Family Today, and emerging precisely from the acknowledgement of the socio-cultural changes that had taken place in the field of sexuality, from the breaking of the ancient link between sexuality and reproduction and the need for the Church to interpret such changes and adapt its teachings.[51] Similar pronouncements were followed by the US, Dutch and Swiss Churches (1963), which went so far as to deny the essential reproductive purpose of the marriage bond: "The physical union of couples, carried out without the intention of procreating, must not be considered a sin: it is one of the main elements of conjugal unity" (cited by Flamigni 2012: 354).

Once again, Europe was thus divided on the religious and moral norms related to sexuality along the demarcation line that separated the Catholic and Protestant religions.

5 The delocalisation of childbirth to hospitals

The years from the 1920s to the 1970s marked a profound revolution in the history of childbirth, with the delocalisation of births to hospitals, not only in cases of dystocia, but also in physiological deliveries. Although at different times and in different ways, over the course of about 50 years, this trend grew in all Western countries, except for the Netherlands. From a place reserved for unmarried and/or poor mothers, hospitals became the place of choice, where women of all extractions and social classes decided to give birth.[52]

The figures of this unstoppable process speak for themselves: in 1924, in Germany, hospital deliveries were 24%; in 1952, they had risen to 72%; ten years later, they reached 95%. In France, particularly Paris, between 1920 and 1939, they went from 30% to 60%.[53] In the US, they rose from 37% in 1935 to 79% in 1945.[54] In Italy, in the first half of the century, the process was slower: in the years between the two wars, 95% of childbirths took place at home; in 1951, these were still 85%.[55] But the increase was steep in the following 20 years: in 1970, almost 90% of women gave birth in maternity hospitals and wards. The only exception in Europe was represented by the Netherlands, where the tradition of home births remained, by virtue of a different model of health organisation that combined tradition and the assurance of emergency assistance.

This change of location actually entailed a radical change in the culture of childbirth itself: from an event internal to the family and community spheres, it became a medical act, regulated by hospital rituals which also redesigned the role of the midwife, further subordinating it to the doctor, deprived of real autonomy and regulated by strict hospital rules.

What led to a change in collective behaviour of this magnitude, one of the most important in the history of childbirth? Why did women decide to go to the hospital to give birth? There are many and complex reasons.

First of all, it must be said that, in those years, medicine had won its long war against puerperal fever, after, as we have seen (see Chapter 9.3), various lost battles. Thanks to the application of the principles of antisepsis, the discovery of sulphonamides first and antibiotics later, which could fight bacterial infections, medicine had managed to defeat one of the fundamental causes of mortality (and of hospital ones in particular), thus making both physiological and dystocic deliveries, which required surgical operations, safer.[56] Starting in the 1930s and 1940s, maternal mortality declined significantly. In England and Wales, it went from 43.3 out of 10,000 live births in 1920 to 26.1 in 1940 and 3.9 in 1960; in the same period, in the Netherlands, it went from 24 in 1920 to 23.5 in 1940 and 3.7 in 1960.[57] In Paris, it dropped from 2-3/1,000 in 1931 to 1.4/1,000 in 1938.[58]

In the countries of Northern Europe, with slight fluctuations, in the 1960s, it settled at around 3–4 cases per 10,000 deliveries, falling even further in the 1970s, also thanks to improvements in living conditions, nutrition and domestic environments. In Italy, the figures were slightly higher, while confirming the same trend: from 30 out of 10,000 live births in 1935 to 5 in 1960, to 2.5 in 1975. Perinatal mortality, also thanks to the development of resuscitation techniques, also dropped from 64/1,000 in 1950 to 36/1,000 in 1965, to 24/1,000 in 1975.[59]

Substantially reformed, often linked to new paediatric wards, in a prenatal childcare perspective, maternity hospitals had become safer places, as were other hospital wards; it must be underlined, in fact, that the hospitalisation of childbirth is part of a more general trend of seeing hospital medicine prevailing.

The prestige of medicine increased: antisepsis became the new beacon of progress, the flag that presented the hospital as the eminent place of care, unlike the home presented as an insidious place where bacterial cultures proliferated: hospitals were no longer just "the refuge for abandoned and suffering people, but the instrument of a policy of health and assistance that watches over the entire population", as Dr René Sand had hoped in the early 19th century (cited by Beauvalet-Boutouyrie 1999: 3).

In addition to public concerns, this medical progress also met the growing expectations of safety by women and families: not only a rejection of death, which had already emerged in the early modern age, but the rejection of any risk, in the perspective of complete prevention, of "perfect" childbirth, which developed in the 1980s and involved children as well, made more and more "precious" by the progressive drop in birth rate.[60]

News stories where women were dying at home because they could not find a doctor in time, when sudden complications arose, made a great impression on the public opinion. In 1955, famous Italian journalist and writer Oriana Fallaci devoted a passionate article in the *Europeo* to one of these stories (*Morire di parto*, Dying in childbirth), reporting the tragic story of a Venetian woman who had bled to death due to the failure to deliver the placenta when having her third child, precisely because none of the four obstetricians called at night by her husband had been willing to call.[61] Also thanks to massive public investments implemented in those years, on the contrary, hospitals guaranteed a ready team of specialists, the immediate availability of obstetric operations in cases of sudden complications, blood transfusions and oxygen if required and the availability of drugs, sheltering women from similar "tragic accidents" (as this particular death was described). They also offered newborns greater protection, thanks to a new device: the incubator which, developed in 1880 by Stéphane Tarnier and gradually perfected, proved to be indispensable for premature or underweight babies.[62]

Safety and the rejection of risk for themselves and for their children therefore played a crucial role in women's choice, and in some places, especially in Anglo-Saxon countries, it was also linked to the tempting prospect of giving birth without pain, thanks to the use of anaesthesia during childbirth, in a kind of mysticism of bacteriology and anaesthesia.[63]

However, in the hospitalisation of childbirth, many other factors of a social and cultural nature were also crucial, which during the course of the century contributed to sustaining and reinforcing this trend: from the upheavals that both wars had caused to housing, to the progressive crisis of the extended family in the second post-war period, to emigration from the countryside to the city, to new housing models, to the increase in female occupation outside the home, with the consequent weakening of traditional networks of social solidarity.[64] The progressive development of a culture that separated birth (and death) from the domestic space, entrusting its management to medicine, should also be emphasised. The suffering, pain, blood and bodily fluids that accompanied childbirth were thus removed from daily life, in the name of an image of health, well-being and happiness that characterised the years of the economic boom in particular. The new view demanded that women hide what they once had to show off or even simulate: pain.[65] The screams of women in childbirth that once flooded the streets were now considered indecent and socially unacceptable. In the 20th century, suffering and death replaced sex as the main taboos and even childbirth was removed from the community because of the burden of pain and physical and emotional upheaval it entailed.

This interweaving of factors also emerged from the motivations of the women who lived through this transition:

> We go to the hospital because we think that they will intervene immediately if necessary, right? And therefore we are safer [...] And also because not being at home you have less embarrassment, because at home there is a bit of ... a bit of upheaval, isn't there? Both in terms of bedding and for many other things.
>
> (Orrù 1994: 217)

But within hospitals, therapeutic practices, relationships and the very perception of the event substantially changed: childbirth was equated to the other admissions, regulated by the same rules that were in force in the other wards, completely losing its precious specificity. Hospital rituals included the separation from the outside, the depersonalisation of patients, the application of standard protocols, the respect of hierarchies, adaptation and acceptance of the rules. The woman giving birth was turned into a "patient"; childbirth was included in the perspective of a mere physiological/pathological process to control, induce and direct in increasingly technological ways.

Hospital protocols required the removal of husbands and relatives from the moment of admission, a series of "purification" interventions (washing/shaving of the pubic area), restriction to lying in bed during the first stage of labour, scheduled obstetric checks and visits; for the delivery, transfer to a room very similar to an operating theatre, to a high bed, with legs strapped in stirrups, in full light. No intimacy or privacy, no consideration of special needs, little information on treatments; the expression of feelings or of suffering was barely tolerated, if not grossly scolded; any anxiety or fear was treated as tantamount to distrust of the medical authority; the doctor–patient relationship was regulated by a sterile affective distance, presented as competence.[66] What was required of women-in-childbirth-patients was their full adaptation "to the expected gestures and behaviours of those who assisted them" (Terzian-Regalia 1992: 106), a total delegation to the medical authority, that is to say their obedient passivity. Those who did not adapt were strongly blamed, as emerging from their testimonies:

> They kept telling me that I was bad, that when we have the chance to have beautiful children we don't cooperate.
>
> (Orrù 1994: 231)

> At one point I could no longer bear to be in the same position, with my legs bent. Enough, I wanted to get up, I wanted to throw myself out of bed! Then they held me down and told me I was crazy.
>
> (Ibidem: 195)

> Every gynaecologist who came rummaged inside me, looked at me [...]
> "Madam," he said, "if you don't stop, we'll call the ... police sergeant and have you arrested now".
>
> *(Ibidem: 165)*

The mother–child relationship at birth was also rigidly codified: the umbilical cord was immediately cut, the child pulled up by his feet, separated from his mother, washed with running water, checked and clothed and finally taken to the nursery, where, together with the other newborns, he remained until he was discharged. Contact with his mother was regulated by strict timetables and intervals, according to the rules of new normative childcare, which aimed to teach a child to respect timetables and to learn specific behaviours from birth.[67] In case of poor adherence to these rules, mothers were instructed to resort to formula milk, which the pharmaceutical industry promoted in the social reality as a panacea for many evils and as a symbol of female emancipation.

The hospitalisation of childbirth is closely connected to the progressive emergence of a technocratic model that made extensive use of tools and techniques, in an extension to eutocic deliveries of the same protocols envisaged for dystocic ones, aimed at the prevention of "possible" disease, even when not ascertained. The practice of inducing and speeding up labour became widespread, with amniorrhexis (the rupture of membranes) and the subsequent administration of oxytocin to accelerate dilation (in the 1920s and 1930s, it was already used in 9% of hospital childbirths in the US).[68] The use of forceps for "prophylactic reasons" intensified, starting in the US, where various obstetricians, such as Franklin S. Newell, argued for the need to use it systematically for women of the "overcivilized type", too fragile to give birth without its help.[69] Even Caesarean sections, made safer, began their progressive ascent to one the most frequent obstetric operations: in the US, they increased from 3.2% in the 1930s (1930–1939) to 6.8% in the 1960s (1960–1969) and 12.8% in the 1970s (1970–1979).[70] The practice of episiotomy also became ubiquitous to prevent spontaneous and displaced perineum lacerations: in Chicago midwifery clinics, as far back as in the 1930s, it was practised in 53% of deliveries.[71] Comparative research, conducted in the second half of the 1970s in four locations (the US, Sweden, Holland and Yucatan), highlighted these hospital practices, stressing their profound rupture with traditional ones.[72]

The issue of breastfeeding deserves special mention, first of all to point out that the years after the Second World War saw the disappearance of the traditional figure of the wet nurse, erased by the establishment of breastfeeding, the success of the model of the housewife devoted to reproduction and care work and above all by the triumph of bottle-feeding.[73] The spread of formula milk, marketed in the UK as early as the mid-1920s, prevailed in the years after the Second World War in the wake of massive propaganda by pharmaceutical companies, which also presented it as an instrument of the new female emancipation.[74]

6 "My womb is mine": contraception and abortion in the feminist movement

The slogan that the women's movement shouted in the streets in the 1970s brought into play an explosive and radically new principle in gender history: the self-determination on one's own body. The change in perspective compared to the large part of the 19th-century emancipation movement was profound: it was no longer just a matter of claiming equality in civil and political rights, but of declaring a freedom of choice that developed both in terms of sexuality and motherhood.[75] The scope of this principle was revolutionary compared to millennia of cultural constructions, norms and regulations. For the first time in history, not just single women, but a widespread, far-reaching movement publicly claimed the right to decide not only "when and how", but also "whether" to have a child, as the slogans of the feminist movement stated; in short, motherhood was no longer seen as a moral duty or biological destiny, but as a conscious choice.[76] Against this background of freedom in sexual behaviour, the link between marriage and procreation, just like the one that united sexuality and motherhood, had been broken.[77]

The discovery of new contraceptive methods provided valid technical support and an important aid in the process of liberation. Hormone-based contraceptives, developed by Gregory Pincus in 1956 with the support of Margareth Sanger and Katherine McCormick ("the Pill"),[78] became popular in the 1960s along with other contraceptive methods (e.g. the diaphragm, the coil), in the context of a new perspective of family planning and progressive reduction in the birth rate, which from the US (where there had already been a steady trend in the middle of the century) arrived in Europe, triggering the "contraceptive revolution" that led to a sizeable reduction in the birth rate.[79]

Even the countries of southern Europe were hit by this phenomenon: in Italy, for example, the birth rate halved in the space of 20 years: from 1964 to 1987, it went from an average of 2.6 to 1.3 children per couple.[80]

Notwithstanding the laws that still existed in various countries, extensive counter-information made available through pamphlets, mimeographs and self-help courses gave women the knowledge indispensable to make informed choices. *Our Bodies Ourselves*, the book published in 1971 by the Boston Women's Health Book Collective and covering topics ranging from physiology to pathology, from sexuality to abortion, from childbirth to breastfeeding, soon became a best-seller, and was translated into 31 languages with four million copies printed.[81]

For some women, this freedom of choice materialised in the rejection of motherhood, which was also affected by the distance from a maternal model considered as subordinate.[82] Many, on the other hand, were looking for new paths that included motherhood and self-fulfilment, motherhood and joy.[83] This gave rise to claims of full social citizenship, requests for services that allowed women to combine work and motherhood (nurseries and nursery schools) and other facilitating initiatives. Inseparable from these demands were also those requesting the repeal of repressive abortion laws and of laws banning contraception and demanding the institution of sexual-health clinics.[84] In Italy, the debate within the movement on the content of the new abortion law was particularly intense, with a division between those who supported the simple decriminalisation of abortion and those who wanted it legalised, with free health support for women, a position which ultimately prevailed.[85]

This theme mobilised the feminist movement into a wide range of initiatives: from mass demonstrations to the organisation of self-managed abortions, from collective self-declarations to mobilisations in abortion trials. In the UK was very active the Abortion Law Reform Association (ALRA), founded as early as 1939 by Janet Chance, Joan Malleson, Stella Browne and Alice Jenkins, author of the complaint book *Law For The Rich* (1960). Thanks to their efforts, the Abortion Act, the first European law, was passed in 1967. The National Abortion Campaign (NAC) was also founded in 1975 in support of this law.

In 1971, in Germany, 375 women denounced themselves to the magazine *Stern* for interrupting their pregnancies, as happened in France in the *Manifeste des 343 salopes*, signed by authoritative intellectuals of the time, Simone de Beauvoir in the first place. The trials of Marie-Claire Chevalier in France (1972) and Gigliola Pierobon in Padua (1973) became opportunities for major demonstrations.[86]

Meanwhile, associations and groups were founded, with the aim of providing legal and practical support to women, such as Mlac (*Mouvement pour la liberté de la avortement et contraception*) in France or CISA (*Centro Informazione Sterilizzazione e Aborto*) in Italy, founded in 1973 by Adele Faccio, Emma Bonino and Maria Adelaide Aglietta.[87]

Between the end of the 1970s and early 1980s, the growing involvement of public opinion and the support from left-wing parties (albeit with distinctions and differentiations) led to the approval of laws on the voluntary termination of pregnancy in most Western countries: in Great Britain and various US states (1967), Germany (1974), France (1975), Portugal and Spain (1984, 1985). In the US, in 1973, a Supreme Court ruling confirmed a woman's right to decide to terminate a pregnancy in the first three months, thus legitimising the legislation already approved in various States.[88]

In Italy, a historic Constitutional Court ruling declared art. 546 of the Criminal Code, which prohibited therapeutic abortion, was in breach of the constitution, thus sanctioning the principle of priority of a mother's life over her foetus' for the first time. Three years later, in 1978, parliament approved law 194 (*Norme per la tutela sociale della maternità e sull'interruzione volontaria della gravidanza.* Norms for the social protection of motherhood and on the voluntary termination of pregnancy). The opposition of the Catholic Church and the Catholic parties was particularly strong: in a climate of serious social conflict, Italians were called to vote in a referendum asking for the law to be repealed (1981). The victory that confirmed the law revealed how the collective mentality had changed, and how the principle of motherhood choice had percolated and found approval even among the women of the popular and Catholic classes.[89]

In the same years, the laws forbidding the advertising and use of contraceptives were repealed: in 1967, the Neuwirth law legalised them in France; in 1971, it was Italy's turn, with the repeal of article 553 of the Criminal Code, for which AIED (*Associazione Italiana Educazione Demografica*, Italian Association for Demographic Education) had strongly fought; in 1975, the establishment of family planning clinics followed (law 405).[90]

These are important laws, which marked a crucial stage in the history of women, a kind of *habeas corpus* that based female citizenship on the principle of self-determination as a body.[91] However, it should be pointed out that in some contexts, such as in Italy, their effective application still finds serious obstacles linked both to the low number of state family clinics and above all to the so-called "conscientious objectors", medical professionals allowed by law to withhold their services.

These transformations were inscribed in a basic framework characterised by the redefinition, in the 1970s, of biopower as outlined by Foucault, which tended to withdraw from the direct control of bodies to be expressed in more refined and indirect forms of control: from punishment to surveillance carried out above all through economic support, the offer of services, the checks and guidance of social and health practitioners.[92] Citizens, recognised as individuals responsible for their own biological destiny, were increasingly expected to manage their own "human capital",[93] especially in Northern Europe and the US, while political power tended to concern itself with offering them the conditions to implement this management and address biological risks, by providing health facilities and social services. The task of medical practitioners then became checking, through counselling, their full self-control and the conformity of their choices.

7 "Of woman born": a new perspective on childbirth

At the beginning, the feminist movement was above all a movement "against", which joined freedom and demands, self-awareness and denunciation of the power that a new term called "phallo-scientific": *Insieme contro* (Together against) was the significant title of a book by Clara Jourdan, where the author invited women to join:

> *Together* to discover that we can take back our bodies, *against* a phallo-scientific power that has tried to turn it into a passive object, poorly known and medicalised. Together to understand our sexuality and our real needs, against a charitable and paternalistic view of state medicine. Self-help, self-awareness, women's health centres: an essential step towards liberation.
> (*Jourdan 1976: back cover*)

Criticism was centred on the Catholic Church on the one hand and on medicine on the other, identified as being responsible for a repression of women which found its most explicit symbol in the figure of the witch.[94] The criticism of medicalisation and of the power exercised by medicine over women's bodies went hand in hand with the concrete work of organising feminist health clinics, self-help courses and alternative medicine.[95]

After this unavoidable phase, towards the end of the 1970s, a more mature feminism embarked on a full reflection on motherhood, recognising it as an important and peculiar experience for female individuals in a perspective of sexual difference. The book by Adrienne Rich, *Of woman born* (1976), marked a significant transition, the beginning of a research path that, in an intense criss-crossing between history and self-awareness, would overthrow not only the traditional canons, but the perspective itself, emphasising the experience of motherhood in its bodily dimension as well as being connotative of the female individual. Analysing the present in the light of history, the author asked, "What did it mean for men to be born of a woman's body?",[96] starting a reflection that would be largely developed, particularly in France and Italy, by the so-called "maternalist" feminism (L. Hirigaray, L. Muraro, A. Cavarero). The fledgling women's history also started investigations on this theme destined to open up new research areas in history, radically redesigning its boundaries.[97]

Meanwhile, another critical front was opening up on this battleground, backed up by a radical proposal to reorganise childbirth care: Frédérick Leboyer, French obstetrician active in the Resistance, director of the obstetric clinic of the University of Paris, published in 1974 a book destined to make history: *Pour une naissance sans violence* (For a birth without violence).[98] The violence denounced by the author was not the one against the mother, but against the other individual involved in the event: the newborn. Backed by his long experience and by observations derived from the comparison with other cultures (in particular the Indian one), Leboyer highlighted in simple language, in the form of dialogues and through the use of images, what was lying in full view of all, without being "seen": the particular suffering of the child during a medicalised birth. Leboyer's analysis aimed to highlight how the physiological fatigue of birth was aggravated precisely by hospital rituals, deaf to the needs of the newborn as to those of the mother, in an unconscious expression of sadism passed off as natural and normal. Harsh lighting, a noisy environment, the sudden severing of the umbilical cord, the lifting by his feet, the immediate separation from his mother, the prompt washing, all procedures carried out in the name of safety and hygiene, were traumatising experiences for the child, who instead needed to be received with delicacy in this difficult transition, smoothing the contrast between the conditions of life inside the womb and the external ones, ensuring quiet, dimmed lights, contact with his mother and an immediate opportunity to latch onto her breast.

Even in this case, it was a new perspective that reviewed hospital protocols in the light of this individual and his needs, as the subtitle to the Italian edition stated: *La nascita, il venire al mondo, il parto dal punto di vista del bambino* (Birth, coming into the world and childbirth from the baby's point of view) (1975). In this perspective, some traditional gestures and cares that 18th- and 19th-century medicine had erased were also retrieved, as well as practices from other, more distant cultures. Leboyer thus opened up the new path to childbirth "without violence".

In this path, feminism also found common ground with other movements, such as the environmentalists and the followers of democratic medicine, in an important and fruitful convergence, even if not without ambiguity and potential differences, which would emerge above all in the following years, when new models and regulatory forms were imposed on mothers in the name of "naturalness" and the needs of the (only) child. The case of the powerful *Leche League*, the American maternal breastfeeding league, with many branches in Europe as well, is a prime example.[99]

While both the criticism of medicalisation and the desire to recover many aspects of traditional childbirth in the name of humanisation and greater female leadership were identical, the priorities of the various movements were actually different. For feminists, in fact, the objective of making women responsible for the choices concerning their bodies, free from impositions and regulations, even those arising from a rediscovered naturalness, was absolutely crucial.

8 Pain-free childbirth: chloroform, epidural anaesthesia and psycho-prophylaxis

Another taboo that fell in the 20th century, on the wave of the relevant processes to secularise society, was the association of suffering with childbirth as an inescapable connection, insofar as it was inscribed in divine laws. After centuries, in the 19th century, a medicine more attentive to the needs of women had begun to address the complex issue of childbirth pain both on the research side and on that of techniques aimed at alleviating it. The path ran through contrasts and controversies, in a real ideological war, which in part continues even today in some Catholic countries.

The first steps in this direction were taken in the mid-19th century in Great Britain, where some doctors (such as James Simpson and Walter Channing) tried to apply the findings on inhalation narcosis experienced in surgery to obstetrics, using ether and chloroform. The reaction of conservative circles was very strong, but the practice still spread, albeit limited to aristocratic and upper-middle-class *milieux*. A contribution to legitimising it came from Queen Victoria herself, who in 1853 asked John Snow to anaesthetise her with chloroform during the birth of her son Leopold, and then again at the birth of her last daughter Beatrice.

Between the end of the 19th and the beginning of the 20th centuries, scientific interest in administering anaesthesia to women in labour rapidly increased, as did experiments with new substances. We can certainly say that in this period, "there (was) no narcotic, anaesthetic, calming substance that alone, or in combination with others […], ha(d) not been tried as an analgesic during childbirth" (Nardi 1954: 440): from ether to a mixture of scopolamine and morphine (which together gave both anaesthesia and oblivion), to ethyl chloride, presented by O.J. Rapin in 1923 at the third Congress of gynaecologists and obstetricians in Geneva, to methylene chloride, proposed by Eduard Arrias, to nitrous oxide, widely used in the US, to cocaine solutions inserted in the nasal cavities, tried by A. S. Mozak in 1936.[100]

Research was evidently also supported by a social demand that was emerging in a female reality made more aware and combative by the spread of emancipation movements, especially in Anglo-Saxon countries. Here, many women explicitly requested it, as does Catherine, the protagonist of the novel *A Farewell to Arms* by Ernest Hemingway, who must have had in mind the reality of his own country, rather than the Italian and Swiss one where the novel is set:

> "I want it now," Catherine said. The doctor placed the rubber mask over her face and turned a dial and I watched Catherine breathing deeply and rapidly. Then she pushed the mask away. The doctor shut off the petcock. [...] She smiled. "I'm a fool about the gas. It's wonderful."
> *(Ernest Hemingway 1929: 337–338)*

The National Twilight Sleep Association was founded in 1915 in the US by feminists Marguerite Tracy, Mary Boyd and Charlotte Carmody. It supported the use of drugs and anaesthetics (morphine and scopolamine) during childbirth, finding consensus and support in the upper middle classes: "The women of America are demanding that the administration of painlessness shall not be left to the decision of the doctor, but of the mother" (Rundi Hutter 2010: 82), wrote Marguerite Tracy, who considered being knocked out with drugs an expression of feminism. Along these lines, Anna Steese Richardson organised the Better Babies movement.[101] Drs. Karl Gauss and Bernhard Kröning from the University of Freiburg had suggested the use of these substances since 1906.

In practice, however, the world of obstetricians was very divided: once again, cultural, religious and social elements deeply divided the Western world between the most favourable to the use of anaesthetics, such as the Anglo-Saxon north, and more decidedly contrary areas, such as the Catholic south, where the ideology of the unavoidable suffering of women in childbirth and of its moral value continued to exist. In the US and the UK, many doctors supported the use of these drugs both for deontological and for professional reasons. The fear of losing a bourgeois clientele that specifically asked for it was a reason openly declared by various American obstetricians,[102] but there were also those, such as Bernhard Kröning, who argued that anaesthesia was now indispensable to women of the bourgeois classes, now incapable of bearing a pain so intense that it might have altered their psychological as well as physical balance.[103]

Other doctors, on the other hand, also objected in view of the consequences this could have on the child and because of the increased medical interventionism. In fact, all these substances had side-effects: they deprived mothers of the awareness of childbirth during the final stage; they increased the need for instruments and had some impact on the liveliness of babies at birth. For a long time, even the physical fragility of Prince Leopold (who in fact suffered from a genetic disease, haemophilia) was attributed to the use of chloroform during his birth. In a perspective that considered the life and health of the child as a priority, these were decisive arguments.

The future path of obstetric anaesthesia was inaugurated by Walter von Stöckel (1909) with the application of local analgesia techniques, codified in the following years by various doctors (Fidel Pagés, Eugen Aburel, Achille Mario Dogliotti, John J. Bonica): spinal epidural anaesthesia (the continuous injection of sedative through a small catheter inserted into the epidural space) had the advantage of relieving the pain, leaving the mother alert during childbirth. Moreover, it could be dosed differently, even if it did not completely solve the problems of increased instrumental support. In the 1950s, this technique became widespread, once again starting with the US and Great Britain, consolidating a trend that would be firmly established in the following years in many European countries.

Between the 1930s and 1960s, a completely different, psychology-based method, which rejected the use of drugs and medication in the name of a "natural childbirth", was developed in the UK by obstetrician Grantly Dick-Read (1890–1959) and in France by Fernand Lamaze.

Based in Woking, in the suburbs of London, and critical of anaesthesia, the British obstetrician was convinced that pain was largely caused by fear, which caused muscle contractions, and had developed a method based on techniques of muscle relaxation and self-control. His first book, *Natural Childbirth* (1933), was at first ridiculed, and he was expelled from the London clinic he had set up with a group of fellow obstetricians, so he set up a private clinic at 25 Harley Street. But his second book, *Revelation of Childbirth* (1942), later entitled *Childbirth without Fear*, became a best-seller in the post-war period and the method spread mainly in Great Britain and the Netherlands.[104]

Totally independently of Dr Dick-Read, a few years later, another similar method was developed in Soviet Russia by psychiatrist I.Z. Velvovsky, a disciple of I.P. Pavlov, supported and assisted by A.P. Nikolaev, a Leningrad obstetrician. Starting from the belief that childbirth, as a physiological act, could not in itself be painful and that suffering was induced by cultural conditioning that acted unknowingly on the female psyche, the psycho-prophylactic method sought to counteract it through breathing and relaxation techniques, so as to "distract" the mother from fear and suffering, giving her an active role in all stages of childbirth. This presupposed the organisation of preparation courses and some training for women during pregnancy. Experimented successfully and received with enthusiasm, it was imposed by law in the USSR in 1951. Its dissemination in Western Europe must be ascribed to French doctor Fernand Lamaze. After meeting Nikolaev and spending some time in Leningrad, he decided to apply the method in Paris, at the *Maternité de la clinique des Métallurgistes* (better known as *Maternité des Bluets*), where he was the director. After some initial distrust, linked to the communist ideology of its inventor and of his French follower, the psycho-prophylactic method was recognised by the French government in 1960.[105]

These methods to achieve a natural birth were received positively in various Catholic countries, including Italy, with the support and approval of the

Church. Pope Pius XII approved them in 1956, judging them to be morally acceptable:

> Science and technology can therefore use the conclusions of experimental psychology, physiology and gynaecology (such as the psycho-prophylactic method) to eliminate the sources of error and make childbirth painless and possible. The Scriptures do not forbit it.[106]

In actual fact, this initial enthusiasm, a little naive according to Yvonne Knibiehler, was destined to fade over the years, in light of the fact that many women, especially during their first childbirths, although prepared, did not achieve the desired objectives: although it might dull the pain, this method certainly did not eliminate it.[107] The two methods, Grantly Dick-Read's and Velvovsky-Nikolaev's, however, had certainly achieved a crucial objective: making women the protagonists of their own childbirths, reassigning to them an active and conscious role.

9 "Let's take childbirth back!"

Riprendiamoci il parto (Let's take childbirth back) was the significant title of the Italian translation of Raven Lang's *Birth Book*, published in the US in 1972 and in Italy in 1978 by Rome's Feminist Group on Childbirth.[108] It expressed a demand widely shared in the feminist movement, even if it was articulated in different forms and ways: for some activists, "taking back childbirth" meant avoiding the experience of a medicalised birth; for others, recovering the emotional charge of the event, and bringing it back within the affective sphere; for others bringing it back within a natural and non-pathological perspective, and respecting the needs of the child as well: for all of them, it meant escaping a destiny of passive suffering. Even for Adrienne Rich, it was a crucial and emblematic passage, with enormous psychological and political implications.[109]

A series of surveys conducted in several countries brought to light the sense of powerlessness and violence experienced by many women in their sexuality, during abortions, in childbirth, but also their firm will to escape, to get out of loneliness and silence: "*Basta tacere!*" (Don't be silent!), for example, was the title of one of these accounts collected in Italy by the *Movimento di lotta femminista* (Feminist Fight Movement) (1972).[110] The public denunciation was intertwined with the desire for profound change involving the whole sphere of sexuality, reproduction and physical motherhood.

It was in this context that alternative experiences of childbirth were tried, arising in most cases from a fruitful synergy between feminists and left-wing obstetricians and/or members of the environmental movement, equally critical of medicalisation, often more in a context of political criticism of capitalism and of a hopeful "return to nature".[111] These were very different experiences, depending on whether one or the other objective prevailed, often arising in suburban hospitals or private clinics, which had become centres of attraction for national and European networks. The *Clinique de Lilla* in Paris was one of these and one of the first in Europe. Established in 1964 on the initiative of two women who had also founded an association, between 1971 and 1976, it became a place where an "alternative" childbirth was practised: pregnant women attended preparatory courses on different methods and at the time of labour and delivery were left free to choose the position and the people participating in the event.

At Pithiviers Hospital, in the Loiret, Michel Odent applied his Leboyer method: women gave birth in the *salle sauvage*, with coloured walls, cushions and sofas, in a silent twilight and with background music; they were left free to move, to take the position they preferred and, if they wished, to have their labour in water. After being born, babies were placed on their mothers' bellies and immediately allowed to breastfeed.[112]

In Great Britain, in 1982, Janet Balaskas promoted the International Active Birth Movement which, in addition to carrying out research on the physiology of childbirth, took care of its preparation following the principle of "active birth", recovering some practices from the most ancient tradition (such as walking during labour). The following year, she published her highly successful book *Active birth*, reprinted and translated several times.[113]

In Italy, one of the first centres was set up at the Monticelli Hospital in Ogina, near Piacenza, by Lorenzo Braibanti, author of the book *Nascere meglio* (Being born better).[114] In Rome, the *Centro Nascita Montessori* (Montessori Birth Centre) was opened by Adele Costa Gnocchi, who from 1969 ran courses in obstetric psycho-prophylaxis using the Lamaze method and, from 1976, RAT (Respiratory Autogenic Training) courses. In 1974, the new Head of Obstetrics at the Fatebenefratelli Hospital in Rome, Romano Forleo, reorganised his ward in the spirit of the principles of humanised childbirth.[115]

It should also be highlighted how, in these experiences, fathers acquired a new role compared to the past, with an involvement that saw them present and participate both during pregnancy and at the birth, as in the directions of the method of natural childbirth developed by Robert A. Bradley, known as "husband-coached childbirth" and popularised by his book *Husband-Coached Childbirth* (1965).[116]

The humanisation of childbirth, therefore, took place in forms that also reflected the new couple relationships. It was an innovative aspect, the expression of new intimacy and solidarity within couples, which led to a clear break with the traditional gender separation in childbirth.[117] Meanwhile, in various cities, feminist midwives' associations were set up to promote home deliveries. This realised the hopes anthropologist Sheila Kitzinger had expressed in her book *Rediscovering Birth*, of an alliance between feminists and midwives to fight the indiscriminate use of technology and reacquire an active role in childbirth.[118]

In 1976, in London, a group of female midwifery students founded the Association of Radical Midwives, which, in contrast with their national representative body, the Royal College of Midwives (RCM), opened private clinics and organised home births.[119]

In Paris, the *Clinique de Lilla* trained a team of midwives who practised home births on request. Other teams were set up in Italy in various cities, such as Florence, Milan, Rome and Venice; they soon joined in a national association, the *Associazione nazionale ostetriche parto a domicilio e case di maternità* (National association of midwives for home births and maternity homes) (1981).[120] A point of reference at the European institutional level was the organisation of childbirth assistance in the Netherlands, which had followed the solitary road of strengthening midwifery home care rather than hospitalisation in the 19th and 20th centuries, achieving levels of safety equal to those of other countries.

In the wake of these campaigns by the feminist movement, even state institutions were beginning to introduce some reforms, accepting and recognising, in different ways throughout Europe, some demands for the renewal of assistance to pregnancy and childbirth. In Great Britain, the Association for Improvements in Maternity Services promoted significant investments in the mother and child welfare sector and in the promotion of home births, while the National Childbirth Trust fought for the empowerment of women in the management of motherhood as well. These principles were implemented by the British government with the Changing Childbirth report (1993), which implemented a policy of maternal assistance based on the principle of woman-centred care.[121]

In Italy, law 405/75 (Istituzione dei Consultori Familiari), which established family planning clinics, in addition to providing information on contraception, had the additional objective of providing psychological and social assistance in preparation to motherhood and responsible parenthood. Based on the model of Birth Centres, some clinics began to offer a halfway option between hospitalised and home births, still guaranteeing maximum safety, as they were located in the grounds of major hospitals, but also offering a more familiar and domestic environment, with limited technology.[122]

In 1985, the World Health Organization, the UN special agency for health, published an important, milestone document, *Appropriate technology for birth*,[123] which made a series of recommendations for the correct assistance to physiological births, criticising excessive medicalisation and a whole series of hospital practices considered lacking in scientific justification. These included the systematic shaving of the pubic area, routine artificial rupturing of membranes, routine foetal monitoring, the requirement to lie down during labour and delivery, and deploring the indiscriminate increase in Caesarean sections (according to the document, there is no justification in any geographical region for having more than 10–15% Caesareans). Recognising the concept of "women's psychological well-being", in the context of a careful preliminary risk assessment, it was positively recommended to have the presence of a familiar person, freedom of movement and the free choice of positions during labour and childbirth (all practices drawn from the oldest tradition), immediate contact with the baby, early breastfeeding and also the respect for the values and culture of every woman, an important emphasis in a reality marked by intense migration. The following year, *Recommendations on Postnatal care* followed, reiterated in 1998, 2004 and 2014.[124]

In 1988, the European Parliament issued the *Charte des droits de la parturiente*[125] (Charter of rights of women in childbirth), where these principles were taken up and developed, recognising the relevance of "cultural" and psychological factors in childbirth and the requirement to respect the needs of women and their personal traits. In this perspective, a profound revision and reorganisation of all legislation related to women during pregnancy and childbirth was advocated and the usefulness of home birth was also recognised, depending on the physical and psychological conditions of mother and child, stressing the need to create women's health centres modelled on the Well Women's Centres opened in various European cities.

These were important recommendations for the authority of the institutions from which they come, even if they were received quite differently in the various European countries.

10 Revealing the secrets of the womb: ultrasound scans

With the development of ultrasound scans, between the 1960s and 1970s, medicine reached what had been first a dream for centuries, then a tenaciously pursued objective: to see what the body conceals, what happens inside the womb. Man's *cupiditas videndi* had been – as we have seen – a crucial trait in the medical approach to the female body since the days of the Scientific Revolution and even more in the age of clinics: a desire for knowledge that was expressed in the pursuit of what could be seen, within a hierarchy of forms of knowledge that placed seeing at the top.[126] This aspect was emphasised even more in the age of 'image'.

In the 19th and 20th centuries, the development of new instruments saw a rapid progress: the ancient *speculum matricis*, which Justine Siegemund (see Chapter 7.2) had vociferously rejected at the end of the 17th century, was joined by the *Lichtleiter* (light conductor), invented by Philipp Bozzini (1807), by x-rays applied to obstetrics (1913) and by the fibrescope (the first optical-fibre endoscope), developed by Basil Hirschowitz (1956). But only the application of ultrasound technology, introduced in 1958 in Glasgow by Ian Donald, and the development of simple machinery with external probes made it possible to take the decisive step in this direction, making in some way visible to the eye what moves and palpitates in the womb.[127] The shift with respect to the past was fundamental: seeing inside no longer meant "looking at death" (as was the case in post-mortems), both as far as the woman's and the foetus' bodies were concerned. The woman's living body became apparently transparent under the probe of the ultrasound system.

In the 1980s and 1990s, more refined instrumentation improved the quality of the images, giving the impression that the barrier of the containing body had been completely overcome, focusing on the foetus not only in the advanced stages of its development, but also in the initial one, in its first uncertain and mysterious origin: the machine allowed the foetus to be seen and measured and pathologies identified. The diagnostic spectrum was expanded and scientific knowledge vastly improved. The instrument's success and dissemination were extraordinary: in France, over a five-year period, its use during pregnancy rose from 11% (1976) to 82% (1981), reaching 90% in 1995.[128]

Ultrasound scans became the best instrument to medically check on pregnancy, to "monitor" it, according to a neologism introduced to the language of obstetrics. It also became essential in the application of other investigation techniques that spread in the 1990s, such as amniocentesis (the collection and analysis of amniotic fluid) and chorionic villus sampling (the analysis of chorionic villi), which allow the diagnosis of prenatal pathologies and the identification of chromosomal defects.[129]

However, not only did their undisputed advantages in diagnostics determine the extraordinary success of ultrasound scans, but so did other motivations and needs that transcended medicine. The instrument clearly both met and at the same time amplified a social demand: parents' desire to see their child before birth, to recognise it emotionally and to identify its gender and features. Unlike other diagnostic tests, in fact, ultrasound scans are shared by doctor and parents, in a new interaction where an obstetrician becomes a mediator of images and knowledge and where different gazes and needs are intertwined: the scientific on the one hand, the emotional on the other, in an overlap of medical imaging and parental imagery. In this sense, we can agree with M.L. Boccia and G. Zuffa that it is a new "cognitive ritual".[130]

The advent of ultrasound also implied a transformation that involved different levels: the representation of the foetus, forms of medical monitoring and the experience of pregnancy. Foetal life was not a "first birth" only in the abstract articulations of theological and scientific thought, as was in the 18th century; it also became such in the common sense, in the affective dimension, precisely by virtue of the extension of visibility to gestation. While birth was traditionally characterised precisely by the creature enclosed in the womb "showing itself to the world", it was the concept of birth itself that had definitively changed into the appearance of the mobile signs of the foetus on the doctor's video screen. In the 1980s, the first photograph many parents put in the child's photo album was no longer that of his first cry, but the snapshot fixed by the ultrasound scan: the black and white profile of the first scan.[131]

Further technological development (e.g. endoscopies using laparoscopy, the use of electron microscopy) captured increasingly detailed and early images, pushing the gaze right up to the moment of conception. Their digital enhancement and dissemination through mass media pushed that process of subjectivation of the foetus initiated by 18th-century embryology to its extreme consequences, generalising its representation. The making of films such as *From Conception to Birth* by Alexander Tsiaras (from the book by the same title written with Barry Werth),[132] the dissemination in magazines and books of sequential photographs, along the path opened up by Lennart Nilsson in *Life* magazine, went hand in hand with the use of the images of foetuses in television commercials, in advertising and in films, with the emergence of the foetus as a media subject, with all the emotional and symbolic repercussions that this transition implied.[133] The consequences were ambivalent, especially when considered from the point of view of a female individual and in a long-term perspective. The undisputed progress in prevention, which responded to the couples' demand for a healthy child (also because he was often an only child), was juxtaposed by the extension of medical control over the whole of pregnancy, starting with conception, with a medicalisation marked by increasingly more detailed protocols, made of multiple scans, laboratory tests and visits. The precautions once reserved for at-risk pregnancies were extended to physiological ones, to all pregnancies.

The experience of pregnancy, the relationship between a woman and her body and her ability to intercept and interpret its messages were profoundly altered. The expression of her perceptions no longer had any value, neither before her community, nor before her obstetrician, when unsupported by technical and diagnostic findings and by the word of the doctor himself: he was the one who explained to the woman what happened in her body, and what she should feel. Thus, the female experience also depended on the response of the clinical report, in a form of delegation that certainly saw her more protected and ensured, but also more impotent and passive.[134] All this went against the needs of re-appropriation of women's body and childbirth declared by feminism.

11 The new frontier of artificial insemination

Out of the radical changes affecting the field of reproduction in the 20th century, artificial insemination has been the most revolutionary and disruptive from the scientific, cultural and social points of view, because it crosses multiple levels of human experience (the social, the imaginary, the symbolic, that of representation) and because it has brought about profound changes involving, in addition to motherhood and birth, also sexual roles and the family, raising a series of bioethical problems. For this reason, in line with the indications of the European Parliament, from the 1990s, permanent National Bioethics Committees have been set up in many countries, with the aim of monitoring and assessing research paths both on the legal and on the deontological-moral levels.

The stages in the advancement of these techniques have been marked by important technical-scientific discoveries that over the century have followed one another at a fast pace, making it possible not only to imagine being able to reveal "the mystery of fertilisation" (as Charles Bonnet wrote to Lazzaro Spallanzani in the 18th century),[135] or reproduce it in the lab, but even to formulate it as a medical therapy, included in health protocols and publicly recognised.

This was the 20th-century "leap", coming after the difficult journey of Lazzaro Spallanzani's, John Hunter's and Michel-Augustin Thouret's bold attempts, the bitter 19th-century debates, the secret experiments and the birth of the first societies for the practice of artificial insemination, at the end of the 19th century. While, in some countries such as the USSR and the US, the spread of artificial insemination was already significant in the 1930s and 1940s, in the 1950s, it reached success rates of thousands of cases per year: more than 5,000 according to a survey promoted in the US.[136] It was not only a question of a quantitative, but also of a qualitative leap, which made this practice a safe procedure in the cure of sterility, in a progressive scientific, professional and moral legitimacy.

What made this transition possible? First of all, the important scientific discoveries of the 19th century: the identification of the functions of the ovaries in the menstrual cycle (with the discovery of spontaneous ovulation), the role played by spermatozoa and the emergence of cell theory (with Oscar Hertwig's discovery of the process of fertilisation) had laid the scientific foundations for an intervention that, from the technical point of view, used the development of cryopreservation in the 1950s and the first seed banks. This process was enabled by the discovery of ovarian hormones, and by the possibility to freeze not only sperm, but also eggs, at the end of the 1990s. All this made it possible for the first time to carry out fertilisation outside the mother's body, *in vitro*, with a further shift in the path of medically assisted conception. On 27 July 1978, thanks to the work of British doctors Robert Edwards and Patrick Steptoe, the first *test-tube baby* was born: Louise Joy Brown.[137]

A plurality of factors of a different nature had promoted this fast-paced technical-scientific research which, once combined, had ended up legitimising it in the social reality. The thrust of eugenic lines of thought is one of them. In some countries, especially in the US, the urgency of a qualitative strengthening of the population had been strongly felt as far back as the 1920s and 1930s, as we have seen (Chapter 11.3): artificial insemination thus fitted within a wider project to fight against the alleged degeneration of the race, to increase the original white-Anglo-Saxon stock, which first resorted to these techniques. In other countries, it appeared to be functional to the project of demographic strengthening which looked at the decline in births as a scourge with dangerous political and social implications. In both perspectives, artificial insemination was an effective cure to heal and/or develop the body of the nation.

But the political was not the only interest. The social demand for these techniques, increasingly present and increased by positive results, stemmed from a desire for parenting that would not surrender to the limits of nature, which considered it legitimate to try and overcome them, even by resorting to the seed of a donor; in short, it highlighted a significant change in culture and ethical criteria.[138] To what extent they were affected by the emphasis on the maternal role, the concept of motherhood as a female fulfilment, the social and political relevance this took on it is difficult to say, but it is significant that, in the public debate, the term "maternity" is articulated with "right" and that it is presented as one of the reasons supporting the practice.[139] Soviet doctor A. Schorowa, the first female doctor to intervene on the topic, in addition to experimenting with the practice, as far back as the 1920s supported the legitimacy of artificial insemination precisely based on the right to motherhood, describing sterility as a disease to be cured.[140]

From the point of view of medicine, the practice fitted within the scientific imagination not only as a way to overcome the limits of nature and control fertilisation *ab origine*, but also to create life itself, as so much literature and philosophy had imagined, starting with Paracelsus and his *homunculus*, and Mary Shelley's Frankenstein. On the social level, it contributed to further promoting the figure of the doctor, who became the "agent" of life, the third protagonist of conception (with father and mother), the one who made their wishes possible, thanks to his technology. In this sense, we speak of "medicine of desire", to which, among other things, substantial economic advantages are connected, with the development of a real fertilisation industry.[141]

These are the factors that determined the legitimacy of the practice in the social reality, preceding legal and political eligibilities: laws on artificial insemination were approved in most European countries between the end of the 1980s and the 1990s (1988 Spain, 1990 UK and Germany, 1994 France, 1997 The Netherlands), when the practice was already widespread. These laws, therefore, arose from the need to regulate it, by setting principles and limits.

Significant differences at the European level also emerged in this area: the USSR, the US and Great Britain were at the forefront of experimentation, while in Catholic countries, or where the authority of the Catholic Church was stronger, it remained limited to single groups and figures, often disputed and criticised. This was a differentiation in practices that was reflected in the different orientations of the two religions: while the Catholic Church had condemned it since 1897, with a pronouncement by the Holy Office (reiterated in 1929), in the mid-20th century, the Protestant Churches had opened up to artificial insemination, albeit limited to the homologous one, with the pronouncement of the Canterbury Commission (*Artificial human insemination* 1948).[142]

It is important to emphasise that artificial insemination, especially after IVF (in vitro fertilisation and embryo transfer), triggered a real social and cultural earthquake within the family, motherhood and in the very representation of birth.

The most obvious outcome was the further breakdown in the relationship between sexuality and reproduction. While contraceptive methods had rendered sexuality independent of reproduction, with artificial insemination techniques, it was reproduction itself which broke away from sexual intercourse, as it could take place *in vitro*, with a dissociation of bodies that removed sexuality in the procreative act. The use of donor sperm or eggs also broke the link between parenting and filiation, creating a dichotomy between biological fathers and/or mothers and social fathers and/or mothers. The outcome was a redesigning of parenting and filiation, for centuries based on blood ties, with a separation between biological and social functions. The access to medically assisted procreation (MAP) by gay couples or single women further introduced unprecedented models of parental couples of the same sex or of single parenting.[143] And while it is true that a woman's body still remains essential to the reproductive process, it is nevertheless clear that it increasingly takes the form of a mere container, a functional medium available on the market. What once took place with wet nurses, paid to breastfeed the children of others, today happens with surrogate mothers, who make their wombs available to the implantation of a fertilised cell, either as a gift (as has occurred in some cases), or, more frequently, for money.[144]

The outcome has been an explosion of motherhood, in the sense of a breakdown in the maternal function, which can be carried out by different female figures: the biological mother, donor of the egg, and the surrogate mother, who receives the zygote (the fertilised cell) in her womb. The fundamental principle of filiation, the certainty of motherhood (*mater semper certa est*), is therefore revoked. The one who gives birth is not necessarily the biological mother. In addition to the father's, the mother figure has also been split between surrogate mother and genetic mother. In this sense, there are those who speak of apparent "cancellation of the female body", of "exploded motherhood"[145] or of the "eclipsing of mothers".[146]

Equally significant have been the changes that have occurred in terms of the representation of birth and death. The advent of "test-tube mothers" marked a further turning point in this path of cultural redefinition: while in the 18th century, birth no longer coincided with "coming into the light", in the 20th century, with the emergence of MAP, it no longer even coincided with the presence of a foetus inside the womb. It was taking place upstream, with fertilisation itself, symbolically uncoupling from the maternal body to become absolute as a biological event in itself, with an extreme retreat in terms of biological development. The use of expressions, such as "born in a test tube", significantly highlighted it. Consequently, the representation of the embryo was also redefined, in a process of personification that reached the fertilised cell.[147] Significantly, the Catholic Church considers the zygote itself as a full individual, as we read in the pronouncement of the Congregation of the Doctrine of the Faith on the *Respect for human life in its origin and on the dignity of procreation* (22-2-1987):

Thus, the fruit of human generation, from the first moment of its existence, that is to say from the moment the zygote has formed, demands the unconditional respect that is morally due to the human being in his bodily and spiritual totality. The human being is to be respected and treated as a person from the moment of conception; and therefore from that same moment, his rights as a person must be recognised, among which, in the first place, is the inviolable right of every innocent human being to life.[148]

The Italian State codified the subject in the controversial law 40/2004, which recognised the embryo as an "individual" equal to the other individuals involved in the reproductive process and as such bearer of rights, paradoxically greater than his mother's, with the resulting legal consequences: the prohibition of heterologous fertilisation, the obligation to implant a maximum of three embryos and all at the same time, the prohibition of preimplantation diagnosis. This law was called "cruel" by feminist associations, which in 2005 promoted protest initiatives and a referendum.[149] A failure to reach the quorum confirmed the law, which, however, was subsequently reviewed by as many as 33 sentences by various Italian courts and thwarted by three pronouncements by the Constitutional Court, in light of the principles of freedom, self-determination of the couple and priority of the mother's health, enshrined in the 1948 Constitution.

Even the specular representation of death has been unhinged. The freezing of sperm and eggs seems to ensure a kind of biological immortality to the individual: the aspiration to individual survival is no longer linked only to real filiation (as Plato observed in his *Symposium*: see Chapter 1.5), but already realised *in nuce* in the "possible" filiation, in the freezing of seed/egg that contains the genetic heritage of the individual. It allows us to preserve in a kind of timeless Limbo what potentially could develop as an individual in the future. Not only that, but it also allows for the combination of two terms that were absolutely irreconcilable in the past: filiation and death. As some news stories have sensationally shown, children can be born from a long-dead father or mother, if their semen/egg has been frozen. The utopia imagined by Dr Paolo Mantegazza in the 19th century, of a fallen soldier who fertilised his wife even after death ("a husband who died on the battlefield might also be able to fertilise his wife even as a corpse", cited by Betta 2012: 61), becomes a reality, with a transfer from the imaginary figure of the hero to that of every common mortal.

12 Conclusions: at the dawn of the third millennium

At the dawn of the third millennium, the social reality of childbirth and birth in Western countries appears to be characterised by ambivalent aspects, which see elements of continuity and tradition alongside profound transformations and innovations, within the framework of the rapid acceleration of reproductive technologies. The struggles of the feminist movement have asserted some basic principles, mostly understood at the legislative level as well, albeit with different relevance and different emphases: a woman's self-determination in her reproductive choices is one of them, as is the right to health. Motherhood is generally no longer recognised as an obligation or a destiny, but as a choice that a woman can make in total freedom, deciding whether, when and how to have a child, as was articulated in the slogans of the feminist movement. Even a country like Ireland, reluctant to accept this principle and firm in its ban of abortion, has recently overturned this position with the referendum of 25 May 2018. To what extent these declarations of rights find effective correspondence in the social reality is very controversial, in a landscape that sees a growing conservative counteroffensive with different faces and articulations. The application of various laws enacted between the 1970s and 1990s is very uneven in Europe, either called into question in some countries or heavily hindered in others. In Alabama, a law was signed on 16 May 2019 that bans abortion even in the case of rape and sexual violence, with severe penalties for doctors who perform it. In Poland, the government's attempt in March 2018 to abolish the restrictive abortion law approved in 1993 was thwarted only by massive women's demonstrations. In Italy, the application of Law 194/78 is seriously hindered by the high number of conscientious objectors

(70–80% in the national average, with peaks of 90% in some regions),[150] so much so as to prompt a warning by the Council of Europe in 2016, for the violation of Article 11 of the European Social Charter.[151] But everywhere, anti-abortion parties have taken up the fight again, as shown by Alexandra Jousset and Andrea Rawlins-Gaston, directors of the reportage *"Avortement – Les Croisés Contre-Attaquent"* produced the Franco-German TV network Arté in 2017.

Medically assisted conception also remains a privilege of the few in some countries, due to its high cost often not covered by the health service, against a growing decrease in fertility in Western countries, whose causes are still little investigated by scientific research.

Moreover, the economic crisis, the proliferation of casualised employment contracts, added to the inadequate provision by social services in the landscape of a welfare crisis, run the risk of compromising precisely the first and fundamental right: to choose motherhood without having to pay a heavy personal price, in terms of work and career.[152]

With regard to childbirth care, to what extent have the innovative recommendations by the WHO in 1985 on the subject of birth assistance (*Appropriate technology for birth*) been received and applied by national governments? The social reality is made of light and shadows, of profound inequalities not only between countries, but also within the same one. In Italy, for example, actual changes are happening in many hospitals that go in the direction of greater humanisation and respect for women in labour, with the presence of fathers during labour and the spread of *roaming-in*,[153] but in others, the situation still seems connoted by heavy medicalisation and a scarce attention to the needs and suffering of women. The campaign against violence in childbirth, *Bastatacere* (Don't be silent!) launched in Italy on the web in 2016, with first-hand evidence and reports, reveals a bewildering reality, which was believed to have disappeared.[154] Various organisations, such as *Human Rights in Childbirth*, are fighting hard on this, even with denunciations, for the respect of the rights of the woman in childbirth in terms of freedom, autonomy and equality.[155]

Beyond these female voices, the figures highlight the heavy medicalisation, with an incidence of Caesarean sections that in various countries, at the dawn of the third millennium, still remains well above the indications of the WHO (which set an acceptable maximum 10–15%), with percentages of 21.5% in Great Britain in 2000, 22% in the US in 1999, 15.9% in France in 1995, 17.6% in Spain in 1995 and 33.2% in Italy in 2000 (but in some regions as high as 60%).[156] These figures reveal a practice that leaves medical directions aside and responds to interests of a different kind: economic, professional protection, clinical planning, safety, etc.

The use of the epidural is characterised by even more marked differences between countries (about 70% of childbirths with epidural in France/Great Britain compared to about 15% in Italy in 2010)[157]: it is routinely done in many countries, almost without asking women, while in others, such as Italy, it is on the contrary heavily hindered by not being included in the LEAs (essential levels of assistance that the national service is required to provide to citizens free of charge): in either case, women are effectively prevented from deciding themselves, based on presumed well-being or forced natural births.

The first attempt to introduce it in Italian public hospitals was made by Health Minister Livia Turco in 2008, but it took almost ten years for the law to be approved, under the Minister of Health Beatrice Lorenzin (12 January 2017), despite pressure from associations that had been formed in support of the epidural, such as the AIPA (Italian Association of birth in analgesia).[158]

Behind this delay, aspects and problems of an economic, cultural and social nature are hidden: from the cost of health care, to the ideological stability of the biblical "you will give birth in pain" or even the fear, in some supporters of natural birth, of a further increase of medicalisation.

The use of technologies has also been extended to the entire reproductive process: assistance to pregnancy is also marked by intense protocols that include clinical examinations, visits, ultrasound scans, echo-doppler and, increasingly frequently, Chorionic villus testing and amniocentesis. One wonders to what extent the use of new reproductive technologies affirms or realises a real choice for women and is an expression of freedom or whether it conceals a more subtle form of "maternal obligation" from which technology makes it even more difficult to escape, as some research has shown.[159]

In fact, there are still forms of conditioning, even more emphasised by a mystical resurgence of motherhood, which presumes – among other things – a mother's full consecration to the needs of her child.[160]

Therefore, permanent features and innovations are also intertwined in women's choices, hiding different situations behind an apparent homogeneity of behaviour. In short, technology is not progressive in itself: it can be a tool or, on the contrary, an obstacle in the path of female liberation, depending on a series of factors, including the crucial weight of the levels of autonomy and awareness and the existence of an organised women's movement. The phenomenon of missing women in Eastern countries (the altering of the natural ratio of genders at birth) reveals how the use of technology can become a dangerous weapon against women, discriminating their birth itself once the gender of the foetus has been revealed, in contexts where gender imbalance is particularly marked and rooted and where the women's movement is absent or weak.

In recent decades, the development of assisted reproduction techniques has certainly been so rapid as not to allow for an adequate cultural re-processing, which needs more time, with the risk of mismatches and splits between material experience and its psychological processing. The debate on these issues is ongoing within the world of women: among feminist theorists, there are those who look at this perspective as a conquest for women, identifying the root of oppression in the reproductive function and liberation in its biological overcoming,[161] as well as those who, on the contrary, see it as another attempt by men to appropriate women's reproductive capacities, also highlighting the risk (connected to the figures of surrogate mothers) of a new type of "reproductive" prostitution on a world scale.[162] The group FINRRAGE (Feminist International Network of Resistance to Reproductive and Genetic Engineering) has emerged in this context.[163] The controversy exploded in France and Italy in December 2015 with the 'No to the womb for rent' petition, launched by the movement Se non ora quando-Libere, who asked for a European law against the practice of motherhood for others.[164]

Some changes appearing in terms of customs seem clearer and more significant. Gender hierarchies at birth, for example, have been disrupted in many Western countries. "Let's hope it's a girl" is not just the title of a successful Italian film by director Mario Monicelli (1986): it is a wish that reveals the weakening of a centuries-old and undisputed priority. According to a survey conducted in Italy in the same year, most couples had no preference as to the gender of their newborn, if anything with a slight preference for girls.[165]

The success of new couple relationships, with cohabitations more and more often outside of marriage and the questioning of the traditional models of conjugality and parenthood, has thwarted the distinction between legitimate and natural children, between "legitimate" and "illegitimate" mothers, freeing unmarried mothers from a centuries-old social marginalisation, the origin – as we have seen – of violence and discrimination.

Even the bodily experience of motherhood is emerging from the dark corner of shame and invisibility where it had been confined for centuries: the increasing value given to the body, the idea that "woman is beautiful" has also been extended to the maternal body, to her physical metamorphosis, opening up a space of citizenship, albeit partial and limited. The naked photograph of heavily pregnant Demi Moore on the cover of Vanity Fair magazine (August 1991),[166] the first of long series of actresses, highlighted a shift in the process of emancipation and public visibility of the pregnant body, which increasingly finds confirmation in the social reality, where young women proudly exhibit their pregnancies: in many contexts, having a baby bump is no longer a source of shame. Childbirth is also filmed and shown in family and friendship groups and even in some television series,[167] attributing to the event an entertainment factor that, however, could cause it to lose its precious emotional, intimate and affective charge.

Above all, the stain of impurity, with its secular rituals, has been removed from new mothers. However, in many contexts, breastfeeding in public remains taboo, as it is still judged to be unseemly and even forbidden in various public places, even in the absence of laws to that effect, while, in Great Britain, the *Equality Act* (2010) allows a woman to breastfeed in public.[168]

On this issue, we also note the innovative position taken by Pope Francis, who invited mothers to breastfeed even in Church, if necessary, during a baptism ceremony in the Sistine Chapel on 10 January 2016.[169] It should be noted that the ancient contradiction between the extolling of the motherly function and the devaluation of the bodily aspect of motherhood (to the extent of making it taboo) re-emerges in relation to this practice: while breastfeeding is increasingly exalted, not only by the WHO, but also by organisations such as the Leche League, the image of a nursing mother continues to be considered unseemly and various news events report acts of discrimination against nursing mothers in public, as denounced in the petition launched by Change.org in 2017 with the slogan "Wherever you want to".[170]

The use of the web is also noteworthy, with the spread of blogs of mothers who not only exchange emotions and information, but also find solidarity and consensus around certain objectives, in new ways of revendication that in some cases look precisely at the feminist movement of the 1970s, with new female agency.[171]

In this animated context, a diachronic perspective can offer precious opportunities for reflection and analysis, allowing us to grasp the complexity of the present starting from its historical construction. This shows us how important it is, especially for women, to be the agents of the choices that affect their bodies, especially in this area, and beyond prescriptive cages of any kind. After all, this was the most revolutionary and innovative conquest of 1970s feminism.

Notes

1. Osteomalacia is the softening of the bones caused by impaired bone metabolism primarily due to inadequate levels of available phosphate, calcium and vitamin D, or because of resorption of calcium.
2. Casati (1871).
3. Vanzan Marchini (1985).
4. Filippini (1999: 107).
5. Bock (1994b: 405–415).
6. Bock (2002: 163).
7. Cova (1997).
8. Bock and Thane (1991); Buttafuoco (1995); Willson (2010: ch. 2); Gazzetta (2018).
9. Vezzosi (1999, 2002).
10. Bock (2002: 168).
11. Buttafuoco (1991); Gazzetta (2018: ch. 4.2).
12. Guzzoni degli Ancarani (1911: 523–544); Scaramuzza (2004).
13. Luc (1997); Rollet (2001: 148–150).
14. Filippini (1999: 103–108).
15. Rollet (2001: 204).
16. Ibidem: 211–216.
17. Rollet (1996).
18. Lewis (1980: ch. 3).
19. Gijswijt-Hofstra and Marland (2003).
20. Quine (2013).
21. Wanrooij (1990: 75).
22. Cova (2011); Géraud (1963); Ronsin (1980); Wanrooij (1990).
23. Clarke (1998: 171–176); Hall (2018).
24. Livi Bacci (1977: ch. 2.2, tables 2.3 and 2.4).
25. Bock (1994b: 422); Vezzosi (2002).
26. As pointed out by Victoria de Grazia (1992: 42).
27. Knibiehler (1997: 319).
28. De Grazia (1992: ch. 3); Minesso (2007: ch. 2); Bettini (2008); La Banca (2013).
29. Gissi (2006a: 112).
30. Pirandello [1917] (1987, vol 2: 597–689).

31 Pancino (1984: 175).
32 Detragiache (1980).
33 Gissi (2006a: 95).
34 Gissi: (2006a: 111–112 and 126 (note 20)– infant mortality; 104 table – maternal mortality).
35 De Grazia (1992: 46, table),
36 Wanrooij (1990); Garcìa Fernandez (2014).
37 Saraceno (1995); Mosse (1996).
38 Hawkins (1997); Mantovani (2004); Cassata (2006: ch. 1); Black (2012).
39 Black (2012).
40 As demonstrated by Vergès (2017).
41 Teitelbaum and Winter (1985: ch. III.1.2).
42 Bock (2002: 208).
43 Bock (1994a: 152).
44 Moriani (1999: 66).
45 Haller (1963); Ronsin (1980); Cova (2011); Hall (2018).
46 Wanrooij (1990).
47 *Casti Connubii. Encyclical of pope Pius XI on Christian Marriage*, 31-12-1930 (par. 108). Taken from the online version: http://w2.vatican.va/content/pius-xi/en/encyclicals/documents/hf_p-xi_enc_19301231_casti-connubii.html.
48 Ibidem: par. 56. See: Pelaja and Scaraffia (2008: ch. 6); Betta (2014).
49 *Discorso di sua santità Pio PP XII alle partecipanti al congresso della Unione cattolica italiana Ostetriche* (29 ottobre 1951), part III. Available online at: http://w2.vatican.va/content/pius-xii/it/speeches/1951/documents/hf_p-xii_spe_19511029_ostetriche.html.
50 Noonan (1965).
51 Flamigni (2012: 351); Hall (2018).
52 Shorter (1882: ch. 7); Wertz and Wertz (1989); Knibiehler and Thébaud (1995); Marland and Rafferty (1997); Knibiehler (1997: ch. II); Al-Gailani, (2018).
53 Knibiehler and Thébaud (1995: 106).
54 Al-Gailani (2018).
55 Livi Bacci (1977: ch. 3.3.2); Oppo (1997: 228–229); Brezinka (1997).
56 Loudon (1992, 2000).
57 Loudon (1992: 152–155).
58 Knibiehler and Thébaud (1995: 106).
59 Terzian and Regalia (1992: 82).
60 Terzian and Regalia (1992).
61 Fallaci (1955).
62 Baker (1996).
63 As pointed out by Al-Gailani (2018).
64 Shorter (1982 ch. 7); Thébaud (1986); Knibiehler and Thébaud (1995); Knibiehler (1997); Oppo (1997); Al-Gailani (2018).
65 As pointed out by Philippe Ariès (1974).
66 Oakley (1980); Pizzini (1981: 62–80 and 1985: 118–143); Knibiehler (1997: 60–63); Kitzinger (1978: ch. 6); Wertz and Wertz (1989); Serini (1992); Brodsky (2008).
67 Knibiehler (1997: 60–63).
68 Shorter (1982: ch. 7).
69 Randi Hutter (2010: 30).
70 Shorter (1982: 162, table); Wolf (2018).
71 Shorter (1982: 172).
72 Jordan (1978).
73 Fildes (1988: ch. 12).
74 Knibiehler and Thébaud (1995: 104); Rollet (1992).
75 Ergas (1994); Petchevsky (1995); Scattigno (1997); Franklin (2018).

76 Knibiehler (1997: ch. V); Perrot (2002: 13–14); Franklin (2018).
77 Saraceno (1997, 2012); Hall (2018).
78 Clarke (1998: 192–195).
79 Lefaucheur (1992: 498); Clarke (1998: 192–195); Olszynko-Gryn (2018).
80 Golini (1988: 364).
81 The first title of the book was *Women and Their Bodies* (1971), then retitled *Our Bodies Ourselves* in 1973 (The Boston Women's Health Book Collective (1973). See Kline (2018).
82 Scattigno (1997: 273–299); Debest (2012: 43–50).
83 Rich (1976).
84 Reagan (1997); Percovich (2005).
85 Baeri (2007: 162–167).
86 Perrot (2002); Le Naour and Valenti (2003); Perini (2014a).
87 Pisa (2017).
88 Bock (2002: 237); Le Naour and Valenti (2003); Olszynko-Gryen (2018).
89 Perini (2014b).
90 Knibiehler and Fouquet (1983: ch. 9); Knibiehler (1997: ch. V); Percovich (2005).
91 Baeri (2007: 154–182).
92 Memmi (2002: 229–252); Héritier (2002); Fassin and Memmi (2004).
93 Memmi (2002: 241–244).
94 Ehrenreich and English (1973).
95 Oakley (1976, 1984).
96 As in the subtitle of the Italian edition of her book (1977).
97 Pomata (1983).
98 Leboyer (1974).
99 Forti and Guaraldo (2006).
100 Nardi (1954: 439–446); Shorter (1982: 145–149).
101 Randi Hutter (2010: 85); on medical experimentation see Wolf (2009).
102 Shorter (1982: 147).
103 Randi Hutter (2010: 78).
104 Thomas (1997); Moscucci (2003); Oakley (2004).
105 Jaubert (1979); Caron-Leulliez and George (2004); Michaels (2014);
106 *Discours du Pape Pie XII sur l'accouchement naturel indolore*, 8 janvier 1956: w2.vatican.va/content/pius-xii/it/speeches/1956.index.html (II, par. 4). (document in French and Spanish only).
107 Knibiehler (1997: 64).
108 Lang [1972] (1978).
109 Rich (1976).
110 Movimento di lotta femminista, Ferrara, *Basta tacere! Testimonianze di donne. Parto, aborto, gravidanza, maternità*, 1972. Available online at: www.femminismo-ruggente.it/femminismo/who.html.
111 Colombo (1985); Cavaglieri (1985); Moscucci (2003).
112 Michaels (2014).
113 Balaskas (1983).
114 Braibanti (1980).
115 Forleo (1983).
116 Bradley (1965).
117 Corridori and Fanos (2009); Caumel-Dauphin (2013).
118 Kitzinger (2000).
119 Spina (1998: 59).
120 Available online at: www.nascereacasa.it/.
121 Williams (1997).
122 'Istituzione dei consultori familiari?, Legge 29 luglio1975, n. 405 (*Gazzetta Ufficiale*, 27 agosto 1975, n. 227).

123 WHO, 'Appropriate technology for birth', *The Lancet*, 326, 24 August 1985: 436–437.
    These recommendations were repeated in 1986, 1998, 2004 and also in 2014 (*Postnatal care of the mother and newborn*).
124 *WHO recommendations on postnatal care of the mother and newborn*. Available online at: www.who.int/maternal_child_adolescent/documents/postnatal-care-recommendations/en/.
125 *Charte des droits de la parturiente* (resolution B2-712-86, juillet 1988), available online at: https://naissance.asso.fr/wiki/pmwiki.php?n=Portail.PortailNaissance.
126 Foucault (1973).
127 d'Yvoire (2006: 143–146).
128 Ibidem: 157.
129 Terzian, Regalia (1992: 83–86); Duden (2002a: ch. 9).
130 Boccia and Zuffa (1998: 73).
131 Fellous (1991).
132 Tsiaras and Werth (2002).
133 Duden (1993).
134 Duden (1993, 2002a).
135 Cited by Betta (2012: 26).
136 Betta (2012: 137–138).
137 Frydman (1986: 121–134); Costa-Lascoux (1994: 618–624); Flamigni (2002); Prasad (2012); Hopwood (2018b and 2018c).
138 Baudouin, Labrusse-Rioux (1987); Frydman (1986: 203–231).
139 Cesbron and Knibiehler (2004: 211–214).
140 Betta (2012: 126).
141 Frydman (1986: 203).
142 Church of England. Commission Appointed to Consider the Practice of Artificial Human Insemination (1948) *Artificial Human Insemination: the Report of a Commission Appointed by His Grace the Archbishop of Canterbury*, London: S.P.C.K.
143 Laqueur (1995: 303–327); Saraceno (1997: 338–351 and 2012); Cesbron and Knibiehler (2004: 198–211); Burton (2015).
144 Giraud (1987).
145 Pizzini (1991); Pizzini and Lombardi (1995).
146 Boccia and Zuffa (1998).
147 Betta (2003: 186–192); Flamigni (2010).
148 *Instruction on respect for human life in its origin and on the dignity of procreation replies to certain questions of the day*, 22-2-1987, I, 1. Taken from the online version:www.vatican.va/roman_curia/congregations/cfaith/documents/rc_con_cfaith_doc_19870222_respect-for-human-life_en.html.
149 Boccia, Busi, Chelo et *alii* (2004); Bonsignori, Dominijanni and Giorgi (2005).
150 Perini (2014b).
151 The warning was in response to a 2013 report by the Cgil union; it was issued on 11th April 2016: 'In Italia è difficile. Il Consiglio d'Europa accoglie il ricorso CGIL', *Rassegna sindacale. Quotidiano del lavoro*, 11th April 2016 (www.rassegna.it/articoli/in-italia-aborto-troppo-difficile-il-consiglio-deuropa-accoglie-il-ricorso-cgil).
152 Piazza (2009); Cirant (2012); Modena and Sabatini (2010).
153 Pizzini and Lombardi (1999, ch. 1.3); Lombardi (2017).
154 *Osservatorio sulla violenza ostetrica in Italia. Basta Tacere, Le madri hanno voce*, which has created the Monitoring Centre of Obstetric violence in Italy (see ovoitalia.wordpress.com).
155 Available online at: http://humanrightsinchildbirth.org/.
156 Figures from: Angela Spinelli, *I parti cesarei in Italia. Andamenti e variabilità regionali*: www.epicentro.iss.it/percorso-nascita/spinelli (Epicentro is the public-health portal of the Italian Istituto superiore di Sanità).

157 *Indagine conoscitiva sul percorso nascita "Nascere sicuri"* (2010) www.senato.it/leg/16/BGT/Testi/Allegati/00000100.pdf.
158 *Decreto del Presidente del Consiglio dei Ministri* (DPCM), Essential levels of assistance from the National Service, 12 January 2017 (*Gazzetta Ufficiale*, 18 March 2017, n. 65 – supplement n.15).
159 Vegetti-Finzi (1991); Rozée and de La Rochebrochard (2010).
160 Forti and Guaraldo (2006); Donath (2017).
161 Haraway (1991); Shalev (1990); Prasad (2012); Kendal (2015).
162 Rothschild (1983); Muraro (2016); Boccia (2018).
163 Pizzini and Lombardi (1995).
164 SNOQ-Libere, *No all'utero in affitto*. Available online at: www.cheliberta.it/2015/12/04/appello-che-liberta.
165 The survey was carried out by the newspaper *La Repubblica*-Unicab, in 1986, on a sample of 50% men and 50% women: 50.4% replied that they had no preference; in the minority, the wish for a girl was prevalent (29.1% against 20.4%): Stefano Clerici, 'Gli italiani vogliono che sia femmina', *La Repubblica*, 4 December 1986. Available online at: https://ricerca.repubblica.it/repubblica/archivio/repubblica/1986/12/04/gli-italiani-vogliono-che-nasca-femmina.html.
166 Photoshoot by Annie Leibovitz. Tina Brown was the editor-in-chief of *Vanity Fair* at the time.
167 See, for example, the series *Call the Midwife* (BBC), based on the memoirs of midwife Jennifer Worth, who worked in the London's East End: *Call the Midwife, Shadows of the Workhouse, Farewell to the East End*), or the reality show *Coppie in attesa*, shown in Italy by Rai2 in 2015 and 2016.
168 The Equality Act 2010 says that it is against the law to treat a woman unfavourably because she is breastfeeding (*Equality Act* 2010, ch. 15, part 2, ch. 2.13 and 17, 'Pregnancy and maternity discrimination'; available online at www.legislation.gov.uk/ukpga/2010/15/pdfs/ukpga_20100015_en.pdf.
169 Domenico Agasso, 'Allattare in Chiesa si può. La più grande eredità da lasciare ai figli è la Fede', *La Stampa*, 10 gennaio 2016. Available online at www.lastampa.it/vatican-insider/it/2016/01/10/news/il-papa-allattare-in-chiesa-si-puo-la-piu-grande-eredita-da-lasciare-ai-figli-e-la-fede-1.36548281.
170 Available online at: www.change.org/p/governo-italiano-allattamento-%C3%A8-ovunque-lo-desideri.
171 Cristianini and Colombo (2011); D'Amelia (2015).

BIBLIOGRAPHY

Accati, Luisa (1987) 'Il padre naturale. Tra simboli dominanti e categorie scientifiche', *Memoria. Rivista di Storia delle Donne*, 21: 79–106.
Accati, Luisa (1998) *Il mostro e la bella. Padre e madre nell'educazione cattolica dei sentimenti*, Verona: Cortina.
Accati, Luisa, Maher, Vanessa and Pomata, Gianna (1980) (eds) *Quaderni storici*, XV, 44 (2) (Special Issue: *Parto e maternità: momenti della biografia femminile*).
Alessi, Giorgia (1989) *L'onore riparato. Il riformismo del Settecento e le ridicole leggi contro lo stupro*, in Fiume (ed): 129–142.
Alessi, Giorgia (1995) *Le gravidanze illegittime e il disagio dei giuristi (sec. XVII–XIX)*, in Fiume (ed): 221–247.
Alfani, Guido (2006) *Padri, padrini, patroni. La parentela spirituale nella storia*, Venice: Marsilio.
Alfani, Guido, Castagnetti, Philippe and Gourdon, Vincent (eds) (2009) *Baptiser: pratique sacramentelle, pratique sociale (XVIe–Xxe siècles)*, Saint-Étienne: Publications de l'Université de Saint-Étienne.
Alfani, Guido, Gourdon, Vincent and Robin, Isabelle (eds) (2015) *Le parrainage en Europe et en Amérique. Pratiques de longue durée (XVI–XXI siècle)*, Bruxelles, Bern, Berlin, Frankfurt a.M., New York, Oxford, Wien: P.I.E-Peter Lang S.A.
Al-Gailani, Salim (2018) 'Hospital Birth', in Hopwood, Flemming and Kassell (eds): chap. 17.
Almaviva, Marziano (1999) 'Storia di un "morbo femminile": il dibattito europeo sulla febbre puerperale tra XVIII e XX secolo")', *Bollettino di demografia storica-S.I.DE.S.*, 30–31: 11–34.
Altieri Biagi, Maria Luisa, Mazzotta, Clemente, Chiantera, Angela and Altieri, Paola (eds) (1992) *Medicina per le donne nel Cinquecento. Testi di Giovanni Marinello e Girolamo Mercurio*, Turin: Utet.
Amalfi, Gaetano (2005) *La culla, il talamo e la tomba nel napoletano*, Naples: Adriano Gallina.
Amato Vincenzi, Diana (1988) 'La famiglia e il diritto', in Melograni (ed): 629–696.
Andò, Valeria (ed and transl.) (2000) *Ippocrate. Natura della donna*, Milan: Rizzoli.
Angelini, Massimo (1997) 'Chimere e singolarità della generazione in età moderna tra pratica dell'impostura e i presunti effetti dell'immaginazione materna', *Anthropos & Iatria*, 1 (2): 27–36.

Arena, Francesca (2013) 'La maternité entre santé et pathologie. L'histoire des délires puerpéraux à l'époque moderne et contemporaine', *Histoire, médecine et santé*, 3: 101–113.

Arena, Francesca (2015) 'Il puerperio. Trasformazioni psichiche e regressioni corporee. Un paradosso della medicina contemporanea', in Chemotti and La Rocca (eds): 959–974.

Arena, Francesca (2016) 'La fièvre de lait et les maladies lactées. Des maladies genrées au XVIIIe siècle', *Cahiers du genre*, 60: 123–139.

Arent, Hanna (1958) *The Uman Condition*, Chicago: University of Chicago Press.

Ariès, Philippe (1960) *L'enfant et la vie familiale sous l'ancien régime*, Paris: Plon (1st English transl. by R. Baldick 1962, *Century of Childhood*).

Ariès, Philippe (1974) *Western Attitudes Toward Death from the Middle Ages to the Present*, transl. by P. Ranum, Baltimore: Johns Hopkins University Press.

Arikha, Noga (2007) *Passions and Tempers: A History of the Humours*, New York: Ecco.

Ascoli, Giulietta (1994) *Balie*, Palermo: Sellerio.

Assael, Baroukh M. (1995) *Il favoloso innesto. Storia sociale della vaccinazione*, Rome, Bari: Laterza.

Asson, Michelangelo (1846) 'Considerazioni sopra l'embriotomia e il taglio cesareo', *Esercitazioni dell'Ateneo Veneto*, 6: 117–132.

Astruc, Jean [1766] (1771) *L'art d'accoucher réduit à ses principes où l'on expose les pratiques les plus sûres et les plus usitées dans les differentes expèces d'accouchements*, Paris: P. Guillaume Cavelier.

Aubert, Jean-Jacques (1989) 'Threatened Wombs: Aspects of Ancient Uterine Magic', *Roman and Byzantine Studies*, 30 (3): 421–449.

Aveling, James H. Hobson (1882) *The Chamberlens and the Midwifery Forceps. Memorial of the Family and Essay on the Invention of the Instruments*, London: Churchill.

Badinter, Elisabeth (1980) *L'amour en plus. Histoire de l'amour maternelle (XVIIe–XXe siècles)*, Paris: Flammarion.

Badinter, Elisabeth (1986) *L'un et l'autre. Des relations entre hommes et femmes*, Paris: Odile Jacob.

Baeri, Emma (2007) 'Cerniere di cittadinanza. Il protagonismo femminile negli anni '70', in N. M. Filippini and A. Scattigno (eds) *Una democrazia incompiuta. Donne e politica in Italia dall'Ottocento ai giorni nostri*, Milan: FrancoAngeli: 154–182.

Baker, Jeffrey P. (1996) *The Machine in the Nursery: Incubator Technology and the Origins of Newborn and Intensive Care*, Baltimore, London: Johns Hopkins University Press.

Balaskas, Janet (1983) *Active Birth*, New York: HarperCollins Publishers.

Baldini, Eraldo (1991) *Riti del nascere. Gravidanza, parto e battesimo nella cultura popolare romagnola*, Longo: Ravenna.

Bardet, Jean-Pierre, Hunecke, Volker, Pérez Moreda, Vicente *et alii* (1991) *Enfance abandonnée et société en Europe, XIVe–XXe siècle. Actes du colloque international de Rome (30 et 31 janvier 1987)*, Rome: École Française de Rome.

Barras, Vincent (2004) 'La naissance et ses recettes en medecine antique', in Dasen (ed): 91–102.

Bartoloni, Stefania and Lombardi, Daniela (eds) (2018) *Genesis. Rivista della società italiana delle Storiche*, 17 (1) (Special issue: *La ricerca della paternità*).

Baruffaldi, Gerolamo (1746) *La mammana istruita per validamente amministrare il Santo Sacramento del Battesimo in caso di necessità alle creature nascenti*, Venice: Recurti.

Baskett, Thomas (2017) *History of Caesarean Birth: From Maternal Death to Maternal Choise*, Bristol: Clinical Press Ltd.

Basso, Rosanna (2015) *Levatrici. L'assistenza ostetrica nell'età liberale*, Rome: Viella.

Baudelocque, Jean-Louis (1781) *L'art des accouchemens par M. Baudelocque, membre du Collége et Adjont au Comité perpétuel de l'Académie Royale de Chirurgie*, Paris: Mequignon.

Baudelocque, Jean-Louis (1787) *Principes sur l'art des accouchemens, par demandes et réponses, en faveur des sages-femmes de la campagne. Nouvelle édition, revue, corrigée; augmentée & enrichie d'un grand nombre de planches*, Paris: chez Méquignon l'aîné, libraire.

Baudelocque, Jean-Louis (1798) *Recherches et Réflexions sur l'opération césarienne suivies d'une note sur l'accouchement de la femme Marville, du procès-verbal de l'ouverture du corps et d'un arrêté de la Société de Médecine de Paris relatif à l'opération césarienne*, Paris: Impr. Société de Médecine.

Baudelocque, Jean-Louis (1833) *Dell'arte ostetricia di J.L. Baudelocque*, P. Leonardi Cattolica (ed), Milan: Gaspare Truffi and Comp.

Baudouin, Jean-Louis and Labrusse-Rioux, Catherine (1987) *Produire l'homme, de quel droit?: étude juridique et éthique des procréations artificielles*, Paris: Presse Universitaire de France.

Beauvalet-Boutouyrie, Scarlett (1995) 'Faut-il supprimer les maternités?', in Gélis, Morel et alii (1995): 64–84.

Beauvalet-Boutouyrie, Scarlett (1999) *Naître à l'hôpital au XIXe siècle*, Paris: Belin.

Becchi, Egle (1994) *I bambini nella storia*, Rome, Bari: Laterza.

Becchi, Egle and Julia, Dominique (eds) (1996) *Storia dell'infanzia*, Rome, Bari: Laterza, vols. 1 and 2.

Bellavitis, Anna (2018) *Women's Work and Rights in Early Modern Urban Europe*, transl. by C. Boscolo, London: Palgrave (1st Italian ed., Rome: Viella 2016).

Bellet, Isaac (1765) *Letters on the Force of Imagination in Pregnant Women. Wherein It Is Proved, by Incontestible Arguments, Drawn from Both Reason and Experience, That It Is a Ridiculous Prejudice to Suppose It Possible for a Pregnant Woman to Mark her Child with the Figure of any Object she has Longed for*, London: W. Griffin (1st French ed. 1765).

Belmont, Nicole (1971) *Les signes de la naissance. Études des représentations symboliques associées aux naissances singulières*, Brionne: Gerard Monfort.

Belmont, Nicole (1982) 'Nascita', in R. Romano (ed) *Enciclopedia*, Turin, Einaudi, vol. 9: 702–714.

Beltrami, Daniele (1954) *Storia della popolazione di Venezia dalla fine del secolo XVI alla caduta della Repubblica*, Padua: Milani.

Bengtsson, Tommy and Saito, Osamu (eds) (2000) *Population and Economy: From Hunger to Modern Economic Growth*, Oxford: Oxford University Press.

Benozio, Michel, Beugnot, Claire, Demoy, Sophie et alii (2004) *La machine de madame Coudray: ou l'art des accouchements au XVIIIe siècle*, Bonsecours (Seine-Maritime): Ed. Point de vues.

Bergamo, Maria (2003) *Da Maria puerpera a Maria adorante. Evoluzione della postura della madre di Dio nelle immagini della natività*, www.engramma.it/engramma_v4/rivista/.../029_nativita_saggio.htm.

Bernardi, Walter (1980) *Filosofia e scienza della vita. La generazione animale da Descartes a Spallanzani (1672–1793)*, Turin: Loescher.

Bernardi, Walter (1986) *Le metafisiche dell'embrione. Scienze della vita e filosofia da Malpighi a Spallanzani (1672–1793)*, Florence: Olschki.

Bernheim, Pierre-Antoine (2010) 'La naissance du divin enfant', in Frydman and Szejer (eds): 39–47.

Bernoni, Domenico Giuseppe [1878] (1980) *Tradizioni popolari veneziane di medicina*, Venice: Filippi.

Berriot-Salvadore, Evelyne (1993) 'The Discourse of Medicine and Science', in Duby and Perrot (dir) (1993): 348–388.

Bertelli, Sergio (2002) *Il re, la Vergine, la sposa. Eros e maternità nella cultura figurativa europea*, Rome: Donzelli.

Berthiaud, Emanuelle (2013) *Enceinte. Une histoire de la grossesse entre art et société*, Paris: Éd. de la Martinère.

Berthiaud, Emanuelle (2015) 'Être enceinte en France aux XVIIIe et XIXe siècles. Une expérience féminine particulière', in Chemotti and La Rocca (eds): 945–958.

Betri, Maria Luisa (2010) 'Itinerari di professionalizzazione sulla scena del parto', in M. Ferrari Monica and P. Mazzarello (eds) *Formare alle professioni. Figure della sanità*, Milan: FrancoAngeli: 143–145.

Betta, Emmanuel (2003) 'La scena tecnologica del parto', *Genesis. Rivista della Società Italiana delle Storiche*, 2 (1): 186–193.

Betta, Emmanuel (2006) *Animare la vita. Disciplina della nascita tra medicina e morale nell'Ottocento*, Bologna: Il Mulino.

Betta, Emmanuel (2010) 'Aborto', in A. Prosperi (dir), *Dizionario storico dell'Inquisizione*, vol. 1, Pisa: Edizioni della Normale: 13–15.

Betta, Emmanuel (2012) *L'altra genesi. Storia della fecondazione artificiale*, Rome: Carocci.

Betta, Emmanuel (2014) *Il Popolo di Romagna*, Il Sant'Uffizio e il controllo delle nascite', *Quaderni storici*, XLIX, 145 (1): 141–182.

Bettini, Maurizio (ed) (1993) *Maschile/femminile. Genere e ruoli nelle culture antiche*, Rome, Bari: Laterza.

Bettini, Maurizio (2008) *Stato e assistenza sociale in Italia. L'Opera Nazionale Maternità e Infanzia, 1925–1975*, Livorno: Erasmo.

Bettini, Maurizio (2013) *Women & Weasels: Mythologies of Birth in Ancient Greece and Rome*, transl. by E. Eisenach, Chicago, London: The University of Chicago Press (1st Italian ed. 1998).

Bettini, Maurizio (2015) *Dèi e uomini nella città. Antropologia, religione e cultura nella Roma antica*, Rome: Carocci.

Bianchi, Giovanni Battista (1741) *De naturali in humano corpore vitiosa morbosaque generatione Historia, cum aeneis tabulis, justisque Rerum Indicibus*, Augustae Taurinorum: Joannis B. Chais.

Bigatto, Luisa (ed) (2000) *Giuseppe Toaldo e il suo tempo. Nel bicentenario della morte. Scienze e lumi tra Veneto e Europa*, Cittadella: Bertoncello Artigrafiche.

Bigeschi, Giovanni (1819) *Elementi di ostetricia a domande e risposte per l'istruzione delle giovani levatrici*, Florence: Stamperia Pagani.

Black, Edwin (2012) *War against the Weak: Eugenics and America's Campaign to Create a Master Race*, New York: Four Walls Eight Windows.

Blondel, James Augustus (1727) *The Strength of Imagination in Pregnant Women Examined; and the Opinion that Marks and Deformities in Children Arise from Thence, Demonstrated to Be a Vulgar Error*, London: J. Peele.

Blum, Carol (2002) *Strength in Numbers: Population, Reproduction, and Power in Eighteenth-Century France*, Baltimore: Johns Hopkins University Press.

Blumenfeld-Kosinski, Renate (1990) *Not of Woman Born. Representations of Cesarean Birth in Medieval and Renaissance Culture*, Ithaca, London: Cornell University Press.

Blunt, John (pseud. of Fores, Samuel William) (1793) *Man-Midwifery Dissected, or the Obstetric Family-Instructor. For the Use of Married Couples, and Single Adults of Both Sexes*, London: S.W. Fores.

Boccia, Maria Luisa (2018) *Le parole e i corpi. Scritti femministi*, Roma: Ediesse.

Boccia, Maria Luisa and Zuffa, Grazia (1998) *L'eclissi della madre. Fecondazione artificiale, tecniche, fantasie e norme*, Milan: Pratiche Editrice.

Boccia, Maria Luisa, Busi, Beatrice, Chelo, Elisabetta *et alii* (2004) *Un'appropriazione indebita. L'uso del corpo della donna nella nuova legge sulla procreazione assistita*, Milan: Baldini e Castoldi.

Bock, Gisela (1994a) 'Nazi Gender Policies and Women's History', in Duby and Perrot (dir) (1994): 149–176.

Bock, Gisela (1994b) 'Poverty and Mothers' Rights in the Emerging Welfare States', in Duby and Perrot (dir) (1994): 402–432.

Bock, Gisela (2002) *Women in European History*, transl. by Brown Allison, Oxford: Blackwell.
Bock, Gisela and Nobili, Giuliana (eds) (1988) *Il corpo delle donne*, Ancona-Bologna: Transeuropa.
Bock, Gisela and Thane, Pat (eds) (1991) *Maternity and Gender Policies: Women and the Rises of the European Welfare States, 1880–1950*, London, New York: Routledge.
Boivin, Marie Gillain (1827) *Mémorial de l'art des accouchemens, ou Principes sur la pratique de l'hospice de la Maternité de Paris et sur celle des plus célebres praticiens nationaux et etrangers*, Paris: Méquignon.
Bonsignori, Simona, Dominijanni, Ida and Giorgi, Stefania (eds) (2005) *Si può. Procreazione assistita, norme, soggetti, poste in gioco*, Rome: Manifestolibri.
Borgeaud, Philippe (2004) 'L'enface au miel dans les récits antiques', in Dasen (ed): 113–126.
Boston Women's Health Book Collective (1973) *Our Bodies Ourselves*, New York: Simon and Schuster.
Botti, Caterina (2000) *Bioetica ed etica delle donne. Relazioni, affetti e potere*, Milan: Zadig.
Boudin, Pierre-Constant (1905) *Manuel pratique d'allaitement. Hygiène du nourrisson*, Paris: Doin.
Boulanger, Paul-Marie and Tabutin, Dominique (eds) (1980) *La mortalité des enfants dans le monde et dans l'histoire*, Liège: Ordina.
Bourgeois, Louise [1609] (1992) *Observations diverses sur la stérilité, perte de fruits, fécondité, accouchements et maladies des femmes et enfants nouveau-né, suivi de Instructions à ma fille*, F. Olive (ed), Paris: Côté-femme éditions.
Bradley, Robert A. (1965) *Husband-Coached Childbirth*, New York: Haper & Row.
Braibanti, Lorenzo and Braibanti, Paride (1980) *Nascere meglio*, Turin: Editori Riuniti.
Braidotti, Rosi (1994) *Nomadic Subjects: Embodiment and Sexual Difference in Contemporary Feminist Theory*, New York: Columbia University Press.
Brambilla, Elena (1984) 'La medicina del Settecento: dal monopolio dogmatico alla professione scientifica', in F. Della Peruta (ed), *Storia d'Italia, Annali 7, Malattia e medicina*, Turin: Einaudi: 6–132.
Breschi, Marco, Derosas, Renzo and Manfedini, Matteo (2000) *Infant Mortality in Nineteenth-Century Italy. Interactions between Ecology and Society*, in Bengtsson and Saito (eds): 457–488.
Brezinka, Christoph (1997) 'The End of Home Births in the Language Islands of Northers Italy', in Marland and Rafferty (eds): 201–217.
Brian, Éric (1994) *La mesure de l'État: Administrateurs et géomètres au XVIIIe siècle*, Paris: Albin Michel.
Brisson, Luc, Congourdeau, Marie-Hélène and Solère, Jean-Luc (eds) (2008) *L'embryon: formation et animation. Antiquité grecque et latine, traditions hébraïque, chrétienne et islamique*, Paris: Librairie Philosophique J. Vrin.
Brodsky, Phyllis L. (2008) *The Control of Childbirth. Mothers versus Medicine through the Ages*, Jefferson (NC): Mcfarland.
Bruit Zaidman, Louise (1992) 'Pandora's Daughters and Rituals in Grecian Cities', in Duby and Perrot (dir) (1992a): 338–376.
Bucarelli, Alessandro and Lubrano, Carlo (2003) *Eutanasia ante litteram in Sardegna: sa femina accabadora. Usi costumi e tradizioni intorno alla morte in Sardegna*, Cagliari: Scuola sarda editrice.
Buffini, Andrea (1844) *Ragionamenti, storici, economici, statistici e morali intorno all'ospizio dei trovatelli*, Milan: Tipografia Pietro Agnelli.
Burkert, Walter (1983) *Homo necans. The Anthropology of Ancient Greek Sacrificial Ritual and Myths*, Berkley, Los Angeles, London: University of California Press.

Burton, Nadya (ed) (2015) *Natal Signs: Cultural Representations of Pregnancy, Birth and Parenting*, Bradford, ON: Demeter Press.

Bussy, Genevois Danièle (1994) 'The Women of Spain from the Republic to Franco', in Duby and Perrot (dir) (1994): chap. 6.

Buttafuoco, Annarita (1985) *Le Mariuccine. Storia di un'istituzione laica: l'asilo Mariuccia*, Milan: FrancoAngeli.

Buttafuoco, Annarita (1991) 'Motherhood as a Political Strategy. The Role of the Italian Women's Movement in the Creation of the Cassa Nazionale di Maternità', in Bock and Thane (1991): 178–195.

Buttafuoco, Annarita (1995) *Questioni di cittadinanza. Donne e diritti sociali nell'Italia liberale*, Siena: Protagon.

Bynum, William. F. and Porter, Roy (eds) (1985) *William Hunter and the Eighteenth-Century Medical World*, Cambridge: Cambridge University Press.

Cacciari, Massimo (2017) *Generare Dio*, Bologna: Il Mulino.

Caffiero, Marina (2004) *Battesimi forzati: storie di ebrei, cristiani e convertiti nella Roma dei papi*, Rome: Viella (1st English transl. 2012).

Caforio, Antonella (ed) (2002) *Figure femminili protettrici della nascita. La baba, la femme qui aide, la levatrice nella cultura europea*, Milan: Pubblicazioni ISU, Università Cattolica.

Calvi, Giulia (1982) 'Manuali delle levatrici (XVII–XVIII sec.)', *Memoria. Rivista di storia delle donne*, 3: 114–116.

Campbell Ross, Ian (1986) *Public Virtue, Public Love: The Early Years of the Dublin Lying-in Hospital, the Rotunda*, Dublin: O'Brien Press.

Campese, Silvia, Manuli, Paola and Sissa, Giulia (1983) *Madre materia. Sociologia e biologia della donna greca*, Turin: Bollati Borighieri.

Campiotti, Marta (1985) 'Partorire a casa: il frutto di una scelta per la donna e l'ostetrica', in Oakley, Romito and Arcidiacono *et alii*. (1985): 141–144.

Cangiamila, Francesco Emanuele [1745] (1751) *Embriologia Sacra, ovvero dell'uffizio de' sacerdoti, medici e superiori circa l'eterna salute de' bambini racchiusi nell'utero*, Milan: Giuseppe Cairoli.

Cangiamila, Francesco Emanuele (1775) *Abrégé de l'embryologie sacrée ou des devoirs des Prêtres, des Médecins, des Chirurgiens et des sages-femmes envers les enfants qui sont dans le sein de leurs mères*, transl. by Dinouart, Paris: Bailly.

Cantarella, Eva (1985) *L'ambiguo malanno: Condizione e immagine della donna nell'antichità greca e romana*, Rome: Editori Riuniti.

Cantarella Eva (2019) *Gli inganni di Pandora. L'origine delle discriminazioni di genere nella Grecia antica*, Milan: Feltrinelli.

Cappelletto, Giovanna (1983) 'Infanzia abbandonata e ruoli di mediazione sociale nella Verona del Settecento', *Quaderni storici*, XVIII, 53 (2): 421–443.

Cappelletto, Tiziano and Filippini, Nadia Maria (1982) 'L'Arte ostetrica a Venezia', *Giornale Veneto di Scienze Mediche*, 34 (1): 37–43.

Carbón, Damian (1541) *Libro del arte de las Comadres o Madrinas y regimiento de las preñadas y paridas y de los niños*, Mallorca: Hernando de Cansoles.

Carol, Anne (2011) 'Sage-femme ou gynécologue? M.-A. Boivin (1773–1841)', *Clio. Histoire, femmes et sociétés*, 33: 237–260.

Caron-Leulliez, Marianne and George, Jocelyne (2004) *L'accouchement sans douleur. Histoire d'une révolution oubliée*, Paris: Éd. de l'Atelier.

Carter, Codell K. and Carter, Barbara R. (2017) *Childbed Fever: A Scientific Biography of Ignaz Semmelweis*, London: Routledge (new ed.).

Casagrande, Tiziana (ed) (1994) *Parto e maternità nel Veneto all'inizio del secolo*, Bassano del Grappa: Ghedina e Tassoni.

Casarini, Maria Pia (1983) 'Il buon matrimonio. Tre casi di infanticidio nell'800', *Memoria. Rivista di storia delle donne*, 7: 275–284.
Casarini, Maria Pia (1988) 'La "madrassa". Malattia e occultamento della gravidanza', in Bock and Nobili (eds) (1988): 85–102.
Casati, Gaetano (1871) *Sulla osteomalacia osservata alla Maternità di Milano e sulle alterazioni apportate alla pelvi, studiate specialmente sotto il rapporto ostetrico per le indicazioni che presentano in gravidanza ed all'atto del parto*, Milano: G. B. Pogliani.
Cassata, Francesco (2006) *Molti, sani e forti. L'eugenetica in Italia*, Turin: Bollati Boringhieri.
Castiglione, Caroline (2017) 'The Non-Naturals and the Vulnerable Body', in S. Cavallo, T. Storey (eds) *Conserving Health in Early Modern Culture. Bodies and Environements in Italy and England*, Manchester: Manchester University Press: 55–79.
Caumel-Dauphin, Francine (2013) 'La place du père dès années 1970 à aujourd'hui', in Morel (ed): 185–190.
Cavaglieri, Rossana (1985) 'Il parto in casa come esperienza di integrazione e continuità', in Oakley, Romito, Arcidiacono *et alii*. (1985):145–150.
Cavallo, Sandra (2007) *Artisans of the Body in Early Modern Italy. Identities, Families, Masculinities*, Manchester: Manchester University Press.
Cavallo, Sandra (2018) 'Pregnant Stones as Wonders of Nature', in Hopwood, Flemming and Kassell (eds): Exibits 17.
Cavallo, Sandra and Cerutti, Simona (1990) 'Female Honor and Social Control of Reproduction in Piedmont between 1600 and 1800', in G. Ruggiero and E. Muir (eds) *Sex and gender in Historical Perspective*, Baltimora: John Hopkins University Press: 73–109.
Cavallo, Sandra and Storey, Tessa (eds) (2017) *Conserving Health in Early Modern Culture. Bodies and Environments in Italy and England*, Manchester: Manchester University Press.
Cavallo Boggi, Pina (ed) (1979) *Trotula de Ruggiero. Sulle malattie delle donne*, transl by M. Nubiè and A. Tocco, Turin: La Rosa.
Cavarero, Adriana (1990a) *Nonostante Platone. Figure femminili nella filosofia antica*, Rome: Editori Riuniti.
Cavarero, Adriana (1990b) 'Dire la nascita', in Diotima (ed) *Mettere al mondo il mondo. Oggetto e oggettività alla luce della differenza sessuale*, La Tartaruga: Milan: 93–122.
Cavarero, Adriana (1995) *Corpo in figure: filosofia e politica della corporeità*, Milan: Feltrinelli.
Cavazza, Marta (1997) '"Dottrici" e lettrici dell'Università di Bologna nel Settecento', *Annali di Storia delle Università italiane* 1: 109–126.
Cavazza, Marta (2003) 'Women's Dialectics, or the Thinking Uterus: an Eighteenth-Century Controversy on Gender and Education', in Daston and Pomata (eds): 237–258.
Cavazza, Silvano (1982) 'La doppia morte. Resurrezione e battesimo in un rito del Seicento', *Quaderni storici*, XVII, 50 (2): 551–582.
Cazzani, Luigi (1863) 'Prospetto clinico dell'Istituto di ostetricia presso la Regia Università di Pavia diretta dal professor ordinario Cav. Teodoro Lovati per gli anni scolastici 1861–62 e 1862–63', *Annali Universali di Medicina*, 183: 450–490.
Céline, Louis-Ferdinand (1937) *The Life and Work of Semmelweis*, transl. by Robert Allerton Parker, Boston: Little, Brown and Company (1st French ed. 1924).
Cesbron, Paul (2010) 'L'histoire de la naissance en Occident', in Frydman and Szejer (eds): 157–170.
Cesbron, Paul and Knibiehler, Yvonne (2004) *La naissance en Occident*, Paris: Albin Michel.
Ceschi, Raffaello (2011) 'Gravidanze illegittime. Prevardazione e interrogatori nelle doglie nella Svizzera italiana (secoli XVI–XVIII)', in Lavenia and Paolin (eds): 43–53.
Chabot, Isabelle (2011) *La dette des familles. Femmes, lignage et patrimoine à Florence aux XIVe et XVe siècle*, Rome: Ecole Française de Rome.

Chamberlain, Geoffrey (2007) *From Witchcraft to Wisdom: A History of Obstetrics & Gynaecology in the British Isles*, Cambridge: RCOG Press.

Charrier, Philippe, Clavandier, Gaëlle, Gourdon, Vincent, Rollet, Catherine and Sage-Pranchère Nathalie (eds) (2018) *Morts avant de naître. La mort périnatale. Dead before being born. About perinatal death*, Paris: Presse Universitaires François Rabelais.

Chauvard, Jean François (2012) 'Madrine, comari e levatrici. Donne e parentela spirituale a Venezia nella seconda metà del Cinquecento', in A. Bellavitis, N. M. Filippini and T. Plebani (eds) *Spazi, poteri, diritti delle donne a Venezia in età moderna*, Verone: Quiedit: 181–196.

Chemotti, Saveria and La Rocca, Cristina (eds) (2015) *Il genere nella ricerca storica*, Atti del VI Congresso della Società Italiana delle Storiche, Padua: Il Poligrafo.

Chinosi, Lia (ed) (1985) *Nascere a Venezia. Dalla Serenissima alla prima guerra mondiale*, Turin: Gruppo Editoriale Forma.

Cicatiello, Clotilde (2013) 'La figura della levatrice a Napoli tra prescrizioni ecclesiastiche e pratica medica (secoli XVII–XIX)', *Ricerche di storia sociale e religiosa*, XLII, 84: 35–60.

Cicatiello, Clotilde (2018) *Rivalità sulla scena del parto. Medici e levarici a Napoli tra Ottocento e Novecento*, Milan-Udine: Mimesis.

Cid Lòpez, Rosa Maria (ed) (2014) *Parir y nacer en el Mediterráneo Antiguo. Entre el mito y la historia*, Oviedo: Trea.

Cid Lòpez, Rosa Maria (2007) 'Imágenes y prácticas de la sumisión femenina en la antigua Roma. El culto de Juno Lucina y la fiesta de Matronalia', *Dossier de Studia Historica. Historia Antigua*, 25: 357–372.

Cid López, Rosa Maria (2015) 'La maternidad in Occidente: reflexiones desde el feminismo y la historia', in Chemotti and La Rocca (eds): 975–995.

Cirant, Eleonora (2012) *Una su cinque non lo fa. Maternità e altre scelte*, Milan: FrancoAngeli.

Clarke, Adele E. (1998) *Disciplining Reproduction. Modernity, American Life Science and the Problems of Sex*, Berkley, Los Angeles, London: University of California Press.

Codice penale universale austriaco coll'appendice delle piu recenti norme generali (1815), Venezia: Francesco Andreola.

Cody Forman, Lisa (2004) 'Living and Dying in Georgian London's Lying-in Hospitals', *Bulletin of the History of Medicine*, 78 (2): 309–348.

Cody, Forman Lisa (2005) *Birthing the Nation. Sex, Science, and the Conception of Eighteenth-century Britons*, Oxford: Oxford University Press.

Cole, Joshua (2000) *The Power of Large Numbers: Population, Politics, and Gender in Nineteenth-Century France*, Ithaca (NY): Cornell University Press.

Colla, Luigi A. (1798) *Principi generali sul parto naturale*, Parma: Fratelli Gozzi.

Colombo Grazia (1985) 'Ai confini dell'istituzione: quali modelli?', in Oakley, Romito and Arcidiacono *et alii*. (1985): 135–140.

Colombo, Grazia, Pizzini, Franca and Regalia, Anita (eds) (1985) *Mettere al mondo. La produzione sociale del parto*, Milan: FrancoAngeli.

Colucci, Silvia (2005) 'Donne di parto. Riflessioni sulla iconografia della nascita a Siena, dal Medioevo alle soglie dell'età moderna', in Vannozzi (ed): 285–357.

Condorelli, Mario (1975) 'Cangiamila, Francesco Emmanuele', in *Dizionario biografico degli italiani*, Rome: Treccani: vol. 18 *ad vocem*.

Conforti, Maria (2009) '"Affirmare quid intus sit divinare est": mole, mostri e vermi in un caso di falsa gravidanza di fine Seicento', *Quaderni storici*, XLIX, 130 (1): 125–152.

Congourdeau, Marie-Hélène (2007) *L'embryon et son âme dans les sources grecques (VIe siècle av. J.-C. - Ve siècle apr. J.-C.)*, Paris: Collège de France-CNRS, Centre Histoire et Civilisation de Bysance.

Congourdeau, Marie-Hélène (2018) 'Debating the Soul in Late Antiquity', in Hopwood, Flemming and Kassell (eds): chap. 8.

Corbier, Mireille (1999) 'Lois, normes, pratiques individuelles et collectives. La petite enfance à Rome', *Annales. HSS*, 54, 6: 1257–1290.
Corbin, Alain, Courtine, Jean-Jacques and Vigarello, Georges (eds) (2011) *Histoire de la virilité*, Paris: Seuil.
Corblet, Jules (1881–1882) *Histoire dogmatique, liturgique et archéologique du sacrement de Baptême*, Paris: V. Palme.
Corradi, Alfonso (1874–1877) *Dell'ostetricia in Italia dalla metà del secolo scorso fino al presente. Commentario di A. Corradi in risposta al programma di concorso della Società Medico-chirurgica di Bologna per l'anno 1871*, Bologna: Gamberini e Parmeggiani.
Corridori, Marinella, Fanos, Thamianos and Fanos, Vassilios (eds) (2009) *Il padre contemporaneo*, Quartu Sant'Elena (CA): Hygeia Press.
Corridori, Marinella and Fanos, Vassilios (2010) 'Birth and the Care of the Newborn in Ancient Rome', in Fanos and Yurdakök (eds): 71–88.
Corsini, Carlo A. (1996) *Infanzia e famiglia nel XIX secolo*, in Becchi and Julia (eds): 250–281.
Corsini, Carlo A. and Viazzo, Pier Paolo (eds) (1997) *The Decline of Infant and Child Mortality. The European Experience 1750–1990*, Kluwer Academic, Kluwer Law International, UNICEF: The Hague.
Corsini, Carlo A. and Sandri Lucia (ed) (1999) 'La nascita della pediatria e ostetricia tra XVIII e XX secolo. Un seminario', *Bollettino di demografia storica*, 30/31: 95–118.
Cosmacini, Giorgio (1987) *Storia della medicina e della sanità in Italia*, Rome, Bari: Laterza.
Cosmacini, Giorgio (1989) *Storia dell'ostetricia. Stato dell'arte dal Cinque all'Ottocento*, Milan: Cilag.
Cosmacini, Giorgio (2002) *Il medico giacobino: la vita e i tempi di Giovanni Rasori*, Rome, Bari: Laterza.
Cosmacini, Giorgio (2007) *L'arte lunga. Storia della medicina dall'antichità a oggi*, Rome, Bari: Laterza.
Costa-Lascoux, Jacqueline (1994) 'Reproduction and Bioethics', in Duby and Perrot (dir) (1994): 567–586.
Coudray Le Boursier, Angélique Marguerite du [1759] (1976) *Abrégé de l'art des accouchemens, dans lequel on donne les préceptes nécessaires pour le mettre heureusement en pratique*, Paris: Dacosta.
Coulon, Gerard (2004) 'Images et imaginaire de la naissance dans l'Occident romain', in Dasen (ed): 209–226.
Cova, Anne (1997) *Maternité et droits des femmes en France (XIXe–XXe siècles)*, Paris: Anthropos.
Cova, Anne (2011) *Féminismes et néo-malthusianismes sous la IIIe République. "La liberté de la maternité"*, Paris: l'Harmattan.
Crainz, Franco (1986) *Il taglio cesareo nel mito e nella leggenda*, Rome: Janssen.
Cristianini, Costanza and Colombo, Grazia (2011) *Di mamma in mamma. Storie di maternità condivise in rete*, Milan: RED Edizioni.
Curatolo, Giacomo Emilio (1901) *L'arte di Juno Lucina in Roma. Storia dell'ostetricia dalle sue origini fino al secolo XX*, Rome: Tip. Sallustiana.
Curi, Umberto (2009) *Miti d'amore: filosofia dell'eros*, Milan: Bompiani.
D'Amelia, Marina (1997) 'La presenza delle madri nell'Italia medievale e moderna', in D'Amelia (ed): 3–52.
D'Amelia, Marina (ed) (1997) *Storia della maternità*, Rome, Bari: Laterza.
D'Amelia, Marina (1999) 'Diventare madre nel XVII secolo: l'esperienza di una nobile romana', in S. Seidel Menchi, J. Schutte and T. Kuehn, *Tempi e spazi di vita femminile tra Medioevo ed età moderna*, Bologna: Il Mulino: 279–310.
D'Amelia, Marina (2005) *La mamma*, Bologna: Il Mulino.
D'Amelia, Marina (2015) 'Meglio un blog oggi che un Prozac domani: le nuove maternità e i blog delle mamme', in Chemotti and La Rocca (eds): 996–1017.

Da Molin, Giovanna (1981) *L'infanzia abbandonata in Italia nell'età moderna. Aspetti demografici di un problema sociale*, Bari: Università degli studi.

Da Molin Giovanna (1993) *Nati a abbandonati. Aspetti demografici e sociali dell'infanzia abbandonata in Italia nell'età moderna*, Bari: Cacucci.

Da Molin, Giovanna (1994) *Trovatelli e balie in Italia (secc. XVI–XIX)*, Bari: Cacucci.

Da Molin, Giovanna and Stella, Pietro (1984) 'Famiglia e infanticidio nell'Europa preindustriale', *Quaderni dell'Istituto di scienze storico politiche. Università di Bari*, 3: 69–97.

Dadà, Adriana (ed) (2002) *Balie da latte. Istituzioni assistenziali e private in Toscana tra 17° e 20° secolo*, with the collaboration of Lucia Sandri, Rome: Morgana edizioni.

Dalarun, Jacques (1992) 'The Clerical Gaze', in Duby and Perrot (dir) (1992b): 15–42.

Dally, Ann (1991) *Women under the Knife. A History of Surgery*, London: Hutchinson Radius.

Daly, Mary (1973) *Beyond God the Father. Toward a Philosophy of Women's Liberation*, Boston: Beacon Press.

Darmon, Pierre (1981) *Le mythe de la procréation à l'âge baroque*, Paris: Seuil.

Dasen, Véronique (ed) (2004a) *Naissance et petite enfance dans l'antiquité*. Actes du colloque de Fribourg, 28 novembre -1 décember 2001, Fribourg: Accademic Press Fribourg.

Dasen, Véronique (2004b) 'Femmes à tiroir', in Dasen (ed): 127–144.

Dasen, Véronique (ed) (2007) *L'embryon humain à travers l'histoire. Images, savoirs et rites*, Paris: Infolio.

Dasen, Véronique (2018) 'A Uterine Amulet from the Roman Empire', in Hopwood, Flemming and Kassell (eds): Exhibits 7.

Daston, Lorraine and Park, Katharine (1998) *Wonders and the Order of Nature, 1150–1750*, New York: Zone Books.

Daston, Loraine and Pomata, Gianna (eds) (2003) *The Faces of Nature in Enlightenment Europe*, Berlin: Verlag.

Davanzo Poli, Doretta (1985) 'L'abbigliamento in gravidanza, parto e puerperio', in Chinosi (ed): 56–79.

Dean-Jones, Lesley Ann (1994) *Women's Bodies in Classic Greek Science*, Oxford: Clarendon Press.

Debest, Charlotte (2012) 'Le refus de maternité. Entre émancipation des assignations patriarcales et idéalisation du rôle de la mère', in Knibiehler, Arena and Cid, López (eds): 43–50.

De Demerson, Paula (1976) 'La cesarea post-mortem en la Espana de la Illustracion', *Asclepio. Archivio ibero–Americano de Historia y antropologia de la medicina y antropologia medica*, 28: 185–233.

De Grazia, Victoria (1992) *How Fascism Ruled Women. Italy 1922–1945*, Berkeley: University of California Press.

De Grazia, Victoria (1994) 'How Mussolini Ruled Italian Women', in Duby and Perrot (dir) (1994): 120–148.

De Gubernatis, Angelo (1878) *Storia comparata degli usi natalizi in Italia e presso gli altri popoli indoeuropei*, Milan: Treves.

DeLacy, Margaret (1989) 'Puerperal Fever in Eighteenth-century Britain', *Bulletin of the History of Medicine*, 63 (4): 521–556.

Delahaye, Marie-Claude (1990) *Tétons et tétines. Histoire de l'allaitement*, Paris: Trame Way.

Della Peruta, Franco (1979) 'Infanzia e famiglia nella prima metà dell'Ottocento', *Studi Storici*, 3: 473–491.

Del Panta, Lorenzo (1994) 'Mortalité infantile et post-infantile en Italie du XVIIIe au XXe siècle: tendances à long terme et différences régionales', *Annales de démographie historique*, 1: 45–60.

Del Panta, Lorenzo, Livi Bacci, Massimo, Pinto, Giuliano and Sonnino, Eugenio (1996) *La popolazione italiana dal Medioevo a oggi*, Rome, Bari: Laterza.

Demand, Nancy (1994) *Birth, Death, and Motherhood in Classic Greece*, Baltimore, London: Johns Hopkins University Press.

Demars-Sion, Véronique (1991) *Femmes séduites et abandonnées au XVIIIe siècle. L'exemple de Chambrésis*, Lille: Ester.

Derosas, Renzo (1999) 'Appesi a un filo. I bambini veneziani davanti alla morte', in Filippini and Plebani (eds): 39–54.

Detienne, Marcel (1976) 'Potagerie de femme, ou comment engendrer seule', *Traverses*, 5–6: 75–81.

Detragiache, Denise (1980) 'Un aspect de la politique démographique de l'Italie fasciste: la répression de l'avortement', *Mélanges de l'École française de Rome*, 92 (2): 211–251.

De Wendy Perkins, Louise (1996) *Midwifery and Medicine in Early Modern France: Louise Bourgeois*, Exeter: University of Exeter Press.

Deyts, Simone (2004) 'La femme et l'enfant au maillot en Gaule: icnographie et épigraphie', in Dasen (ed): 227–238.

Dickmann, Elisabeth (2013) 'The Passing of the Civil Code in Italy in 1865 and Anna Maria Mozzoni's Criticism of the Traditional Family Concept', in Ch.-E. Mecke and S. Meder (eds) *Family Law in Early Women's Rights Debates: Western Europe and the United States in the Nineteenth and Early Twentieth Centuries*, Köln, Weimar, Wein: Böhlau Verlag: 143–169.

Dick-Read, Grantly (1933) *Natural Childbirth*, London: W. Heinemann, Medical Books.

Di Robilant, Andrea (2008) *Lucia in the Age of Napoleon*, London: Faber and Faber.

Di Segni, Riccardo (1990) 'Colei che non ha mai visto sangue. Alla ricerca delle origini ebraiche della concezione virginale di Maria', *Quaderni Storici*, XXV, 75: 757–789.

Dinouart, Joseph Antoine Toussaint (1775) *Préface du traducteur*, in Cangiamila (1775): III–X.

Donath, Orna (2017) *Regretting Motherhood: A Study*, Berkeley: North Atlantic Books.

Donnison, Jean (1977) *Midwives and Medical Man: A History of the Struggle for the Control of Childbirth*, London: Heineman Education Books.

Donovan, James M. (1991) 'Infanticide and the Juries in France, 1825–1913', *Journal of Family History*, 16 (2): 157–176.

Drobot, Georges (1980) *Icone de la nativité: un corollaire et un moyen de formation du dogme de l'Incarnation*, Begrolles-en-Mauges: Abbaye de Bellefontaine.

Drobot, Georges (2000) *La lettura delle icone: introduzione storico-teologica all'icona della Natività*, Bologna: Edizioni Dehoniane Bologna.

duBois, Page (1988) *Sowing the Body: Psychoanalysis and Ancient Representations of Women*, Chicago: University of Chicago Press.

Duby, Georges and Perrot, Michèle (dir) (1992a) *History of Women in the West*, vol. I, P. Schmitt Pantel (ed) *From Ancient Goddesses to Christian Saints*, transl. by Goldhammer Arthur, Cambridge (MA): Belknap Press of Harvard University Press.

Duby, Georges and Perrot, Michèle (dir) (1992b) *History of Women in the West*, vol. II, C. Klapisch-Zuber (ed) *Silences of the Middle Ages*, transl. by Goldhammer Arthur, Botsford Clarissa, Schneider Deborah Lucas, Cambridge (MA): Belknap Press of Harvard University Press.

Duby, Georges and Perrot, Michèle (dir) (1993) *History of Women in the West*, vol. III, N. Zemon Davis, A. Farge (eds) *Renaissance and the Enlightenment Paradoxes*, transl. by Goldhammer Arthur Botsford Clarissa, Cambridge (MA): Belknap Press of Harvard University Press.

Duby, Georges and Perrot, Michèle (dir) (1994) *History of Women in the West*, vol. V, F. Thébaud (ed) *Toward a Cultural Identity in the Twentieth Century*, transl. by Goldhammer Arthur and Bond Sax Joan, Cambridge (MA): Belknap Press of Harvard University Press.

Duby, Georges (1996) *Dames du XIIe siècle*, Paris: Gallimard, vol. III (Eve et les prêtres).

Duchesneau, Francois (1985) 'Vitalism in Late Eighteenth-Century Physiology: the Cases of Barthez, Blumenbach and John Hunter', in Bynum and Porter (1985): chap. 9.

Duden, Barbara (1991) *The Woman Beneath the Skin: A Doctor's Patients in Eighteenth-Century Germany*, transl. by Thomas Dunlap, Cambridge (MA), London: Harvard University Press (1st German ed. 1987).

Duden, Barbara (1993) *Disembodying Women. Perspectives on Pregnancy and the Unborn*, transl. by Lee Hoinacki, Cambridge (MA): Harvard University Press (1st German ed. 1991).

Duden, Barbara (2002a) *Die Gene im Kopf - der Fötus im Bauch. Historisches zum Frauenkörper*, Hannover: Offizin-Verlag.

Duden, Barbara (2002b) 'Zwichen wahrem Wissen und Phophetie: Konzeptionen des Ungeborenen', in Duden, Schlumbohm, and Veit (eds): 11–48.

Duden, Barbara, Schlumbohm, Jürgen and Veit, Patrice (eds) (2002) *Geschichte des Ungeborenen. Zur Erfahrungs-und Wissenschaftsgeschichte der Schwangerschaft, 17.-20. Jahrhundert*, Göttingen: Vendenhoeck e Ruprecht.

Dumont, Marial and Morel, Pierre (1968) *Histoire de l'obstétrique et de la gynécologie*, Lyon: Simep, éditions.

Dupaquier, Jacques et Michel (1985) *Histoire de la démographie. La statistique de la population dès origines à 1914*, Paris: Perrin.

Durbach, Nadja (2004) *Bodily Matters: The Anti-Vaccination Movement in England, 1853–1907*, Raleigh (NC): Duke University Press.

d'Yvoire, Jean (2000) 'La placenta: un oggetto dallo statuto epistemologico problematico', in Pancino (ed): 83–101.

d'Yvoire, Jean (2006) 'L'irruzione del feto nel mondo dell'immagine e dell'immaginario (ovvero lo svelamento del segreto?', in Pancino and d'Yvoire (eds): 127–189.

Ehrard, Jean (1963) *L'idée de nature en France dans la première moitié du XVIIIe siècle*, Paris: Albin Michel.

Ehrenreich, Barbara and English, Deirdre (1973) *Witches, Midwives, and Nurses. A History of Women Healers*, Old Westbury (NY): Feminist Press.

Ekholm, Karin (2018) 'Pictures and Analogies in the Anatomy of Generation', in Hopwood, Flemming, Kassell (eds): chap. 15.

Enciclopedia Mariana "Theotócos" (1958) Genova: Bevilacqua e Solari.

Enke, Ulrike (2002) 'Von der Schönheit der Embryonen: Samuel Thomas Soemmerrings Werk *Icones embryonum humanorum* (1799)', in Duden, Schlumbohm, and Veit (eds): 205–236.

Ehrard Jean (1963) *L'idée de nature en France dans la première moitié du XVIIIe siècle*, Paris: Albin Michel.

Ergas, Yasmine (1994) 'Feminisms of the 1970s', in Duby and Perrot (dir) (1994): 527–547.

Etzioni, Amitai (ed) (1969) *The Semi-Professions and Their Organization: Teachers, Nurses, Social Workers*, New York: The Free Press.

Evenden, Doreen (1993) 'Mothers and Their Midwives in Seventheenth-Century London', in Marland (ed): 9–26.
Fallaci, Oriana (1955) 'Morire di parto', *L'Europeo*, 8.
Fanos, Vassilios, Corridori, Marinella and Cataldi, Luigi (eds) (2003) *Pueri, puerorum, pueris. Miti, storia e credenze sui bambini attraverso i secoli*, Lecce: Agorà.
Fanos, Vassilios and Yurdakök, Murat (eds) (2010) *Children of the Mother Goddess. History of Mediterranean Neonates*, Quartu Sant'Elena (CA): Hygeia Press.
Fanos, Vassilios, Atzei, Alessandra and Corridori, Marinella (2010) 'Birth and Care of the Newborn in Ancient Greece', in Fanos and Yurdakök (eds): 37–50.
Fanos, Vassilios, Fanos, Thamianos and Corridori, Marinella (2010) 'Extraordinary Births in the Gods' Delivery Room', in Fanos and Yurdakök (eds): 51–62.
Farge, Arlette (1976) 'Accouchement et naissance au XVIIIe siècle', *Revue de medecine psycomathique*, 1: 19–28.
Fasbender, Heinrich (1906) *Geschichte der Geburtshülfe*, Jena: Gustav Fischer.
Fassin, Didier and Memmi, Dominique (eds) (2004) *Le gouvernement des corps*, Paris: Éditions de l'Ehess.
Fattorini, Emma (1999) *Il culto mariano tra Ottocento e Novecento: simboli e devozione. Ipotesi e prospettive di ricerca*, Milan: FrancoAngeli.
Fazzari, Michela (2013) 'La siringa di Mauriceo e le complicanze del parto', in L. Guidi and M. R. Pelizzari (eds), *Nuove frontiere per la storia di genere*, vol. 3, Salerno: Università degli studi di Salerno-Libreria universitaria.it: 671–677.
Feldman, Davis M. (1970) *Marital Relations, Birth Control and Abortion in Jerwish Law*, New Jork: Schoken books.
Felici, Lucia, (2005) 'L'assistenza alle madri nell'Europa del Cinquecento', *Storia delle donne*, 1: 221–238.
Fellous, Michèle (1991) *La première image. Enquête sur l'échographie obstétricale*, Paris: Nathan.
Ferrario, Joanne M. (2008) *Nefarious Crimes, Contested Justice. Illicit Sex and Infanticide in the Republic of Venice, 1557–1789*, Baltimore: Johns Hopkins University Press.
Fildes, Valerie (1988) *Wet Nursing: A History from Antiquity to the Present*, Oxford: Basil Blackwell.
Filippini Cappelletto, Nadia Maria (1983) *Noi, quelle dei campi. Identità e rappresentazione di sé nelle autobiografie di contadine veronesi del primo Novecento*, Turin: Gruppo editoriale Forma.
Filippini, Nadia Maria (1984) 'Con le mani disarmate: la vicenda di una levatrice-chirurgo veneziana (1800–1802)', *Sanità, scienza e storia*, 2: 156–173.
Filippini, Nadia Maria (1985a), 'Levatrici e ostetricanti a Venezia tra Sette e Ottocento', *Quaderni Storici*, XX, 58 (1): 149–180.
Filippini, Nadia Maria (1985b) 'Il bambino prezioso. Maternità e infanzia negli interventi istituzionali del primo Ottocento', in Chinosi (ed): 28–40.
Filippini, Nadia Maria (1985c) 'L'assistenza al parto nel primo Ottocento: appunti sull'intervento istituzionale', in Oakley, Romito and Arcidiacono *et alii*. (1985): 63–70.
Filippini, Nadia Maria (1990) 'Il medico e la levatrice', *Quaderni Storici*, XXV, 73 (1): 291–297.
Filippini, Nadia Maria (1992a) 'Ospizi per partorienti e cliniche ostetriche tra Sette e Ottocento', in M. L. Betri and E. Bressan (eds) *Gli ospedali in area padana fra Settecento e Novecento*, Milan: FrancoAngeli: 395–411.
Filippini, Nadia Maria (1992b) *Ostetricia naturale, ostetricia chirurgica: uno scontro di culture e di scuole nella Parigi di fine Settecento*, in Sbisà (ed): 49–79.
Filippini, Nadia Maria (1993) 'The Church, the State and Childbirth: The Midwife in Italy during the Eighteenth Century'. in Marland (ed): 152–175.

Filippini, Nadia Maria (1995) *La nascita straordinaria. Tra madre e figlio, la rivoluzione del taglio cesareo (sec. XVIII–XIX)*, Milan: FrancoAngeli.

Filippini, Nadia Maria (1997) 'Il cittadino non nato e il corpo della madre', in D'Amelia (ed): 111–137.

Filippini, Nadia Maria (1998) 'Die 'erste Geburt': Eine neue Vorstellung vom Fötus und vom Mutter-leib (Italien, 18. Jahrhundert)', in Duden, Schlumbohm, and Veit (eds): 99–128.

Filippini, Nadia Maria (1999) '"Come tenere pianticelle". L'educazione della prima infanzia: asili di carità, giardinetti, asili per lattanti', in Filippini and Plebani (eds): 91–112.

Filippini, Nadia Maria (2002a) 'Sous le voile: les parturientes et les recours aux hospices de maternité à Turin, au milieu du XIXe siècle', *Revue d'Histoire moderne et contemporaine*, 49 (1): 173–194.

Filippini, Nadia Maria (2002b) 'Die erste geburt: Eine neue Vorstellung vom Fötus und vom Mutterleib (Italien, 18. Jahrhundert)', in Duden, Schlumbohm and Veit (eds): 99–128.

Filippini, Nadia Maria (2003a) '"Sanctuaire de la nature ou prison du fœtus": nature et corps féminin sous le combat sur la césarienne (France, fin du XVIIIe siècle)', in Daston and Pomata (eds): 259–282.

Filippini, Nadia Maria (2003b) 'La personificazione del feto e l'eclisse della madre', *Genesis. Rivista della Società Italiana delle Storiche*, 2 (1): 182–185.

Filippini, Nadia Maria (2010) 'Extraordinary Birth. History of the Caesarean Section in the Western World', in Fanos and Yurdakök (eds): 147–162.

Filippini, Nadia Maria (2012) 'Stupro presunto, lo stereotipo duro a morire', *Il manifesto*, 6 settembre.

Filippini, Nadia Maria (2018) 'Les prêtres et les mort-nés: à propos d'un registre spécial des avortements et des enfants mort-nés d'une paroisse vénitienne (XIXe siècle)', in Charrier, Clavandier, Gourdon, Rollet and Sage-Pranchère (eds): 65–82.

Filippini, Nadia Maria and Plebani, Tiziana (eds) (1999) *La scoperta dell'infanzia. Cura, educazione e rappresentazione. Venezia 1750–1930*, Venice: Marsilio.

Filippini, Nadia Maria, Plebani, Tiziana and Scattigno, Anna (eds) (2002) *Corpi e storia. Donne e uomini dal mondo antico all'età contemporanea*, Rome: Viella.

Fine, Agnès (1994) *Parrains, marraines: la parenté spirituelle en Europe*, Paris: Fayard.

Fine, Agnès (2001) 'Maternité et identité féminine', in Y. Knibiehler (ed) *Maternité, affaire privé, affaire publique*, Paris: Bayarde: 61–76.

Fiocca, Giorgio (1983) 'Mammane e medici a Roma tra Sette e Ottocento', in A. Lazzarini (ed) *Economia e società nella storia dell'Italia contemporanea. Fonti e metodi di ricerca*, Rome: Edizioni di storia e letteratura: 143–153.

Fischer, Jean-Louis (2010a) 'Naissances monstrueuses: l'enfant anormal à travers les âges', in Frydman and Szejer (eds): 201–211.

Fischer, Jean-Louis (2010b) 'La représentation de l'embryon et du foetus de l'antiquité à nos jours', in Frydman and Szejer (eds): 113–122.

Fissell, Mary E. (2018) 'Man-Midwifery Revisited', in Hopwood, Flemming and Kassell (eds): chap. 22.

Fiume, Giovanna (1995) 'Madri snaturate. La mania puerperale nella letteratura medica e nella pratica clinica dell'Ottocento', in Fiume (ed): 98–99.

Fiume, Giovanna (1997) 'Nuovi modelli e nuove codificazioni: madri e mogli tra Sette e Ottocento', in D'Amelia (ed): 76–110.

Fiume, Giovanna (ed) (1989) *Onore e storia nelle società mediterranee*, Palermo: La luna.

Fiume, Giovanna (ed) (1995) *Madri. Storia di un ruolo sociale*, Venice: Marsilio.

Flamigni, Carlo (2002) *La procreazione assistita*, Bologna: Il Mulino.

Flamigni, Carlo (2006) *Il controllo della fertilità. Storia, problemi e metodi dall'antico Egitto a oggi*, Turin: Utet.
Flamigni, Carlo (2010) *La questione dell'embrione. Le discussioni, le polemiche, i litigi sull'inizio della vita personale*, Milan: Dalai.
Flamigni, Carlo (2012) *Storia della contraccezione. Ignoranza, superstizione e cattiva coscienza di fronte al problema del controllo delle nascite*, Milan: Dalai.
Flandrin, Jean-Louis (1973) 'L'attitude à l'egard du petit enfant et les conduites sexuelles dans la civilisation occidentale: structures anciennes et évolution', *Annales de démographie historique*, 1: 143–210.
Flandrin, Jean-Louis (1975) *Les amours paysannes. Amours et sexualité dans les campagnes de l'ancienne France, XVIe–XIXe siècle*, Paris: Gallimard-Julliard.
Flandrin, Jean-Louis (1976) *Familles, parenté, maison, sexualité dans l'ancienne société*, Paris: Hachette.
Flandrin, Jean-Louis (1981) *Le Sexe et l'Occident: Évolution des attitudes et des comportements*, Paris: Éditions du Seuil.
Flandrin, Jean-Louis (2006) *L'Église et la contraception*, Paris: Imago (e-book).
Flemming, Rebecca (2018a) 'Introduction to Part I', in Hopwood, Flemming and Kassell (eds).
Flemming, Rebecca (2018b) 'Galen's Generations of Seeds', in Hopwood, Flemming and Kassell (eds): chap. 7.
Flügge, Sibylla (1998) *Hebammen und heilkundige Frauen. Recht und Rechtswirklichkeit im 15. und 16. Jahrhundert*, Frankfurt: Stroemfeld Verlag.
Forbes, Thomas R. (1966) *The Midwife and the Witch*, New Haven, London: Yale University Press.
Forleo, Romano and Giulia (1983) *Figlio figlia: guida ad una gravidanza e a un parto felice*, Milan: Feltrinelli.
Fornasa, Silvano (2018) *Il tempo di un respiro. Il miracolo del ritorno alla vita in terra vicentina*, Venice: Marsilio.
Forti, Simona and Guaraldo, Olivia (2006) 'Rinforzare la specie. Il corpo femminile tra biopolitica e religione materna', *Filosofia politica*, 20 (1): 57–76.
Foscati, Alessandra, Gislon Dopfel, Costanza and Parmeggiani, Antonella (eds) (2017) *Nascere. Il parto dalla tarda antichità all'età moderna*, Bologna: Il Mulino.
Foscati, Alessandra (2014) 'La scena del parto. Nascita del corpo e salvezza dell'anima tra religione e "magia" nell'alto medioevo', in C. Terranova, *La presenza dei bambini nelle religioni del Mediterraneo antico: la vita e la morte, i rituali e i culti tra archeologia, antropologia e storia delle religioni*, Rome: Aracne: 311–337.
Foscati, Alessandra (2019) 'Nonnatus dictus quod caeso defunctae matris utero prodiit. Postmortem Caesarean Section in the Late Middle Ages and Early Modern Period', *Social History of Medicine*, 32 (3): 465–480.
Fossier, Robert (eds) (1997) *La petite enfance dans l'Europe médiévale et moderne*, Toulouse, Presse Universitaire du Mirail.
Foucault, Michel (1973) *The Birth of the Clinic. An Archaeology of Medical Perception*, transl. by A. M. Sheridan Smith, London: Tavistock Publications (1st French ed. 1963).
Foucault, Michel (2008) *The Birth of Biopolitics: Lectures at the Collège de France, 1978–79*, transl. by G. Burchell, Basingstoke: Palgrave Macmillan (1st French ed. 2004).
Foucault, Michel, Barret Kriegel, Blandine, Thalamy, Anne *et alii* (1976) *Les machines à guerir: aux origine de l'hôpital moderne*, Paris: Impr. de l'Institut de l'environnement.
Fortunius Licetus (1634) *De monstrorum caussis, natura, et differentiis libri duo: in quibus ex rei natura monstrorum historiae, caussae, generationes, & differentiae plurimae a sapientibus*

intactae, cum generatim & in plantarum, & belluarum genere, tum seorsum in humana specie tractantur, Patauii: apud Paulum Frambottum (1st ed. 1634).
Franceschini, Chiara (2017) *Storia del Limbo*, Milan: Feltrinelli.
Franchetti, Daniela (2012) *La scuola ostetrica pavese tra Otto e Novecento*, Noviglio (MI): Cisalpino-IEU.
Franchetti, Daniela (2013) 'La formazione sanitaria delle levatrici in Lombardia', in C. G. Lacaita and M. Fugazza (eds) *L'istruzione secondaria nell'Italia unita 1861–1901*, Milan: FrancoAngeli: 374–396.
Frank, Johann Peter [1779] (1976) *A System of Complete Medical Police: Selections from Johann Peter Frank*, E. Lesky (ed), transl. by E. Vilim, Baltimore: Johns Hopkins University Press.
Frank, Johann Peter [1779] (1825) *Sistema compiuto di polizia medica*, transl. it, Milan: Pirotta.
Franklin, Sarah (2018) 'Feminism and Reproduction', in Hopwood, Flemming and Kassell (eds): chap. 42.
Frazer, James George (1922) *The Golden Bough. A Study in Magic and Religion*, London: Macmillan.
Fredj, Claire (2009) 'Concilier le religieux et le médicalles médicins, la césarienne post-mortem et le baptême au XIX siècle', in Alfani, Castagnetti and Gourdon (eds): 125–143.
Frugoni, Chiara (1992) 'The Imagined Woman', in Duby and Perrot (dir) (1992b): 336–422.
Frydman, René (1986) *L'irrésistible désir de naissance*, Paris: Presse Universitaire de France.
Frydman, René, Papiernik, Émile, Crémière, Cédric and Fischer, Jean-Louis (eds) (2009) *Avant la naissance. 5000 ans d'images*, Le Havre: Éd. de Conti.
Frydman, René and Szejer, Miriam (eds) (2010) *La naissance: histoire, cultures, pratiques d'aujourd'hui*, Paris: Michel Albin.
Galán, García Sonia, Medina Quintana, Silvia and Suárez, Carmen (eds) (2014) *Nacimientos bajo control. El parto en las edades Moderna y Contemporánea*, Madrid: Trea.
Galen, Claudius (1548) *De sanitate tuenda, libri sex, Thoma Linacro Anglo interprete*, Lugduni: Guliel. Rouillium.
Galen (1951) *A translation of Galen's Hygiene (de sanitate tuenda)* by Robert Montraville Green, Springfield: Charles Thomas publisher.
Galeotti, Giulia (2003) *Storia dell'aborto. I molti protagonisti e interessi di una lunga vicenda*, Bologna: Il Mulino.
Gall, Pietro (1922) *Il taglio cesareo addominale. Studio storico-clinico*, Bologna: Cappelli.
Gall, Pietro (1939) 'Le vicende storiche del forcipe', *Annali di ostetricia e ginecologia*, 76.
Garcìa Fernandez, Sonia (2014) "Parir para la patria". El control del embarazo y el parto en las primeras décadas del franquismo (1939–1955), in Galán García and Medina Quintana (eds): 129–148.
Garofalo, Fausto (1949) *L'ospedale di San Rocco delle partorienti e delle celate*, Rome: Arti Grafiche S. Anna.
Gazzetta, Liviana (2018) *Orizzonti nuovi. Storia del primo femminismo in Italia (1865–1925)*, Rome: Viella.
Galen, Claudius, Pergameni (1548) *De sanitate tuenda*, Thoma Linacro anglo interprete, Lugduni: Guliel. Rouillium.
Gelbart Rattner, Nina (1998) *The King's Midwife. A History and Mystery of Madame du Coudray*, Berkeley, Los Angeles: University of California Press.
Gélis, Jacques, Laget, Mireille and Morel, Marie-France (1978) *Entrer dans la vie. Naissance et enfances dans la France traditionelle*, Paris: Gallimard.

Gélis, Jacques, Morel, Marie-France, Loux, Françoise et alii (1995) *"L'heureux événement": une histoire de l'accouchement*, Paris: Musée de l'assistance publique-Hôpitaux de Paris.

Gélis, Jacques (1984a) *L'arbre et le fruit. La naissance dans l'Occident moderne (XVIe–XIXe siècle)*, Paris: Fayard (English transl. by R. Morris 1991, *History of Childbirth: Fertility, Pregnancy, and Birth in Early Modern Europe*).

Gélis, Jacques (1984b) 'Refaire les corps. Le deformation volontaires du corps de l'enfant la naissance', *Ethnologie française*, 1: 7–28.

Gélis, Jacques (1987) 'La tentation d'opérer: la symphyséotomie en Europe au XVIIIe siècle', *Contraception, fertilité, sexualité*, 15: 347–350.

Gélis, Jacques (1988) *La sage-femme ou le médecin. Une nouvelle conception de la vie*, Paris: Fayard.

Gélis, Jacques (2006) *Les enfants des Limbes. Mort-nés et parents dans l'Europe chrétienne*, Paris: Audibert.

Géraud, Roger (1963) *La limitation médicale des naissances*, Paris: Union Général d'Éditions.

Giacomini, Mariuccia (1985) 'Il parto in casa. Resoconti orali di ostetriche veneziane', in Chinosi (ed): 129–140.

Giani Gallino, Tilde (ed) (1989) *Le grandi madri*, Milan: Feltrinelli.

Gijswijt-Hofstra, Marijke and Marland, Hilary (eds) (2003) *Cultures of Child Health in Britain and the Netherlands in the Twentieth Century*, Amsterdam: Rodopi.

Gimbutas, Marija (1982) *The Goddesses and Gods of Old Europe, 6500–3500 BC, Myths and Cult Images*, Berkeley: University of California.

Ginzburg, Carlo (1983) *The Night Battles: Witchcraft & Agrarian Cults in the Sixteenth & Seventeenth Centuries*, transl. by J. and A. Tedeschi, Baltimore: Johns Hopkins University Press (1st Italian ed. 1966).

Ginzburg, Carlo (1992) *Ecstasies: Deciphering the Witches' Sabbath* (1st Italian ed. 1989).

Giordano, Scipione (1876) *Degli spedali in genere e delle maternità in particolare. Ragionamenti e proposte*, Milan: Rechiedei.

Giraud, François (1987) *Mère porteuse et droit de l'enfant*, Paris: Publisud.

Gislon Dopfel, Costanza, Foscati, Alessandra and Burnett, Charles (eds) (2019) *Pregnancy and Childbirth in the Premodern World European and Middle Eastern Cultures, from Late Antiquity to the Renaissance*, Turnhout: Brepols Publishers.

Gissi, Alessandra (2006a) *Le segrete manovre delle donne. Levatrici in Italia dall'Unità al fascismo*, Rome: Biblink.

Gissi, Alessandra (2006b) 'La più celebre antica borsa": ovvero il capitale della levatrice', *Genesis. Rivista della Società Italiana delle Storiche*, 5 (1): 79–96.

Gissi, Alessandra (2015) 'L'aborto procurato come questione sociale: modelli e paradigmi nell'Italia liberale', *Genesis. Rivista della Società Italiana delle Storiche*, 14 (1): 141–161.

Golini, Antonio (1988) 'Profilo demografico della famiglia italiana dall'Ottocento a oggi', in Melograni (ed): 327–382.

González, Carlos Ignacio (1988) *María evangelizada y evangelizadora*, Bogotá: Celam.

Gordon, Linda (1976) *Woman's Body, Woman's Right: The History of Birth Control Politics in Americ*, New York: Grossman/Viking.

Gorni, Mariagrazia and Pellegrini, Laura (1974) *Un problema di storia sociale: l'infanzia abbandonata in Italia nel secolo XIX*, Florence: La Nuova Italia editrice.

Gourdon, Vincent (2003) 'Le baptême catholique à Paris dans les premières décennies du XIXe siècle. Entre prescriptions religieuses et objectifs familiaux', *Cahiers de l'I.E.R.P.*, 1, Saint-Etienne, Publications de l'Université de Saint-Etienne: 58–96.

Gourdon, Vincent, Georges, Céline and Labéjof, Nicolas (2004) 'L'ondoiement en parroisse à Paris au XIXe siècle', *Histoire urbaine*, 10: 141–179.

Gourdon, Vincent (2009) 'L'hygiénisme français et les dangers du baptême précoce. Petit parcours au sein d'un topos médical du XIXe siècle', in Alfani, Castagnetti and Gourdon (eds): 103–124.

Gourdon, Vincent (2014) *Les Révolution du baptême en France de 1789 à nos jours, mémoire original du dossier Métamorphoses de la famille en France XVIIIe–XIXe siècle: hiérachies, réseau, ritualisation*. Habilitation à diriger des recherches, Université Paris-Sorbonne (unpublished thesis).

Gourdon, Vincent and Rollet, Catherine (2009) 'Stillbirth in Nineteenth-Century-Paris: Social, Legal and Medical Implications', *Population*, 64 (4): 601–632.

Gourdon, Vincent and Sage Pranchère, Nathalie (2018) 'Enregistrer et gérer mort-nés et fausse couches en France (époque moderne-XIXe siècle)', in Charrier, Clavandier, Gourdon, Rollet and Sage-Pranchère (eds): 41–64.

Gourevitch, Danielle (1984) *Le mal d'être femme. La femme et la médecine dans la Rome antique*, Paris: Belles Lettres.

Gourevitch, Danielle (2004) 'Chirurgie obstétrical dans le mond romain: césarienne et embryotomie', in Dasen (ed): 239–264.

Gourevitch, Danielle and Raepsaet-Charlier, Marie-Thérèse (2001) *La femme dans la Rome antique*, Paris: Hachette.

Gourevitch, Danielle, Morini, Anna and Rouquet, Nadine (ed) (2003) *Maternité et petite enfance dans l'antiquité romaine*. Catalogue de l'exposition, Bourges: ed. de la ville de Bourges.

Grandi, Casimira (ed) (1997) *Benedetto chi ti porta, maledetto chi ti manda. L'infanzia abbandonata nel Triveneto (secoli XV–XIX)*, Treviso: Ed. Fondazione Benetton.

Graves, Robert (1948) *The With Goddess. A Historical Grammar of Poetic Myth*, London: Faber & Faber.

Graves, Robert [1955] (1992) *The Greek Myts*, London: Penguin Book.

Green, Monica H. (ed and transl) (2001) *The Trotula: A Medieval Compendium of Women's Medicine*, Philadelphia: University of Pennsylvania Press.

Green, Monica Helen (2007) 'Reconstructing the Oeuvre of Trota of Salerno', in Jacquart and Paravicini Bagliani (eds): 183–233.

Green, Monica Helen (2008) *Making Women's Medicine Masculine: The Rise of Male Authority in Pre-Modern Gynaecology*, Oxford: Oxford University Press.

Green Monica H. (2009) 'The Sources of Eucharius Rösslin's 'Rosegarden for Pregnant Women and Midwives (1513)', *Medical History*, 53, 2: 167–192.

Gregorio, Maria Giuseppina and Cataldi, Luigi (2010) 'Childhood Protection: Amultets and Talismans', in Fanos and Yurdakök (eds): 175–187.

Grevembroch, Giovanni [1754] (1981) *Gli abiti dei veneziani di quasi ogni età con diligenza raccolti e dipinti nel secolo XVIII (1754)*, Venice: Filippi (anastatic reprint).

Griffini, Romolo (1868) 'Sul progetto di regolamento organico nell'ospizio provinciale degli esposti e delle partorienti in Milano', *Annali Universali di Medicina*, 70, 618: 465–563.

Grillenzoni, Carlo (1868) 'Relazione statistica ostetrica sull'ospizio di maternità di Ferrara per gli anni 1863, 64, 65, 66 del direttore prof. Grillenzoni C.', *Annali Universali di Medicina*, 204: 525–609.

Grundy, Isobel (1994) 'Sarah Stone: Enlightenment Midwife', *Clio Medica*, 29: 128–144.

Guarnieri, Patrizia (1999) 'E la mamma dov'è? Medici, donne e bambini nell'Ottocento', *Bollettino di demografia storica*, 30–31 (Special Issue: 'La nascita della pediatria e ostetricia tra XVIII e XX secolo): 95–118.

Guarnieri, Patrizia (2001a) 'Ospedali e ambulatori per l'infanzia tra '800 e '900', *Rivista italiana di Pediatria*, 27: 182–185.

Guarnieri, Patrizia (2001b) 'Piccoli, poveri e malati. Gli ambulatori per l'infanzia a Roma nell'età liberale', *Italia contemporanea*, 223: 225–257.

Guarnieri, Patrizia (2005) 'Madri che uccidono. Diritto, psicologia e mentalità sull'infanticidio dal 1810 ad oggi', in M. Bresciani Califano (ed) *Sapere e narrare. Figure della follia*, Florence: Olschki: 145–174.

Guarnieri, Patrizia (ed) (2009) *Maternità, nascite e aborti tra esperienze e bioetica*, Rome: Carocci.

Guidi, Laura (1986) 'Parto e maternità a Napoli. Carità e solidarietà spontanee, beneficenza istituzionale (1840–1880)', *Sanità, scienza e storia*, 1: 111–147.

Guttormsson, Loftur (2002) 'Parent-Child Relations', in Kertzer, David I. and Barbagli Marzio (eds) (2002) *Family Life in the Long Nineteenth Century, 1789–1913*, New Haven, London: Yale University Press: chap. VIII.

Guzzoni degli Ancarani, Arturo (1903) *I trattati di ostetricia pubblicati in Italia sino al 1900*: nota bibliografica, Naples: Stab. tip. N. Jovene e C.

Hacke, Daniela (2004) *Women, Sex and Marriage in Early Modern Venice*, Aldershot: Ashgate.

Hall, Lesley A. (2018) 'Movements to Separate Sex and Reproduction', in Hopwood, Flemming, Kassell (eds): chap. 29.

Haller, Mark M. (1963) *Eugenics: Hereditarian Attitudes in American Thought*, New Brunswick: Rutgers University Press.

Hanafi, Nahema (2017) *Le Frisson et le baume. Expériences féminines du corps au siècle des Lumières*, Rennes et Paris: Presses universitaires de Rennes.

Hanlon, Gregory (2003) 'L'infanticidio in Toscana nella prima età moderna', *Quaderni storici*, XXXVIII, 113: 453–498.

Hanson, Ann Ellis and Green, Monica H. (1994) 'Soranus of Ephesus: Methodicorum princeps', in W. Haase and H. Temporini (eds), *Aufstieg und Niedergang der römischen Welt*, Teilband II, Band 37.2, Berlin and New York: Walter de Gruyter: 968–1075.

Haraway, Donna (1991) *Simians, Cyborgs, and Women: The Reinvention of Nature*, London: Routledge.

Harley, David (1993) 'Provincial midwives in England: Lancashire and Cheshire, 1660–1760', in Marland (ed): 27–48.

Harris-Stoertz, Fiona (2012) 'Pregnancy and Childbirth in Twelfth-and Thirteenth-Century French and English Law', *Journal of the History of Sexuality*, 21, 100: 263–281.

Harris-Stoertz, Fiona (2017) 'La figura dell'ostetrica nei testi dell'alto medioevo', in Foscati, Gislon Dopfel and Parmeggiani (eds): 33–45.

Hartland, Edwig Sidney (1894) *The Legend of Perseus. A Study of Tradition in Story Custom and Belief*, London: David Nutt.

Hartland, Edwig Sidney (1909) *Primitive Paternity. The Myth of Supernatural Birth in Relation to the History of the Family*, London: David Nutt.

Hawkins, Mike (1997) *Social Darwinism in European and American Thought*, Cambridge: Cambridge University Press.

Hecht, Jacqueline (1980) 'L'évolution de la mortalité aux jeunes âges dans la littérature économique et démographique de l'ancien régime', in P. M. Boulanger and D. Tabutin (eds) *La mortalité des enfants dans le mon-de et dans l'histoire*, Liège: Ordina: 29–84.

Hemingway, Ernest (1929) *A Farewell to Arms*, New York: Charles Scribner's Sons.

Héritier-Augé, Françoise (1993) 'La costruzione dell'essere sessuato. La costruzione sociale del genere e le ambiguità dell'identità sessuale', in Bettini (ed): 113–140.

Héritier, Françoise (1996) *Masculin-féminin. La pensée de la différence*, Paris: Jacob.

Héritier, Françoise (2002) *Masculin-féminin II. Dissoudre la hiérarchie*, Paris: Jacob.

Hibbard, Bryan (2000) *The Obstetrician's Armamentarium. Historical Obstetric Instruments and their Inventors*, S. Anselmo (CA): Norman Publishing.

Hoffer, Peter Charles and Hull, Natalie N. E. H. (1981) *Murdering Mothers: Infanticide in England and New England 1558–1803*, New York: New York University Press.

Hopkins, Keith (1983) *Death and Renewal*, Cambridge: Cambridge University Press.

Hopwood, Nick (2018a) 'The Keywords "Generation" and "Reproduction"', in Hopwood, Flemming, Kassell (eds): chap. 20.

Hopwood, Nick (2018b) 'Artificial Fertilization', in Hopwood, Flemming, Kassell (eds): Chap. 39.

Hopwood, Nick (2018c) 'It's a Girl', in Hopwood, Flemming, Kassell (eds): Exhibits 38.

Hopwood, Nick, Flemming, Rebecca and Kassell, Lauren (eds) (2018) *Reproduction: antiquity to the present day*, Cambridge: Cambridge University Press (ebook).

Hull, John (1799) *A Defence of the Cæsarean Operation, with observations on Embryulcia and the section of the Symphysis Pubis, addressed to Mr. W. Simmons*, Manchester.

Hunecke, Volker (1987) *Die Findelkinder von Mailand: Kindsaussetzung und aussetzende Eltern vom 17. bis zum 19. Jahrhundert*, Stuttgart: Klett-Cotta (1st Italian ed. 1989, *I trovatelli di Milano*, Bologna: Il Mulino).

Hunecke, Volker (1991) 'Intensità e fluttuazioni degli abbandoni dal XV al XIX secolo', in Bardet, Hunecke, Pérez Moreda *et alii*: 27–72.

Hunecke, Volker (1994) 'The Abandonment of Legitimate Children in Nineteenth Century Milan and the European Contex', in J. Henderson and R. Wall (eds) *Poor Women and Children in the European Past*, London: Routledge: 117–138.

Hunter, William (1774) *Anatomia uteri humani gravidi tabulis illustrata*, Birmingham: John Baskerville.

Institor, Heinrich (Krämer), Sprenger, Jacob [1487] (see Mackay).

Jackson, Mark (ed) (2002) *Infanticide. Historical Perspectives on Child Murder and Concealment, 1550–2000*, Aldershot: Ashgate.

Jacobson-Schutte, Anne (1980) '"Trionfo delle donne": tematiche di rovesciamento dei ruoli nella Firenze rinascimentale', *Quaderni storici*, XV, 44 (2): 474–496.

Jacquart, Danielle and Paravicini Bagliani, Agostino (eds) (2007) *La Scuola medica Salernitana: gli autori e i testi*, Florence: Edizioni del Galluzzo.

Jaubert, Marie-José (1979) *Les Bateleurs du mal joli. Le mythe de l'accouchement sans douleur*, Paris: Balland.

Jordan, Brigitte (1978) *Birth in Four Cultures: A Crosscultural Investigation of Childbirth in Yucatan, Holland, Sweden, and the United States*, Montreal: Eden Press Women's Publications.

Jordanova, Ludmilla (2018) 'Man-Midwifery Dissected', in Hopwood, Flemming, Kassell (eds): Exhibits 22.

Jourdan, Clara (1976) *Insieme contro. Esperienze dei consultori femministi*, Milan: La Salamandra.

Joubert, Laurent (1578) *Erreurs populaires au fait de la medecine et régime de santé*, Bourdeaux: Millanges.

Julia, Dominique (1996) 'L'infanzia agli inizi dell'epoca moderna', in Becchi and Julia (eds): 231–311.

Kapparis, Konstantinos (2002) *Abortion in the Ancient World*, London: Duckworth.

Kassell, Lauren (2018) 'Fruitful Bodies and Astrological Medicine', in Hopwood, Flemming, Kassell (eds): chap. 16.

Kendal, Evie (2015) *Equal opportunity and the Case for State Sponsored Ectogenesis*, Basingstoke: Palgrave.

Kertzer, David (1993) *Sacrificed for Honor: Italian Infant Abandonment and the Politics of Reproductive Control*, Boston: Beacon Press.

Ketham, Johannes de [1491] (1988) *The Fasciculus medicinae of Johannes de Ketham, Alemanus: facsimile of the first (Venetian) edition of 1491*, transl. by Luke Demaitre, commentary by

Karl Sudhoff; transl. and adapted by Charles Singer, Birmingham: The Classics of Medicine Library.
King, Helen (1998) *Hippocrates Woman. Reading the Female Body in Ancient Greece*, London: Routledge.
King, Helen (2013) *The One Sex on Trial: The Classic and Early Modern Evidence*, London: Routledge.
King, Helen (2018) 'Women and Doctors in Ancient Greece', in Hopwood, Flemming, Kassell (eds): chap. 3.
Kitzinger, Sheila (2000) *Rediscovering Birth*, London: Little Brown and Company.
Kitzinger, Sheila (1978) *Women as Mothers*, Glasgow, Fontana-Collins.
Klapisch-Zuber, Christiane (1980) 'Genitori naturali e genitori di latte nella Firenze del Quattrocento', *Quaderni Storici*, XV, 44 (2): 543–563.
Klapisch-Zuber, Christiane (1985) *Women, Family and Ritual in Renaissance Italy*, transl. by L. Cochrane, Chicago, London: University of Chicago Press.
Klapisch-Zuber, Christiane (1996) 'Il bambino, la memoria e la morte', in Becchi and Julia (eds): vol. I: 155–181.
Kline, Wendy (2018) 'Our Bodies, Ourselves', in Hopwood, Flemming, Kassell (eds): Exhibits 35.
Knibiehler, Yvonne (1997) *La révolution maternelle. Femme, maternité, citoyenneté depuis 1945*, Paris: Perrin.
Knibiehler, Yvonne (2000) *Histoire des mères et de la maternité en Occident*, Paris: Puf.
Knibiehler, Yvonne (2003) 'L'allaitement et la société', *Érudit. Recherches féministes*, 16 (2): 11–33.
Knibiehler, Yvonne (2007) *Accoucher. Femmes, sages-femmes et médecins depuis le milieu du 20e siècle*, Rennes: Éditions de l'École nationale de la Santé publique.
Knibiehler, Yvonne and Fouquet, Catherine (1982) *Histoire des mères du moyen âge à nos jours*, Paris: Montalba.
Knibiehler, Yvonne and Fouquet, Catherine (1983) *La femme et le medecins. Analyse Historique*, Paris: Hachette.
Knibiehler, Yvonne, Arena, Francesca and Cid López, Rosa Maria (eds) (2012) *La maternité à l'épreuve du genre. Métamorphoses et permanence de la maternité dans l'aire méditerranéenne*, Rennes: Presses de l'École des Hautes Études en Santé Publique (EHESP).
Knibiehler, Yvonne and Thébaud, Françoise (1995) *La médicalisation de l'accouchement dès années 1920 aux années 1970*, in Gélis, Morel *et alii* (1995): 101–113.
Köves-Zulauf, Thomas (1990) *Römische Geburtsriten*, München: Beck.
Krämer, Heinrich and Sprenger, Jacob (1487)(see Mackay).
Kreager, Philip (2018) 'The Emergence of Population', in Hopwood, Flemming, Kassell (eds): chap. 8.
La Banca, Domenica (2013) *Welfare in transizione. L'esperienza dell'ONMI (1943–1950)*, Naple: Edizioni Scientifiche Italiane.
Labouvie, Eva (1998) *Andere Umstände. Eine Kulturgeschichte der Geburt*, Köln-Weimar-Wien: Böhlan Verlag.
Lachapelle, Marie-Louise (1821) *Pratique des accouchements, ou Mémoires et observations choisies, sur les points les plus importants de l'art*, Paris: J.B. Baillière.
Laget, Mireille (1979) 'La césarienne ou la tentation de l'impossible, XVIIe–XVIIIe siècle', *Annales de Bretagne et des pays de l'Ouest*, 86 (2): 177–189.
Laget, Mireille (1982) *Naissances: l'accouchement avant l'âge de la clinique*, Paris: Seuil.
Lalli, Chiara (2016) 'La fecondazione eterologa resta un diritto per pochi privilegiati', *Internazionale*, 21 aprile.
La Motte, Guillaume Mauquest de [1715] (1989) *Accoucheur de campagne sous le Roi-Soleil. Le Traité de G. Mauquest de La Motte*, J. Gélis (ed), Paris: Editions Imago.

Lang, Raven (1972) *Birth book*, Felton: Genesis Press (1st Italian ed. 1978: *Riprendiamoci il parto. Esperienze alternative di parto: resoconti, testimonianze, immagini*, Rome: Savelli).
Langer, William L. (1973) 'Infanticide. A History Survey', *History of Childhood Quartely*, 1: 353–366.
Lanzardo, Liliana (1985) *Il mestiere prezioso. Racconti di ostetriche*, Turin: Gruppo editoriale Forma.
Laqueur, Thomas (1992) *Making Sex. Body and Gender from the Greeks to Freud*, Cambridge (MA): Harvard University Press.
Laqueur, Thomas (1995) 'Da una generazione all'altra. Alla ricerca di nuovi legami nell'era delle tecnologie riproduttive', in Fiume (ed): 303–327.
Laslett, Peter (1977) *Family Life and Illicit Love in Earlier Generations: Essay in Historical Sociology*, Cambridge: Cambridge University Press.
Laslett, Peter, Oosterveen Karla and Smith, Richard M. (1980) *Bastardy and Its Comparative History: Studies in the History of Illegitimacy and Marital Nonconformism in Britain, France, Germany, Sweden, North America, Jamaica and Japan*, Cambridge (MA): Harvard University Press.
Laubenheimer, Fanette (2004) 'La mort de tous petits dans l'Occident romain', in Dasen (ed): 293–315.
Laurent, Sylvie (1989) *Naître au Moyen âge. De la conception à la naissance: la grossesse et l'accouchement, XIIe–XVe siècles*, Paris: Léopard d'or.
Lavenia, Vincenzo and Paolin, Giovanna (eds) (2011) *La fede degli italiani. Per Adriano Prosperi*, vol. 3, Pisa: Edizioni della Normale.
L'Estrange, Elizabeth (2010) '"Quand femme enfante…". Remèdes pour l'accouchement au Moyen Âge', in McClive and Pellegrin (eds): 167–182.
Le Fort, Léon (1866) *Des maternités. Étude sur les maternités et les Institutions charitables d'accouchement à domicile dans les principaux États de l'Europe*, Paris: Masson.
Le Goff, Jacques (1984) *The Birth of Purgatory*, transl. by A. Goldhammer, Chicago: University of Chicago Press (1st French ed. 1981).
Le Naour, Jean-Yves and Valenti, Catherine (2003) *Histoire de l'avortement. X1Xe–XXe siècles*, Paris: Seuil.
Leboyer, Frédérick (1974) *Pour una naissance sans violence*, Paris: Seuil (1st English ed.: *Birth Without Violence*, London: Wildwood House, 1975; 1st Italian ed. 1975: *Per una nascita senza violenza. La nascita, il venire al mondo, il parto dal punto di vista del bambino*, Milan: Bompiani).
Lefaucheur, Nadine (1994) 'Maternity, Family, and the State', in Duby and Perrot (dir) (1994): 433–452.
Lefaucheur, Nadine (2010) 'L'abandon en Occident', in Frydman and Szejer (eds): 212–221.
Leperchery, Félix (2010) *L'approche de l'embryon humain à travers l'histoire. Une exemplarité épistémologique éloquente*, Paris: L'Harmattan.
Leroy, Fernand (2001) *Histoire de naître: de l'enfantement primitif à l'accouchement médicalisé*, Bruxelles: De Boeck.
Lett, Didier (1997) 'De l'errance au deuil. Les enfants morts sans baptême et la naissance du Limbus Puerorum aux XIe–XIIIe siècles', in Fossier (eds): 77–92.
Lett, Didier (1998) *L'enfant des miracles. Enfance et famille au Moyen Âge (XIIe–XIIIe s.)*, Paris: Flammarion.
Lett, Didier and Morel, Marie France (2006) *Une histoire de l'allaitement*, Paris: Éd. de la Martinière.
Levack, Brian P. (1987) *The Witch Hunt in Early Modern Europe*, London: Longman.
Levret, André (1761) *L'art des accouchemens démonstré par des principes de physique et méchanique, pour servir d'introduction et de base à des leçons particulières*, Paris: Le Prieur.

Lewis, Jane (1980) *The politics of Motherhood: Child and Maternal Welfare in England, 1900–1939*, London: Croom Helm.
Li Causi, Piero (2005) 'Generazione di ibridi, generazione di donne. Costruzioni dell'umano in Aristotele e Galeno (e Palefato)', *Storia delle donne*, 1: 89–114.
Liceti, Fortunio (Fortunius Licetus) [1616] (1665) *De monstris. Ex recensione Gerardi Blasii, m.d. & p.p. Qui monstra quædam nova & rariora ex recentiorum scriptis addidit*, Amstelodami: Andreæ Frisii.
Livi Bacci, Massimo (1977) *A History of Italian Fertiliy During the Last Two Century*, Princeton: Princeton University Press.
Lombardi, Daniela (ed.) (1997) *Ricerche storiche*, 27 (2) (Special Issue: Legittimi e illegittimi. Responsabilità dei genitori e identità dei figli tra Cinque e Ottocento).
Lombardi, Daniela (2018) 'La Déclaration de grossesse; l'obbligo degli alimenti e la tutela delle madri nubili. Francia e Italia XVI–XVIII secolo', *Rivista Storica Italiana*, 130 (1): 5–43.
Lombardi, Lia (2017) 'Fathers and Fathering. Men Inside the Delivery Room', *AG-AboutGender. International Journal of Gender Studies*, 6 (11): 204–222.
Longo, Oddone (2000) 'La morte per la patria', in Tucidide, *Epitafio di Pericle per i caduti del primo anno di guerra*, O. Longo (ed), Venice: Marsilio: 9–28.
Lonni, Ada (1984) 'Il mestiere di ostetrica al confine tra lecito e illecito', *Società e storia*, 25: 563–590.
Loraux, Nicole (1982) 'Pónos. Sur quelques difficultés de la piene comme nom du travail', *Annali dell'Istituto Orientale di Napoli*, 4: 171–192.
Loraux, Nicole (1995) *The Experiences of Tiresias. The Feminine and the Greek Man*, transl. by P. Wissing, Princeton: Princeton University Press (1st French ed., 1989).
Loudon, Irvine (1992) *Death in Childbirth: An International Study of Maternal Care and Maternal Mortality 1800–1950*, Oxford: Clarendon Press.
Loudon, Irvine (2000) *The Tragedy of Childbed Fever*, Oxford: Oxford University Press.
Loux, Françoise (1998) *Traditions et soins d'aujourd'hui. Anthropologie du corps et professions de santé*, Paris: Masson.
Lovato, Guerrino (2012) *La levatrice incredula nella leggenda della Natività*, Venice: Lupi e Sirene.
Luc, Jean-Noël (1997) *L'invention du jeune enfant au XIXe siècle. De la salle d'asile à l'école maternelle*, Paris: Belin.
Lurie, Samuel (2013) *The History of Caesarean Section*, New York: Nova Science Publishers.
Lynch, Katherine A. (2000) 'Infant Mortality, Child Neglect and Child Abandonment in European History: A Comparative Analysis', in Bengtsson and Saito (eds): 133–164.
Mackay, Christopher S. (2009) *The Hammer of Witches: a Complete Translation of the Malleus maleficarum*, Cambridge: Cambridge University Press.
Maclean, Ian (1980) *The Renaissance Notion of Woman: A Study in the Fortunes of Scholasticism and Medical Science in European Intellectual Life*, Cambridge: Cambridge University Press: 28–46.
Magli, Ida (1978) *La donna. Un problema aperto. Guida alla ricerca antropologica*, Florence: Vallecchi.
Magli, Ida (1987) *La Madonna*, Milan: Rizzoli.
Magli, Ida (1989) *La sessualità maschile*, Milan: Mondadori.
Maher, Vanessa (1992) *Il latte materno. I condizionamenti culturali di un comportamento*, Turin: Rosenberg & Sellier.
Mahon, Paul-Augustin-Olivier (1820) *Medicina legale e polizia medica. Traduzione dal francese esattamente corretta, notabilmente accresciuta di annotazioni ad adattata ai vigenti Codici pel regno Lombardo Veneto da G. Chiappari*, Milan: Pirotta.
Maire, Brigitte (2004) 'Conception, retentio et cotylédon. On quelques aspects de la vie intra-utérine', in Dasen (ed): 207–221.

Malacarne Vincenzo (1808) *Dialoghetti per istruzione delle levatrici idiote*, Padue: No Publisher.
Manetti, Renzo (2005) *Le Madonne del parto. Icone templari*, Florence: Polistampa.
Mantegazza, Raffaele (2017) *Narrare l'inizio. Gravidanza, parto, nascita tra natura e culture*, Rome: Castelvecchi.
Mantovani, Claudia (2004) *Rigenerare la società: l'eugenetica in Italia dalle origini ottocentesche agli anni Trenta*, Soveria Mannelli: Rubettino.
Manuli, Paola (1980) 'Fisiologia e patologia del femminile negli scritti dell'antica ginecologia greca', in M. D. Grmek (ed) *Hippocratica: Actes du Colloque hippocratique de Paris 1978*, Paris: Éditions du C.N.R.: 393–408.
Manuli, Paola (1983) 'Donne mascoline, femmine sterili, vergini perpetue: la ginecologia greca tra Ippocrate e Sorano', in Campese, Manuli and Sissa (1983): 149–204.
Marinello, Giovanni [1563] (1574) *Le medicine partenenti alle infermità delle donne*, Venice: Giovanni Valgrisi.
Marland, Hilary (ed) (1993) *The Art of Midwifery. Early Modern Midwives in Europe*, London: Routledge.
Marland, Hilary (1993) 'The Burgerlijke Midwife of 18th Century Holland', in Marland (ed): 192–213.
Marland, Hilary (2004) *Dangerous Motherhood: Insanity and Childbirth in Victorian Britain*, Basingstoke, New York: Palgrave Macmillan.
Marland, Hilary, and Rafferty, Anne Marie (eds) (1997) *Midwives, Society and Childbirth: Debates and Controversies in the Modern Period*, London: Routledge.
Marti Casado, Tamara and Savva, Maria (2017) 'Whats is a Embryo? A Lexical Study of Hippocrates' and Galen's Theories on Its Creation and Development', *Postgraduate Journal of Medical Humanities*, 4: 32–54.
Martin, Emily (1989) *The Woman in the Body. A Cultural Analysis of Reproduction*, Stratford: Open University Press.
Mauriceau, François [1668] (1681) *Traité des maladies des femmes grosses et des celles qui sont accouchées*, Paris: chez l'Auteur.
Mazzarello, Paolo (2015) *E si salvò anche la madre. L'evento che rivoluzionò il parto cesareo*, Turin: Bollati Boringhieri.
McClive, Cathy and Pellegrin, Nicole (eds) (2010) *Femmes en fleurs, femmes en corps. Sang, santé, sexualités, du Moyen Âge aux Lumières*, Saint-Étienne: Publications de l'Université de Saint-Étienne.
McClive, Cathie and King, Helen (2007) 'When is a foetus not a foetus? Diagnosing false conceptions in early modern France', in Dasen (ed): 223–238.
McTavish, Lianne (2018) 'A Birthing Chair', in Hopwood, Flemming, Kassell (eds) (2018): Exhibits 18.
Medina Quintana, Silvia (2015) 'El momento de dar a luz. Normas y prácticas en torno al parto', in Chemotti and La Rocca (eds): 931–944.
Meldini, Piero (1975) *Sposa e madre esemplare. Ideologia della donna e della famiglia durante il fascismo*, Florence: Guaraldi.
Meldolesi, Anna (2011) *Mai nate. Perché il mondo ha perso 100 milioni di donne*, Milan: Mondadori.
Melli, Sebastiano (1721) *La comare levatrice istruita nel suo ufizio secondo le regole più certe, e gli ammaestramenti più moderni*, Venice: stamperia Carlo Palese.
Melograni, Piero (ed) (1988) *La famiglia italiana dall'Ottocento a oggi*, Rome, Bari: Laterza.

Memmi, Dominique (2002) 'Verso una confessione laica? Nuove forme di controllo pubblico dei corpi nella Francia contemporanea', in Filippini, Plebani and Scattigno (eds): 229–252.
Merchant, Carolyn (1980) *The Death of Nature: Women, Ecology, and the Scientific Revolution*, San Francisco: Harper & Row.
Mercuriale, Girolamo (1587) *De morbis muliebribus prælectiones ex ore Hieronymi Mercurialis iam dudum à Gaspare Bauhino exceptæ, nunc vero per Michaelem Columbum ex collatione plurimum exemplarium consensu auctoris locupletiores, & emendatiores factæ*, Venetiis: Felicem Valgrisium.
Mercurio, Scipione (Girolamo) (1658) *Degli errori popolari d'Italia libri sette*, Padua: Matteo Cadorino.
Mercurio, Scipione (Girolamo) [1596] (1713) *La Commare o raccoglitrice dell'eccellentissimo signor Scipion Mercurio, filosofo, medico e cittadino romano, divisa in tre libri*, Venice: Domenico Lovisa.
Metz-Becker, Marita (1997) *Der verwaltete Körper. Die Medikalisierung schwangerer Frauen in den Gebärhäusern des frühen 19. Jahrhunderts*, Frankfurt a.M.: Campus Verlag.
Michaels, Paula A. (2014) *Lamaze. An International History*, Oxford: Oxford University Press.
Milanesi, Claudio (1989) *Mort apparente, mort imperfaite. Médecine et mentalités au XVIIIe siècle*, Paris: Payot.
Minesso, Michela (2007) *Stato e infanzia nell'Italia contemporanea: origini, sviluppo e fine dell'Onmi, 1925–1975*, Bologna: Il Mulino.
Miralles, Carles (1993) 'Le spose di Zeus e l'ordine del mondo nella Teogonia di Esiodo', in Bettini (ed): 17–44.
Mitterauer, Michael (1993) *Ahnen und Heilige: Namengebung in der europäischen Geschichte*, München: C.H. Beck.
Modena, Francesca and Sabatini, Fabio (2010) *I Would if I Could: Precarious Employment and Childbearing Intentions in Italy*, MPRA, Munich Personal RePEc Archive: https://mpra.ub.uni-muenchen.de/26117/.
Modershon, Mechtild (1977) *Natura als Goettin im Mittelalter. Ikonographische Studien zu Darstellungen der personifizierten Natur*, Berlin: Akademie Verlag.
Molmenti, Pompeo (1928) *La storia di Venezia nella vita privata*, Bergamo: Istituto d'arti grafiche.
Montani, Patrizia (1995) 'Madri nubili e tribunali. Legislazione e sentenze in età liberale', *Italia contemporanea*, 200: 455–468.
Montani, Patrizia (1998) 'Amori, seduzioni e mancate promesse. Le madri nubili e il dibattito sulla ricerca della paternità nella legislazione italiana tra Otto e Novecento', in S. Clementi and A. Spada (eds) *Norma e contrarietà. Una storia del nubilato in età moderna e contemporanea*, Bolzano: Folio: 205–230.
Morel, Marie-France (2007) 'Histoire du maillot en Europe occidentale', in D. Bonnet, L. Pourchez, *Du soin au rite dans l'enfance*, Toulouse: Érès: 61–84.
Morel, Marie France (2010a) 'Les représentations de la naissance dans l'art occidentale', in Frydman and Szejer (eds): 67–85.
Morel, Marie France (2010b) 'Soigner les tout-petit: histoire de la puericulture et de la pédiatrie', in Frydman and Szejer (eds): 172–189.
Morel, Marie France (ed) (2013) *Accueillir le nouveau-né d'hier à aujourd'hui*, Toulouse: Érès.
Morgagni, Giobatta [1761] (1837) *Delle sedi e cause delle malattie anatomicamente investigate da Giobatta Morgagni*, prima versione italiana di Pietro Maggesi, Milan: Rusconi.
Moriani, Gianni (1999) *Il secolo dell'odio. Conflitti razziali e di classe nel Novecento*, Venice: Marsilio.

Mortara, Giorgio (1925) *La salute pubblica in Italia durante e dopo la guerra*, Bari, Rome: Laterza.
Moscucci, Ornella (1990) *The Science of Woman. Gynaecology and Gender in England. 1800–1929*, Cambridge: Cambridge University Press.
Moscucci Ornella (2003) 'Holistic Obstetrics: The Origins of "Natural Childbirth" in Britain', *Postgraduate Medical Journal*, 79: 168–173.
Mosse, George L. (1996) *The Image of Man: The Creation of Modern Masculinity*, Oxford: Oxford University Press.
Moulinier-Brogi, Laurence (2005) 'Conception et corps féminin selon Hildegarde de Bingen', *Storia delle donne*, 1: 139–157.
Moulinier-Brogi, Laurence (2007) 'La science des urines de Maurus et les Sinthomata magistri Mauri inédits', in Jacquart and Paravicini Bagliani (eds): 261–281.
Moulinier-Brogi, Laurence (2010) 'Virginité, maternité et maux de corps féminin au prisme de l'uroscopie médiévale', in McClive, Cathy and Pellegrin, Nicole (eds): 21–36.
Müller, Gerhard L. (1989) *Was heißt: Geboren von der Jungfrau Maria? Eine theologische Deutung*, Freiburg, Basel, Wien: Freiburg im Breisgau Herder.
Müller, Wolgang (2012) *The Criminalization of Abortion in the West. Its Origins in Medieval Law*, Ithaca: Cornell University Press.
Munno, Cristina (2015) 'De Marco Cao au *Il Popolo di Romagna*. Le baptême et les parrainage en Vénétie entre 1830–2010', in Alfani, Gourdon and Robin (eds): 429–458.
Muraro, Luisa (2016) *L'anima del corpo. Contro l'utero in affitto*, Brescia: La Scuola.
Murgia, Michela (2011) *Ave Mary. E la Chiesa inventò la donna*, Turin: Einaudi.
Murray, Jones Peter (2018) 'Generation between Script and Print', in Hopwood, Flemming and Kassell (eds): chap. 13.
Muzzarelli, Maria Giuseppina (2013) *Nelle mani delle donne. Nutrire, guarire, avvelenare dal medioevo a oggi*, Rome, Bari: Laterza.
Nardi, Enzo (1971) *Procurato aborto nel mondo greco romano*, Milan: Giuffrè.
Nardi, Michele Giuseppe (1954) *Il pensiero ostetrico-ginecologico nei secoli*, vols. 2, Milan: Thiele-REMI.
Nessi, Giuseppe (1797) *Arte ostetricia teorico pratica*, Venice: No Publisher.
Niccoli, Ottavia (1980) '"Menstruum quasi Monstruum": parti mostruose tabù sessuali nel '500', *Quaderni storici*, XV, 44 (2): 402–428.
Niccoli, Ottavia (1988) *Il corpo femminile nei trattati del Cinquecento*, in Bock and Nobili (eds): 23–44.
Niccoli, Ottavia (2005) *Rinascimento anticlericale. Infamia, propaganda e satira in Italia tra Quattro e Cinquecento*, Rome, Bari: Laterza.
Nietzsche, Friedrich [1881–88] (1995) *Thus Spoke Zarathustra: a Book for All and None*, transl. by W. Kaufmann, New York: Modern Library Edition.
Nihell, Elizabeth (1760) *A Treatise on the Art of Midwifery: Setting Forth Various Abuses Therein, Especially as to the Practice with Instruments*, London: A. Morley.
Noonan, John T. (1965) *Contraception: A History of Its Treatment by the Catholic Theologians and Canonists*, Cambridge (MA): Harvard University Press.
Noonan, John T. (1970) *The Morality of Abortion. Legal and Historical Perspectives*, Cambridge (MA): Harvard University Press.
Nuland, B. Sherwin (2003) *The Doctors' Plague: Germs, Childbed Fever, and the Strange Story of Ignác Semmelweis*, New York: W. W. Norton.
Oakley, Ann (1976) 'Wisewoman and Medicine Man: Change in the Management of Childbirth', in J. Mitchell, A. Oakley (eds) *The Rights and Wrongs of Women*, Harmondsworth: Penguin: 45–47.

Oakley, Ann (1980) *Women Confined: Towards a Sociology of Childbirth*, Oxford: M. Robertson.
Oakley, Ann (1984) *The Captured Womb: A History of the Medical Care of Pregnant Women*, Oxford: Basil Blackwell.
Oakley, Ann (2004) 'Who Cares For Women? Science Versus Love in Midwifery Today', in Van Teijlingen, Lois, McCaffery and Porter (eds): 319–328.
Oakley, Ann, Romito, Patrizia, Arcidiacono, Caterina *et alii* (1985) *Le culture del parto*, Milan: Feltrinelli.
Olive, Françoise (1992) 'Preface', in Bourgeois [1609] (1992): 7–25.
Olsan, Lea T. (2018) 'A Medieval Birth Girdle', in Hopwood, Flemming, Kassell (eds): Exhibits 11.
Olszynko-Gryn, Jesse (2018) 'Technologies of Contraception and Abortion', in Hopwood, Flemming, Kassell (eds): chap. 36.
Opitz, Claudia (1992) 'Life in the Late Middle Ages (1250–1500)', in Duby and Perrot (dir) (1992b): chap. 9.
Oppo, Anna (1997) 'Concezioni e pratiche della maternità tra le due guerre del Novecento', in D'Amelia (ed): 208–239.
Orrù, Luisa (1994) 'Partorire in casa e partorire in ospedale. Testimonianze biografiche orali di donne madri', in Orrù and Putzolu (eds): 153–242.
Orrù, Luisa and Putzolu, Fulvia (eds) (1994) *Il parto e la nascita in Sardegna tra tradizione e medicalizzazione*, Cagliari: Cuec.
Ortiz, Teresa (1993) 'From Hegemony to Subordination: Midwives in Early Modern Spain', in Marland (ed): 95–114.
Palumbo, Berardino (1991) *Madre, madrina. Rituale, parentela e identità in un paese del Sannio (S. Marco dei Cavoti)*, Milan: FrancoAngeli.
Pancino, Claudia (1984) *Il bambino e l'acqua sporca. Storia dell'assistenza al parto dalle mammane alle ostetriche (sec. XVI–XIX)*, Milan: FrancoAngeli.
Pancino, Claudia (1996) *Voglie materne. Storia di una credenza*, Bologna: Clueb.
Pancino, Claudia (2000) (ed) *Corpi. Storia, metafore, rappresentazioni fra medioevo ed età contemporanea*, Venice: Marsilio.
Pancino, Claudia (2006) 'La rappresentazione del nascituro nell'iconografia anatomica fra Cinque e Ottocento', in Pancino and d'Yvoire (2006): 17–125.
Pancino, Claudia (2009) 'Comari, levatrici, ostetriche. Alcune tappe della storia di un'antica professione femminile', in S. Chemotti, *Donne al lavoro. Ieri, oggi, domani*, Padua: Il Poligrafo: 115–128.
Pancino, Claudia (2010) 'Le baptême catholique des nouveau-nés', in Frydman, Szejer (eds): 423–430.
Pancino, Claudia (2011) '"Puerpera pura parens". Per una storia del rito di purificazione dopo il parto', in Lavenia and Paolin (eds): 55–66.
Pancino, Claudia (2015) *La natura dei bambini. Cura del corpo, malattie e medicine della prima infanzia tra Cinque e Settecento*, Bologna: Bononia University Press.
Pancino, Claudia and d'Yvoire, Jean (2006) *Formato nel segreto. Nascituri e feti fra immagini e immaginario dal XVI al XXI secolo*, Rome: Carocci.
Pancino Claudia and Pillon Daniela (1985) 'La nascita nelle tradizioni popolari veneziane dell'Ottocento', in Chinosi (ed): 114–128.
Panseri, Guido (1981) 'La nascita della polizia medica: l'organizzazione sanitaria nei vari stati italiani', in G. Micheli (ed) *Storia d'Italia, Annali 3, Scienza e tecnica*, Turin: Einaudi: 157–196.
Panzani, Jacopo (1774) 'Un parto difficile. Osservazioni del Sig. Dott. J. Panzani', *Giornale di medicina*, XII, 32.

Pardo-Tomàs, José and Martinez-Vidal, Alavar (2007) 'The Ignorance of Midwives: The Role of Clergyment in Spagnish Enlightenment Debates on Birth Care', in A. Cunningham (ed) *Medicine and Religion in Enlightenment Europe*, London: Routledge: 49–60.

Paré, Ambroise [1573] (1664) 'De la Génération de l'homme', in *Les Œuvres d'Ambroise Paré, conseiller et premier chirurgien du Roi*, Lyon: chez Iean Gregoire (XII ed.): 586–644.

Paré, Ambroise [1573] (1664) 'Des monstres et prodiges', in *Les Œuvres d'Ambroise Paré, conseiller et premier chirurgien du Roi*, Lyon: chez Iean Gregoire (XII ed): 645–701.

Park, Katharine (2006) *Secret of Women. Gender, Generation and the Origin of Human Dissection*, New York: Zone Books.

Park, Katharine (2018) 'Managing Childbirth and Fertility in Medieval Europe', in Hopwood, Flemming, Kassell (eds): chap. 11.

Parma, Anna (1981) 'La lunga noia della gravidanza. La medicina del Settecento di fronte alle donne incinte', *DWF. Donnawomanfemme*, 17: 90–102.

Parma, Anna (1984) 'Didattica e pratica ostetrica in Lombardia (1765–1791)', *Sanità, scienza e storia*, 2: 101–154.

Pascal Eugenie (2010) 'L'attente de l'héritier. Désir d'enfant, grossesse et délivrance dans les lettres de princesses (1560–1630)', in McClive and Pellegrin (eds): 139–166.

Pasi, Antonia (1992) *Contare gli uomini. Fonti, metodi, temi*, Milan: LED.

Pasi Antonia (1995) 'Mortalità infantile e cultura medica in Italia nel XIX secolo', *Bollettino di demografia storica*, 23: 71–96.

Passerini, Luigi (1853) *Storia degli stabilimenti di beneficenza della città di Firenze*, Florence: Tipografia Le Monnier.

Pastorello, Luigi (1838) 'Storia di una gastroisterotomia e riflessioni critiche siulla preferenza di lei all'embriotomia', *Memoriale della medicina contemporanea*, 1: 78–86.

Pastorello, Luigi (1854) *Trattato di ostetricia*, Pavia: Tip. Bizzoni.

Pedrini Diego, Dubbini Lucia (2018) 'The Accidental Smothering of Infants between the Sixteenth and Seventeenth Century through the Case of the Diocese of Jesi', *Annales Démographie Historique*, 136 (2): 159–177.

Pelaja, Margherita (1994) *Matrimonio e sessualità a Roma nell'Ottocento*, Rome, Bari: Laterza.

Pelaja, Margherita and Scaraffia, Lucetta (2008) *Due in una carne. Chiesa e sessualità nella storia*, Rome, Bari: Laterza.

Pennacchi Josephum (1884) *De abortu et embriotomia, seu de Commentarium in cap. 2 sect. 3 const. Apostolicae Sedis procurantes abortum effectu sequuto*, Romae: ex Typographia propaganda.

Perco, Daniela (1984) *Balie da latte. Una forma peculiare di migrazione temporanea*, Feltre: DCP.

Perco, Daniela (1999) 'Balie da latte e balie asciutte. Figure femminili nelle famiglie aristocratiche e borghesi di Venezia', in Filippini and Plebani (eds): 185–192.

Percovich Luciana (2005) *La coscienza del corpo. Donne, salute e medicina negli anni Settanta*, Milan: FrancoAngeli.

Perini, Lorenza (2014a) *Il corpo del reato. Parigi 1972-Padova 1973. Storia di due processi per aborto*, Bologna: BraDypUS.

Perini, Lorenza (2014b) *Dopo la 194. Un tempo storico, un dibattito culturale, la geografia di un territorio*, Rome: Aracne.

Perkins, Wendy (1996) *Midwifery and Medicine in Early Modern France: Louise Bourgeois*, Exeter: University of Exeter Press.

Perrella, Salvatore M. (2003) *Maria Vergine e Madre. La verginità feconda di Maria tra fede, storia e teologia*, Cinisello Balsamo (MI): Edizioni S. Paolo.

Perrot, Michelle (2002) *Donne in lotta per i diritti del loro corpo*, in Filippini, Plebani and Scattigno (eds): 3–18.

Pesenti, Tiziana (1985) 'Editoria medica tra Quattro e Cinquecento: L'Articella e il Fasciculus medicine', in E. Riondato (ed) *Trattati scientifici nel Veneto fra il XV e XVI secolo*, Venice: Università Internazionale dell'Arte: 1–28.

Personé, Girolamo (1781) *Della sezione della sinfisi del pube e del taglio cesareo. Trattato*, Venice: Milocco.

Petchesky Pollack, Rosalind (1995) 'The Body as Property: A Feminist Re-Vision', in F. D. Ginsburg, R. Rapp (eds) *Conceiving the New Order: The Global Politics of Reproduction*, Berkeley: University of California Press: 387–406.

Phan, Marie Claude (1975) 'Les déclarations de grossesse en France (XVIe–XVIIIe siècles). Essai institutionnel', *Revue d'histoire moderne et contemporaine*, 22: 61–88.

Phan, Marie Claude (1986) *Les amours illégitimes. Histoires de séduction en Languedoc (1676–1786)*, Paris: Éd. du CNRS.

Phan, Marie-Claude (1989) 'La séduction impunie ou la fin de la recherche de paternité', in M. F. Brive (ed) *Les femmes et la Révolution française*. Actes du colloque international de Toulouse, 12–14 avril 1989, Toulouse: Presses Universitaires du Mirail: vol II, 53–64.

Piazza, Marina (2009) *Attacco alla maternità. Donne, aziende, istituzioni*, Portogruaro: Nuovadimensione.

Pillon, Daniela (1981) 'La comare istruita nel suo uffizio. Alcune notizie sulle levatrici tra il '600 e il '700', *Atti dell'Istituto Veneto di Scienze, Lettere e Arti*, 140: 65–78.

Pinto-Correia, Clara (1997) *The Ovary of Eve. Egg and Sperm and Preformation*, Chicago: The University of Chicago Press.

Pirandello Luigi [1917] (1987) 'Donna Mimma', in M. Costanzo (ed) *Novelle per un anno*, Milan: Mondadori: 597–689.

Pirovano, Franca (1985) *Momenti di folklore in Brianza*, Palermo: Sellerio.

Pisa, Beatrice (2017) *Il Movimento Liberazione della Donna nel femminismo italiano. La politica, i vissuti, le esperienze (1970–1983)*, Rome: Aracne.

Pitch, Tamar (1998) *Un diritto per due. La costruzione giuridica di genere, sesso e sessualità*, Milan: Il Saggiatore.

Pizzini, Franca (ed) (1981) *Sulla scena del parto: luoghi, figure, pratiche*, Milan: FrancoAngeli.

Pizzini, Franca (1981) 'Il parto in ospedale: tragitto della donna e rituali dell'istituzione', in Pizzini (ed): 129–149.

Pizzini, Franca (1985) 'La partoriente come paziente', in Colombo, Pizzini, and Regalia (eds) (1985): 118–143.

Pizzini, Franca (1991) 'I movimenti internazionali delle donne e le tecniche riproduttive', in Resi, Costantini, Parolari *et alii* (1991): 69–77.

Pizzini, Franca and Lombardi, Lia (eds) (1995) *Madre provetta. Costi, benefici e limiti della procreazione artificiale*, Milan: FrancoAngeli.

Pizzini, Franca and Lombardi, Lia (1999) *Corpo medico e corpo femminile. Parto, riproduzione artificiale e menopausa*, Milan: FrancoAngeli.

Ployant, Teresa [1797] (1803) *Breve compendio dell'arte ostetricia di madama Teresa Ployant ostetrice maggiore e maestra negl'Incurabili di Napoli*, Fermo: Bazzi.

Politi, Marco (2008) 'Dignità da tutelare, ma la vita va difesa. Barragan: la Ivg è sempre un peccato', *la Repubblica*, 14 febbraio 2008.

Pomata, Gianna (1980) 'Madri illegittime tra Otto e Novecento', *Quaderni storici*, XV, 44 (2): 497–542.

Pomata, Gianna (1983) 'La storia delle donne: una questione di confine', in N. Tranfaglia (ed), *Il mondo contemporaneo. Gli strumenti della ricerca*, vol. 10, Florence, La Nuova Italia: 1435–1469.

Pomata, Gianna (1994a) *La promessa di guarigione. Malati e curatori in antico regime*, Rome, Bari: Laterza.

Pomata, Gianna (1994b) 'Legami di sangue, legami di seme. Consanguineità e agnazione nel diritto romano', *Quaderni storici*, XXIX, 86, (2): 299–334.

Pomata, Gianna (1995) *La "meravigliosa armonia". Il rapporto tra seni e utero dall'anatomia vascolare all'endocrinologia*, in Fiume (ed): 45–82.

Pomata, Gianna (1996) 'Blod Ties and Semen Ties': Consanguinity and Agnation in Roman Law', in M. J. Maynes, A. Waltner, B. Soland and U. Strasser (eds) *Gender, Kinship and Power: A Comparative and Interdisciplinary History*, New York, London: Routledge: 43–64.

Pomata, Gianna (2002) *Donne e Rivoluzione scientifica: verso un nuovo bilancio*, in Filippini, Plebani and Scattigno (eds): 165–192.

Pomata, Gianna (2013) 'Was there a Querelle des Femmes in Early Modern Medicine?', *Arenal*, 20: 313– 341.

Pomata, Gianna (2018) 'Innate Heat, Radical Moisture and Generation', in Hopwood, Flemming, Kassell (eds): chap. 14.

Portal, Paul (1685) *La pratique des accouchements, soutenue d'un grand nombre d'observations*, Paris: G. Martin.

Porter, Roy (ed) (1985) *Patiens and Practitioners. Lay Perceptions of Medicine in Pre-Industrial Society*, Cambridge: Cambridge University Press.

Povolo, Claudio (1978–1979) 'Note per uno studio dell'infanticidio nella Repubblica di Venezia nei secoli XV–XVIII', *Atti dell'Istituto Veneto di Scienze, Lettere e Arti*, 137: 106–130.

Pozzi, Lucia and Barona, Josep L. (2012) 'Vulnerable Babies. Late foetal, Neonatal and Infant Mortality in Europe (18th–20th Centuries)', *Annales Démographie Historique*, I, 123: 11–24.

Prasad, Aarathi (2012) *Like a Virgin: How Science Is Redesigning the Rules of Sex*, Richmond: Oneworld.

Premuda, Loris (1958) *Personaggi e vicende dell'ostetricia e della ginecologia nello studio di Padova*, Padua: Ediz. Attualità di ostetricia e ginecologia.

Preussler, Susanne (1985) *Hinter verschlossenen Türen. Ledige Frauen in der Münchner Gebäranstalt (1832–1853)*, München: Anthofer's Satz.

Prosperi, Adriano (2005) *Dare l'anima. Storia di un infanticidio*, Turin: Einaudi.

Prosperi, Adriano (ed) (2006) *Salvezza delle anime, disciplina dei corpi. Un seminario sulla storia del battesimo*, Pisa: Edizioni della Normale.

Pullan, Brian M. (2016) *Tolerance, Regulation and Rescu. Dishonoured women and abandoned children in Italy, 1300–1800*, Manchester: Manchester University Press.

Pulz, Waltraud (1996) 'Aux origines de l'obstétrique moderne en Allemagne (XVIe–XVIIIe siècle): accoucheurs contre matrones?', *Revue d'histoire moderne et contemporaine*, 43 (4): 593–617.

Pulz, Waltraud (1998) 'Gewaltsame Hilfe? Die Arbeit der Hebamme im Spiegel eines Gerichtskonflikts (1680–1685)?', in Schlumbohm, Duden, Gélis, Veit (eds): 68–83.

Pundel, Paul J. (1969) *Histoire de l'opération césarienne: Étude historique de la césarienne dans la médecine, l'art et la littérature, les religions et la législation*. Bruxelles: Presses académiques européennes.

Putzolu, Fulvia (2006) *Is levadoras. Levatrici della Sardegna tra Otto e Novecento*, Cagliari: Cuec.

Quine, Maria-Sophia (2013) *Population Politics in Twentieth Century Europe. Fascist Dictatorships and Liberal Democracies*, London, New York: Routledge.

Raffaele, Giovanni (1841) *Ostetricia teorico-pratica con atlante di figure tratte dai piu pregiati autori e migliorate secondo i progressi della scienza*, vols. 3, Naple: Battelli.

Ramazzini, Bernardino [1700] (2009) *The Diseases of Workers*, in F. Carnevale, M. Mendini and G. Moriani (eds) *Works* (English transl. by Christina Cawthra), Sommacampagna (VR): Cierre.

Randi Hutter, Epstein (2010) *Get Me Out: A History of Childbirth from the Garden of Eden to the Sperm Bank*, New York: W. W. Norton & Co Inc.

Rangoni, Laura (2005) *La grande madre. Il culto del femminile nella storia*, Milan: Xenia.

Ranisio, Gianfranca (1996) *Venire al mondo. Credenze, pratiche e rituali del parto*, Rome: Meltemi.

Rattner Gelbart, Nina (1998) *The King's Midwife. A History and Mystery of Mme du Coudray*, Berkeley, Los Angeles: University of California Press.

Reagan, Leslie J. (1997) *When Abortion Was a Crime: Women, Medicine, and Law in the United States (1867–1973)*, Berkeley: University of California Press.

Regolamento della Casa di Dio (1759) *Degli statuti e regolamenti del grande spedale degl'infermi di Modena ed opere annesse libri tre stesi, e compilati per comando di s.a.s. il signor duca Francesco Terzo*, Modena: Bartolomeo Soliani: I, XIV.

Reggiani, Flores (2008) 'La famiglia dell'Ospedale nei secoli', in M. Canella, L. Dodi and F. Reggiani (eds) *"Si consegna questo figlio". L'assistenza all'infanzia e alla maternità dalla Ca' Granda alla Provincia di Milano (1456–1920)*, Milan: Università di Milano-Skira: 35–103.

Reggiani, Flores (2014) *Sotto le ali della colomba. Famiglie assistenziali e relazioni di genere a Milano dall'Età moderna alla Restaurazione*, Rome: Viella.

Reggiani, Flores (2018) 'Padri naturali fra tribunali civili e brefotrofi (Milano 1816–1880)', *Genesis. Rivista della Società Italiana delle Storiche*, 17 (1): 81–104.

Remotti, Francesco (2008) *Contro natura. Una lettera al papa*, Rome, Bari: Laterza.

Renzetti, Emanuela (1988) 'La sessualità nei libri dei segreti del XVI e XVII secolo', in Bock and Nobili (eds): 45–68.

Resi, Isetta, Costantini, Walter, Parolari, Letizia *et alii* (1991) *Tra tecnologia e desiderio. Un figlio*, Cagliari: La Tarantola.

Revelli, Nuto (1985) *L'anello forte. La donna: storie di vita contadina*, Turin: Einaudi.

Ribero, Aida (ed) (2011) *Procreare la vita, filosofare la morte. Maternità e femminismo*, Padua: Il Poligrafo.

Rich, Adrienne (1976) *Of Woman Born. Motherhood as Experience and Institution*, New York: W. W. Norton & Co Inc. 1976 (transl. it. 1977: *Nato di donna. Cosa significa per gli uomini esser nati da un corpo di donna*, Milan: Garzanti).

Riddle, John M. (1992) *Contraception and Abortion from the Ancient World to the Renaissance*, Cambridge (MA): Harvard University Press.

Rifkin, A. Benjamin, Ackerman, J. Michael and Folkenberg, Judith (2006) *Human Anatomy. Depicting the Body from the Renaissance to Today*, London: Thames & Hudson.

Rigau-Pérez, José G. (1995) 'Surgery at the Service of Theology: Postmortem Cesarean Sections in Puerto Rico and the Royal Cedula of 1804', *Hispanic American Historical Review*, 75, 3: 377–404.

Rigon, Ferdinando (1985) 'La tazza della comare', in Chinosi (ed): 80–83.

Rigotti, Francesca (2010) *Partorire con il corpo e con la mente. Creatività, filosofia, maternità*, Turin: Bollati Boringhieri.

Rituale Romanum [1614] (1740), *Pauli V Pont. Max. Jussu editum in quo quae parochis ad administrationem Sacramentorum, ad Benedictiones, Conjurationes necessaria censentur accurate sunt posita*, Venetiis: Pezzana.

Riva, Giuseppe (1860) *Manuale di Filotea del sacerdote milanese Giuseppe Riva*, Milan: Serafino Maiocchi (10th ed.).

Rizzo, Sebastiano (1776) *Della origine e dei progressi dell'arte ostetricia prolusione di Sebastiano Rizzo. recitata il giorno 17. settembre 1776*, Venezia: stamperia Carlo Palese.

Robilant, Andrea Di (2008) *Lucia in the age of Napoleon*, London: Faber and Faber.

Roger, Jacques (1997) *The Life Sciences in Eighteenth-Century French Thought*, K. R. Benson (ed), transl. by R. Ellrich, Stanford (CA): Stanford University Press (1st Franch ed. 1963).

Rollet, Catherine (1978) 'Allaitement, mise en nourrice et mortalité infantile en France à la fin du XIXe siècle', *Population*, 6: 1190–1203.

Rollet, Catherine (1983) 'L'allaitement artificiel des nourrissons avant Pasteur', *Annales de démographie historique*, 1: 81–91.

Rollet, Chaterine (1990) *La politique à l'egard de la petite enfance sous la Troisième republique*, Paris: INED éditions.

Rollet, Catherine (1992) 'Biberon d'hier et d'aujourd'hui: une page de l'histoire de l'enfance', *Cahiers de la puéricultrice*, 4: 35–42.

Rollet, Catherine (1996) 'Pierre Budin, l'obstétricien pédiatre ou le début de la médecine périnatale', *Devenir*, 8 (3): 61–75.

Rollet, Catherine (2001) *Les enfants au XIXe siècle*, Paris: Hachette.

Rollet, Catherine and Morel, Marie-France (2000) *Des bébés et des hommes. Traditions et modernité des soins aux tout-petits*, Paris: Albin Michel

Ronchi, Ermes M., Ravasi, Marco, Montagna, Davide M. *et alii* (2000) *La Madonna nell'attesa del parto. Capolavori del patrimonio italiano del '300-'400*, Milan: Scheiwiller.

Ronchi, Ermes M. (2000) 'Iconografia della Madonna del parto', in Ronchi, Ravasi, Montagna *et alii* (2000): 27–33.

Ronsin, Francis (1980) *La Grève des ventres. Propagande malthusienne et baisse de la natalité en France, XIXe–XXe siècles*, Paris: Aubier Montaigne.

Roschini, Gabriele M. (1969) *Maria Santissima nella storia della salvezza: Trattato completo di mariologia alla luce del Concilio Vaticano II*, Isola del Liri: Pisani ed.

Rose, Lionel (1986) *The Massacre of the Innocents: Infanticide in Britain, 1800–1939*, London: Routledge.

Rosen von Rosenstein, Nils (1776) *The Diseases of Children, and Their Remedies*, transl. by A. Sparrman, London: T. Cadell (1st Swedish ed. 1764).

Rösslin, Eucharius (Rodhion) [1513] (1910) *Der Swangern Frauwen und Hebammen Rosengarten* (1513), München: Carl Kunhn, 1910 (fac-similar reprint).

Rösslin, Eucharius ('Rodhion) (1537) *De partu hominis et quae circa ipsum accidunt. Libellus, D. Eucharii Rodhionis*, Venetiis: ex Ion. Bapt. Pederzani (latin transl. of Eucharius Rösslin junior).

Rothschild, Joan (ed) (1983) *Machina ex dea: Feminist Perspectives on Technology*, New York, Oxford: Pergamon.

Rousselle, Aline (1980) 'Observation féminine et idéologie masculine: Le corps de la femme d'après les médecins grecs', *Annales: Économies, Sociétés, Civilisations*, 35: 1089–1115.

Rousselle, Aline (1992) 'Body Politics in Ancient Rome', in Duby and Perrot (dir) (1992a): 296–336.

Rousset, François (1581) *Traitté nouveau de l'hystérotomotokie ou enfantement caesarien qui est extraction de l'enfant par incision latérale du ventre et matrice de la femme grosse ne pouvant autrement accoucher. Et ce sans préjudicer à la vie ny de l'un ny de l'autre, ny empécher la faecondité maternelle par après*, Paris: Denys du Val.

Rozée, Virginie and de La Rochebrochard, Elise (2010) 'L'accès à l'assistance médicale à la procréation en France: reflet de la norme sociale procréative?', *Santé, société et solidarité*, 9 (2): 109–114.

Rubiera Cancelas, Carla (2015) 'Uso y abuso del cuerpo femenino. Mujeres y reproduccción en las sociedades greco-romanas', in Chemotti and La Rocca (eds): 918–930.

Rueff, Jacob (1580) *De conceptu et generatione hominis, de matrice et heius partibus, nec non de conditione infantis in utero et gravidarum cura et officio*, Francofurti ad Moenum: Georgium Coruinum (1st German edition *Ein schön lustig Trostbüchle von den Empfengknussen und Geburten der Menschen*, 1554).

Rusnock, Andrea (1999) 'Biopolitics: Political arithmetic in the Enlightenment', in W. Clark, J. Golinski and S. Schaffer (eds) *The Sciences in Enlightened*, Chicago: University of Chicago: 49–69.

Rusnock, Andrea (2002) *Vital Accounts: Quantifying Health and Population in Eighteenth-Century England and France*, Cambridge: Cambridge University Press.

Rusnock, Andrea (2018) 'Biopolitics and the Invention of Population', in Hopwood, Flemming, Kassell (eds): chap. 23.

Sacombe, Jean-François (1792) *La Luciniade, ou l'Art des accouchemens, poème didactique par le citoyen Sacombe*, Paris: Garnéry, Devaux, Levigneur.

Sacombe, Jean-François (1798a) *Plus d'opération césarienne, ou le Voeu de l'humanité*, Paris: Impr. de H.-L. Perronneau.

Sacombe Jean-François (1798b) *Les douzes mois de l'Ecole anti-césarienne. Ouvrage périodique*, Paris: chez Gabon.

Sage Pranchère, Nathalie (2017) *L'école des sages-femmes. Naissance d'un corps professionnel (1786–1917)*, Tours: Presses universitaires François Rabelais.

Sanchez Arcàs, Ruperto (1950) *Historia de la Operaciòn cesarea en Espana*, Madrid: Marbàn.

Sánchez Romero, Margarita and Cid López, Rosa (eds) (2018) *Motherhood and Infancies in the Mediterranean in Antiquity*, Oxford: Oxbow Books.

Saint-Germain, Charles (de) (1651) *Traitté de fausse couches, enseignant la nature de faux germes, embryons, avortons et moles, les accidens qui précèdent et accompagnent les fausses couches, le prognostic, les precautions et les remedes neccessaires pour assister et secourir les femmes*, Paris: Cardin Besogne.

Saraceno, Chiara (1995) 'Costruzione della paternità e della maternità', in Angelo, Del Boca, Massimo, Legnani and Mario, G. Rossi (eds) *Il regime fascista. Storia e storiografia*, Rome, Bari: Laterza: 475–506.

Saraceno, Chiara (1997) 'Verso il 2000: la pluralizzazione delle esperienze e delle figure materne', in D'Amelia (ed): 218–351.

Saraceno, Chiara (2012) *Coppie e famiglie. Non è una questione di natura*, Milan: Feltrinelli.

Sardi, Paolo (1975) *L'aborto ieri e oggi*, Brescia: Paideia.

Saverio Trincia, Francesco (2003) 'Procreazione assistita e diritti dell'embrione', *Genesis. Rivista della Società Italiana delle Storiche*, 2 (1): 197–202.

Savonarola, Michele [1460?] (1952) *Il trattato ginecologico-pediatrico in volgare di Michele Savonarola. Ad mulieres ferrarienses de regimine pregnantium et noviter natorum usque ad septennium Michaelis Savonarolle Patavi liber incipit feliciter*, L. Belloni (ed), Milan: Società italiana di ostetricia e ginecologia.

Sbisà, Marina (ed) (1992) *Come sapere il parto. Storia, scenari, linguaggi*, Turin: Rosenberg & Sellier.

Sbisà, Marina (1992) 'Parlando di parto. Vissuti e saperi nei discorsi delle donne', in Sbisà (ed): 185–237.

Scaramuzza, Emma (2004) *La santa e la spudorata. Alessandrina Ravizza e Sibilla Aleramo: amicizia, politica e scrittura*, Naples: Liguori.

Scattigno Anna (1997) *La figura materna tra emancipazionismo e femminismo*, in D'Amelia (ed): 273–299.

Schiebinger, Londa (1989) *The Mind Has No Sex? Women in the Origins of Modern Science*, Cambridge (MA): Harvard University Press.
Schiebinger, Londa (1993) *Nature's Body. Gender in the Making of Modern Sciences*, Boston: Rutgers University Press.
Schlumbohm, Jürgen, Duden, Barbara, Gélis, Jacques and Veit, Patrice (1998) (eds) *Rituale der Geburt. Eine Kulturgeschichte*, München: C.H. Beck.
Schlumbohm, Jürgen (1998) 'Der Blick des Arztes, oder: wie Gebärende zu Patientinnen wurden. Das Entbindungshospital der Universität Göttingen um 1800', in Schlumbohm, Duden, Gélis and Veit (eds): 170–191.
Schlumbohm, Jürgen (2001) 'The Pregnant Women are Here for the Sake of the Teaching Institution': The Lying-in Hospital of Göttingen University, 1751 to c. 1830', *Social History of Medicine*, 14 (1): 59–78.
Schlumbohm, Jürgen (2007) 'The Practice of Practical Education: Male Students and Female Apprentices in the Lying-in Hospital of Göttingen University, 1792–1815', *Medical History*, 51: 3–36.
Schlumbohm, Jürgen (2012) *Lebendige Phantome. Ein Entbindungshospital und seine Patientinnen 1751–1830*, Göttingen: Wallstein Verlag.
Schlumbohm Jürgen (2018) *Verbotene Liebe, verborgene Kinder. Das Geheime Buch des Göttinger Geburtshospitals, 1794–1857*, Göttingen: Wallstein Verlag.
Schmid, Verena (1992) 'Figura e compiti dell'ostetrica: problemi aperti e possibilità di evoluzione', in Sbisà (ed): 117–138.
Schmitt, Jean-Claude (1994) *Les revenants. Les vivants et les morts dans la société médiévale*, Paris: Gallimard.
Schrader, Catharina [1693] (1987) *Mother and child were saved. The Memoirs (1693–1740) of the Frisian Midwife Catharina Schrader*, transl. and annotated by H. Marland, Amsterdam: Rodopi.
Schweber, Libby (2006) *Disciplining Statistics: Demography and Vital Statistics in France and England, 1830–1885*, Durham (NC): Duke University Press.
Seidel Menchi, Silvana (2000) 'Les pèlerinages des enfantes mort-nés. Des rituels correctifs pour un dogme impopulaire?', in Ph. Boutry, P. A. Fabre and D. Julia (eds) *Rendre ses vœux. Les identités pèlerines dans l'Europe moderne (XVIe–XVIIIe siècles)*, Paris: Éditions de l'EHESS: 139–158.
Selmini, Rossella (1987) *Profili di uno studio storico sull'infanticidio*, Milan: Giuffré.
Semmelweis Ignác [1861] (1983) *The Etiology, Concept and Prophylaxis of Childbed Fever*, transl. by C. K. Carter, Madison: The University of Wisconsin Press.
Serini, Rosalba (1992) 'Dalla casa all'ospedale: l'istituzionalizzazione della nascita', *I quaderni dell'associazione culturale Livia Laverani Donini*, V, 8–9: 21–49.
Shalev, Carmel (1990) *Birth Power: The Case for Surrogacy*, New Haven: Yale University Press.
Sharpe, James A. (1984) *Crime in Early Modern England: 1550–1750*, London: Longman.
Shorter, Edward (1975) *The Making of the Modern Family*, New York: Basic Books.
Shorter, Edward (1982) *History of Women's Bodies*, New York: Basic Books.
Shorter, Edward (1985) 'The Management of Normal Deliveries and the Generation of William Hunter', in Bynum and Porter (1985): chap. 13.
Siebold, Eduard Caspar. J. von (1891–1892) *Essai d'une histoire de l'obstétricie*, Paris: G. Steinheil (1st German ed. 1839).
Siegemund, Justine [1690] (2005) *The Court Midwife*, ed. and transl. by Lynne Tatlock, Chicago: Chicago University Press.
Simon, Jean-François (1743) 'Recherches sur l'opération Césarienne', *Memoires de l'Accademie Royale de Chirurgie*, I: 210–254.

Simmons, Williams (1798) *Reflections on the Propriety of Performing the Caesarean Operations: To Wich are Added Observations on Cancer and Experiments on the Supposed Origin of Cow-Pox*, Manchester, London: Clarkes.
Sissa, Giulia (1983) 'Il corpo della donna: lineamenti per una ginecologia filosofica', in Campese, Manuli and Sissa (1983): 83–148.
Sissa, Giulia (1987) *Le corps virginal. La virginité féminine en Grece*, Paris: Vrin (1st Engl. Transl. 1990).
Sissa, Giulia (1992) 'The Sexual Philosophies of Plato and Aristotle', in Duby and Perrot (dir) (1992a): 46–81.
Söll, Georg (1981) *Storia dei dogmi mariani*, Rome: Las.
Sömmering, Samuel Thomas (1799) *Icones embryonum humanorum*, Frankfurt: Varrentrap.
Speert, Harold (1973) *Iconographia gyniatrica: A Pictorial History of Gynecology and Ostetrics*, Philadelphia: F.A. Davis.
Sperling, Jutta Gisela (ed) (2013) *Medieval and Renaissance Lactations. Images, Rhetorics, Practices*, Aldershot: Ashgate.
Spina, Elena (1998) *Ostetriche e Midwives. Spazi di autonomia e identità corporativa*, Milan: FrancoAngeli.
Spinks, Jennifer (2018) 'Monstrous Births and Diabolical Seed', in Hopwood, Flemming, Kassell (eds): Exhibits 13.
Steffani, Carlo (1839) *Manuale pei mm. rr. Arcipreti e parroci, contenente le leggi sovrane le antiche e le vicereali risoluzioni, i decreti, i regolamenti, le istruzioni relative alle incombenze che furono loro appoggiate per ciò che riguarda l'amministrazione dello stato*, Padova: Tip. Seminario.
Stone, Lawrence (1977) *The Family, Sex and Marriage in England 1500–1800*, London: Weidenfeld and Nicolson.
Stone, Sarah (1737) *A Complete Practice of Midwifery. Consisting of Upwards Forty Cases or Observations in That Valuable Art, Selected from Many Others, in the Course of a Very Extensive Practice*, London: T. Cooper.
Tassoni, Giovanni (1973) *Arti e tradizioni popolari. Le inchieste napoleoniche sui costumi e le tradizioni nel Regno d'Italia*, Bellinzona: Casagrande.
Teitelbaum, Michael S. and Winter, Jay M. (1985) *The Fear of Population Decline*, London: Accademic Press.
Terpstra, Nicholas (2005) *Abandoned Children of the Italian Renaissance: Orphan in Florence and Bologna*, Baltimore: Johns Hopkins University Press.
Terzian, Emanuela and Regalia, Anita (1992) 'Né arte, né scienza: stereotipi e ambiguità dei modelli di assistenza ostetrica', in Sbisà (ed): 82–116.
Testart, Alain (2010) *La Déesse et le Grain. Trois essais sur les religions néolithiques*, Paris: Errance.
Tetsa, Marcella and Tsotra, Kyriaki (2010) 'History of Breasteeding', in Fanos and Yurdakök (eds): 97–108.
Thébaud, Françoise (1986) *Quand nos grand mères donnaient la vie. La maternité en France dans l'entre deux-guerres*, Lyon: Presses Universitaires de Lyon.
Thirion, Marie (2010) 'Histoire de l'allaitement', in Frydman and Szejer (eds): 232–241.
This, Bernard (1982) *La Requête des enfants à naître*, Paris: Seuil.
Thomas, Mary (ed) (1997) *Post War Mothers: Childbirth Letters to Grantly Dick-Read (1946–1956)*, Rochester: University of Rochester Press.
Thomasset, Claude (1992) 'The Nature of Woman', in Duby and Perrot (dir) (1992b): 43–69.
Toaldo, Giuseppe (1787) *Tavole di vitalità composte da d. Giuseppe Toaldo preposito della SS. Trinità professore e accademico di Padova*, Padua: stamperia Gio. Antonio Conzatti.

Totelin, Laurence M.V. (2009) *Hippocratic Recipes. Oral and Written Transmission of Pharmacological Knowledge in Fifth and Fourth-Century Greece*, Leiden, Boston: Brill: 127–128.

Towler, Jean T. and Bramall, Joan B. (1986) *Midwives in History and Society*, London: Croom Helm.

Trevisan, Francesco (1823) *Della preservazione dei bambini. Memoria pubblicata nell'occasione delle nozze Andretta Bernardi-Francesco Trevisan*, Treviso: Tip. Trento.

Trexler, Richard (1973) 'Infanticide in Florence. New Sources and First Results', *History of Childhood Quarterly*, 1 (1): 98–116.

Tsiaras, Alexander and Werth, Barry (2002) *From Conception to Birth. A Life Unfolds*, Doubleday- New York: Doubleday Books ed.

Turner Éduard (1880) 'Bibliographie de Francois Rousset', *Annales de Gynécologie*, 14: 1–25.

Van der Lugt, Maaike (2004) *Le ver, le démon et la Vierge: Les théories médiévales de la génération extraordinaire: Une étude sur les rapports entre théologie, philosophie naturelle et médecine*, Paris: Les Belles Lettres.

Van der Lugt, Maaike (2018) 'Formed Fetuses and Healthy Children in Scholastic Theology, Medicine and Law', in Hopwood, Flemming, Kassell (eds): chap. 12.

Van Gennep, Arnold [1909] (2019) *The Rites of Passage*, David I. Kertzer (intr.), transl. by Monika B. Vizedom, Gabrielle L. Caffee (1st French ed. 1909).

Van Teijlingen, Edwin, Lois, George W., McCaffery, Peter and Porter, Maureen (eds) (2004) *Midwifery and the Medicalization of Childbirth. Comparative Perspectives*, New York: Nova Science Publishers.

Vannozzi, Francesca (ed) (2005) *Figure femminili (e non) intorno alla nascita. La storia in Siena dell'assistenza alla partoriente e al nascituro XVIII–XX secc.*, Siena: Protagonisti Editori.

Vantini, Vignola, Lucia (2007) 'Maria', in Diotima (ed) *L'ombra della madre*, Naples: Liguori: 101–115.

Vasset, Sophie (2013) 'La querelle des accocheurs et des sages-femmes en Grande-Bretagne: l'exemple d'Elizabeth Nihell', *Littérature Classique*, 81: 243–255.

Vegetti, Finzi, Silvia (1991) *Scenari dell'immaginario*, in Resi, Costantini and Parolari (eds): 79–90.

Velpeau, Alfred Armand (1835) *Traité complet de l'art des accouchemens, ou tocologie théorique et pratique, avec un abrégé des maladies qui compliquent la grossesse, le travail et les couches, et de celles qui affectent les enfans nouveau-nés*, Bruxelles: H. Dumont (Third ed.).

Venturi, Franco (1969) *Settecento riformatore. Da Muratori a Beccaria*, vol. 1, Turin: Einaudi.

Verardo Zeviani, Giovanni (1775) *Su le numerose morti dei bambini. Dissertazione accademica*, Verone: stamperia Moroni.

Verdier, Yvonne (1979) *Façon de dire, façon de faire. La laveuse, la couturière, la cuisinière*, Paris: Gallimard.

Verdon, Thimoty (2005) *Mary in Western Art*, Washington: Pope John Paul II Center.

Vergès, Françoise (2017) *Les ventres des femmes. Capitalisme, racialisation, féminisme*, Paris: Albin Michel.

Vernant, Jean-Pierre (2001) *La mort héroïque chez les Grecs*, Nantes: Pleins Feux.

Vernant, Jean-Pierre (2005) *Pandora, la première femme*, Paris: Bayard.

Vezzosi, Elisabetta (1999) 'The Language of Motherhood and Welfare: Mothers' Letters to the Children's Bureau', in B. Bosco Tedeschini Lalli and M. Vaudagna (eds), *Brave New Words. Strategies of Language and Communication in the United States of the 1930s*, Amsterdam: VU University Press: 30–43.

Vezzosi, Elisabetta (2002) *Madri e Stato. Politiche sociali negli Stati Uniti del Novecento*, Rome: Carocci.

Viana, Odorico and Vozza, Francesco (1933) *L'ostetricia e la ginecologia in Italia*, Milan: Società italiana di ostetricia e ginecologia.

Vicarelli, Giovanna (1997) *Alle radici della politica sanitaria in Italia. Società e salute da Crispi al fascismo*, Bologna: Il Mulino.
Vidossi, Giuseppe (1960) *Saggi e scritti minori di folklore*, Turin: Bottega d'Erasmo.
Vienne, Florence (2018) 'Eggs and Sperm as Germ Cells', in Hopwood, Flemming, Kassell (eds): chap. 28.
Vigarello, Georges (1993) *Le sain et le malsain: santé et mieux-être depuis le Moyen-Age*, Paris: Seuil.
Villani, Stefano (2006) 'Il battesimo nel Book of Common Prayer', in Prosperi (ed): 551–571.
Visentin, Maria Cecilia (2000) 'La Madonna del parto nella pietà popolare', in Ronchi, Ravasi, Montagna *et alii* (2000): 38–41.
Vitiello, Angelica (2006) 'Il tempo delle ostetriche condotte: formazione e autonomia professionale. Un percorso di ricerca tra carte d'archivio e racconti', in E. Fasano Guarini, A. Galoppini and A. Peretti (eds) *Fuori dall'ombra. Studi di storia delle donne nella provincia di Pisa*, Pisa: Plus-Università di Pisa: 461–514.
Wanrooij, Bruno P. F. (1990) *Storia del pudore. La questione sessuale in Italia 1860–1940*, Bologna: Il Mulino.
Warner, Marina (1976) *Alone of All Her Sex: The Myth and the Cult of the Virgin Mary*, London: Weidenfeld and Nicolson.
Wertz, Richard W. and Wertz, Dorothy C. (1989) *Lying-In: A History of Childbirth in America*, New York: The Free Press.
Wiesner, Merry E. (1993) *Women and Gender in Early Modern Europe*, Cambridge: Cambridge University Press.
Williams, Susan A. (1997) *Women in the Twentieth Century: A History of the National Birthday Trust Fund 1928–93*, Thrupp: Sutton Publishing.
Willson, Perry (2010) *Women in Twentieth-Century Italy*, New York: Palgrave MacMillan.
Wilson, Adrian (1985) 'William Hunter and the Varieties of Man-Midwifery', in Bynum and Porter (eds): chap. 12.
Wilson, Adrian (1995) *The Making of Man-Midwifery: Childbirth in England, 1600–1770*, Cambridge (MA): Harvard University Press.
Witkowski, Gustave-Joseph (1887) *Histoire des accouchements chez tous les peuples*, Paris: Steinheil.
Witkowski, Gustave-Joseph (1890) *Les accouchements à la cour*, Paris: Steinheil.
Witkowski, Gustav-Joseph (1891) *Accoucheurs et sages-femmes célèbres: esquisses biographiques*, Paris: Steinheil.
Wolf, Jacqueline H. (2009), *Deliver Me from Pain: Anesthesia and Birth in America*, Baltimore: Johns Hopkins University Press.
Wolf, Jacqueline H. (2018) *Caesarean Section. An American History of Risk, Technology, and Consequence*, Baltimore: Johns Hopkins University Press.
Woods, Robert (2009) *Death Before Birth: Fetal Health and Mortality In Historical Perspective*, Oxford: Oxford University Press.
Woods, Robert and Gallery, Chris (2014) *Mrs Stone & Dr Smellie: Eighteenth-Century Midwives and Their Patients*, Liverpool: Liverpool University Press.
Woolf, Stuart (1986) *The Poor in Western Europe in the Eighteenth and Nineteenth Centuries*, London: Methuen.
Yan, Thomas (1992) 'The Division of the Sexes in Roman Law', in Duby and Perrot (dir) (1992a): 83–137.
Young, John H. (1944) *Cesarean Section. The History and Development of the Operation from the Earliest Times*, London: H. K. Lewis & Company.

Zanetti, Zeno (1892) *La medicina delle nostre donne*, Città di Castello: Lapi.

Zanotto, Andrea (1996) 'Una forma di controllo della natalità illegittima nel granducato di Toscana: la circolare "de tuendo foetu"', *Bollettino di demografia storica*, 26 (2): 183–202.

Zglinicki, Friedrich (1983) *Geburt: eine Kulturgeschichte in Bildern*, Dusseldorf: Vestermann V.

Zocchi, Paola (1999) 'L'assistenza agli esposti e alle partorienti nell'ospedale maggiore di Milano e nell'ospizio di S. Caterina alla Ruota tra Sette e Ottocento', *SIDES. Bollettino di demografia storica*, 30–31: 165–184.

Zocchi, Paola (2003) 'Nascita innaturale e parto cesareo: problemi e paure tra Sette e Ottocento', in A. Menzione (ed) *Specchio della popolazione. La percezione dei fatti e problemi demografici nel passato*, Udine: Forum: 81–104.

Zucal, Silvano (2017) *Filosofia della nascita*, Brescia: Morcelliana.

Zuccolin, Gabriella (2017) 'E cussi se fanno homicidiale di propri fioli': i parti genellari tra teorie mediche e implicazioni morali dall'antichità al tardo Medioevo', in Foscati, Gislon Dopfel and Parmeggiani (eds): 77–94.

INDEX

Note: Page numbers followed by "n" denote endnotes.

abandonment of newborns 123–125; *see also* foundling hospitals
abortion: in the ancient world 66–67; in the feminist movement 248–249; fight against in medieval and early modern Christianity 53, 67–69; forced in Hitler's Germany 241; increased repression during Fascism 239; and midwives 143, 148–149; therapeutic 219, 220, 221, 249; *see also* foetus; midwives
Abortion Act 249
Abortion Law Reform Association (ALRA) 249
Abraham 130
Aburel Bogdan, Eugène 254
Académie de Médecine (Paris) 28, 201, 215, 219
Académie des Sciences (Paris) 177, 179
accoucheur 77, 166, 174, 183, 184, 197, 216, 219
Adimari Strozzi, Fiammetta 153
Adonis 21
adsestrices (assestrices) 145
Aeschylus 11, 22
afterbirth *see* placenta
Agatha, Saint 112
Aglietta, Maria Adelaide 249
Agnodice (or Agnodike) 145
Agrippa, Marcus Vipsanius 107
Agripino birth 107
Akin, Todd William 17

Albertus Magnus (Albert the Great) 47
Alcmena 80
Alfonso II d'Este, Duke of Ferrara 70
Ambrose of Milan, Saint 31, 59
amniorrhexis 247
amniotic sac 97–98, 107; fluid 259
Amphidromía 118, 129
amulets and talismans 61, 116, 148
Anabaptists 135
anaesthesia during childbirth: differences in use in geographical areas 265–266; epidural 254; experimentations 252–254; and increased hospitalisation 245; *see also* drugs; Italian Association of birth in analgesia; National Twilight Sleep Association
analogical medicine *see* sympathetic medicine
anatomical wax dummies 167
anatomic-mathematical school 180–182
Anaxagoras 13, 18
animalculi 207
animalculism 207–208
Anne of Austria (of Habsburg), Queen of France 82
Anne, Saint 79, 82
Anthony of Padua, Saint (Fernando Martins de Bulhões) 61
antibiotics 202
antisepsis and lower mortality 202, 244
Antoninus Pierozzi of Florence, Saint 96

Apatourìa 129
Apocalypse of Ezra 64
Apollo 12, 139
Appropriate technology for birth 257, 265
Arabic medicine 19, 45
Aranzi, Julius Caesar 51
Arcanum divinae sapientiae, encyclical 222
arcuccio 123
Areopagus of Athens 12, 22
Aristophanes 149
Aristotle: *Generation of Animals* 13, 14, 17, 26, 65; generation theories 14–15; hierarchies in generation 17–18; and Scholasticism 16; women as the colder sex 14; *see also* generation
Armstrong, George 224
Arrias, E. 252
arrière-faix 97
Artemis 23
artificial insemination 261–264; differences between the Catholic and the Protestant Churches about 262; first experiments 241, 260; laws on 262
artificial premature labour 180, 217, 219, 220
Asclepius 21, 139
Association for Improvements in Maternity Services 257
Associazione Italiana Educazione Demografica (AIED) 250
Associazione nazionale ostetriche parto a domicilio e case di maternità (National association of midwives for home births and maternity homes) 257
Asson, Michelangelo 220
Astruc, Jean 180, 224
Athena: her birth 21–22
Augustine Aurelius of Hippo, Saint 32, 33, 46, 47, 53, 63, 131, 135, 136, 137
Aussegnung der Wöchnerin 119
Avicenna (*Abū ʿAlī Ibn Sīnā*) 16, 19, 41, 45, 55, 88, 107

baby-farming 225
Balaskas, Janet 256
balia 110
balio 110
Ballexserd, Jacques 224
baptism: "conditional" 66, 134, 136, 138, 150; the Council of Trent on 117, 132, 134–136; during labour 141; Luther's Sermon on 135; as "social birth" 130–132; *see also* rituals; Limbo; post-mortem Caesarean section; sanctuaries *à répit*
Barragan, Javier Lozano 221

barrenness *see* infertility
Barthez, Paul-Joseph 181
Bartholin, Caspar (junior) 208
Bartholin, Thomas 208
Baruffaldi, Girolamo 134, 141
bath: daily recommended by Enlightenment paediatricians 224; in a difficult birth 85; of newborn 103, 106–107
Baudelocque, Jean-Louis 174, 176, 177, 179, 180, 181, 183
Beatrice Mary Victoria Feodore, Princess of the UK 252
Beauvalet-Boutouyrie, Scarlett 198
Beauvoir, Simone de 249
bed: after childbirth 103, 116–118; delivery in 85, 88; and medicalisation 198
Bellet, Isaac 209, 229n17
belts: holy protecting 46, 61, 82; husbands' in childbirth 46; removed in pregnancy and childbirth 46, 58, 79; *see also* relics
Benedict XIV (Prospero Lorenzo Lambertini), Pope 121, 139, 212
Benedict XVI (Joseph Aloisius Ratzinger), Pope 137, 222
Bequet, Marie 235
Berengario, Jacopo da Carpi 52
Beretta Molla, Gianna, Saint 222
Better Babies movement 253
Bettini, Maurizio 45
Bianchi, Giovanni Battista 209–212
Bible 26, 28, 114, 118, 123, 130, 135; *see also* Genesis; Leviticus
Bigeschi, Giovanni 66
biopower 3, 5, 13, 160, 161–162, 236, 250
birth *see* childbirth
birth decrease data (20th century) 236
birthing chair 84–86; described by Soranus 88; its spread in the early modern age 87–88; as a symbol of the midwife's profession in Venice 146–147; *see also obstetricalis sella*
birthmarks *see* cravings
Blondel, James 209, 228n16
blood, menstrual *see* menstruation
bloodletting during pregnancy 60–61, 62
Blunt, John (pseud. of S. W. Fores) 184, 186, 187
Boccia, Maria Luisa 259
bodily humours *see* humours
body: female as colder and humid 14; female as earth/field 10–13; one-sex model 15; representation in Hobbes 180–181; self-determination in feminism

248; social body in the Enlightenment 161–162
Boër, Johann Lucas 176, 180, 182
Bonica, John 254
Bonino, Emma 249
bonne mère 144
Bonnet, Charles 260
Borgia, Lucrezia 153
Borromeo, Carlo, Cardinal of Milan 123, 150
Boston Women's Health Book Collective 248
bottle-feeding 247
Bourgeois, Louise Boursier 43, 60, 61
Boyd, Mary 253
Boyle, Robert 65
Bozzini, Philipp 258
Bradley, Robert A. 256
Braibanti, Lorenzo 256
Braibanti, Paride 256
Braidotti, Rosi 18
breast milk: formation in ancient medicine 109; puerperal fever caused by a stagnation of 102–103; see also breastfeeding; colostrum
breastfeeding by the Virgin Mary 33–34; duration of 47; Enlightenment campaign to promote it 222–223; rules and prohibitions during 59, 109; as symbolic representation of charity 109; taboo in public 267–268; see also breast milk; Leche League
Brit Milah 130
Brown, Louise Joy 261
Browne, Stella 249
Burkert, Walter 24

Cadogan, William 224
Caesar, Gaius Julius, legendary birth of 21
Caesarean section in myth and legend 21
Caesarean section on living women: increase in the 20the century 265; maternal mortality rates in 18th–19th centuries 218, 220, 221; as option in favour of the child's life (maternal sect) 218; scientific debate in early modern age 216–217, 219–220; see also maternal sect; Porro Operation
Caesarean section post mortem: the campaign by F. E. Cangiamila 211–213; Lex Regia 139–140; in medieval Councils 140; in the Romanum Ritual 140; see also Caesar Gaius Julius; Cangiamila; nonnati children
Calvin, John 135

Cangiamila, Francesco Emanuele: on Caesarean section on living women 218; Embriologia Sacra and the campaign for post-mortem Caesarean sections 211–213; representation of the embryo 210; see also Nuova Prammatica siciliana del taglio cesareo e dell'aborto
Capitoli circa il medicare e comporre medicamenti (Venice) 152
Capuron, Joseph 181
Caracalla (Marcus Aurelius Antoninus), Roman Emperor 67
Carbòn, Damian 154
Carmina in childbirth protection 61, 88
Carmody, Charlotte 253
Casati, Gaetano 233
Casti Connubi, encyclical 222, 242
Catherine de' Medici, Queen of France, delivery of 84
Catullus 20
Cavallini, Giulia 220
Cavarero, Adriana 251
Cazzani, Luigi 195
Celsus, Aulus Cornelius 94
Centro Informazione Sterilizzazione e Aborto (CISA) 249
chair/stool for delivery see birthing chair
Chamberlens (family), Peter the Elder; Hugh; William 177
Chance, Janet 249
Changing Childbirth report (UK) 257
Channing, Walter 252
Chapman, Edmund 186
Charles III Bourbon, King of Spain 213
Charles V Habsburg, Holy Roman Emperor 122
Charlotte Augusta, Princess of Wales 178
Charte des droits de la parturiente 258
Chevalier, Marie-Claire 249
child: monitoring laws of 227; reform in defence of 226–228; resemblance to parents according to Aristotle 17–18; secrets to have a male one 54–55; see also childcare; death; mortality; newborn
Childbed Fever see puerperal fever
childbirth: at court 103; natural/unnatural 90–94; new feminist perspective on 250–252; pain-free 252–253; political interests on 161–163; scene/setting of 42, 76, 82–83, 87–89; symbolic removal of 9–10; as women's "war" 22–26; see also delivery; labour
childcare new forms of in 18th century 224–225
Children's Bureau 234

chirurgo-ostetricante 174
chloroform, use in childbirth 252
chòrion 49
Churching of Women 119; *see also* purification rituals
circumcision 130; *see also* rites
Clement of Alexandria 13
Clément, Jules 184
coitus interruptus 68, 236; *see also* contraceptive methods
College of Physicians (Protomedicato, Bologna) 152
College of Physicians and Surgeons (Venice) 184, 186
College of Surgeons (Barcelona) 167
College of Surgery (Madrid) 167
colostrum, as harmful 108
comare 118, 132, 134, 148, 152
conception: in Aristotle 15–16; and closure of the womb 45; Hippocratic theories of 14; and sexual pleasure 13–14, 16–17, 19, 55; *see also* artificial insemination; generation; procreation; reproduction
concussio in a difficult birth 83, 85
Constitutio Criminalis Carolina 122
contraceptive methods/practices: in the ancient world 66–67; "contraceptive revolution" 248–249; difference between the Catholic and Protestant Churches on the use of 242–243; laws forbading 140; spread and reduction in the birth rate (first half of the 20th century) 236; *see also* malthusian practices
Cooper, William 219
copulation between animals and women in myth 18, 63
Cornelia, mother of the Gracchi 80
Corpus Iuris Civilis by Emperor Justinian 32, 140
Corradi, Alfonso 178, 218, 220
Cosimo III de' Medici 69
Costa Gnocchi, Adele 256
Costantini, Giuseppe Antonio 225
Coudray le Boursier, Angélique Marguerite du 145, 154, 167, 168
craniotomes *see* instruments
cravings in pregnancy 57–58; scientific debate in the 18th century 209–211
Cremonini, Lucia 122
Crispi, Francesco 169
Cronus 21
crotchets *see* instruments
culbute 53

cups: new mothers' or midwives' (*tazze della comare*) 118
Curatolo, Giacomo Emilio 88

Dalle Donne, Maria 167
Dangerous Drugs Act (UK) 227
Dante Alighieri 16, 137
Daret, Jacques 31
Daughters of the American Revolution (DAR) 240
De Demerson, Paula 229n25
De La Vallière, Louise 184
De Marinis, Maddalena 164, 183
Dea Nutrix 109
death in childbirth: of the child without baptism (the "dual death") 137–138; in Greek funerary reliefs 24; *see also* infanticide; Limbo; mortality
degeneration of race: fear of 240
delivery: etymology of the term 80; modesty in 42, 62, 76, 146, 171, 184, 185, 193, 196; postures in 85–88; separate room in lying-in hospitals 195–196, 246; Zeus' cephalic 21–22; *see also* childbirth; placenta
délivre 97
delocalisation of childbirth to hospitals 243–247; different timing of 243–244; social and cultural factors 244–245, 247
Demeter 9, 22, 112
Democritus 13
demographic growth policies (18th century) 159, 161–163; battle for during Fascism 236–237; fears of demographic decline 163, 236; *see also* biopower
Denman, Thomas 180
Deputazione dei Projetti 213
Descartes, René 180
Deschi da parto (birth trays) 117
Desessartz, Jean-Charles 22
Detienne, Marcel 22
Diana, Roman Goddess 78
Dies Lustricus 130
Dinouart, Joseph Antoine Toussaint 217
Dionis, Pierre 85, 216
diseases: of midwives 114, 147; of newborns/children in modern paediatrics 224; in pregnancy and bleeding 60–61; *see also* hysteria; chidbed fever; puerperal insanity
Dogliotti, Achille Mario 254
Dominic of Osma (also of Caleruega, de Guzmán), Saint 46
Donald, Ian 258

Drelincourt, Charles 208
drugs: in delivery 143; given to babies 227; and the National Twilight Sleep Association 253; *see also* anaesthesia; Dangerous Drugs Act; opiates
Dubois, Antoine 198, 219
duBois, Page 11
Duden, Barbara 48, 221
dystocia *(dystokìa)* in Hippocratic texts and in Soranus 92; and delocalisation of births to hospitals 200, 143, 145; and man-midwives 185–186

École anti-symphyso-césarienne 183; *see also* Sacombe
Edward I, King of England 68
Edwards, Robert Geoffrey 261
Egeria 79
eggs: discovery of 207–208; freezing of 261; *see also* Ovism; artificial insemination
Eileithyiae 22
Elisabeth of Valois, Queen of Spain 84
Elisabeth, Saint 13
emancipation movement *see* women's emancipation movement
embryo *see* zygote
embryology: birth of 208–211
embryotomy: conflict in the modern medical world 217–218; Holy Office verdict on 219; as mother's life choice 95–97; *see also* instruments; *maternal sect*
Empedocles 13
endoscopy 259
Ephrem the Syrian, Saint 31
Epictetus 67
epidural anaesthesia *see* anaesthesia
episiotomy 179, 190n24, 247
Epitaph of Pericles see Thucydides
Erinyes 12, 22
Esquirol, Jean-Étienne-Dominique 203
Estienne, Charles 50
eugenics 240–242; *see also* sterilisation
Euripides 22, 24
Ex-votos 77, 79, 112

Fabrici d'Acquapendente, Girolamo (Fabricius Hieronimus) 16
Faccio, Adele 249
Failed forceps outside (FFO) 178; *see also* forceps
Fallaci, Oriana 245
Fedeli Trevisan, Benedetta 166, 186
female emancipation movement *see* women's emancipation movement

feminism "maternalist" 234, 251; *see also* women's emancipation movement
Feminist International Network of Resistance to Reproductive and Genetic Engineering (FINRRAGE) 267
Fidel Pagés, Miravé 254
Fiorentini, Girolamo (Hieronymus Florentinius) 54
Firdowsi (Abul-Qâsem Ferdowsi Tusi), Persian poet 21
Flandrin, Jean-Louis 13
Foetal sect 218; *see also* Caesarean section
foetus: development and ensoulment in ancient medicine 49–54; gender differences 48–49, 53, 55; somersault of 53; new embryology research on 209–211; as "unborn citizen" 213–214; ultrasound scanning and new representation of 259–260; vegetal representation of 12–13, 53, 84, 85, 90, 95, 181; *see also* abortion; baptism; imaginative virtue; miscarriage
food during pregnancy 58; during quarantine 103; in labour 85; wet nurses' 112
forceps: European differences and polemics on use 182–183; invention of 176–177; rate of maternal mortality due to their use 178; *see also* instruments; *failed forceps outside* (FFO); man-midwives
Fores, S. W. *see* Blunt
Forleo, Romano 256
Foucault, Michel 174, 250
Foucquet de Maupeou, Marie 61
foundling hospitals 69, 123–124, 155, 193, 194; in Milan 124, 194; mortality data in some European cities (18th century) 125; 19th-century reforms 227, 238
Franci, Filippo 70
Francis de Paola, Saint 33
Francis de Sales, Saint 27, 79
Francis I (Jorge Mario Bergoglio), Pope 267
Francis of Assisi, Saint 29
Frank, Johann Peter 13, 60, 73n62, 83, 117, 162, 213, 214, 223
Frari, Michele 189
Fried, Johann Jakob 175
fumigations, vaginal 58, 79, 80, 85, 98

Gaddi, Taddeo 33
Galen: *On the Anatomy of the Uterus* 153; and the development of the foetus 49; and inversion of genitals 15; as "proto-feminist" 16; and theory on the

combination of seeds (*De semine*) 15, 16; *see also* one-sex model; seeds
Galli, Giovanni Antonio 166, 167, 176, 185
Gauss, Karl 253
Geburtshelfer 174, 198
Gélis, Jacques 53, 77, 82, 139, 176
gender violence and miscarriage or foetal malformations 60
generation: gender hierarchy in 17–19; man as origin of in Aristotle 14–15; preformationist theories about 207–209; *see also* conception; procreation; reproduction
Genesis 26, 28
genitals (or Genitalia): correspondence between male and female 15; manipulation in newborns by midwives 107; *see also* one-sex model
Giffard, William 183
Giordano, Scipione 194, 195, 197
Giotto 31, 33
girdles *see* belts
godparents 132–134, 135, 136; midwife as godmother 134, 148
Goldmann, Emma 236
Gonzaga, ruling family in Mantua 64
Gooch Robert 203
Graaf, Régnier de (or Reinier) 207
Grantly, Dick-Read 254, 255
Green, Monica 35n18
Green Scott, Julia 240
Gregory IX (Ugolino di Anagni), Pope 53
Gregory of Nyssa, Saint 31
Grevembroch, Giovanni 56, 87, 111, 147, 226
guardadonne 145
gyné 23

Hanlon, Gregory 123
Harris, Walter 224
Harvey, William 93, 180, 207, 216
Hebamme 148
Hebammenordung 151
Hecht, Jacqueline 113
Hécquet, Philippe 180, 185
Heister, Lorenz 88, 209
Hemingway, Ernest 95, 253
Henry II of Valois, King of France 68
Henry III of Valois, King of France 68
Henry IV of Valois, King of France 82
Hephaestus 22
Hera 22, 112
Heracles 11, 23
Hermes 22
Hesiod 21, 22, 86

Hestia 129
Hildegard of Bingen 18, 49, 85
Hippocratic corpus/Hippocratic collection/texts 12, 13, 14, 15, 18, 41, 46, 47, 53, 60, 91, 92, 109; *Barrenness* 55, 65; *Excision of the foetus* 96; *On Generation* 45, 48; *Jusiurandum* 67; *Nature of the child* 49, 90; *Superfetation* 54
Hirigaray, Luce 251
Hirschowitz, Basil Isac 258
Hitler, Adolf 241
Hobbes, Thomas 180
Holy Office [Supreme Sacred Congregation of the Roman and Universal Inquisition] 28, 139, 215, 219, 221, 242, 262
hooks *see* instruments
Hopwood, Nick 162
hormones ovarian 248, 261; *see also* ovulation
Hospice des Enfants-Trovés 125
hospitalisation of childbirth *see* delocalisation
hospitals *see* foundling hospitals; lying-in hospitals
Hull, John 217
Human Rights in Childbirth 265
humours theory 14, 58, 60, 202
Hunecke, Volker 124
Hunter, John 260
Hunter, William 174, 180, 182, 209
huperétides 145
husband: his garments in childbirth scene 82; "husband-coached childbirth" method 256; of midwives 145, 148; role in childbirth 83, 88; of wet nurse (*balio*) in medieval Florentine families 110–111
hygiene books and almanacs (18th century) 224; courses for mothers 238; *see also* childcare
hystéra see womb
hysteria 46

illnesses *see* diseases
imaginative virtue of pregnant women 44, 57–58; debate between imaginationists and anti-imaginationists 209–211; *see also* performative force
impagliolata (or *impagiolata*) 117
Impallomeni, Giovan Battista 204
impurity of women after childbirth 112–115; in the Jewish religion 114; and *post-partum* period 115–118
incantamenta see spells

incubator by Stéphane Tarnier 245
infanticide: in the ancient world 120–121; in Christianity 67, 95, 121–122, 149; gender-selective 123; laws against in the early modern age 68, 122; and magic rituals 121; public initiatives to prevent 69, 192, 193; and puerperal insanity 202–204; trials in some cities of modern age 127n81; trials between 19th and 20th centuries 204–205; *see also* puerperal insanity
infertility: antidote against 100; as divine punishment 63; repudiated wife because of 76; *see also* artificial insemination
Innocent III (Lothar of Segni), Pope 53, 68
Innocent XI (Benedetto Odescalchi), Pope 70
insanity *see* puerperal insanity
insemination *see* artificial insemination
instruments: controversies about their abuse 164–165, 180–183; first obstetrical 96, 97, 141, 146, 176; prerogative of the guilds of barber-surgeons 76, 146, 152; prohibitions of use by midwives 168, 170; *see also* crotchets; embryotomy; forceps; pelvimeter, speculum, vectis
intercourse: abstain from during breastfeeding 109; banned during menstruation 64; banned during pregnancy 13, 59, 63
International Theological Commission about Limbo 137
Ishtar 9
Isidore of Seville 45, 139
Isis 9, 109
Italian Association of birth in analgesia 266

Jacobs, Aletta 236
James I Stuart, King of England and Ireland (James VI as King of Scotland) 68, 122
James II Stuart, King of England and Ireland (and James VII as King of Scotland) 84
James's gospel 31
Jenkins, Alice 249
Joan of Arc 23, 146
John the Baptist, Saint 48, 105
John XXIII (Giuseppe Angelo Roncalli), Pope 243
Joseph II, Emperor of Austria 176, 193
Jourdan, Clara 250
Jousset, Alexandra 265
Julian (the Apostate), Emperor 41

Juno, Lucina 78, 80, 109, 112, 175; *Solvizona* 112
Justinian (Flavius Petrus Sabbatius Iustinianus Augustus), Roman Emperor 16, 32, 140

Kassel, Lauren 93
Katharina von Braunschweig-Lüneburg 154
Kehrer, Adolf 221
Ketham, Johannes de 25
Kilian, Hermann Friedrich 177
King, Helen 36n35
Kitzinger, Sheila 256
Klapisch-Zuber, Christiane 110, 113, 123
Klein, Johann 201
Knaus, Hermann 242
Knibiehler, Yvonne 29, 255
knives *see* instruments
Krämer, Heinrich (Institoris Henricus) 121, 149
Kröning, Bernhard 253

labour: food and drink during 85; movement during 84; *see also* childbirth; delivery; *pònos*
Lachapelle, Marie-Louise 154, 189, 197
lactation *see* breastfeeding
Laennec, René Théophile-Marie-Hyacinthe 179
Laget, Mireille 136
Lamaze, Fernand 254, 256
Lambeth Conference 243
laparoscopy 259
Laqueur, Thomas 15, 19, 55, 36n35
Law for the Protection of German Blood 241
Le Fort, Léon 200
Leboyer, Frédérick 251, 256
Leche League 252; *see also* breastfeeding
lechói 88
Leclerc de Buffon 209
Legitimation League 205
Leo I, the Great, Pope and Saint 31
Leo XIII (Vincenzo Gioacchino Raffaele Luigi Pecci), Pope 222, 242
Leonardo da Vinci 50, 52
Leopold Prince, son of Queen Victoria 252, 253
Leroy, Alphonse-Louis-Vincent 179
levatrice/comare levatrice 148, 239
Leviticus 114, 118
Levret, André 60, 166, 177, 180
Liceti, Fortunio 64

limbo, theological construction of 136–137; *see also* baptism; International Theological Commission about
Lister, Joseph 202
lochia: as impure and corrosive 114; incompatibility with breast milk 108
lóchos 23
Loraux, Nicole 23
Lorenzin, Beatrice 266
Loudon, Irvine 77, 206n31
Louis XIII Bourbon, King of France 108
Louis XIV Bourbon, King of France 82, 184
Lucina *see* Juno, Lucina
Lucrezia d'Este, sister of Alfonso II 70
Luke, the Evangelist 13, 48, 130
lustratio 130
Luther Martin 135
lying-in hospitals: anonymity of illegitimate mothers 193; distribution in Europe 197; establishment and objectives 192–193; organisation and training 194–198; percentages of unmarried mothers 194; *see also* foundling hospitals; infanticide; puerperal fever
Lynch, Katherine 123

Macduff 140
Madonna *see* Mary, the Virgin
Madonne del parto (Pregnant Madonnas) **33**
madrona 148
Magli, Ida 34
maîa 20, 143, 153
Maidalchini Eugenia 49, 79
maieutics 20
Majno, Ersilia 234
Malacarne, Vincenzo 176, 185
Malebranche, Nicolas 208
malformations of the foetus: due to gender violence 60; and mother's performative force 65, 211; *see also* imaginative virtue; monsters
Malleson, Joan 249
Malleus maleficarum 149
Malpighi, Marcello 208
malpresentations of the foetus during delivery 43, 93–94, 146; *see also* presentations of the foetus; version
Malthusian theories 222, 235–236, 242
mammana 148
Mammes of Caesarea, Saint 112
Mangiagalli, Luigi 234
man-midwives: controversies with midwives 182, 185–189; differences in Europe 183–185; disputes over midwifery 180–183; their establishment 174–176; their instruments 176–179; *see also* biopower; medicalisation; instruments
Mantegazza, Paolo 225, 264
manual intervention/manoeuvres *see* version
Manzolini, Anna e Giovanni 167; *see also* Morandi
Manzoni, Alessandro 20
Marbeau, Firmin 234
Marcus Aurelius, Roman Emperor 68
Margaret of Antioch, Saint 46
Maria de' Medici, Queen of France 61, 82, 84, 87, 145
Maria Lactans see Mary, the Virgin
Maria Theresa of Habsburg, Empress 19
Marie Louise of Habsburg Lorraine, wife of Napoleon Bonaparte 219
Marinello, Giovanni 55, 60, 99, 148, 154
Marinello, Lucrezia 154
Marland, Hilary 203
Martini, Carlo Maria, Archbishop of Milan 222
Mary of Burgundy, Duchess 117
Mary of Modena, wife of James II of England and Ireland 84
Mary the Virgin: conception and virgin delivery in theology 29–33; in feminist thinking 34–35; and the "incredulous midwife" 31; as patroness of childbirth 79; representations of her motherhood in art 33; *see also* ex-votos; relics
maternal sect 218; *see also* Caesarean section on living women
maternity *see* motherhood
Mauquest de la Motte, Guillaume 60, 65, 99, 183
Mauriceau, François 51, 58, 60, 92, 103, 141, 177, 216
McCormick, Katherine 248
Mechanism, application to midwifery 180–181
medical "police" 161–163; *see also* biopower
Medical Society (London) 219
medicalisation of childbirth 172, 192, 197–198, 213, 246–247; criticism by feminists 250–251; *see also* instruments; lying-in hospitals
Melania, the Younger, Saint 82
Melli, Sebastiano 112, 154, 225
Memmo Martinengo, Paolina 78
Memmo Mocenigo, Lucia 78, 163, 222
menstruation: absence of as a sign of pregnancy 47–48, 65; cause of in ancient medicine 14; intercourse during 63, 63
Mercuriale, Girolamo 148

Mercurio, Scipione (Girolamo) 11, 15, 28, 47, 51, 58, 59, 78, 80, 82, 85, 88, 92, 93, 94, 98, 103, 106, 107, 108, 112, 144, 147, 150, 154, 165, 217
Métis 21
Michaelis, Gustav Adolf 190n24
Michiel Giustinian, Elisabetta 234
midwifery: manuals of 28, 88, 141, 150, 154–155, 176, 180; schools of 166–170; *see also* lying-in hospitals
midwives: Church control of 149–151; increased repression of during Fascism 139; Plato on 143; public regulation of in early modern age 151–153; qualified versus unlicensed 170–172; traditional features and skills of 144–147; as suspected witches 148–149; on trial (18th century) 163–164; variety of figures 153–155; *see also* Agnodice; midwifery
milk stones/caves 112
ministrae see huperétides
Miralles, Carles 21
miscarriage: causes of 58–59; remedies to prevent 58, 61
Modena, Leone, Rabbi 107
Moderata Fonte (Modesta Pozzo De' Zorzi) 78
moles, formation theories 65–66
Monitoring Centre of Obstetric Violence in Italy 271n154
Monot, Charles 228
monsters: medical investigations about 64–65; representations of 62–64; and sexual intercourse during menstruation 63, 64; *see also* malformations; imaginative virtue
Montesquieu, Charles-Louis de Secondat 20
Montessori Birth Centre 256
Moore, Demi 267
Morandi Manzolini, Anna 167
Morgagni, Giovanni Battista 93, 94, 208
mortality: data of its decline in the 20th century 244; fight against as a political objective (18th century) 161–162; infant in the *ancien régime* 113; maternal rate in childbirth in early modern age 77; progressive decrease in the 19th and 20th centuries 228, 244; *see also* death; Caesarean section
Moscati, Giuseppe 185, 186
Moses 123
Mosse, Bartholomew 196
motherhood: new feminist perspective on 250–252; as "patriotic" duty during Fascism 236–238; as proof of womanhood 23; public enhancement of in the 18th century 222–225; right to 261; as a social function 233–235; *see also* rights
mothers, unmarried: charitable initiatives for destitute 69; control over in early modern age 68–69; "guarantor of childbirth" 69; institutions/workhouses for 69–72; surrogate 236–238; *see also* foundling hospitals; lying-in hospitals
Mouvement pour la liberté de la avortement et contraception (Mlac) 249
Movimento di lotta femminista (Feminist Fight Movement) 255
Mozak, A. S. 252
Mulieris dignitatem, pastoral letter 222
Muraro, Luisa 251
Muratori, Ludovico Antonio 163, 166, 185
Musatti, Cesare 164, 233, 234, 235
Muscio (Mustio or Mustione) 41, 50
Mussolini, Benito 25, 236, 237

Nachgeburt 97
Naegele, Franz Carl 181
Napoleon Bonaparte 219
Napoleonic Code 71, 139, 193, 226
National Abortion Campaign (NAC) 249
National Childbirth Trust 257
National Congress for the Health of Mercenary Breastfeeding 235
National Twilight Sleep Association 253; *see also* drugs
nativity scene in painting 29, 82, 103–106
nature: representations of 64–65, 93, 181–182; state of (in the Enlightenment) 25, 182; violence to 182; wonders of 64
Nessi, Giuseppe 90
Neuwirth Lucien, law 250
newborns: laws in defence of (18th century) 226–228; post-natal care by midwife in early modern age 103–108; protection rituals of 116, 118, 128; representation in medieval age 113–114; *see also* bath; breastfeeding; social birth
Newell, Franklin S. 247
Newton, Isaac 181
Nicholls, Frank 183
Nietzsche, Friedrich Wilhelm 183
Nigrisoli, Giovanni Maria 208
Nihell, Elizabeth 145, 154, 182
Nikolaev, Anatoly P. 254, 255
Nilsson, Lennart 259
nodriza 110
nonnati 140
nourrice 110

Numa Pompilius, King of Rome 139
Nuova Prammatica siciliana del taglio cesareo e dell'aborto 212, 214
nurseries 226, 233–235, 238, 248
nursing *see* wet nursing
nutrix lactaria 110

obstetric instruments *see* instruments
obstetric machine by Madame du Coudray 167
obstetricalis sella 86; *see also* birthing chair
obstetricians *see* man-midwives
obstetrics: active versus 'waiting' 180–183; *see also* midwifery
Odent, Michel 256
Oedipus 34, 123
Ogino, Kyusaku 242
one-sex model *see* body
opiates (to babies) laws banning 227; *see also* Dangerous Drugs Act
Oribasius (or Oreibasius) 41
Origen of Alexandria 31
Osiander, Friedrich Benjamin 198, 182
Ould, Fielding 190n24
ovaries: discoveries related to them in the 17th century 207–208; as "female testicles" in ancient medicine 15, 19; and menstrual cycle 261; *see also* eggs; hormones; ovulation
Ovid (Ovidius, Naso Publius) 20, 67
ovism 207–208

paediatrics as a new branch of medicine 228
pain in childbirth 23–24; as divine punishment 26–28; its expression in Christian society 88–90; *see also* anaesthesia; labour; *pònos*
Palasciano, Ferdinando 196
Palfijn, Jan (or Palfyn, Jean) 177
Palletta, Gian Battista 224
Pancino, Claudia 115, 176
Pandora 26
Panzani, J. 85
Paracelsus (*Philippus Aureolus Theophrastus Bombastus Paracelsus*) 262
Paré, Ambroise 55, 64, 66, 91, 94, 145, 216
Park, Katharine 156n14, 16n18, 190n24
Parmenides of Elea 13, 18
Parocchi, Lucido Maria 221
Pascal, Eugénie 78
Pasteur, Louis 201
Pastorello, Luigi 214, 218
paternity: the prohibition of searches in 19th-century codes 72, 124, 193, 205; search of 70–71; *see also* Legitimation League
Paul IV (Gian Piero Carafa), Pope 32
Paul V (Camillo Borghese), Pope 135
Paul VI (Giovanni Battista Montini), Pope 243
Paul of Merida, Saint 140
Paul of Tharsus, Saint 21
Pavlov, Ivan Petrovič 254
pelvimeter by Baudelocque 179, 181, 216
Penitentials 13, 67, 121, 131
Pepys, Samuel 48
performative force of pregnant women 55, 64–65; *see also* imaginative virtue
Perondi, Giuliano 239
Perseus 123
Personé, Girolamo 179
Petition of the Unborn Babies 183
Phaenarete, mother of Socrates 20, 143
pharmakia 148
Philip II, King of Spain 84
piacula 149
pica (kissa) 47
Piccoli, Antonio 166
Piero della Francesca 33
Pierobon, Gigliola 249
Pinard, Adolphe 202, 233
Pincus, Gregory 248
Pinel, Philippe 203
Pius VI (Angelo Onofrio Melchiorre Natale Giovanni Antonio Braschi), Pope
Pius X (Giuseppe Melchiorre Sarto), Pope 137
Pius XI (Achille Ambrogio Damiano Ratti), Pope 222, 242
Pius XII (Eugenio Maria Giuseppe Giovanni Pacelli), Pope 243, 255
placenta, the "second delivery" 91–98; disposal of 100; magic and healing powers of 98, 100; manual extraction of 99; sympathetic union with the newborn 98
Plato 12, 19, 20, 46, 67, 143, 145, 148
Pliny the Elder (Gaius Plinius Secundus) 46, 61, 63, 66, 67, 81, 92, 121, 139, 149, 153
Ployant, Teresa 155, 170, 183, 185, 188
Plutarch 23
pónos 23, 79
Porro, Edoardo 195, 205, 220; "Porro operation" 220–221
Portal, Paul 93, 183
post-mortem Caesarean section see Caesarean section post-mortem
Prayer of an Expectant Mother 27, 79

preformationist theories about generation 207–208
pregnancy: bodily signs and manifestations in Hippocratic medicine 47; medical advice and care during 58–59; medical check of (20th century) 258–259; ritualistic prohibitions during 61–62; test of 48; see also miscarriage; ultrasound scans
presentations of the foetus during childbirth 91–93; in Baudelocque 181; drawing in Muscio 50; see also foetus; malpresentations
prevardatio 68–69
procreation desire in Plato 19–20; see also conception; generation, reproduction
Prosperi, Adriano 68, 122, 135
Provveditori alla Sanità (Health Magistrates, Venice) 152
Provvidenza baliatica 235
Pseudo-Matthew gospel 31
psychology-based method 254
puerperal fever 200–202; mortality rates in some lying-in hospitals 200; see also Semmelweis' discovery
puerperal insanity 202–204; and infanticide laws 204–205; see also infanticide
Pulz, Waltraud 165
Purgatory 137
purification rituals 118–120
Puzos, Nicolas 203

quarantine *post-partum* 44, 115–118

raccoglitrice (or *ricoglitrice*) 148
Radford, Thomas 218
Raffaele, Giovanni 19, 52, 178, 188, 199
Ramazzini, Bernardino 43, 114, 147
Rapin, Oscar 252
Rasori, Giovanni 73n65
Raven, Lang 255
Ravizza, Alessandrina 234
Rawlins-Gaston, Andrea 265
Raymond of Peñafort, "Nonnatus", Saint 140
Realdo, Colombo 97
Recommendations on Postnatal care (WHO) 257
Regio Supremo Tribunale di Sanità (Royal Supreme Health Court in Venice) 186
relevailles 119
relics in childbirth setting 46, 61, 82; see also belts
remedies: during childbirth 81, 163; for placental delivery 98–99; to prevent miscarriages 42, 43; *Remedia* books 61

reproduction: dissemination of the term 162; *see also* conception; generation; procreation
Revelli, Nuto 25
Rich, Adrienne 251, 255
rickets and difficult childbirth 77, 95, 177, 179, 218
rights: to motherhood 261; of women in childbirth 234, 257–258, 265; *see also Charte des droits de la parturiente*; Children's Bureau; *Human Rights in Childbirth*
Rigotti, Francesca 20
rites: new medical in lying-in hospitals 244; of passage 128–129; of purification after childbirth 118–120; to replace baptism 137–139; *see also Aussegnung der Wöchnerin*; baptism; circumcision; *Churching of Women; relevailles*
Rituale Romanum 66, 115, 119, 126n51, 135, 136, 140, 150
rituals *see* rites
Rizzo, Sebastiano 162
Rocco, Alfredo (Italian Criminal Code) 204, 237, 239
Rodin, Pierre 174
Romulus and Remus, Rome founders 123
Roonhuyzen, Endrich van 177, 179
Rose of Jericho 81
Rosén von Rosenstein, Nils 224
Rösslin (or Roesslin), Eucharius (Rodion) 87, 91, 92, 93, 106, 154
Rousseau, Jean-Jacques 26, 182, 223
Rousset, François 216
Rouzade, Leonie 234
Royal College of Medicine (London) 183
Royal College of Midwives (RCM) (London) 256
Royal Edinburgh Asylum 203
Rueff, Jacob 50, 51, 62, 65, 86, 88, 89, 93, 94, 144
Ruysch, Frederick 208
Rymsdyk, Jan van 209

Sacchi, Giuseppe 234
Sacombe, Jean-François 181–182, 217, 219; and the *École anti-symphyso-césarienne* 183
sage-femme 148
Sanchez Arcàs, R. 229n25
Sànchez, Tomàs 17
sanctuaries à *répit* 229n25; *see also* baptism
Sand, René 245
Sanger, Margareth 236, 248
Sänger, Max 221
Sansovino, Francesco 117

Savonarola, Michele 11, 45, 54, 88, 93, 107, 111–112
Schiff, Paolina 234
Schmid, Verena 38n108
Schola Medica Salernitana 12
schools of midwifery *see* midwifery schools
Schorowa, A. A. 261
Schrader, Catharina 145, 154, 155
Schreinmadonnen see Vierges ouvrantes
second delivery *see* placenta
seed, male and female in the Hippocratic texts 13–14; in Galen 15, 18; *see also* semen
Selmini, Rossella 205
semen in Aristotle 14; *see also* sperm
Semmelweis, Ignàc Fülop discovery by 201–202
Sennert, Daniel 63
Septimius Severus, Roman Emperor 67
sex determination: bets to guess (Venice) 55–56; theories in embryos 17–19
sexual organs *see* genitals
Shakespeare, William 140
Shelley, Mary 262
Shorter, Edward 77, 78, 100n7, 178, 182
Siegemund, Justine 154, 164
Sigault, Jean-René 179
Simon, Jean-François 216
Simpson, James Young 252
Skoda, Joseph 201
Smellie, William 166, 175, 177, 182, 184
Smith, William Tyler 218
Snow, John 252
social birth *see* baptism; circumcision; rites, of passage
Société de l'allaitement maternel 235
Socrates 19, 20, 143
Solayrès, François Louis Joseph de Renhac 181
Solera Mantegazza, Laura 234
Sömmering, Samuel Thomas von 209
Sophocles 11
Soranus of Ephesus: on abortion 66, 148; on childbirth 79, 81, 82, 87, 90, 92, 94, 95; on embryotomy 96; on foetal development 49; *Gynaecia* 12, 79, 81, 94; on midwives 144, 145, 146, 153; on newborn care 107, 108; on pregnancy 45, 46, 55, 58, 59, 65
Spada Maildachini, Eugenia 49
Spada, Maria 79
Spallanzani, Lazzaro 208, 260
spasimo 113
speculum matricis and J. Siegemund's controversy against 164–165, 258
sperm: donor of 262; freezing of 161, 264; use of the term 207; *see also animalcule*; semen
spermatozoa 261; *see also animalcule*; sperm
Sprenger, Jacob 121, 149
Stearns, Sarah 79
Steese Richardson, Anna 253
Steptoe, Patrick Christopher 261
sterilisation laws of 241–242; *see also* eugenics
sterility *see* infertility
stethoscope 47, 179
Stoeckel, Walter von 254
Stone, Sarah 154
Stopes, Marie 236
Storch, Johann 48
strophé 53
Strozzi, Filippo 153
suffocation of newborns in their parents' bed 123, 127n89, 146
sulphonamides 202
surgeons: and courses for midwives 166–167; guild/corporation of 96, 146, 167, 174, 184, 186, 188; and post-mortem caesarean sections 140, 152, 214, 218; their role in difficult childbirths in the medieval and early modern age 62, 76, 96–97, 152, 153, 164, 165, 168, 176; *see also* instruments; man-midwives
surgical instruments *see* instruments
surrogate mother *see* mother
swaddling clothes/bands use of 81, 103, 107–108, 145, 170, 224, 225; the Enlightenment campaign against 223–224
Swammerdam, Jan 208
sympathetic medicine 61
symphysiotomy 179; *see also École anti-symphyso-césarienne*

Tarnier, Stéphane-Etienne 178, 202, 245
Tertullian 27, 53, 95
testicles, male and "female" *see* body, one-sex model
test-tube baby 261
Theodosius I (Flavius Theodosius), Roman Emperor 131
Theophrastus of Eresus 114
Thomas Aquinas, Saint 16, 30, 53, 59, 96, 137, 140
Thouret, Michel-Augustin 260
Thucydides, *Epitaph of Pericles* 23, 24
Toaldo, Giuseppe 227
Todd Akin, William 17
Toniolo, Giuseppe 233

Tracy, Marguerite 253
Trevisan, Francesco 227
Trexler, R. 123
Trotula (or Trota) de Ruggiero 12, 35n18, 47; *see also* Schola medica Salernitana
Tsiaras, Alexander 259
Tuke, William 203
Turco, Livia 266

ultrasound scan 48, 258–260
unmarried mothers *see* mothers, unmarried
uroscopy 47
uterus *see* womb

Valota, Orazio 186
Van Gennep, Arnold 44, 115
Van Leeuwenhoek, Antony 207
Van Putten, Elisabeth and Neeltje 188
vectis 97, 176, 177, 178–179; *see also* forceps; instruments
Velpeau, Alfred Armand Louis Marie 94, 177
Velvovsky, Il'ya Zakharovich 254, 255
Verri, Pietro 223
version in case of malpresentations 43, 94, 146, 166, 170; ban on midwives 185–189
Vesalius, Andreas 41, 53, 97
Vespa, Giuseppe 176, 198
Vestal virgins, priestesses of Vesta 32
Viardel, Cosme 99, 175
Victoria (Alexandrina Victoria), Queen of England 252
Vierges ouvrantes 33
violence *see* gender violence
Virgil (Virgilius, Publius Maro) 137
virginity of Mary *see* Mary the Virgin
Visconti, Bianca Maria 153

Vitalism: implications in obstetrics 11, 181–182
Vitruvius, Marcus Pollio 47
Voltaire (François-Marie Arouet) 65, 161
vroedmeester/stere 188

war and masculine identity 22–26
Well Women's Centres 258
Werth, Barry 259
wet nurse 110–112; disappearance of the figure 247; *see also* breast milk
wet nursing 110–112; new agencies in the 19th century 235
Wickelfrauen 170
Willis, Thomas 200
Willughby, Percivall 85, 87, 93
Winslow, Jacobus-Beninius 209
wise woman 148
Wollstonecraft, Mary 109
womb: closure after conception 45–46; as a mobile organ 46; naturalistic metaphors of 10–12; separate chambers of 15, 18; as "sanctuary of Nature" 216; *see also* hysteria
women's diseases *see* diseases; hysteria
women's emancipation movement: battle in favour of unmarried mothers 205; battles for the protection of motherhood 233–235; *see also* feminism; nurseries
Worth, Jennifer 272n166
Wunderkammern 64

Young, John Harley 218

Zanardelli, Italian Criminal Code 204
Zeno of Verona, Saint 31
Zeviani, Giovanni Verardo 227
zygote: view of the Catholic Church 263